THE REGULATION OF UNFAIR COMMERCIAL PRACTICES UNDER EC DIRECTIVE 2005/29

This book represents the fruit of a conference held in Oxford on 3 March 2006 under the auspices of the Institute of European and Comparative Law in the Oxford University Law Faculty. Directive 2005/29 is an important new measure in the construction of a legal framework apt to promote an integrated economic space in the European Union. It establishes a harmonised regime governing the control of unfair commercial practices. As such it represents an important exercise in the use of new rules and new techniques, and therefore poses new challenges to EU lawyers. The purpose of this book is to inform and to explore the issues raised by the Directive, issues which are of academic and practical interest in helping to understand the evolution of European consumer law within the broader programme of European market regulation. The intense practical significance of this Directive, which heralds a new regime, is likely to provoke commercial operators to seek to exploit opportunities to pursue practices previously suppressed.

The Regulation of Unfair Commercial Practices under EC Directive 2005/29

New Rules and New Techniques

Edited by

Stephen Weatherill and Ulf Bernitz

·HART·
PUBLISHING

OXFORD AND PORTLAND, OREGON
2007

Published in North America (US and Canada) by
Hart Publishing
c/o International Specialized Book Services
920 NE 58th Avenue, Suite 300
Portland, OR 97213-3786
USA
Tel: +1 503 287 3093 or toll-free: (1) 800 944 6190
Fax: +1 503 280 8832
E-mail: orders@isbs.com
Website: www.isbs.com

Hart Publishing, 16C Worcester Place, OX1 2JW
Telephone: +44 (0)1865 517530 Fax: +44 (0)1865 510710
E-mail: mail@hartpub.co.uk
Website: http://www.hartpub.co.uk

British Library Cataloguing in Publication Data
Data Available

ISBN-13: 978-1-84113- 699-8 (hardback)
ISBN-10: 1-84113-699-9 (hardback)

Typeset by Compuscript Ltd, Shannon
Printed and bound in Great Britain by
Biddles Ltd, King's Lynn, Norfolk

Preface

This book represents the fruit of a conference held in Somerville College Oxford on 3 March 2006 under the title 'The Regulation of Unfair Commercial Practices under EC Directive 2005/29: New Rules and New Techniques'. The conference was organised by Stephen Weatherill and Ulf Bernitz under the auspices of the Institute of European and Comparative Law in the Oxford University Law Faculty. It was generously supported by the Wallenberg Foundation, Stockholm. All involved wish to express their warm thanks to the Wallenberg Foundation.

Directive 2005/29 is an important new measure in the construction of a legal framework apt to promote an integrated economic space in the European Union. It establishes a harmonised regime governing the control of unfair commercial practices. We strongly believe, as the title of this book claims, that it represents an exercise in new rules and new challenges. And the purpose of this book is to inform and to explore.

The issues are of academic interest and they are central to understanding the evolution of European consumer law within the broader programme of European market regulation. But these issues carry intense practical significance too. The advent of this new regime will provoke commercial operators to seek to exploit opportunities to pursue practices previously suppressed. We therefore present this book in the confident expectation that it will attract a wide readership.

Jenny Dix helped a great deal in the organisation of the conference and we would like to thank her. Dorota Leczykiewicz undertook the task of editing the papers under severe time pressure, and did a splendid job for which we are very grateful. As ever, Hart Publishing have offered an exemplary service.

Stephen Weatherill,
Ulf Bernitz and
Stefan Vogenauer

Contents

Preface v

List of Contributors ix

1. Introduction 1
   Stephen Weatherill and Ulf Bernitz

2. The Unfair Commercial Practices Directive and its General
   Prohibition 11
   Giuseppe B Abbamonte

3. The Unfair Commercial Practices Directive: Its Scope,
   Ambitions and Relation to the Law of Unfair Competition 33
   Ulf Bernitz

4. An End to Fragmentation? The Unfair Commercial Practices Directive
   from the Perspective of the New Member States from Central and
   Eastern Europe 47
   Antonina Bakardjieva Engelbrekt

5. The Unfair Commercial Practices Directive in Context 91
   Ida Otken Eriksson and Ulf Öberg

6. Unfair Commercial Practices Directive—A Missed Opportunity? .. 103
   Geraint Howells

7. Who is the 'Average Consumer'? 115
   Stephen Weatherill

8. The Relationship of the Unfair Commercial Practices
   Directive to European and National Contract Laws 139
   Simon Whittaker

9. The Unfair Commercial Practices Directive and its Consequences
   for the Regulation of Sales Promotion and the Law of Unfair
   Competition 159
   Jules Stuyck

10. The Case for Reclaiming European Unfair Competition Law from
    Europe's Consumer Lawyers 175
    Christopher Wadlow

viii *Contents*

11. Unfair Commercial Practices: Stamping out Misleading
    Packaging...191
    Vanessa Marsland

12. The Challenges Posed by the Implementation of the
    Directive into Domestic Law—a UK Perspective...........................215
    Christian Twigg-Flesner and Deborah Parry

13. Transborder Law Enforcement—Does it Exist?..............................235
    Hans W Micklitz

Appendix—Directive 2005/29.EC..255

Index...281

List of Contributors

Giuseppe Abbamonte is the head of the unit in the European Commission, DG SANCO, responsible for the consumer *acquis*, including the Unfair Commercial Practices Directive.

Antonina Bakardjieva Engelbrekt holds a degree in law from Sofia University, an LLM degree from the European University Institute, Florence, and a doctoral degree in law from Stockholm University. She is Associate Professor at Örebro and Stockholm Universities and is currently a Jean Monnet Fellow at the European University Institute, Florence. Her research focuses on European and comparative market, consumer and intellectual property law, with particular interest in the impact of Europeanisation on national law and institutions.

Ulf Bernitz is Professor of European Law at Stockholm University and Director of the Oxford/Stockholm Wallenberg Venture in European Law at the Institute of European and Comparative Law, University of Oxford. He has written books and articles in the fields of marketing, competition and consumer law and chaired the Commission that prepared the present Swedish Marketing Practices Act.

Ida Otken Eriksson is a Doctoral Candidate in the University of Stockholm. Previously she was a legal secretary at the European Court of Justice (Cabinet Gulmann), and in private practice.

Geraint Howells is professor of Law at Lancaster University and a barrister at Gough Square Chambers. He has written and lectured widely on consumer law and regularly acts as consultant to various governmental and non-governmental bodies. With Hans Micklitz and Thomas Wilhemsson he has written *European Fair Trading Law: The Unfair Commercial Practices Directive*.

Vanessa Marsland is a partner at Clifford Chance LLP.

Hans-W Micklitz occupies the Lehrstuhl für Privat- und Wirtschaftsrecht, Jean Monnet Chair on European Economic Law at the University of Bamberg, and is Head of VIEW (Institute for European Consumer and Economic Law).

Ulf Öberg is founder of and partner in Öberg & Associés AB; he is a doctoral candidate at Stockholm University; and former *référendaire* to Judge Hans Ragnemalm at the European Court of Justice.

Deborah Parry is an independent consultant in consumer law, and was formerly a Senior Lecturer in Law at the University of Hull.

Jules Stuyck is Professor of European and Economic Law at the K U Leuven (where he is director of the Study Centre for Consumer Law and of the LL M programme), Professor of European law at the Radboud Universiteit Nijmegen, Visiting Professor of EU Competition Law at the Central European University, Budapest, and partner in Liedekerke.Wolters. Waelbroeck.Kirkpatrick, Brussels.

Christian Twigg-Flesner is a Senior Lecturer in Private Law at the University of Hull.

Christopher Wadlow MA, PhD (Cantab) is a Reader at the Norwich Law School, University of East Anglia. He was previously a member of the intellectual property department of Simmons & Simmons. He is the author of *The Law of Passing-off: Unfair Competition by Misrepresentation* (3rd edn London, Sweet & Maxwell, 2004).

Stephen Weatherill is the Jacques Delors Professor of European Law in the University of Oxford, a Fellow of Somerville College and Deputy Director for European Law in the Institute of European and Comparative Law.

Simon Whittaker is Fellow and Tutor in Law at St John's College, Oxford, and Reader in European Comparative Law at the University of Oxford. His interests lie in the areas of the English law of contract and tort, comparative law and the European harmonisation of private law.

1

Introduction

STEPHEN WEATHERILL AND ULF BERNITZ

The title of this book promises an inquiry into 'new rules' and 'new techniques' under the EC's Directive 2005/29 on Unfair Commercial Practices (UCPD).[1] The purpose of this brief Introductory Chapter is to sketch the background to the adoption of the Directive, to situate the measure in the context of the existing literature on EC activity in the field and to set the scene for the Chapters to follow: what really are these 'new rules' and 'new techniques'?

1. CONSUMER LAW: THE GROWTH OF THE LEGISLATIVE ACQUIS

IT IS WELL known that the bulk of the EC's legislative *acquis* in the field of consumer law concerns the harmonisation of contract law. The EC has always possessed a competence to harmonise laws for defined (market-making) ends. Originally the relevant provision was Article 100, which became Article 94 on the renumbering effected by the Treaty of Amsterdam. In practice the key provision today is Article 95 EC, which was Article 100a in its pre-Amsterdam guise. In so far as national laws vary, the argument has typically proceeded that the construction of a unified trading space within the EU was hindered. Therefore harmonisation of laws at EC level was required—'common rules for a common market'. So the strict constitutional purpose of harmonisation was rule-making designed to make an integrated market, but its effect was to allocate to Community level (albeit by virtue of the commonly used minimum formula, typically not exclusively) the competence to decide on the substance of the rules in question. So the subjection of any rule of national law to the discipline of harmonisation carries with it the inevitable implication that the area previously regulated (in different ways) within the Member States will acquire

---

[1] In full: Directive 2005/29/EC of the European Parliament and of the Council, of 11 May 2005, concerning unfair business-to-consumer commercial practices in the internal market and amending Council Directive 84/450/EEC, Directives 97/7/EC, 98/27/EC and 2002/65/EC of the European Parliament and of the Council and Regulation (EC) 2006/2004 of the European Parliament and of the Council [2005] OJ L 149/22.

a common 'Europeanised' regulatory footprint. In this sense harmonisation performs a dual function, first by integrating and deregulating markets (through the reduction of up to 25 different regulatory regimes to one common regime) and secondly by regulating, or more precisely *re*-regulating, them according to the chosen EC-level regulatory technique.

Harmonisation breaks open traditional national regulatory structures, but also stimulates a search for understanding of its 'Europeanising' character. Harmonising contract law is not simply a technical process. It unavoidably means the shaping of a species of European contract law. Choices have to be made by the EC's legislature about the content or the *quality* of the EC's contract law *acquis*. What is ultimately produced is not an EC contract law system on the orthodox model of national systems—but it is a set of rules that force adjustment of national systems and cause reflection on the purpose of the EC's own contribution. There are thematic connections that bind together the EC's interventions. So one may identify within the contract law *acquis* visible and emerging principles and techniques, such as information disclosure, party autonomy and inquiry into substantive unfairness. Important work has been devoted to exploration of how much 'system' is at stake and, still more ambitiously and doubtless controversially, to the recommendation of ways to develop law and practice further.[2] Moreover, it is the complex interaction of harmonised EC contract law and broader systems of deep-rooted national contract law that has triggered the quest for greater 'coherence' to which the Commission is currently dedicated.[3]

So the EC (re-)regulates package travel,[4] unfair terms in consumer contracts,[5] timeshare,[6] and so on. But the consumer law legislative *acquis* stretches beyond contract law. The 'Product Liability Directive' takes the EC's influence into the field of non-contractual liability.[7] Admittedly, there are aspects of this broad and broadening programme of harmonisation which seem more vigorously driven by a unanimous political commitment among the Member States to a species of EC consumer policy than by a

---

[2] Eg, with varying points of emphasis, J Stuyck, 'European Consumer Law after the Treaty of Amsterdam: Consumer Policy in or beyond the Internal Market?' (2000) 37 Common *Market Law Review* (*CMLRev*) 367; G Howells and T Wilhelmsson, 'EC Consumer Law: Has It Come of Age?' (2003) 28 *European Law Review* 370; S Grundmann, 'Information, Party Autonomy and Economic Agents in European Contract Law' (2002) 39 *CMLR* 269; HW Micklitz, 'De la Nécessité d'une Nouvelle Conception pour le Développement du Droit de la Consommation dans la Communauté Européenne' in J Calais-Auloy (ed), *Liber amicorum Jean Calais-Auloy, Études de droit de la consommation* (Paris, Dalloz, 2004); H Rösler, *Europäisches Konsumentenvertragsrecht* (Munich, CH Beck, 2004); K Riesenhuber, *Europäisches Vertragsrecht* (Berlin, de Gruyter, 2003).

[3] For examination of this process see S Vogenauer and S Weatherill (eds), *The Harmonisation of European Contract Law: Implications for European Private Laws, Business and Legal Practice* (Oxford, Hart Publishing, 2006).

[4] Directive 90/314 [1990] OJ L 158/59.

[5] Directive 93/13 [1993] OJ L 95/29.

[6] Directive 94/47 [1994] OJ L 280/83.

[7] Directive 85/374 [1985] OJ L 210/29, amended by Directive 99/34 [1999] OJ L 141/20.

constitutionally pure focus on the role of Article 95 as an instrument for promoting economic integration through legislative harmonisation.[8] And quite how this body of European private law meshes with orthodox understandings of autonomy and individual rights under private law represents another profound challenge.[9] But, as a general observation, the practical impact of the EC's harmonisation programme on consumer law has been substantial.

2. EC ADVERTISING LAW

The EC's harmonisation programme also stretches into advertising law; and, beyond that, into law related to broader types of commercial practice to which the Directive under examination in this book is dedicated. The influence of the EC's legislative *acquis* is significant and growing.

Directive 84/450 on misleading advertising was the EC's first adventure into the field.[10] This applied a harmonised control over misleading advertising and therefore served both to achieve an integrated market, by establishing a common rule for the whole territory of the EU, and to establish the EC's own chosen standards of consumer protection. The Directive was subsequently amended by Directive 97/55,[11] the principal purpose of which is to lay down common criteria according to which comparative advertising is permitted in the EC.

The EC also possesses some product- and sector-specific controls over advertising. Directive 2001/37 harmonises laws concerning the manufacture, presentation and sale of tobacco products.[12] It deals with rules governing warnings on packets, as well as the maximum tar yield of tobacco products. Directive 2003/33 harmonises rules governing advertising of tobacco products in the press and other media.[13] Directive 89/552, the 'Television without Frontiers' Directive, harmonises national laws concerning the pursuit of television broadcasting activities.[14] Its primary purpose is the removal of obstacles to free movement of television broadcasting services within the Community, but, as part of its re-regulatory choice,

---

[8] Cf S Weatherill, 'European Private Law and the Constitutional Dimension' in F Cafaggi (ed), *The Institutional Framework of European Private Law* (Oxford: Oxford University Press, Collected Courses of the Academy of European Law, 2006) 79.

[9] Cf O Cherednychenko, 'EU Fundamental Rights, EC Fundamental Freedoms and Private Law' (2006) 14 *European Review of Private Law* 23.

[10] [1984] OJ L 250/17.

[11] [1997] OJ L 290/18.

[12] [2001] OJ L 194/26.

[13] [2003] OJ L 152/16. This is the (more narrowly drawn) successor to Directive 98/43, annulled by the Court in Case C–376/98 *Germany v Parliament and Council*: Tobacco Advertising [2000] ECR I–8419.

[14] [1989] OJ L 298/23, amended by Directive 97/36 [1997] OJ L 202/60.

it prohibits 'all forms of television advertising and teleshopping for ciga-
rettes and other tobacco products' and prohibits sponsorship by tobacco
product manufacturers, while also controlling television advertising for
and sponsorship by medicinal producers and manufacturers of alcoholic
beverages.[15]

There is, then, a recognisable 'EC advertising law'. The focus on market
integration distinguishes the package of rules from what one would normally expect to find in a national system, but the content reveals a clear
concern to curtail the perceived pernicious effects of (in short) irresponsible
advertising.

3. THE IMPETUS FOR A DIRECTIVE ON UNFAIR COMMERCIAL PRACTICES

Advertising is an important element in successful marketing of goods and
services. But there is a wider scope to the range of commercial practices
that may be deployed by traders. In 2001 the Commission published a
Green Paper on Consumer Protection which tracked the heap of diverse
national laws that are relevant to the regulation of marketing practices.[16]
It described the sheer number of legal obligations that arise in the Member
States as 'off-putting' to 'nearly all businesses but those who can afford to
establish in all Member States', and, in addition, as a brake on consumer
confidence. This was plainly intended to establish EC competence to set
harmonised rules in the field pursuant to Article 95 EC, as well as to make
the substantive case in favour of an EC intervention into the regulation of
marketing practices in business-to-consumer transactions.

A follow-up document in 2002 reported that consultation had shown
strong support for the adoption of a framework Directive in the field.[17] This
in turn was followed by a Draft Directive published by the Commission in
June 2003.[18] This proposed a prohibition against unfair business-to-consumer commercial practices. In April 2004 a supportive legislative resolution was adopted by the Parliament,[19] and in May 2004 the Council reached
a political agreement on the Directive[20] which was duly welcomed by the
Commission.[21] In November 2004 the Council reached a common position
on the adoption of a Directive, which was transmitted to the Parliament.[22]

---

[15] See in detail ch 8 of S Weatherill, *EU Consumer Law and Policy* (Cheltenham, Elgar European Law, 2005).
[16] COM(2001)531, 2 Oct 2001.
[17] COM(2002)289, 11 June 2002.
[18] COM(03)356, 18 June 2003.
[19] A5-0188/2004, 20 Apr 2004.
[20] 2003/0134 (COD), 25 May 2004.
[21] IP/04/658, 18 May 2004.
[22] 2003/0134 (COD), 9 Nov 2004.

Directive 2005/29/EC on unfair commercial practices between business and consumers in the internal market was definitively adopted by the European Parliament and Council in May 2005. The Member States are required to transpose the Directive into national law by 12 December 2007, subject only to certain limited derogations.

4. NEW RULES AND NEW TECHNIQUES—AND NEW CHALLENGES

And so to return to the promise made in the title of this book: what really are the 'new rules' and 'new techniques' contained in this Directive? There are issues of general policy, and there are issues of more detailed 'fit' and interpretation. In combination, these new rules and new techniques hoist this Directive close to the top of the list of the EC's consumer law legislative *acquis* when judged against the standards of intellectual excitement and practical importance in mapping an integrated system of consumer protection for the EC's internal market. And, since the Directive falls for implementation by the Member States only in December 2007, the adventure is only just beginning. There are, in short, enduring challenges to face. The following merely serves to sketch the nature of the challenges. All the issues raised are addressed more fully in one or more of the contributions to this book.

The Directive's central policy choice to set a broad standard of required commercial behaviour in a 'general clause' is of great significance. The Directive prohibits practices which contrary to 'professional diligence' 'materially distort the economic behaviour' of an average consumer.[23] This is a break with the past record of the EC's legislative *acquis* dealing with unfair commercial practices, which has been a good deal more specific, tackling matters such as 'doorstep selling'[24] and timeshare.[25] The selected broader style of the UCPD is plainly more apt to permit regulatory and enforcement flexibility. It may be taken as a refreshingly new approach to tackling the general phenomenon of 'unfairness'. No longer must one 'fit' the practice within a restrictively defined category in order to assert a basis under EC law to supervise it. No longer can rogue traders deftly slide around the detailed rules and escape action when they harm consumers. And yet with flexibility comes unpredictability and imprecision. How can the required legal standard really be understood by traders? Might enforcement practice be compromised by detailed argument about whether a particular practice really counts as 'unfair'? These are concerns that plague any regime employing a general clause, but of course the anxiety returns with extra force when

---

[23] Art 5.
[24] Directive 85/577 [1985] OJ L 372/31.
[25] Directive 94/47, above n 6.

one takes into account the Directive's concern to promote market integration in Europe. How can this be achieved if different approaches are taken to the notion of unfairness in different Member States?

These are indeed challenges, but the Directive is by no means barren of solutions to such concerns. It fleshes out the notions of 'misleading' and 'aggressive' practice.[26] Its Annex contains a 'Black List' of practices considered unfair in all circumstances. So the regime is given firmer shape—it is by no means entirely soft-edged. Moreover, the Directive's preference not slavishly to follow any existing national model for controlling unfair commercial practices reduces the risk—endemic to the EC Directive as a legal act—that established national assumptions will infect the interpretation and application of provisions designed to transpose the Directive into national law. In addition, the EC has increased its attention to the importance of enforcement co-operation across borders as a necessary element in the construction and the management of a truly reliable internal market. This is particularly visible in the shape of Regulation 2006/2004 on Consumer Protection Cooperation, which is intended as an important component in the practical management of the EC's policies.[27]

These devices in many ways represent impressive attempts to create a structure within which a common rule governing unfair business-to-consumer practices will be established at EC level and in which in addition a common application of that rule will be secured at national level. And yet one can expect a degree of unevenness to emerge as the Directive's lifecycle develops. The idea that 'unfairness' may be viewed differently by different adjudicators is much more than merely a technical matter. A commercial practice may conceivably have different effects in different parts of Europe. There is in principle a European standard of unfairness created by this Directive, but there is not a homogenous European market, and a practice may cause damage in one part of the EU but no damage elsewhere where, for example, consumers happen to be a good deal more resistant to the seductive vice of the particular impugned practice. How does one cope? The Directive employs the core notion of an 'average consumer' as a benchmark for identifying 'unfairness'.[28] This choice presents its own profound regulatory and intellectual challenges, given that there is certainly no such thing as an average (European) consumer to be found anywhere in real life! The European Court's treatment of the issue will doubtless be important—and one should appreciate that the types of cases that first reach the Court under the Directive may serve to establish a pattern that will be difficult later to dislodge. Who litigates, and which courts refer, will do much to determine what type of 'vision of the consumer' emerges.

---

[26] Art 6–7, 8–9.
[27] [2004] OJ L 364/1.
[28] Art 5.

For enforcement in particular, the Directive's assumption of a common EU-wide standard of protection underpinned by a reliance on administration of the rules by national (and frequently regional or local) agencies presents challenges. Is the contrast between the reality of a European market and the absence of European consumer protection enforcement agencies a basis for anxiety that administrative diversity will generate practical neglect of effective enforcement of these rules? One may optimistically hope that a process of cross-border institution-building and practical co-operation will develop to underpin this Directive (and others), but one may reflect realistically on the height of the hurdles to such trends which are composed of cultural and institutional heterogeneity across Europe, coupled with the bare fact that most enforcement agencies are poorly resourced and cannot readily take on cases with a costly cross-border dimension.

Another novelty—though one that fits within general policy development in the consumer field—concerns the effect of the Directive on residual national competence in the field. The norm for EC Directives harmonising rules protecting the economic interest of consumers in the past has been minimum harmonisation.[29] That means the EC sets a required floor of regulatory protection in a Directive but the Member States may exceed that level, should they so choose, and may set stricter rules of consumer protection in the relevant field up to the ceiling set by primary rules of EC law, most of all the Treaty rules governing free movement. So market integration is advanced (there is a common rule) but diverse standards of consumer protection persist (in so far as states choose stricter intervention above the common rule). The UCPD rejects this model. It is a measure of maximum harmonisation—or 'maximal' or 'full' harmonisation. It is, in short, a floor, and it is also a ceiling. Member States are locked into the standard required by the Directive—they must prohibit practices that fall below the standard expected by the Directive, but they must allow practices that comply with the Directive. The task of transposition at national level accordingly requires a good deal more attention to detail than in the case of a minimum harmonisation measure, where there is no call to review stricter national measures. Under a maximum measure, stricter rules must be conscientiously sliced away by the national lawmaker. More generally, this 'maximum' or 'full' approach to harmonisation has lately been promoted by the Commission as essential to the regeneration of EC consumer policy in the light of its contribution to the integration of markets in Europe.[30]

---

[29] Cf J Stuyck, 'Patterns of Justice in the European Constitutional Charter: Minimum Harmonisation in the Field of Consumer Law' in L Krämer, H Micklitz and K Tonner (eds), *Law and Diffuse Interests in the European Legal Order* (Baden-Baden, Nomos, 1997); M Dougan, 'Minimum Harmonisation and the Internal Market' (2000) 37 *CMLRev* 853.

[30] The Commission's Consumer Policy Programme for 2002–6 (COM(02)208, [2002] OJ C137/2) provided an important impetus.

Under this perspective, minimum harmonisation fails to eliminate costly regulatory fragmentation between the Member States. The UCPD is an important example of a new strong preference for a *complete* transfer of regulatory responsibility from Member States to the EC in matters of consumer protection in the service of the project of deeper market integration. This, of course, reinforces the point that fixing the standard of protection under the Directive has to be carefully negotiated, well understood and effectively applied. For if a Member State considers the Directive sets too low a standard, it has nowhere to go (other than to seek to induce legislative reform at EC level): the maximum model prevents it upgrading protection within its own territory. This, as the title of the book suggests, is indeed a challenge! Is maximum harmonisation viable? Is it desirable? Does it suppress choice and opportunities for regulatory learning to an extent that is troubling? Or should we rather celebrate the gains from a more efficiently functioning competitive European market, which is regulated to suppress unfairness prejudicing the consumer? The 'maximum harmonisation' model deserves the closest attention (and receives it in this book) for it is central to the choices about how best to balance the interests in free(d) markets and regulatory protection in the European Union.

The issues are of rich academic interest and they are central to understanding the evolution of European consumer law within the broader programme of European market regulation. But these issues carry intense practical significance too. Of course the advent of this new regime will provoke commercial operators to seek to exploit opportunities to pursue practices previously suppressed. How—to take the example of the United Kingdom—will the existing rules on, say, passing-off be affected by the new regime? Will brand-owners lose protection, to the advantage of marketers of copycat products? There is no overt intention on the part of the EC legislature that this will follow—but a legislative instrument is perfectly capable of acquiring an unforeseen momentum of its own as it is driven by ingenious litigants and imaginative jurists. This deserves attention, and receives it in this book.

There is much more! The Directive does not land on an empty field. The sector-specific Directives prevail over the more general Unfair Commercial Practices Directive where their material scope overlaps.[31] Here is another challenge: does this contribute to damaging persisting fragmentation of the EU's regulatory landscape, and what does this imply for review of the legislative *acquis* in this area? The search for coherence does not stop at the existing legislative *acquis*—the inter-relation with the Treaty freedoms demands attention too. The famous rulings in *Keck and Mithouard*[32] and

---

[31] Art 3(4).
[32] Cases C–267 & C–268/91 *Keck and Mithouard* [1993] ECR I–6097.

in *Cassis de Dijon*[33] cannot be ignored. In fact, in many areas the Directive seeks to carve out its own niche in a densely populated legal environment. The Directive is stated to apply 'without prejudice to contract law'.[34] EC consumer policy has long been a patchwork, and one of its features has been that it laps on the shores of not only private law but also public or administrative law. Yet the UCPD asserts a division between these waters in its claim to apply 'without prejudice to contract law'. Is this sustainable or even intellectually coherent? Commercial practices are so very close to contract law—commonly they induce entry into contracts. One may readily imagine that the Directive is capable at least of influencing patterns of thinking in the field of contract law, albeit that its impact is contingent on a number of factors including national legislative and judicial attitudes. Here too the impression is that this Directive—like all Directives but this one likely more than most—will have intended and unintended effects that will not be capable of satisfactory measurement for many years to come. EC Directives can 'irritate' national legal orders.[35]

Remember too that the field of business-to-consumer commercial practices, to which this Directive is devoted, is connected to other important fields of law, albeit certainly in different ways in different Member States. Unfair competition law generally . . . competition law . . . a further challenge for the UCPD is to demonstrate a coherent and operational relationship with these rules. Moreover, Member States remain free to take action against commercial practices where matters of 'taste and decency' are at stake.[36] Precisely where this limit to the scope of the Directive falls promises to provoke debate and litigation. The 'shock tactics' of some advertisers are notorious. Where lies the margin between a decision on a campaign's unfairness, which must correspond to the requirements of the Directive on Unfair Commercial Practices, and a decision directed at preserving national notions of decency and dignity in the face of a lurid advertising campaign, where compliance with primary Community law, in particular the free movement rules, is the principal issue at stake?[37]

The EU's enlargement in 2005 from 15 to 25 Member States adds another rich vein of inquiry. Indeed one justification for the adoption of the Directive on Unfair Commercial Practices was precisely the need to strengthen the regulatory framework underpinning the internal market in the light of the challenge of enlargement. And yet how can this measure be absorbed into the legal and institutional culture of the states of Central and

---

[33] Case 120/78 *Rewe-Zentrale AG v Bundesmonopolverwaltung für Branntwein* [1979] ECR 649.

[34] Art 3(2).

[35] Cf G Teubner, 'Legal Irritants: Good Faith in British Law or How Unifying Law Ends Up in New Divergences' (1998) 61 *Modern Law Review* 11.

[36] Recital 7.

[37] Cf Case C–36/02 *Omega Spielhallen* [2004] ECR I–9609.

Eastern Europe which have bounced and been bounced so rapidly from the command economy to the market economy and which are now called on to absorb a regime of the complexity and ambition of the Directive on Unfair Commercial Practices? What can consumer protection *really* mean in such circumstances, beyond the emphasis on checking compliance with the EC *acquis* by ticking boxes on Commission-prepared questionnaires?

These, then, constitute the formidably awkward and formidably interesting challenges presented by Directive 2005/29 on unfair commercial practices between business and consumers in the internal market. They are the meat on which this book feasts. One academic speaker at our conference in Oxford in March 2006 admitted to having begun with a sceptical attitude to the Directive, but had finished up rather liking the Directive as a new and interesting development in the promotion of a true internal market. The reader is now invited to form his or her own value judgement.

2

The Unfair Commercial Practices Directive and its General Prohibition

GIUSEPPE B ABBAMONTE[1]

1. INTRODUCTION

D IRECTIVE 2005/29/EC ON unfair commercial practices between business and consumers in the internal market (the 'Directive') was proposed by the Commission on 18 June 2003 and adopted by the European Parliament and Council almost two years later on 11 May 2005.[2] The Member States, subject to some limited derogations, shall apply the national measures implementing the directive by 12 December 2007.

The Directive represents the outcome of a long consultation process on the future of consumer policy which began with the publication by the Commission of the Green Paper on Consumer Protection in October 2001 (the 'Green Paper').[3] The Green Paper made the case for a reform of the European legislation of consumer protection based on a framework directive prohibiting unfair commercial practices between business and consumers. The case for reform was that European consumers were not taking full

---

[1] The author is the head of the unit in the Health and Consumer Department of the European Commission dealing with the regulation of unfair commercial practices and other consumer protection legislation. This chapter was drafted following a meeting in Washington, DC, on 6–7 Oct 2005 where the author presented the newly adopted Unfair Commercial Practices Directive to the Federal Trade Commission. The chapter describes the structure, objectives and justification of the Directive in terms of better regulation, liberalisation of the Internal Market and consumer protection. It then analyses the main Articles of the Directive and briefly compares them with the corresponding provisions of the US Federal Statements on Deception and Unfairness. The views expressed are purely personal.

This chapter is largely based on the article 'The Unfair Commercial Practices Directive: An Example of the new European Consumer Protection Approach' by the same author [2006] *Columbia Journal of European Law* (forthcoming).

[2] Directive 2005/29/EC of the European Parliament and of the Council, of 11 May 2005, concerning unfair business-to-consumer commercial practices in the internal market and amending Council Directive 84/450/EEC, Directives 97/7/EC, 98/27/EC and 2002/65/EC of the European Parliament and of the Council and Regulation (EC) 2006/2004 of the European Parliament and of the Council [2005] OJ 2005 L 149/22.

[3] Green Paper on Consumer Protection, 2 Oct 2001, COM(2001)531 final.

advantage of the Internal Market.[4] There was strong evidence that the Internal Market was more a reality for business-to-business transactions. By contrast, a European business-to-consumer market was far from achieved. One of the primary reasons for such failure was a lack of consumer confidence in cross-border transactions.

In the Green Paper, the Commission noted that, in general, there were significant differences in the regulation of consumer protection by the Member States.[5] For example, some Member States[6] had a general legal principle of fair trading or good and honest business practices (ie the general clause) supported by specific rules (eg on misleading advertising). Others[7] did not have such a general principle but only specific rules.

The Commission found that there was a causal link between this regulatory fragmentation and the lack of consumer confidence in the Internal Market.[8] It argued that these differences would make the regulatory environment very unpredictable for consumers and strengthen their belief that they could not rely on the same level of protection when dealing with foreign traders. The argument for reform was even easier to make for businesses. Legal fragmentation created significant Internal Market barriers for business by increasing their compliance and research costs.

Specific examples of such barriers were the ban on certain forms of advertising to children in Sweden[9] and the ban on door-step selling in Luxembourg.[10] A more general and, therefore, more serious obstacle derived from the fact that the courts and enforcement agencies of certain Member States applied different benchmarks to assess whether a commercial practice was unfair. This was especially true for the assessment of misleading advertising.[11] In a number of cases, the advertiser was asked to remove the product from the market of the consumer because certain aspects of the

---

[4] Ibid.

[5] Ibid.

[6] Eg Sweden, Finland, Denmark and Belgium.

[7] Eg the UK, Italy, Ireland and France.

[8] Green paper on Consumer Protection, above n 4, at para 3.1.

[9] In Sweden certain forms of advertising cannot be directed to children. Since 1983, the Market Court has banned, on the basis of Art 4 of the Marketing Act (ie the general clause) direct advertising addressed to children under the age of 16, see eg MD (Marknads-domstol) 1983:16, MD 1999:26. One of the reasons for the ban is that children lack legal competence and may therefore not enter into a purchase agreement without the consent of a parent or guardian. Moreover, under the Swedish Radio and TV Act (1996:844), Chap. VII, ss 4 and 7(3), JB: § 4 '[a]dvertising during a TV broadcast may not have as its objective capturing the attention of children under 12 years of age'.

[10] In its law of 16 July 1987 on 'Door-step selling and itinerary trade', Luxemburg banned door-step selling in its territory, making use of the minimum clause in the Door-step selling Directive: see Art 8 of Council Directive 85/57/EEC, of 20 Dec 1985, to protect the consumer in respect of contracts negotiated away from business premises [2005] OJ L 372/31.

[11] The courts of certain Member States, disregarding the case law of the Court of Justice, did not apply the average consumer test (see section on general clause below).

packaging[12] or the name of the product[13] were considered misleading to the consumers in that country. It is worth noting that, in many of these cases, the advertisers were the European subsidiaries of American companies that were legitimately marketing products in the same way in the United States and other Member States.

These barriers raised obstacles to the free movement of goods and to the freedom to provide services and thus generated distortions of competition. As a result, the elimination of these obstacles and distortions justified a regulatory initiative under Article 95 of the Treaty.[14] The Directive was preceded by an impact assessment,[15] which was one of the first ever carried out by the Commission in accordance with the EU better regulation principles. One of the legislative options considered in the assessment was a framework directive establishing general rules for judging unfair commercial practices. The impact assessment reiterated the first findings of the Commission that justified the proposal in terms of better regulation and completion of the Internal Market. It confirmed that a framework directive would be the best tool for getting rid of the abovementioned Internal Market barriers.

In order to understand the innovations introduced by the Directive, one must recall that, before this Directive, the EU had largely followed a vertical approach, based on minimum harmonisation, in regulating consumer

---

[12] Case C–99/01 *Linhart & Biffl v Unabhängiger Verwaltungssenat* [2002] ECR I–09375. In this case the administrative chamber of Vienna had found that the statement 'dermatologically tested' on the packaging of Colgate products (shampoo and soap) was misleading. This was because the absence of explicit references to the content and outcome of the medical assessment to which the products were subject could give consumers the erroneous impression that these products had curative effects. The products with the statement had been lawfully marketed in other member States.

[13] Eg Case C–220/98 *Estée Lauder v Lancaster* ('Lifting') [2000] ECR I–00117. Estée Lauder had asked for the removal from the German market of a cosmetic product whose name incorporated the word 'lifting', as this the term could mislead consumers. Consumers could get the impression that the use of the product would obtain results comparable to surgical lifting. Also in this case the product had been lawfully marketed with that labelling in other Member States. See also Case C–315/92 *Verband Sozialer Wettbewerb v Clinique et Estée Lauder* ('Clinique'), [1994] ECR I–00317. Clinique had been asked to withdraw its cosmetic products from the German market as the name 'Clinique' could mislead consumers as to the curative effects of the products. Clinique products were lawfully marketed in all the other Member States.

[14] These are the conditions that need to be met for a Directive to be adopted under Art 95 EC. On these conditions, see Case C–376/98 *Germany v European Parliament and Council of the EU* [2000] ECR I–08419, at para 95, on advertising and sponsorship of tobacco products.

[15] Commission Staff Working Paper, Extended Impact Assessment, of 18 June 2003, on the Directive of the European Parliament and of the Council concerning unfair business-to-consumer commercial practices in the internal market and amending Council Directive 84/450/EEC, Directives 97/7/EC, 98/27/EC of the European Parliament and of the Council, SEC(2003)724. The impact assessment is a process by which the Commission analyses *ex ante* the economic, social and environmental impacts of its main actions.

protection. With few exceptions, most of the existing directives regulate consumer rights in relation to specific products (eg timeshare and package travel) or specific selling modes (distance selling and door-step selling). This approach led to a number of problems. First, given its specificity, sectoral legislation often contains prescriptive provisions that can easily be circumvented by dishonest but creative traders. They may design their contract terms and selling methods so that they escape the regulations and elude the consumer protection afforded by them. A typical example is that of quasi-timeshare products, which are timeshares designed to avoid the Timeshare Directive by specifying a contract duration of less than three years, the minimum duration necessary to fall within the scope of the Directive. The risk of too-specific sectoral legislation is that it may constantly run a step behind market developments and rapidly become obsolete.

Secondly, different regulations of different selling modes may lead to fragmentation and generate confusion. As a result, consumers can enjoy different rights, or the modalities for the exercise of these rights may vary, depending on whether consumers buy a product or a service and on the selling method employed by the trader.[16] These differences are often not justified on economic or legal grounds. Moreover, given that most of the existing Directives contain a minimum harmonisation clause,[17] there may still be regulatory differences between the Member States which generate fragmentation and legal uncertainty in the fields harmonised by these Directives.

A third problem derives from the fact that, as indicated above, these sectoral regulations regulate the product (ie the rights for consumers in relation to a certain product), but do not regulate the practice (ie how the product is actually marketed and sold to the consumer). Most of the problems experienced by consumers are the result of unfair commercial practices carried out by dishonest traders. For example, aggressive pressure techniques after the sale, such as threatening telephone calls, may have the effect of dissuading consumers from exercising their rights of withdrawal.

For these reasons, the Directive moves away from the vertical, minimum harmonisation approach. It is a framework directive providing for full harmonisation. It applies to both goods and services, to all sectors and all marketing and selling methods. It takes a liberal approach: everything that

---

[16] Eg under the Distance Selling Directive the consumer has at least 7 working days in which to withdraw from the contract: see Art 6 of Directive 97/7/EC of the European Parliament and of the Council, of 20 May 1997, on the protection of consumers in respect of distance contracts [1997] OJ L 144/19; under the Door-step Selling Directive the consumer has at least 7 days to withdraw from the contract: see Art 5 of Directive 85/577/EEC, above n 11.

[17] Ie a provision enabling the Member States to adopt or maintain provisions which are more favourable to the consumer in the field covered by the Directive.

is not explicitly prohibited is allowed. The Directive is principle-based, being founded on the principle not to trade unfairly and on a general prohibition of unfair commercial practices. Given its very broad scope, the general prohibition should not easily be circumvented even by the most imaginative rogue traders.

2. THE SCOPE (ARTICLE 3)

Article 3 specifies what is within the scope of the Directive and, equally important, what is not.[18] The Directive applies to commercial practices both before and after any purchase by a consumer. The post-sale application is necessary to capture situations where the consumer has a continuing relationship with the trader, such as in the case of a magazine subscription or the purchase of a car from a dealer. It ensures that aspects of the relationship which are not governed by the underlying contract can be dealt with and that, where promises made to consumers pre-sale are not honoured, this unfair practice can be resolved per se, in addition to any contractual remedies available to the consumer. Take, for example, an Internet service provider which promises in its advertising free 24-hour online service availability. If, after the consumer has subscribed to the contract, the ISP does not provide such a service or does not answer the consumer's telephone calls, this will be an unfair practice. Another clear-cut example of an unfair commercial practice conducted after the sale is a unilateral breach of contract.[19]

The Directive protects the economic interests of consumers, and as such harmonises only the business-to-consumer economic aspects of the marketing laws of the Member States.[20] Issues of taste and decency are outside its scope. These issues are rooted in the cultural traditions of the Member States and can hardly be harmonised at the European level. Ethical issues, such as corporate social responsibility, are also outside its ambit, but they become relevant if the trader establishes a clear link between its commitments in these areas and the marketing of its products. For example, if the

---

[18] Art 3 of the Directive, above n 2.

[19] In the US Orkin, a company providing disinfecting and pest control services, had entered into contracts with consumers to provide lifetime termite protection services for a fixed annual fee. There was no contractual basis for Orkin to raise these fees. In 1980, Orkin unilaterally breached 207,000 of these contracts by raising the annual fee. In 1986 The Federal Trade Commission found that this widespread, unilateral breach of contract was unfair: see *Orkin Exterminating Co. Inc.*, 108 FTC 263 (1986); affirmedin, *FTC v Orkin*, 849 F 2d 1354 (11th Circ, 1988).

[20] For the purpose of this chapter, marketing laws may be defined as those which regulate how products and services can be lawfully marketed. These laws cover a boundless number of issues ranging, eg, from the protection of the economic interests of consumer (eg misleading advertising addressed to consumers), to unfair competition, to food law.

trader falsely states in its advertising that it does not use child labour for the manufacture of its products, this will be misleading under the Directive.

Consumer health and safety aspects of products and services are also outside its scope, but they become relevant when the corresponding information is provided to the consumer in a way that is unfair under the Directive. For example, the Directive does not regulate the safety requirements of goods and services and is not concerned with the consequences stemming from placing unsafe products on the market. However, if a trader makes a false or otherwise misleading claim as to the safety of a product (eg in relation the quantities of fat in food), the claim will be misleading under the Directive. This is because misleading claims can impair the consumer's ability to make an informed economic choice and, thus, may harm his economic interests.

The Directive does not deal with contract law and has no bearing on the conditions of formation, validity or effect of the contract. This means that the fact that a consumer has concluded a contract because, for example, he has been misled by an unfair commercial practice is irrelevant under the Directive, which provides for no remedies to invalidate the contract. Of course, the Directive will not limit the general contract law remedies (eg rescission of the contract or appropriate reduction of the price) available to the consumer who has entered into a contract upon being misled. In that case, the consumer will have to institute an action in a civil court, and the fact that the contract has been preceded by a misleading practice will be an important factor that the court will have to take into account.

A more complex matter is the relationship between the Directive and the laws of the Member States on unfair competition. The immediate aim of the Directive is to protect the economic interests of consumers from unfair commercial practices. In doing so, it also protects legitimate business from unfair competition, ensures the integrity of the market and facilitates lawful competition. If a company misleads consumers about its product, it could unlawfully steal business from its fair-dealing competitors who abide by the rules in their dealings with consumers. Unfair commercial practices may also cause an atmosphere of consumer distrust, which can reduce total welfare in several ways. These unlawful practices carried out by a group of traders may:

> lead consumers to doubt the integrity of an entire industry or to distrust markets generally. Deception by Internet sellers, for example, could discourage consumers from using the Internet to gather information and make purchases. Truthful sellers must resort to extraordinary measures to persuade consumers of their honesty.[21]

---

[21] TJ Muris, 'The Interface of Competition and Consumer Protection', Prepared Remarks at the Fordham Corporate Law Institute's 29th Annual Conference on International Antitrust Law and Policy, New York City, 31 Oct 2002, available at www.ftc.gov/speeches/muris/021031fordham.pdf, at 5.

The protection of competitors from unfair competition is, however, an indirect effect of the Directive. The precondition for applying the Directive is the economic harm to the consumer. If a commercial practice harms only the competitor but does not hurt the consumer, it will fall outside the scope of the Directive. As a result, an act may violate the standard of unfair competition in certain Member States but still not be subject to the Directive. This is, for example, the case with denigration and slavish imitation (ie slavish copying independent of the risk of confusion for the consumer). The latter is forbidden in certain countries as an act of unfair competition because they consider that the company copying the product is taking undue advantage of the reputation or expenditure of a competitor. [22] Consumers may derive an advantage from the placing on the market of such products, which may be substitutes having the same quality as the branded products but lower prices. Therefore, such an action does not all foul of the Directive. Practices that are classified as unfair competition and do harm the economic interests of consumers, such as confusing marketing (ie marketing which generates a risk of confusion with the products and distinctive signs of a competitor), fall within the scope of the Directive.

It goes without saying that the Directive does not deal with antitrust matters, such as anti-competitive agreements, abuses of dominant positions, mergers and acquisitions. The Directive also does not call into question the laws of the Member States establishing the conditions of establishment or the authorisation regimes for the exercise of professions. It does not affect the codes of conduct and other specific rules governing regulated professions that the Member States may impose on professionals.

The Directive is a framework law which applies only when there is no sector-specific legislation regulating unfair commercial practices. In application of the principle *lex specialis derogat legi generali*, when such specific legislation exists and harmonises the subject matter in an exhaustive manner, its provisions will prevail over those of the Directive. For example, the special provisions on labelling of cosmetic products contained in Article 6 of Directive 76/768 take precedence over the Directive.[23]

Where a sectoral legal instrument regulates only certain elements of commercial practices, such as the pre-contractual information requirements, the Directive will be applicable for the other outstanding elements. For example, the Directive will come into play if the general information to be provided by service providers under the E-commerce Directive is provided

---

[22] Eg It is prohibited in France: Art 1382 of the Code civil, but not in the UK.
[23] Council Directive 76/768/EEC of 27 July 1976 on the approximation of the laws of the Member States relating to cosmetic products [1976] OJ L 262/169, as amended by Council Directive 93/35/EEC of 14 June 1993, [1993] OJ L 151/32. On this *lex specialis* issue see Case C–99/01 *Linhart & Biffl v Unabhängiger Verwaltungssenat* [2002] ECR I–09375, paras 17–21.

in a misleading way.[24] In this context, the Directive may be described as a gap-filler, since it will fill the consumer protection lacunas in existing sector-specific legislation.

3. INTERNAL MARKET (ARTICLE 4)

Article 4 is an important provision that enables the Directive to achieve its Internal Market effects in full.[25] By enshrining the principle of mutual recognition, it prevents the Member States from restricting the free movement of goods and services on grounds falling within the field coordinated by the Directive. This means that the Member State of the consumer (the country of destination) will not be able to stop, or make it more difficult for, a trader operating from another Member State (the country of origin) to market its product on account of differences between its national law transposing the Directive and the law of the trader.

Mutual recognition applies in the field harmonised by the Directive. It does not apply to matters which are outside the scope of the Directive (eg taste and decency). The Directive is the first European consumer protection law containing a mutual recognition clause. The Commission included such a clause in the Directive because it considered that the full harmonisation and the high common level of consumer protection introduced by the Directive created the conditions to make mutual recognition politically acceptable and workable in this field.

Unlike the original proposal of the Commission,[26] the Directive contains no choice of law rules. In private actions, the applicable law (ie the law determining the extra-contractual liability of the trader) will, therefore, have to be determined on the basis of the international private law rules.[27]

---

[24] Directive 2000/31/EC of the European Parliament and of the Council, of 8 June 2000, on certain legal aspects of information society services, in particular electronic commerce in the Internal Market [2000] OJ L 178/1.

[25] Art 4 of the Directive, above n 2.

[26] Under Art 4(1) of the Commission proposal, '[t]raders shall only comply with the national provisions falling within the field approximated by this Directive, of the Member State where they are established. The Member State in which the trader is established shall ensure such compliance': Proposal for a Directive of the European Parliament and of the Council, concerning unfair business-to-consumer commercial practices in the internal market and amending Council Directive 84/450/EEC, Directives 97/7/EC, 98/27/EC, COM(2003)356 final. Art 4(1) was deleted during the legislative procedure.

[27] Once adopted, in the EU these will be the rules contained in the Proposal for a European Parliament and Council Regulation of 22 July 2003 on the law applicable to non-contractual obligations ('Rome II'), COM(2003)427 final. Under Art 5 of the Proposal, 'the law applicable to a non-contractual obligation arising out of an act of unfair competition shall be the law of the country where competitive relations or the collective interests of consumers are or are likely to be directly and substantially affected'. This means that legal actions originating from cross-border disputes involving the provisions of the Directive will normally be subject to the law of the country of destination, which is the country of the consumer.

The principle of mutual recognition in Article 4, it is argued, should be applied regardless of whether the applicable law, designated by the international private law rules, is the law of the country of destination. If the commercial practice is in conformity with the law of the country of origin, but the applicable law is the law of the country of destination and the practice is not in conformity with this law, the court hearing the case will have to disregard the law of the country of destination. In this case, the law of the country of destination insofar as it restricts the practice, for example by imposing additional requirements on the trade, will be an Internal Market barrier incompatible with Article 4.

Given the maximum harmonisation brought about by the Directive and its level of detail, the question of the applicable law should become much less relevant.[28] The Directive should reduce considerably the differences between the laws of the Member States and so make the issue of whether the law of the country of origin or of the country of destination is applicable in cross-border cases of little importance. This point is illustrated by the recent *Duchesne* case, where the UK Office of Fair Trading ('OFT') sought the first ever cross-border injunction in Europe.[29] The OFT obtained the injunction against the Duchesne company in the Brussels Commercial Court to stop a Belgian trader from sending Misleading Prize Notifications to consumers in the UK. The OFT brought proceedings for breaches of the Belgian and English laws implementing the Misleading Advertising Directive. In granting the injunction, the Belgian court ruled that the applicable law was English law. Duchesne appealed against the injunction. The Court of Appeal upheld the original ruling, but took the view that the applicable law was Belgian law.[30] This case shows that unfair cross-border practices will normally constitute an offence under the laws both of the country of origin and of the country of destination.[31] Nevertheless, there may still be

---

[28] The substantive provisions of the Directive, it is submitted, could in theory be directly applicable without requiring any transposition act of the Member States. These provisions are imperative and sufficiently precise as to confer individual rights on consumers and, therefore, in accordance with the case law of the Court of Justice, could be directly applied even if the Directive were not transposed: eg see Case C–431/92 *Commission v Germany* [1995] ECR I–2189, at 2224.

[29] The OFT initiated the action under s 8 of the Enterprise Act 2002, which gives effect to the Injunctions Directive. This directive gives an enforcement body or organisation designated by one Member State (such as the OFT in the UK) the power to take action before a court in another Member State (eg Belgium) against traders based in that Member State. The precondition for seeking the injunction is that the trader through an infringement of certain EU consumer protection laws is harming the collective interests of the consumers of the country of the enforcer (eg the UK): Directive 98/27 of the European Parliament and of the Council of 19 May 1998, on injunctions for the protection of consumers' interests [1998] OJ L 166/51.

[30] *D Duchesne v OFT*, Court of Appeal, Brussels, 8 Dec 2005.

[31] The conclusion that is drawn from *Duchesne*, which is about the cross-border application of the Minimum Harmonisation Directive on Misleading Advertising, is *a fortiori* valid for the Directive, which provides for full harmonisation.

some differences in the transposition laws of the Member States or in their interpretation of the Directive. For example, Article 7(3) of the Directive regulates the information that a trader must provide in advance when he makes an invitation to purchase.[32] In this information, the trader has to indicate the main characteristics of product. Now, the Member States may have different views as to the main characteristics of products. For example, Member State X may issue guidelines under which the main characteristics of cars are A, B and C, while Member State Y may choose A, B, C and D. In this case, if the trader established in X addresses an invitation to purchase to consumers in Y, it will not be possible to challenge the invitation because it does not contain item D.[33]

4. THE STRUCTURE

The Directive can be depicted as an inverted pyramid having the general prohibition or general clause at the apex, as illustrated in Figure 2.1.

The general prohibition is the key element of the Directive.[34] It prohibits unfair commercial practices between businesses and consumers and defines the conditions for determining whether a commercial practice is unfair. In addition, the Directive regulates the main categories of unfair commercial practices: misleading and aggressive practices. The corresponding provisions reproduce with certain adaptations the tests of the general prohibition.

The general prohibition has an autonomous regulatory function in the sense that a practice which is neither misleading nor aggressive can still be captured by the general prohibition if it meets its criteria. In practice, most unfair practices are either misleading or aggressive, and it is expected that they will be assessed under these more specific provisions. The autonomous functioning of the general prohibition means that it serves as a safety net

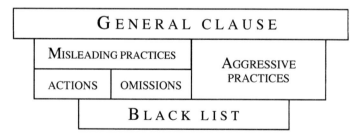

Figure 2.1 The Structure of the Directive

---

[32] Art 7(3) of the Directive, above n 2.
[33] This case is further discussed in the section on the average consumer below.
[34] Art 5 of the Directive, above n 2.

to catch any current or future practices that cannot be categorised as either misleading or aggressive. The primary motivation is to ensure that the Directive is future-proof.

Consumer protection enforcers around the world are coming across different commercial practices in the Internet-based economy that can be defined only with great difficulty as misleading or aggressive but are equally unfair. An example of this is modem hijacking, which consists of rerouting Internet modem connections in a way that causes the consumer to pay disproportionate telephone bills. An Internet user clicks on a banner to run a program on his computer and, without alerting the consumer, the program disconnects his modem from the local server and reconnects it to a distant server. This results in higher telephone fees compared with ordinary dial-up Internet connections. Another example of a commercial practice that could be covered under the general prohibition is given below.[35]

Finally, the Directive contains an exhaustive blacklist of practices that will be regarded in all circumstances as unfair.[36] These unquestionably unfair practices will be prohibited at the outset in all Member States. Of course, a number of practices not explicitly included in the list could also be unfair. These practices will have to be assessed under the provisions on misleading and aggressive practices as well as those of the general prohibition. The blacklist is an integral part of the Directive and can be amended only by a revision of the Directive by means of the legislative procedure under Article 251 of the EU Treaty. The list has to be implemented in the same or an equivalent way by the Member States, which are prevented from adding to the list. If the Member States were allowed to do so, this could have the effect of circumventing the maximum harmonisation introduced by the Directive and would frustrate the objective of legal certainty pursued by the Directive.

5. THE GENERAL PROHIBITION (ARTICLE 5)

The general prohibition contains two conditions for determining whether a practice is unfair. These conditions are cumulative:

(1) The practice must be contrary to the requirements of professional diligence, and

---

[35] See below on the autonomy of the general clause.

[36] See Annex 1: 'Commercial Practices which are in all circumstances considered unfair', of the Directive, above n 3. Examples of these practices are:
— claiming to be a signatory to a code when the trader is not;
— displaying a trust mark, quality mark or equivalent without having obtained the necessary authorisation;
— creating the impression that the consumer cannot leave the premises until a contract is formed.

(2) The practice must materially distort or be likely materially to distort the economic behaviour of the average consumer whom it reaches or to whom it is addressed or of the average member of the group in cases where a commercial practice is directed at a particular group of consumers.[37]

(a) Professional Diligence

Article 2(h) defines professional diligence as 'the standard of special skill and care which a trader may reasonably be expected to exercise towards consumers, commensurate with honest market practice and/or the general principle of good faith in the trader's field of activity'.[38] The concept of professional diligence is broader than subjective good faith since it encompasses not only honesty but also competence on the part of the trader. For example, the behaviour of an honest but incompetent antique dealer who sells fakes, believing them to be originals, would not be in conformity with the requirements of professional diligence.

Professional diligence is broadly equivalent to the common law concept of duty of care. It is a measure of the diligence that a good businessman can reasonably be expected to exercise and must be commensurate with the duty to be performed and the individual circumstances of each case. Professionals are expected to comply with good standards of conduct and approved practices. It is a measure of diligence above that of an ordinary person or non-specialist. The boundaries of professional diligence are not always clear-cut; in certain cases assessing the diligence of a trader may require a close examination of all the relevant facts. For example, the manager of a restaurant has a duty to ensure that the ingredients used are fresh and meals properly prepared. A manager will clearly fail to comply with the professional diligence requirement if he does not ensure that food is properly handled, prepared, and served (eg that it is kept at the proper temperature or is in contact only with plates or utensils that are clean). However, if a customer becomes ill because he is allergic to a particular type of food that he has eaten in that restaurant, the manager will not be held responsible. Restaurant managers are not doctors and cannot be responsible for every accident that occurs to their customers.

(b) Material Distortion

According to Article 2(e), 'to materially distort the economic behaviour of consumers' means 'using a commercial practice to appreciably impair the

---

[37] Directive 2005/29/EC, above n 2.
[38] Art 2(h) of ibid.

consumer's ability to make an informed decision and thereby causing the consumer to take a transactional decision that he would not have taken otherwise'.[39] The material distortion test aims to verify whether the practice has the potential to distort the consumer's economic behaviour. This concept is at the core of the consumer protection legal systems in the Member States[40] and abroad. The US Federal Statement on Deception also covers illegitimate commercial practices that are likely to deceive the consumer and thereby affect his economic behaviour.

The rationale of most of these systems is that unfair commercial practices distort consumer preferences by impairing their capacity or freedom of choice. Consumers buy unwanted products, accept terms and conditions that they would not have accepted, or turn to products that, absent the unfair practice, they would have regarded as inferior substitutes. This causes a market failure that marketing laws aim to redress.

The test, however, does not require proof that consumers have suffered economic damage (eg monetary harm). In some cases, unfair commercial practices will cause economic damage to the consumer as, for example, when sellers coerce the consumer to pay a disproportionately high price or to buy a defective product. However, the insertion of an economic damage requirement as a precondition to acting under the Directive would have been inappropriate as it would significantly have diminished the current level of consumer protection in the EU. Claimants would have to prove not only that the commercial practice caused the consumer to purchase something that he would otherwise not have purchased, but also that the consumer is worse off after the transaction. This is clearly unacceptable and impractical. In most cases, it would be extremely difficult, if not impossible, to prove and quantify the financial loss. This is particularly true where consumers have not yet bought the product because the practice (eg a misleading advertising campaign) has not yet been launched or has only recently been launched.

The use of the adverb 'appreciably' in the definition introduces a threshold. Practices falling below this threshold will be considered *de minimis* and, thus, legitimate under the Directive. For example, the offer of refreshments at the commercial premises of the trader could have a

---

[39] Art 2(f) of ibid.

[40] This concept is also present in the Misleading Advertising Directive. Art 1(2) of the Misleading Advertising Directive defines misleading advertising as 'any advertising which in any way, including its presentation, deceives or is likely to deceive the persons to whom it is addressed or whom it reaches and which, by reason of its deceptive nature, is likely to affect their *economic behaviour* and for these reasons injures or is likely to injure competitors': see Council Directive 84/450/EEC of 10 Sept 1984 concerning misleading and comparative advertising, [1984] OJ L 250/17, as amended by Directive 97/55/EC of the European Parliament and of the Council [1997] OJ L 290/18.

moderate influence, but it is not likely to change consumer behaviour or cause him to make a transactional decision that he would not have otherwise made.

(c) The Average Consumer

The average consumer is the benchmark against which the unfairness of a commercial practice needs to be assessed. The average consumer test is a creation of the European Court of Justice. The Court confirmed the concept in a number of preliminary rulings on the interpretation of Articles 30 and 36 of the EC Treaty (now, after amendment, Articles 28 and 30 EC) and of provisions of secondary legislation (ie the Misleading Advertising Directive and the Community Trade Mark Regulation[41]). Most of the cases were about restrictions on the sale or marketing of a product on the basis of consumer protection from misleading advertising. According to the Court, 'in order to determine whether a particular description, trade mark or promotional description or statement is misleading, it is necessary to take into account the presumed expectations of an average consumer who is reasonably well informed and reasonably observant and circumspect'.[42]

The test is based on the principle of proportionality. A national measure prohibiting claims (eg puffery) that might only deceive a few 'simpleton' and superficial consumers would be disproportionate to the objective pursued and create an unjustified barrier to trade. The test strikes the right balance between the need to protect consumers and the promotion of free trade in an openly competitive market. It is based on the standard of a hypothetical consumer and assumes that consumers should behave like rational economic operators. They should inform themselves about the quality and price of products and make efficient choices. The Court of First Instance has confirmed the test in many instances and, in assessing the likelihood of confusion of certain trade marks, has given some indications as to the behaviour of the average consumer. According to the Court of First Instance, '[t]he average consumer normally perceives a mark as a whole and does not proceed to analyse its various details . . . In addition, account

---

[41] See Art 28 and 30 of the Treaty establishing the European Community; Directive 84/450/EEC, above n 41; Council Regulation (EC) No 40/94 of 20 Dec 1993 on the Community Trademark [1994] OJ L 11/1.

[42] The case law on the average consumer is vast. The test has been recently confirmed in the judgment of 9 Mar 2006 in Case C–421/04 *Matrazen Concord*, not yet reported. Some leading cases on the average consumers are Cases C–210/96 *Gut Springenheide, Rudolf Tusky* [1998] ECR I–04657; C–220/98 *Estée Lauder v Lancaster* ('Lifting') [2000] ECR I–00117; C–99/01 *Linhart & Biffl v Unabhängiger Verwaltungssenat* [2002] ECR I–09375, para 31.

should be taken of the fact that the average consumer only rarely has the chance to make a direct comparison between the different marks but has to place his trust in the imperfect image of them that he has retained in his mind. It should also be borne in mind that the average consumer's level of attention is likely to vary according to the category of goods and services in question'.[43]

The Directive codifies the average consumer test, which was not applied by the courts of certain Member States.[44] Transposition of the test into national law should significantly reduce the scope for divergent assessments of similar practices across the EU and enhance legal certainty.

The Directive represents a good example of constructive dialogue between the Court and the legislator. An original feature of the Directive is that it not only turns this jurisprudence into law, but refines this jurisprudence by modulating the average consumer test when the interests of specific groups of consumers are at stake. First, when the practice is addressed at a specific group of consumers, such as children or rocket scientists, it will be assessed from the perspective of the average member of the group. In the case of an advertisement of a toy during a TV programme for children, for example, one will have to take into account the expectations and the likely reaction of the average child of the group targeted and disregard those of an exceptionally immature or mature child belonging to the same group.

A second refinement of the test concerns those commercial practices that are likely materially to distort the economic behaviour of only a clearly identifiable group of consumers who, for various reasons, are particularly vulnerable to the practice or the underlying product in a way that the trader could reasonably be expected to foresee. In this case, the practice will be assessed from the perspective of the average member of that vulnerable group. This provision does not require traders to do more than is reasonable, both in considering whether the practice would have an unfair impact on any clearly identifiable group of vulnerable consumers, *and in taking steps to mitigate any such impact.* Some consumers because of their extreme naïvety or ignorance may be misled by, or otherwise act irrationally in response to, even the most honest commercial

---

[43] See eg Joined Cases T–183/02 and T–184/02 *El Corte Inglés v Office for Harmonisation in the Internal Market (Trade Marks and Designs)* ('Mundicolor') [2004] ECR II–00965, para 68. See also Case T–20/02 *Interquell GmbH v Office for Harmonisation in the Internal Market (Trade Marks and Designs)* ('Happydog') [2004] ECR II–1001, para 37.

[44] Eg the Belgian Cour de Cassation in *Saint Bryce* (2000) maintained that 'the consumer who needs protection is the least attentive consumer who accepts without criticism the representations made to him and who is not in a position to see through the traps, exaggerations or the manipulative silences' (translation from French into English by the author); the Italian court responsible for misleading advertising (TAR (Tribunale Administrative Regionale) Lazio) refused to apply the test, holding that 'the verification and enforcement powers of the Autorità Garante (the Italian public enforcement body) would be deprived of any effectiveness for the practical impossibility to determine on a case by case basis the average IQ of the consumer reached by the advert': see TAR Lazio, decisions of 27 July 1998 No 2281 and of 18 June 2003 and order of 15 January 2003, No 241 (translation from Italian into English by the author).

practice. There may be, for example, a few simple-minded consumers who may believe that 'Spaghetti Bolognese' are actually made in Bologna or 'Yorkshire Pudding' in York. Traders, however, will not be liable for every interpretation of or action taken in response to their commercial practices by consumers. The real aim of the provision is to capture cases of outright fraud, such as the offer of winning lottery numbers to credulous consumers, and other practices that reach the generality of consumers but are likely to affect only vulnerable consumers. An example of the latter is aggressive door-to-door selling methods that do not affect the average consumer but are likely to intimidate certain groups of consumers, such as the elderly, who may be vulnerable to pressure-selling. The common characteristic of these practices is that it is not possible to prove that they are targeted at the vulnerable group, since they reach the generality of consumers and are not explicitly addressed to the vulnerable ones. In reality, the intent of these practices is to reach the vulnerable ones. A charlatan may sell winning lottery numbers on his website that is open to the general public but he knows that only the credulous consumers will be attracted to his site and lured into the scam.

At the same time, in order to avoid overzealous application of the provision and holding advertisers liable for 'puffery',[45] the Directive clarifies that it does not affect the common and legitimate advertising practice of making exaggerated statements or statements that are not meant to be taken literally.[46]

According to the case law of the Court of Justice on the average consumer,[47] in order to apply the average consumer test, several considerations, including but not limited to social, linguistic and cultural factors, must be borne in mind. This reflects the fact that, in certain cases, peculiar social, linguistic and cultural features in a Member State may justify a different interpretation of the message contained in the commercial practice. Returning to the example given above, it could be argued that, on the basis of the average consumer test, requiring the foreign trader to provide the additional piece of information, D, could be justified in the light of social, cultural or linguistic factors. In other words, because of these factors, the consumers of the country of destination, unlike those in the country of origin, would be misled by the omission of D. This argument, it is argued, should be dismissed. According to the Court of Justice, social, linguistic and cultural factors are not the only ones to be taken into account in applying the average consumer test.[48] For example, the fact that a commercial

---

[45] Puffery consists of statements which are not capable of measurement or which consumers do not take seriously. It is about subjective or hyperbolic statements, such as 'the ultimate driving machine' or 'Red Bull gives you wings'.

[46] Art 5(3) of the Directive, above n 2.

[47] Case C–220/98 *Estée Lauder v Lancaster* ('Lifting') [2000] ECR I–00117, para 29.

[48] For a list of factors to be considered when applying the average consumer test, see the Opinion of Fennely AG, in Case C–220/98 *Estée Lauder v Lancaster* ('Lifting') [2000] ECR I–00117, para 30.

practice has freely circulated without causing consumer protection concerns in the country of origin is another consideration.[49] Given the internal market clause and the full harmonisation of the Directive, this factor should be given prominence over other factors. Therefore, the fact that a commercial practice has circulated legitimately in the country of origin should create a strong presumption about its legality in the country of destination.

(d) The Autonomy of the General Prohibition

The following is an example that illustrates how the general prohibition may operate in practice. It is an unjustified discrimination by a trader to discriminate on the basis of nationality or place of residence of the consumer in the EU. This could be the case of the manager of a hotel who, without any objective reasons, applies different conditions (eg price) according to the nationality or residence of the customers. The manager may apply higher prices to European consumers who are resident abroad or do not have the nationality of the country where the hotel is situated. This type of behaviour would be contrary to the tests of the general clause because:

— an unjustified refusal to sell or discrimination cannot be considered as compatible with the measure of diligence to be expected of a good businessman. A diligent businessman must deal openly and not engage in any unjustified discrimination that could offend prospective purchasers. This consideration must *a fortiori* be valid in the Internal Market and the European Union, which promotes the general principle of non-discrimination;[50] and

— an unjustified refusal to sell or discriminatory treatment can materially distort the economic behaviour of the average consumer. Because of refusal or discriminatory treatment, the preferences of the consumer may be altered. He could, for example, decide not to buy that product or to turn to a competitor whose products he considered to be lower substitutes.

---

[49] Ibid.

[50] See Art 12 of the Treaty establishing the European Community. For an application of the principle of non-discrimination to agreements between individuals see Case C–281/98 *Angonese v Cassa di Risparmio di Bolzano SpA* [2000] ECR I–04139, para 30 ff. In this case the Court applied the principle of non-discrimination set out in Art 48 of the EC Treaty (now, after amendment, Art 39 EC), which regulates the freedom of movement of workers. The Court stated that 'the principle of non-discrimination set out in Article 48 is drafted in general terms and is not specifically addressed to the Member States' (para 30 of the judgment). It is submitted that the same considerations must be applicable, *a fortiori*, to Art 12 EC, which sets out a general prohibition of discrimination, which cannot be restricted to the actions of public authorities.

(e) The Articulation of the Wording of the General Prohibition with the Provisions on Misleading and Marketing Practices

As indicated above, the tests of the general prohibition are reproduced with adaptations in the provisions on misleading and aggressive practices.

The provisions on misleading and aggressive practices do not contain a separate reference to the concept of professional diligence. This is because misleading consumers or treating them aggressively is considered in itself contrary to the requirements of professional diligence. If a practice is misleading or aggressive it will not have to pass the professional diligence test in order to be declared unfair. According to the Directive, misleading and aggressive practices automatically violate the requirements of professional diligence. This means that in practice the professional diligence test will have to be applied only when the practice is assessed under the general prohibition.

The same considerations apply to the 'distortion' element of the material distortion test. Under the Directive misleading and aggressive practices are per se deemed to distort or be likely to distort the consumer's ability to make an informed decision. In other words, these practices will always 'appreciably impair' the consumer's ability to make an informed decision. The concept of distortion, which is based on the broad concept of appreciable impairment of the consumer's ability to make informed decisions (see Article 2(e)), has been adapted to fit the provisions on misleading and aggressive practices. This is why, for example, Article 6, which regulates misleading actions, replaces the appreciable impairment concept with the narrower concept of deception ('deceives or is likely to deceive').

The 'materiality' condition of the material distortion test is contained in the requirement in Articles 6, 7 and 8 that the commercial practice 'thereby causes or is likely to cause the average consumer to take a transactional decision that he would not have taken otherwise'.

The impact of misleading and aggressive commercial practice on consumers will be assessed in line with the requirements of the general prohibition on the average consumer and the vulnerable consumer. This means, for example, that where a particular group of consumers is directly targeted the impact of the misleading or agressive practice will be assessed, under Article 5.2(b), from the perspective of the average member of that group.

6. THE ROLE OF SELF-REGULATION AND THE NEED FOR A REGULATORY BACKSTOP

Certain European countries have a long-established tradition of self-regulation. Codes of conduct, which are not defined in legislation, are used to set standards of good business behaviour in a particular sector. Codes of conduct may be used by business to give sector-specific application to some general legislative requirements. For example, in the field covered by the Directive, codes could bring added value by implementing the principles of the Directive in relevant sectors. In this context, well-established codes of conduct could reflect good business practice and be used to identify the requirements of professional diligence in concrete cases. One of the advantages of self-regulation is its flexibility. Codes may be modified much more rapidly than regulation in order to respond to market developments and to tackle new unfair commercial practices swiftly. Moreover, the control exercised by code owners to eliminate unfair commercial practices may avoid recourse to administrative and/or judicial enforcement. This should be encouraged on grounds of expediency. Whereas in certain countries an action before a court may last several years, in the first instance, a self-regulatory body is normally able to reach a decision much more quickly.[51]

The main disadvantage of codes of conduct is that they apply only to the firms that have committed themselves to abide by them. Codes of conduct do not apply to non-members and rogue trades who do not belong to any legitimate self-regulatory association. This is the main reason a regulatory backstop is always needed. Article 10 of the Directive, by stating that the Directive does not exclude the control of unfair commercial practices by codes, implicitly recognises the role of codes of conduct.[52] The Directive, however, encourages self-regulation, not as a substitute but as a means of supplementing regulation. Proceedings before self-regulatory bodies should occur in addition to the ordinary court or administrative proceedings. Under Article 10(2), recourse to the self-regulatory control bodies shall never be deemed the equivalent of forgoing a means of judicial or administrative recourse.[53] The Directive will not interfere with the important role played by self-regulation in certain countries in applying and enforcing the laws on unfair commercial practices. In these countries, the Directive will represent the regulatory backstop that is available when self-regulation does not yield the desired outcomes.

An important provision in connection with codes of conduct is contained in Article 6, which regulates misleading actions. Article 6.2(b) defines as misleading the non-compliance by a trader with commitments

---

[51] Eg, in Italy an action before a court may last up to 4 or more years at first instance, while the Giuri, which is the tribunal established by the Italian Advertising Code (Codice dell'Autodisciplina Pubblicitaria) gives its decisions in an average of 30 days: see *Study on the Feasibility of a General Legislative Framework on Fair Trading by the Institut für Europäisches Wirtschafts- und Verbraucherrecht eV* (Nov 2000), part III, at 143, available at http://europa.eu.int/comm/consumers/cons_int/safe_shop/fair_bus_pract/ studies_en.htm.

[52] Art 10 of the Directive, above n 2.

[53] Art 10(2) of ibid.

contained in codes of conduct by which the trader has undertaken to be bound, where:

(i) the commitment is not aspirational, but firm and is capable of being verified, and
(ii) the trader indicates in a commercial practice that he is bound by the code.[54]

By recognising the value of codes of conduct as marketing tools, this provision creates a direct link between the provisions on misleading advertising and the failure by traders to honour the promises set out in codes of conduct. It will be particularly significant when the commitment in the code goes beyond the legal requirements. For example, a European timeshare association undertakes in a code of conduct to give a reflection period of 14 days, during which consumers may exercise their right of withdrawal. This period may be longer than the minimum (eg 10 days) under the legislation of certain Member States. If the code is used by a trader as a marketing tool (eg if the code is available or distributed to consumers visiting the commercial premises of the trader) and the trader subsequently refuses to abide by the 14-day commitment, this will be misleading under Article 6.

7. ENFORCEMENT

The Directive fully harmonises the substantive laws of the Member States related to unfair commercial practices. It does not harmonise the enforcement mechanisms that are in place in the Member States to combat these unfair practices. Member States must organise their own enforcement system, designate the persons and bodies having the right to bring legal actions under the Directive, and determine the sanctions for infringement of the provisions of the Directive.

Effective enforcement is critical to achieving the full potential of the Directive. For this reason, it would be desirable if the Member States delegated all necessary powers to enforce the Directive to one public agency. Only an effective system of public enforcement can provide the necessary guarantees in terms of impartiality and independence that private enforcement by definition cannot ensure. Moreover, under some circumstances, only a public agency has the incentive and the powers to carry out certain enforcement actions.[55] These considerations are even stronger in the light

---

[54] Art 6(2)b of ibid.
[55] This is demonstrated by the disappointing experience with the application of the Injunctions Directive in cross-border cases. Most of the organisations designated by the Member States under the Directive are consumer associations. To date none of these associations has sought an injunction abroad. The only case that has been brought so far is *Duchesne*, above n 31.

of the recently adopted Regulation 2006/2004 on cooperation between national authorities responsible for the enforcement of consumer protection laws.[56] The Regulation creates a European network of public authorities responsible for the enforcement of consumer protection laws in case of cross-border infringements (ie unlawful acts or omissions by a trader established in one country that harm or are likely to harm a consumer in another country). The Regulation obliges the Member States to appoint one or more public bodies responsible for the repression of such cross-border infringements. This gives Member States who do not already have a public enforcement system in place a golden opportunity to set up a consumer protection enforcement agency dealing also with national infringements.

8. CONCLUSIONS

The Directive should considerably increase the overall level of consumer protection and legal certainty in the EU and remove a number of barriers to cross-border trade in the EU. In order to achieve these objectives, it is key that the Directive be implemented correctly by the Member States so that their laws achieve equivalent results. In this context, it is particularly important that the Member States recognise the specificity of consumer protection, as compared to unfair competition. The Directive relies on no particular national model and to a large extent, uses novel concepts that have not been taken from the legal systems of any particular Member State. In order to achieve the full harmonisation goal of the Directive it is essential that in transposing it the Member States follow its wording closely. Domestication (ie changing the language of the Directive and replacing its concepts with similar national concepts) should be resisted as this could create legal uncertainty, especially in cross-border situations. It is also necessary for the Member States to establish effective enforcement bodies and mechanisms to make sure that the Directive is properly enforced.

---

[56] Regulation (EC) 2006/2004, of 27 Oct 2004, [2004] OJ L 364/1.

3

The Unfair Commercial Practices Directive: Its Scope, Ambitions and Relation to the Law of Unfair Competition

ULF BERNITZ

1. SOME BASIC FEATURES

THE NEW UNFAIR Commercial Practices Directive (UCPD)[1] constitutes a major new piece of European legislation. Few directives
in the consumer law field have such a broad scope of application
and represent such a high level of legislative ambition. This chapter will
discuss primarily certain aspects relating to the legislative model chosen,
among them the maximum harmonisation model and the fundamental
decision to limit the scope of the Directive to business-to-consumer (B2C)
transactions. As is well-known, business-to-business transactions (B2B)
have been left out of the Directive,[2] and in this area the far less ambitious 1984 Directive on Misleading Advertising will continue to apply,
however including its comprehensive addition of 1997 on Comparative
Advertising.[3]

This solution has been and still is the object of much criticism. It is in
particular contrary to the German concept of a unitary unfair competition

---

[1] Directive 2005/29/EC [2005] OJ L 149/22. The Directive is to be implemented in the
Member States by 12 Dec 2007 (Art 19 of the Directive). See for a comprehensive presentation, J Stuyck *et al*, 'Confidence through Fairness? The New Directive on Unfair Business-to-
consumer Commercial Practices in the Internal Market' (2006) 43 *CMLRev* 107.

[2] Recital 6 of the Directive states that the Directive neither covers nor affects the national
laws on unfair commercial practices which harm only competitors´ economic interests or
which relate to a transaction between traders.

[3] Directive 84/450/EEC [1984] OJ L 250/17, as amended by Directive 97/55/EC [1997]
OJ L 290/18.

law which has been largely accepted in a substantial number of Continental EU countries.[4] Historically, the German unfair competition concept has focused on protection against unfair practices in B2B transactions, but it has gradually been widened and the new German Unfair Competition Act of 2004 aims at offering B2B and B2C protection on the same level, balancing conflicting business and consumer interests, when necessary. Also in the Scandinavian countries the marketing practices legislation has comprised both B2B and B2C protection, albeit with a more pronounced emphasis on protection of consumers than has been the case in Germany. However, there are other models within Europe, eg the solution to include legislation against unfair marketing practices in a broadly framed consumer code. This is the model of the French Code de la Consommation of 1992. In England, on the other hand, there has never developed any coherent legal principle of unfair competition, and consumer legislation on unfair practices is scattered and lacking systematisation.[5]

Against this background and contrary to many of my countrymen, I think the Commission has taken a wise decision when limiting the new directive to B2C transactions. It is worth remembering that the original study and drafting work for the Commission was conducted during the 1960s by the Max Planck Institute for Intellectual Property and Competition Law in Munich (the Ulmer project)[6] on the assumption that the traditional German unfair competition law should serve as the primary model. In my opinion, the fairly quick and smooth acceptance by the European Parliament and the Council of the Commission's proposal for such a comprehensive directive is a remarkable achievement. A primary explanation why the Commission was able to succeed so well is probably the decision taken not to follow the model of any particular EU country but to found its proposal for the Directive[7] on a new systematic formation, based on functional considerations fitting EC law.

By concentrating on the consumer protection aspect, the Commission was able to establish a strong connection to other consumer law directives, eg the E-Commerce Directive[8] and make it part of the developing European consumer law. In line with these Directives, the Unfair Practices

---

[4] See in particular on national unfair commercial practices law in the EU Member States, R Schulze and H Schulte-Nölke, 'Analysis of National Fairness Laws Aimed at Protecting Consumers in relation to Commercial Practices' (June 2003), a study for the EU Commission (with further references), available at caption 'Consumer', www.ec.europa.eu The study includes a number of national reports, among them my own Report on Sweden. See also, eg, H Micklitz and J Kessler, *Marketing Practices and Consumer Protection in the EC Member States and the US* (Baden-Baden, Nomos, 2002).

[5] S Weatherill, 'United Kingdom Report' in Schultze and Schulte-Nölke, above n 4, and S Weatherill *EU Consumer Law and Policy* (Cheltenham, Edward Elgar, 2005) 191.

[6] *Das Recht des unlauteren Wettbewerbs in den Mitgliedstaaten det EWG.*

[7] COM(2003)356 final, 18 June 2003.

[8] 2000/31/EC [2000] OJ L 178/1.

Directive limits the scope of the concept of a consumer to natural persons acting for non-business purposes.[9] In addition, by using a new systematic approach, the Commission was able to adapt its model to the particular need of removing barriers to cross-border advertising and marketing, thus furthering European integration. For obvious reasons, this aspect is lacking in the different national legislative models, but was also largely lacking in the original proposals of the Max Planck Institute.

The successful enactment of the Directive is all the more remarkable considering the breadth of its coverage. The Directive gives a broad definition of what is a commercial practice, including all types of advertising, marketing and commercial communication.[10] It requires full harmonisation on the basis of Article 95 EC (functioning of the internal market), aiming at creating a single regulatory framework regulating all aspects of unfair commercial practices across the EU.[11] This is claimed to create a high common level playing field of consumer protection[12] and eliminate the barriers stemming from the present fragmentation of the rules on unfair commercial practices.[13] Thus, the Directive is compelling Member States to bring their legislation fully into line with the provisions of the Directive, a fundamental difference compared to the present 1984 Directive on Misleading Advertising.

In order to reach this result, the Commission had to compromise and drop its original proposal to introduce the country of origin principle into the marketing practices field. The main thrust of the original Green Paper on Commercial Communication in the Internal Market of 1996[14] was the liberalisation of commercial communication and promotion of free movement of advertising and marketing services throughout the Community, using the country of origin and mutual recognition principles as the main instruments. As is well-known, this principle has been accepted in the E-Commerce Directive: 'Member States may not, for reasons falling within the coordinated field, restrict the freedom to provide information services from another Member State'.[15] However, although kept in the Green Paper of 2001 on EU Consumer Protection[16] and in the proposed text of the Directive as first presented, the country of origin principle stumbled on massive criticism from certain Member States wanting to have the possibility to enforce stricter national standards. As the Directive prescribes

---

[9] Art 2(a).
[10] Art 2(d).
[11] Recital 12.
[12] Recital 11.
[13] Recital 12.
[14] COM(96)192 final.
[15] Art 3.2 of the E-Commerce Directive, above n 8.
[16] COM(2001)531 final.

maximum harmonisation, there should be no room for such differences except in cases in which differences can be established between Member States in consumers' perception or understanding of a certain type of marketing practice.[17] However, the realities may be somewhat different. I will return to the issue of full harmonisation in the concluding part of this chapter.

The Directive is limited to unfair commercial practices harming consumers' *economic* interests (Article 1); a limitation well in line with its primary harmonisation object. Thus, the Directive excludes practices affecting matters of taste and decency where the requirements are said to vary widely between the Member States.[18] Obviously, the latter area has been considered more difficult to harmonise.

Basically, the architecture of the substantive provisions of the Directive is based on a division into four parts:

(I) A general clause prohibiting unfair commercial practices contrary to the requirements of professional diligence, provided the practice is able to distort consumers' economic behaviour (Article 5),

(II) A prohibition on misleading commercial practices, divided into two statutory provisions, one on misleading actions (Article 6) and another on misleading omissions (insufficient information: Article 7),

(III) A prohibition on aggressive commercial practices, likewise divided into two statutory provisions, one directed against the use of aggressive commercial practices (Article 8) and the other against the use of harassment, coercion and undue influence (Article 9),

(IV) A black list comprising 31 types of commercial practices considered to be prohibited as unfair in all circumstances (Annex I). Thus, the blacklisted practices are prohibited per se and do not require an assessment of their effects in the individual case.

The prohibited practices described under II–IV are particularly important examples of unfair commercial practices. It seems somewhat unclear to what extent the general clause in Article 5 is intended to be independently applicable to practices which fall outside the scope of the specific prohibitions, in particular in relation to cases where the commercial practice would be of a different type. This is probably an issue which has to wait for clarification by the ECJ. Primarily, the general clause can be expected to cover practices which are well in line with such practices that fall under any of the two prohibitions on misleading and aggressive practices or the blacklisted practices, but do not fully fit the specific criteria of these provisions. However, it will be perfectly possible for the ECJ to find the general clause

---

[17] The issue is discussed in Stuyck *et al*, above n 1, at 115. Possible derogations and exemptions will be discussed in part 4, below. As pointed out by Stuyck, the interpretation of Art 4 remains unclear.

[18] Recital 7.

applicable to other types of commercial practices regarded as contrary to the requirements of professional diligence, in particular if the Court finds the unfairness of the practice to be a widely held view in the Member States.

2. REDUCED OR RAISED LEVEL OF CONSUMER PROTECTION?

The level of protection offered is a crucial element of the Directive, closely related to its legislative history. Albeit that the Directive presents itself as a consumer protection measure aiming at establishing a high level of protection for consumers across the Union, this picture is not entirely true. Basically, the Directive is aiming at liberalisation and the enhancement of open markets. An important factor, explaining the Commission's interest in having the Directive enacted, is the object of achieving deregulation of national unfair competition law in such Member States where the applied standard has been regarded as too strict and restrictive, thus eliminating barriers to the development of the internal market. The primary target in this regard is undoubtedly the traditionally restrictive German Unfair Competition Act as applied in German case law. However, the consumer protection standards applied in particular areas in, eg, Sweden, have also been found too restrictive, in particular in relation to advertising directed towards children and young people. The risk of lowered consumer protection standards was the reason the Danish and Swedish governments (but no others) voted against the adoption of the Directive in the Council. On the other hand, the Directive will probably introduce stricter standards of protection in certain other Member States. The fundamental idea behind the Directive is to create a common level playing field for advertising and marketing throughout the Union.

The issue of a reduced or raised level of protection is closely linked to the relationship between B2B and B2C protection, particularly in German law. In Germany, many cases alleged to be dealing with consumer protection have a strong flavour of being primarily based on the interests of competitors in getting rid of competition of an uncomfortable character, particularly low-price competition. However, the ECJ, applying a free competition approach, has reacted against these tendencies, and this has caused a certain clash in relation to German case law. A few examples of illustrative ECJ cases may be mentioned.

A well-known early misleading advertising case in the ECJ is the *Nissan* case[19] about the parallel import from Belgium to France of Nissan cars which were sold in France by a small retailer at a cut price. The cars, sold as 'new', had never been driven but were registered for import purposes. They had fewer accessories than the basic models sold in France. A French court asked the ECJ for a preliminary ruling whether or not the marketing of the

---

[19] Case C–373/90 *Criminal Proceedings against X* [1992] ECR I–131.

cars was in conformity with the 1984 Directive on Misleading Advertising. The ECJ demonstrated a tolerant attitude towards the advertising claims made and succeeded in reconciling the Directive with its ambition to keep parallel import channels open. The ECJ found it correct to advertise the cars as 'new', as they had not been driven on the highway, and found the claim that the cars were cheaper to be misleading only if it could be established that the decision to buy on the part of a significant number of consumers to whom the advertising was addressed was made in ignorance of the fact that the lower price of the cars was matched by a smaller number of accessories.

Another illustrative case is the *Estée Lauder* case[20] about labelling a firming cream as 'lifting'. The Estée Lauder Cosmetics Co argued before a German court that the use of the term 'lifting' was misleading because it gave the impression that the use of the firming cream would obtain results identical or comparable to surgical lifting. The ECJ, asked for a preliminary ruling, was obviously not impressed by the argument and stated, citing in particular another well-known case in the same field, *Gut Springenheide*:[21]

> when it has fallen to the Court, in the context of the interpretation of Directive 84/450 [on misleading advertising] to weigh the risk of misleading consumers against the requirements of the free movement of goods, it has held that, in order to determine whether a particular description, trade mark or promotional description is misleading, it is necessary to take into account the presumed expectations of an average consumer who is reasonably well informed and reasonably observant and circumspect.[22]

The ECJ continued:

> Although, at first sight, the average consumer—reasonably well informed and reasonably observant and circumspect—ought not to expect a cream whose name incorporates the term 'lifting' to produce enduring effects, it nevertheless remains for the national court to determine, in the light of all the relevant factors, whether that is the position in the case.[23]

As a third example, among rather many, I may mention the *Hartlauer* case[24] on comparative price advertising. This case is about the interpretation of the provisions on comparative advertising which were made part

---

[20] Case C–220/98 *Estée Lauder Cosmetics v Lancaster Group* [2000] ECR I–117.
[21] Case C–210/96 *Gut Springenheide and Tusky* [1998] ECR I–4657.
[22] Recital 27.
[23] Recital 30.
[24] Case C–44/01 *Pippig Augenoptik v Harlauer Handelsgesellschaft et al* [2003] ECR I–3095.

of the Misleading Advertising Directive in 1997 and which will continue to be in force also in relation to B2C advertising. The Hartlauer company, a well-known price-cutter marketing spectacles in Austria, had made a direct price comparison with spectacles sold by the Pippig company at a much higher price. Without going into all the details, the ECJ, asked by the Austrian court for a preliminary ruling, basically accepted the type of comparative advertising at issue and underlined that Member States were precluded from applying stricter standards as far as the form and content of the comparison were concerned. Referring to the *Estée Lauder* case, the ECJ noted that the national court should take into account the presumed expectations of an average consumer who is reasonably well informed and reasonably observant and circumspect.

The cases mentioned, and many others, reveal the characteristic pro-competition approach taken by the ECJ and its policy not to apply too strict a standard when assessing whether or not consumers are likely to be misled. These basic features of the case law have been carried forward into the new Directive which refers to the average consumer as benchmark. The general clause on unfair commercial practices and the prohibitions in the Directive on misleading and aggressive practices all refer to the average consumer as the person likely to be mislead, having his freedom of choice restricted, etc.[25] The Recitals refer to the notional, typical consumer and the benchmark is described as:

> The average consumer, who is reasonably well-informed and reasonably observant and circumspect, taken into account social, cultural and linguistic factors, as interpreted by the Court of Justice.[26]

However, it is possible to offer extended protection to particularly vulnerable target groups, such as children and sick people. The Directive's text speaks of clearly identifiable groups of consumers who are particularly vulnerable to the commercial practice or the underlying product because of their mental or physical infirmity, age or credulity. The need for special protection of particular groups of consumers in a weak position was particularly observed by the Nordic countries during the deliberations on the text of the Directive.[27]

As is explicitly stated in the Recitals, the average consumer test is not a statistical one. National courts and authorities will have to exercise their own faculty of judgement to determine the typical reaction of the average consumer.[28] This is fully in line with existing case law in the Nordic

[25] See Arts 5(2)(b), 6(1) sentences 1 and 8.
[26] Recital 18.
[27] Recitals 18 and 19, Art 5.3.
[28] Recital 18, last sentences.

countries but certainly different from what has been the common approach in Germany. In German unfair competition case law consumer research pools or other statistical market surveys are very much used as evidence and it has often been considered sufficient that some 10–15 percent of the consumers, or the relevant group of specific addressees, have been misled by the advertising. However, the ECJ took a reserved attitude towards this type of evidence in the *Gut Springenheide* and *Estée Lauder* judgments and the Directive confirms this sceptical position.

Normally, traders carry the burden of proof as to the accuracy of factual claims they have made.[29] However, it is for national law and courts to determine where to place this burden, and it is to be expected that differences between national procedural law in the Member States will have an impact on this issue.

Further, in order to counteract over-excessive use of fairness standards in Europe, eg in Germany, the Directive requires material distortion of consumer economic behaviour as a prerequisite for considering a commercial practice to be unfair.[30] This requirement of commercial effect functions as a threshold and constitutes a de minimis rule. It requires that a commercial practice causes or is likely to cause the average consumer to take a transactional decision he would not otherwise have taken.[31] The requirement excludes misleading representations of an irrelevant or petty character. Taking a tolerant position, the text of the Directive talks explicitly about:

> The common and legitimate advertising practice of making exaggerated statements or statements which are not meant to be taken literally.[32]

Likewise, the material distortion requirement is applicable to the omission of relevant information. According to the text of the Directive omission of information is prohibited only if the omission causes or is likely to cause the average consumer to take a transactional decision he would not otherwise have taken.[33]

To conclude, the primary ambition of the Directive has been to continue and further develop the basic, pro-competition principles of assessment formulated by the ECJ. The Directive believes in the informed consumer, 'reasonably observant and circumvent' to quote the often used phrase of the ECJ, who is able to take exaggerations in advertising *cum grano salis*. This general approach of the Directive seems designed to reduce the level of protection offered under German unfair competition law and comparable

---

[29] Recital 21, second sentence.
[30] Art 5(2)(b).
[31] Art 6.1 first sentence.
[32] Art 5.3 *in fine*.
[33] Art 7.1.

legal systems. At best, the standard established by the Directive will represent a European middle course between reduced or raised levels of protection depending on the present state of the law of the particular Member State. However, much will depend on the forthcoming development of the case law interpreting the Directive, in particular to what extent differences relating to national cultural and social factors will be accepted. The average European consumer will remain a fiction.

3. PROTECTION OF COMPETITORS' INTERESTS UNDER THE DIRECTIVE

When one takes a closer look at the provisions of the Directive, the exclusion of B2B transactions is not as radical and total as one might be inclined to think. Many marketing practices are unfair both from the viewpoint of the competitors or other business firms and from a consumer protection perspective, albeit often with a somewhat different emphasis in the assessment of the character of the unfairness. Such practices are normally covered by the Directive; the sometimes heard view that the Directive fully disregards B2B transactions is not correct. It is noted in the recitals that unfair advertising which directly harms consumers' economic interests also indirectly harms the economic interests of legitimate competitors.[34] This indirect protection of the interests of competitors has different facets. Often, the same advertising or other type of marketing practice is directed to consumers and to other customers, and in such cases national law based on the Directive will in effect offer protection covering a wider circle of addressees. Misleading advertising, having consumers as well as commercial purchasers as addressees, is the obvious example. Another aspect is the indirect beneficial effects for those competitors who stick to honest practices. As stated in the recitals, the Directive indirectly protects 'legitimate businesses from their competitors who do not play by the rules of the Directive.'[35] This approach to regarding the interests of competitors as indirect or complementary to the interests of consumers has much in common with the structure of Scandinavian marketing practices legislation but is unfamiliar to the German unfair competition law tradition.

  The object of the Directive also to offer, within its general limits of application, protection of the interests of competitors and the business community in general is demonstrated clearly by the provision that competitors, as well as organisations, shall be regarded under national law as having a legitimate interest in combating unfair practices. This shall include the right to take legal action against such practices and to initiate other appropriate legal

---

[34] Recital 6 first sentence.
[35] Recital 8.

proceedings.[36] Orders for the cessation of unfair commercial practices shall be available.[37] The wording and structure of the Directive do not support the proposition that it would be sufficient to offer competitors the possibility to submit claims to administrative authorities in charge of consumer protection.

There are certain practices, explicitly included in the Directive, which have a particularly strong link to the interests of competitors and which might be regarded as inclusions in the Directive of protection of unfair B2B practices. Thus, the use of brands, trade names, packaging, etc which mislead the average consumer about the commercial origin of the products and cause him or her to purchase the products on the basis of that misconception (passing off in a general sense) is covered by the Directive.[38] The black list includes as a prohibited practice the promotion of a product similar to one made by a particular manufacturer in such a manner as deliberately to mislead the consumer into believing that the product is made by the same manufacturer when it is not.[39] Obviously, the Directive includes the packaging (get-up) of products. Of particular practical importance would be misleading advertising or misleading exposure of products or their packaging in sales outlets causing consumers to purchase look-alikes.

The standard of assessment is touched upon in one of the Recitals, which declares that it is not the intention of the Directive to reduce consumer choice by prohibiting the promotion of products which look similar to other products unless this similarity confuses consumers as to the commercial origin of the product and is therefore misleading.[40] This recital can be read as a pronouncement in favour of a rather restrictive view of the scope of protection offered, indicating the priority of consumer perception and thus possibly confining the application of the Directive to instances of clear deception of consumers looking for a particular brand or the like. This would be more in line with the rather restrictive view on passing-off prevailing in English law than with the elaborate German case law. In this much observed and economically important area, it will be the task of the ECJ to clarify and develop the legal standards to be applied. Most likely, the ECJ will use its present trade mark law jurisprudence on confusion and deception as an important point of departure.

Practices misleading as to the geographical origin of a product are also mentioned as a type of misleading action covered by the Directive, provided

---

[36] Art 11 on enforcement. Recital 21 first sentence has to be understood in the light of the text of the Directive itself.

[37] Art 11.2(a).

[38] See, in particular, Art 6.2(a) which comprises 'any marketing of a product, including comparative advertising, which creates confusion with any products, trade marks, trade names or other distinguishing marks of a competitor'. See also Art 6.1(b), referring to misleading information about commercial origin of a product.

[39] Recital 13.

[40] Recital 14.

the representation deceives or is likely to deceive the average consumer and is likely to cause him to take a transactional decision he would not have taken otherwise.[41] Thus, the Directive is not offering full protection of unauthorised use of protected appellations of origin or particular geographical denominations, a well developed particular area of law, but the provisions of the Directive might function in the future as a useful complement to existing, more detailed regulation in the field.

Misleading use of attributes, qualifications, connections to other undertakings, ownership of intellectual property rights and similar misleading actions all constitute typical examples of unfair B2B practices.[42] However, they fall under the Directive as long as they are contrary to the standards laid down in the Directive of what is misleading to the consumer and having an economic effect.

Misleading use of commercial or geographical origin and misleading use of attributes, etc, are examples of types of practices considered unfair both from consumers' and competitors' point of view. However, misleading practices addressed only to business customers clearly fall outside the scope of the Directive. Here, as already mentioned, the less comprehensive, already existing Directive on Misleading and Comparative Advertising remains in force.

Other types of unfair B2B commercial practices, not affecting consumers and thus falling outside the scope of the Directive, are normally not subject to harmonised EC regulation. An example is denigrating statements in advertising about other businesses (normally competitors) which are not misleading and have no bearing on consumer interests.

4. THE EFFECTS OF THE DIRECTIVE ON SPECIFIC NATIONAL PROVISIONS

The legal implications of the principle of full or maximum harmonisation adopted in the Directive are far-reaching, in particular in view of the broad definition of the commercial practices concept which, as already mentioned, includes all types of advertising, marketing and commercial communication.[43] As a consequence, national legislation or established case law on commercial communication to consumers of a more restrictive character than the Directive prescribes cannot be upheld after the Directive has taken legal force, unless there is an exemption or temporary derogation. Without

---

[41] Art 6.1, in particular (b).

[42] Art 6.1(f) reads: '[t]he nature, attributes and rights of the trader or his agent, such as his identity and assets, his qualifications, status, approval, affiliation or connection and ownership of industrial, commercial or intellectual property rights or his awards and distinctions.'

[43] Art 2(d).

adopting this principle, it would not have been possible to establish a level playing field.

There are different exemptions and derogations which will not be covered in detail here. The most important one is that Member States are allowed a limited, six-year transition period to dismantle national provisions which are more restrictive or prescriptive than the Directive, provided the specific national measures applied are proportionate.[44] The text of the Directive gives a certain, vaguely phrased, opening for prolongation of such Member State exemptions which seems to offer an opening for future negotiations and controversy. A derogation for national rules on commercial practices by the regulated professions has been admitted, without time limitation.[45] In this area, different types of advertising bans still exist on the Member State level. Member States may impose more restrictive or prescriptive national rules on financial services and immovable property, ie these areas are within the ambit of the Directive but not covered by the full harmonisation principle.[46]

The Directive is confined to collective consumer interests, does not interfere with contract law and is without prejudice to individual actions brought by a consumer.[47] Thus, the relationship between the pre-contractual marketing and advertising stage and the European contract law established by the different consumer protection Directives has been left open to be developed by case law, normally as a matter for national courts. For good reason, this legally tricky area has been found too difficult to regulate.

The Directive is without prejudice to Community or national rules relating to the health or safety aspects of products.[48] Examples are national provisions in relation to alcohol, tobacco and pharmaceuticals. Thus, the Directive does not address specific advertising bans in the Member States, provided they relate to health and safety. However, such bans must be legitimate under the general Community law rules on free movement of goods and services. It follows from the case law that such national provisions must satisfy basically three tests, viz. that they are truly non-discriminatory, that they pursue important public health or safety interests and, thirdly, that they are proportionate, ie appropriate to ensure their aim and do not go beyond what is necessary to achieve such an objective.[49]

Specific Community directives continue to apply and take precedence within their specific fields of application (*lex specialis derogat lex generalis*).[50]

---

[44] Art 3.5.
[45] Art 3.8.
[46] Art 3.9.
[47] Art 3.2 and Recital 9.
[48] Art 3.3.
[49] Note, in particular, Cases C–405/98 *Consumer Ombudsman v Gourmet International Products* [2001] ECR I–1795 and the *Bacardi* Cases, C–262/02 *Commission v France*, C–429/02 *Bacardi France v Télévision Francaise 1 (TF 1) et al* [2004] ECR I–6569.
[50] Art 3.4.

The most important examples are the Television Without Frontiers Directive,[51] presently the subject of revision, and the E-Commerce Directive.[52]

As follows from this overview, it has been possible to limit the scope of derogations and exemptions to only a few areas, apart from the six-year adjustment period. In particular, the inclusion of different sales promotion practices is notable. At present, many continental Member States apply specific prohibitions of particular types of promotional practices, eg different types of combined offers, gifts, etc. Normally, these prohibitions are primarily aimed at offering protection for small business. The Community proposal for a specific, liberalising regulation on sales promotion activities[53] seems to have been dropped.[54] As the Directive explicitly includes marketing directly connected with the promotion of a product to consumers,[55] it should cover sales promotions and be able to tackle the need for harmonisation in this area. As already indicated, the Directive focuses on offering consumers protection against misleading or aggressive promotional practices, eg by marketing pyramid promotional schemes,[56] making persistent and unwanted solicitations or by creating the false impression that the consumer has won a prize or equivalent benefit.[57] The Directive seems to have achieved much of the pro-integrative object of the proposed but contested Sales Promotion Regulation via the back door.

5. WILL FULL HARMONISATION BE ACHIEVED?

The ambitions of the Directive are indeed far-reaching. In one single piece of legislation, it aims at harmonising at the European level the legal framework for the Central Part of advertising and marketing practices, which is an area characterised by very considerable differences in national legal tradition. As it is a maximum Directive, it requires full harmonisation and normally accepts, as has been discussed, only national derogations of a temporary nature. Will the Directive succeed? Will it create an environment permitting companies to make use of the same advertising and marketing practices all over Europe?

It would have been easier to answer this question if it had been possible to keep the original proposal to base the Directive on the country of origin principle. In that case, advertising fulfilling the legal requirements of its

---

[51] 89/552/EEC [1989] OJ L 298/23.
[52] 2000/31/EC [2000] OJ L 178/1.
[53] Proposal for a European Parliament and Council Regulation Concerning Sales Promotions in the Internal Market, COM(2002)585 final.
[54] Stuyck *et al*, above n 1, at 141.
[55] Art 2(d).
[56] Recital 14.
[57] Points 26 and 31 in the black list.

country of origin would have had to be accepted in all the other Member States (save for specific exemptions). However, as finally accepted, it is up to the Member States to implement the Directive by making the necessary changes in their national legislation, and for national courts and administrative agencies to apply the new legislation loyally respecting the spirit of the Directive and its integrative aims. Most certainly, very different techniques will be applied in the Member States when implementing the Directive and it is to be expected these different techniques will reflect the national differences in legal tradition. For example, it makes a very great difference if the legislative starting point in a Member State is an Unfair Competition Act of the German model or a scattered system of detailed, non-systematised statutes as in England. It is also highly likely that courts in the Member States will connect to their well-known national legal concepts and case law when interpreting and applying concepts of the Directive, such as 'professional diligence', 'average consumer' or cause the consumer 'to take a transactional decision'.

Thus, in reality, a quick and full harmonisation is not to be foreseen. Most likely, companies will find that, also after successful implementation of the Directive in the Member States, identical advertising and marketing practices will meet legal hindrances in certain Member States while considered completely acceptable in others. It will probably be necessary to have had quite a considerable number of cases referred to the ECJ for preliminary ruling before a level playing field will emerge. This legal process may very well also involve future Commission interventions against Member States trying to keep specific legal provisions contravening the Directive.

However, the Unfair Commercial Practices Directive fulfils a very important pro-integrative function and will be here to stay. It can be predicted that it will form the legal foundation for a most intriguing and important pattern of legal development to come. European marketing law will develop into an important sub-discipline of European law.

4

An End to Fragmentation? The Unfair Commercial Practices Directive from the Perspective of the New Member States from Central and Eastern Europe

ANTONINA BAKARDJIEVA ENGELBREKT[1]

1. INTRODUCTION

ALTHOUGH NEGOTIATED WITH remarkable speed and efficiency and stirring up relatively limited political debate, the recently adopted Unfair Commercial Practices Directive (hereinafter UCPD) represents a veritable revolution in the field of fair trading law.[2] Rarely has a Community legislative initiative been announced with such open intent to recast national legal systems and traditions in a given field of regulation. According to the press release accompanying the initial Commission proposal the Directive was said to advance a single set of rules which were expected to do nothing less than 'replace the existing multiple volumes of national rules and court rulings on commercial practices'.[3] Indeed, the Directive sets out to introduce a comprehensive regulative regime in an area marked by considerable divergences in national policy, style and enforcement technique.[4] In contrast to the colourful patchwork of Community

---

[1] Antonina Bakardjieva Engelbrekt holds a degree in law from Sofia, 'St. Kliment Ohridski' University, an LLM degree from the European University Institute, Florence, and a doctoral degree in law from Stockholm University. She is Associate Professor at Örebro University and Stockholm Universities and is currently a Jean Monnet Fellow at the EUI, Florence. Financial support from the STINT foundation is gratefully acknowledged.
[2] In the following the terms 'fair trading law' and 'marketing practices law' will also be used for the sake of simplicity.
[3] EU Press release IP/03/857, Brussels, 18 June, 2003.
[4] See HW Micklitz et al., *Study on the Feasibility of a General Legislative Framework on Fair Trading*, Vol I–II, Institut für Europäisches Wirtschafts- und Verbraucherrecht eV (Nov 2000) (hereinafter 'Micklitz, Feasibility Study').

directives regulating various industry-, media- and distribution-specific aspects of marketing in a vertical manner, the UCPD takes a horizontal approach and aims at providing general solutions with an effect across business sectors. It seeks to achieve full harmonisation, thus trying to overcome years of fragmentation and piecemeal harmonisation. In a political climate of constitutional sensitivity, where subsidiarity and new (less intrusive) modes of governance within the European Union (EU) are the terminology of the day, this bold approach deserves attention reaching beyond the narrow community of consumer law experts.

This chapter does not aim at a general analysis of the UCPD,[5] but instead looks at the Directive from the perspective of the New Member States from Central and Eastern Europe (CEE). Given the number of these states and the differences in their legal traditions and regulative frameworks one can, of course, question whether there are sufficient commonalities associated with the continuing implementation of the UCPD in these countries to justify special attention and joint treatment. After all since May 2005 eight of the original 10 candidate states from CEE have been fully fledged members of the Union.[6] Their legal systems have been acknowledged largely to comply with the Community *acquis* following a rigorous scrutiny by the European Commission. Insisting on a particular CEE perspective may be perceived as an unnecessary gesture of political correctness, or, alternatively, as an expression of lingering suspicion as to these states' capacity to shoulder their newly gained responsibilities as Union members.

Nevertheless, I shall argue that bringing in the perspective of the CEE countries is necessary and valuable for several reasons. The first, and more evident, one is the persisting differences in historical legacies and in political and economic realities in the 'new', when compared to the 'old', EU Member States. These differences can be expected to trigger some context-related problems in transposing Community law which merit special attention. Secondly, the regulative framework of commercial practices in these states has evolved only recently, and has been the testing ground for experimental institutional design. Hence, it provides a rich illustration of the variety of institutional dilemmas involved in this legal field and in its harmonisation.

---

[5] For such analysis see A Bakardjieva Engelbrekt, 'EU and Marketing Practices Law in the Nordic Countries—Consequences of a Directive on Unfair Business-to-Consumer Commercial Practices', Report for the Nordic Council of Ministers, Committee on Consumer Affairs (2005:424), available at: www.norden.org/pub/sk/showpub.asp?pubnr=2005:424; J Stuyck, E Terryn and T van Dyck, 'Confidence Through Fairness? The New Directive on Unfair Business-to-Consumer Commercial Practices in the Internal Market' (2006) 43 *CMLRev* 107.

[6] The 8 Central and East European States that joined the European Union on 1 May 2004 are the Czech Republic, Estonia, Hungary, Latvia, Lithuania, Poland, the Slovak Republic and Slovenia. Two more CEE countries, namely Romania and Bulgaria are in the antechamber of the Union. The laws of these latter countries are also going to be discussed since they were exposed to the same pre-accession strategy and are soon expected to become part of the Community legal order.

Last, but not least, the relevant laws and institutions of fair trading in the CEE countries have over the course of the last decade been powerfully influenced by, and are to a large extent a product of, the recent eastward enlargement of the Union. It is generally acknowledged that the last accession process has been unique in many ways, notably through power asymmetry, the conditionality requirement and the massive transfer of both rules (the *acquis communautaire*) and institutional practices from the EU to the accession states.[7] The outcome of this process can therefore in a sense be regarded as a condensed reflection, a reverse image, of the Europeanisation process as a whole. Whereas much has naturally got 'lost in translation', still I believe that a closer analysis of the legislative and institutional results of accession may help unravel paradoxes and tensions in Community law and policy-making that otherwise remain hidden due to the discrete and selective character of processes of positive and negative integration. Going further, I shall suggest that the enlargement process has occasionally functioned as an 'incubator' for changes at the Community level, and one reason to study enlargement policies is that they may serve as precursors of new developments. In this sense, the chapter does not claim to be a comprehensive review of the implementation process in the CEE Member States, but rather uses developments in these states as an analytical prism through which the strengths and weaknesses of the Community approach to harmonisation in this and related fields can be identified and more rigorously studied.

2. FRAGMENTATION AND ENLARGEMENT AS MAIN PREMISES FOR THE UPC DIRECTIVE

A more specific reason to look at the new Member States from CEE is offered by the policy document which paved the way for the UCPD, namely the Green Paper on Consumer Protection of 2001. The Green Paper itself used enlargement as a main justification for embarking on a new and ambitious harmonisation project. Its starting point was the already familiar theme of fragmentation in the Community regulative regime of consumer protection:

> consumer protection in the internal market is faced with a fragmented set of regulations and a fragmented system of enforcement.[8]

---

[7] F Schimmelfennig and U Sedelmeier, 'Governance by Conditionality: EU Rule Transfer to the Candidate Countries of Central and Eastern Europe' [2004] *Journal of European Public Policy* 661; F Schimmelfennig and U Sedelmeier (eds), *The Europeanisation of Central and Eastern Europe* (Ithaca, NY, London, Cornell University Press, 2005); H Grabbe, *The EU's Transformative Power: Europeanization through Conditionality in Central and Eastern Europe* (Basingstoke, Palgrave, 2006).

[8] Green Paper on European Union Consumer Protection, COM(2001)531 final, at 3.

Against this backdrop the imminent eastward enlargement was employed as a two-fold argument to advance the new harmonisation endeavour. On the one hand, enlargement was depicted as enhancing the risk of fragmentation of rules and in particular of enforcement. 'The prospect of enlargement brings *the risk* of further fragmentation of the internal market and additional enforcement problems.'[9]

With a high number of new states with notorious flaws in existing institutional and enforcement frameworks, the risk of imperfect implementation of complex and dispersed Community legislation is admittedly growing exponentially, and with it the likelihood of new barriers to intra-Community trade. In this inward-bound perspective enlargement is seen as an external source of destabilisation to the Community multi-level system of governance, for which the Community has to prepare.

On the other hand, legal harmonisation is in the same document described as a chance and an opportunity for enhancing consumer protection in the accession states. 'It [enlargement] is also an *opportunity* to endow candidate countries that do not always have a long history of consumer protection with simple and effective rules.'[10]

In this outward-bound perspective the proposed harmonisation-cum-simplification of Community consumer law is portrayed as a step in a broader law-transfer and institution-building project with the Community as the main donor. Apparently the Commission sees no contradiction in the two perspectives. The improvement of the coherence of Community law is expected immediately to generate coherence and effectiveness at the national level as well. I will return to this point in the end of this chapter.

Given these premises, it appears that the effect of the UCPD in the New Member States can be used as the ultimate touchstone for measuring the success of the Directive in achieving its main goals. The questions to be asked are consequently: (i) to what extent has the Directive been successful in reducing the fragmentation of consumer protection regulation at the Community level in terms of substantive rules and enforcement techniques taking into account the situation in the new Member States, and (ii) to what extent can it help endow the new Member States with clear and effective rules?

In the following pages I will first give a brief account of the history of harmonisation of unfair commercial practices law in the Community in order to sketch the trajectory of change in policy and harmonisation technique. Then I will turn to the CEE Member and candidate States and trace the evolution of unfair commercial practices law and of related

---

[9] Ibid, at 3, emphasis added by the author.
[10] Ibid, at 10, emphasis added by the author.

institutions in these states. This necessarily schematic overview starts with a broad-brush picture of the relevant legal and institutional legacies from the past and presents several patterns of regulation of unfair commercial practices in the CEE states that emerged in the initial period of transition to democracy and market economy. It goes on to describe the main points on the accession check-list, focusing on the effect of extending the Community *acquis* to the fair trading law and institutions in the candidate states. In view of the variety of approaches and of regulative frameworks, the chapter does not attempt a systematic comparative analysis, but rather seeks to elicit tendencies and commonalities. The task is to identify the main directions of Community leverage (intended and not intended) and to try and disentangle the logic behind Community influence. In a final section the chapter attempts to gauge the effects of the implementation of the UCP Directive in the CEE Member States and to offer a critical analysis of the Directive from this perspective.

What I hope to show on a more general level with the analysis is that the substantive law of unfair commercial practices is intrinsically linked to issues of institutional choice and design, which in turn determine patterns of enforcement and ultimately the way the rules are employed by interested actors and their effect on society at large. It is therefore suggested that a greater sensitivity for the national institutional context on the part of Community institutions will help streamline the Community legislative process, calibrate the control of the implementation of Community law and bring more realism in the political expectations from new harmonisation initiatives.

3. THE FRAGMENTATION OF COMMUNITY RULES ON COMMERCIAL PRACTICES PRIOR TO THE UCPD

The observation that Community consumer protection law has been in a state of fragmentation does not need much substantiation. Fragmentation has likewise plagued the narrower field of unfair commercial practices law. This does not mean that there were no aspirations for greater coherence: quite the contrary! Already from the beginning of the 1960s different Community institutions and scholarly think-tanks have been engaged in spelling out the formula for comprehensive, and at the same time practicable, harmonisation of unfair commercial practices law at Community level. The road to harmonisation has, however, proved long and winding. Although the saga is fairly familiar, it will be briefly recapitulated below in order both to demonstrate the interrelationship of this legal field with other Community polices and regulative choices and to trace possible spill-over in accession policy.

(a) From 'Unfair Competition' to 'Consumer Protection': Market-building *v* Market-correcting Approaches

As is well known, initiatives for harmonisation of fair trading law were launched as early as the early 1960s and were then considered as a natural complement to a strong Community competition law and to ongoing projects for harmonisation of intellectual property law. Particularly in German legal doctrine a harmonised unfair competition law was regarded as an important element of the European Economic Constitution (*Wirtschaftsverfassung*) and thus as a building block of the Common Market.[11] The comprehensive study of the laws of unfair competition in the then six Member States carried out for the Commission by Eugen Ulmer ambitiously proposed harmonisation in the form of a Convention, and not a Directive.[12] The 'unfair competition' concept was considered sufficiently uncontroversial, given its presence in the 1883 Paris Convention for Protection of Industrial Property, to which all Community Member States were parties, to be taken as a starting point of most serious proposals.[13]

Despite its broad comparative character the outcome of the study was markedly influenced by the German way of legal thinking in this field. The analytical grid applied in the comparative study closely followed the categorisations traditionally used in analyses of the German Unfair Competition Act (*Gesetz gegen den unlauteren Wettbewerb*, or UWG). The interests placed at the centre of the draft were those of competitors, and, in a consequential manner, the interests of the consumers and the general public. This largely corresponded to the traditions and then dominant policy views of the founding states of the European Communities. In terms of legislative technique the Ulmer study was constructed on a general clause on unfair competition, fleshed out by a catalogue of more specific factual situations, which in some respects was a direct reflection of the German law while at the same time corresponding to the Paris Convention.[14]

---

[11] PC Müller-Graff, 'Ordnungspolitische Divergenzen und wettbewerbliche Lauterkeit in der Verfassung des Gemeinsamen Marktes' in B Börner, H Jahreiss and K Stern (eds), *Einigkeit und Recht und Freiheit: Festschrift für Karl Carstens* (Cologne-Berlin, Heymann, 1984) 209.

[12] The study was carried out by the Max Planck Institute for Foreign and International Patent, Copyright and Competition Law (MPI) in Munich under the leadership of its Director Prof Eugen Ulmer. It consisted of multiple volumes of country analyses and a concluding comparative report with recommendations.

[13] E Ulmer, *Das Recht des unlauteren Wettbewerbs in den Mitgliedstaaten der EWG. Band I. Vergleichende Darstellung* (Munich, CH Beck, 1965) 15; cf G Schricker, 'Die Arbeiten zur Angleichung des Rechts des unlautere Wettbewerbs in den Ländern der Europäischen Wirtschaftsgemeinschaft' [1973] *Gewerblicher Rechtsschutz und Urheberrecht Internationaler Teil (GRUR Int)* 141.

[14] The suggested rules included: causing risk of confusion, disparagement (*Anschwärzung*), including personal and comparative advertising, misleading advertising and, finally, the protection of trade secrets (*Geschäfts- und Betriebsgeheimnisse*): Ulmer above n 13, 250–6.

Yet in the course of the preparatory work, and especially after the Community acquired three new members in 1973—the UK, Ireland and Denmark—it became clear that it would be very difficult to find a basis for a compromise. Whereas in Germany the UWG was a well-developed and intensively applied body of law, in the UK and Ireland a general concept of 'unfair competition' was almost unknown and, moreover, unacceptable for a number of dogmatic and legal policy reasons.[15] More importantly still, while the Max Planck institute was preparing its impressive study, consumerism was gaining ground in the Community Member States. In this respect too, the German unfair competition law approach clashed with higher British and Danish preoccupation with consumer interests.

Growing rapidly into an independent sphere of public concern, consumer protection was also 'discovered' as a policy area at the Community level, partly also as an opportune response to ongoing developments in European integration.[16] In 1975 a first Preliminary Programme for a Consumer Protection and Information Policy of the (then) European Economic Community was adopted by the Council.[17] The programme was an idiosyncratic soft law document, which however proved decisive for the future of consumer policy in the Community. It proclaimed the famous catalogue of consumer rights (the right to protection of health and safety, the right to protection of economic interests, the right to redress, the right to information and education, the right to representation (the right to be heard)) and mapped a variety of measures through which the Community could help promote those rights. Parallel to these policy developments a significant institutional redistribution of competences in the European Commission took place. After the accession of the three new Member States in 1973 an independent Commission service for environment and consumer protection was set up, which in 1981 was transformed into a Directorate.[18]

These political changes called for greater recognition of consumer interests also in the process of harmonisation of fair trading law. Importantly for our discussion, within the broader objective of protecting consumers' economic interests the 1975 Programme identified several areas with relevance for fair trading law. Among them were protection of consumers from misleading and unfair advertising (item 22) and protection of consumers from unfair commercial practices (item 24), such as doorstep selling, terms

---

[15] For a detailed analysis of English law, see A Ohly, *Richterrecht und Generalklausel im Recht des unlauteren Wettbewerbs* (Cologne, Carl Heymanns, 1997) 73. See also L Krämer, *EEC Consumer Law* (Brussels, Story Scientia, 1986).

[16] For a detailed account see T Bourgoignie, 'Consumer Law and the European Community: Issues and Prospects' in T Bourgoignie and D Trubek *Consumer Law, Common Markets and Federalism* (Berlin, de Gruyter, 1987).

[17] Council Resolution of 14 Apr 1975 on a preliminary programme of the European Economic Community for a consumer protection and information policy [1975] OJ C 92/1.

[18] Krämer, above n 15.

of contracts, conditions in guarantees, door-to-door sales, premium offers, unsolicited goods and services, information given on labels and packaging.[19] Institutionally, the newly founded consumer protection entities gradually replaced the Directorate on internal market in the work on fair trading. From the beginning of the 1970s the Consumer Protection Service was actively involved in the legislative work, and after 1977 became fully in charge of this work.

This process of institutionalisation and organisational development inevitably influenced the general spirit and direction of harmonisation. Unfair competition was gradually abandoned as a conceptual framework and was replaced with the more neutral and limited term 'advertising'. After several unsuccessful attempts to reach a common understanding on a directive on unfair advertising, a Misleading Advertising Directive was adopted as a modest compromise solution underscoring the need to pay due regard to the interests of consumers.[20] Thus, the main rationale for regulating fair trading underwent a perceptible shift from ensuring fair competition throughout the Community to protecting consumers from the harmful effects of incorrect and misleading marketing practices. One can say that there was a move from a market-building to a market-correcting approach.

(b) From Comprehensive to Piecemeal Harmonisation: the Road to Fragmentation

In effect, the change in policy rationale implied the abandonment of plans for comprehensive harmonisation on the basis of an unfair competition law approach, and instead paved the way to piecemeal harmonisation of specific regulatory issues. A multilayered patchwork of Community fair trading law consisting of different categories of acts and revealing a variety of harmonisation techniques began slowly to take shape. Particularly sluggish has been the development in the area of acts of general application. The 1984 Misleading Advertising Directive based on minimum harmonisation was complemented only in 1997 by exhaustively harmonising the conditions for the permissibility of comparative advertising.[21]

---

[19] [1975] OJ C 092/2.
[20] A bolder proposal on unfair advertising was discarded, having been paradoxically perceived in Germany to be influenced by English legal thinking and in England accused of a German bias: see [1978] OJ C 70/4. An even earlier draft, Doc XO/C/94/75, was submitted in 1975. The proposal envisaged the prohibition as unfair of any advertising building on sexual, social or religious discrimination, which was plainly *avant-garde*. Likewise a general requirement that advertising does not exploit trust, credulity and lack of experience was taking a decisive step towards a consumer-oriented view on advertising: see Krämer, above n 15.
[21] Directive 97/55/EC [1997] OJ L 290/18.

The legislative work in areas of special application has been more intensive. Thus, the Doorstep Selling Directive and the Distance Selling Directive addressed two particular methods of selling, deviating from the classical situation of purchase in a shop of the consumer's choice.[22] The Television without Frontiers Directive and the Directive on Electronic Commerce devoted attention to harmonisation of marketing and advertising provisions specific to these media.[23] Moreover, a large number of Community acts were adopted governing advertising and marketing in separate industry sectors, like foodstuffs, medicinal products, cosmetics, tobacco, financial services, etc.[24]

Clearly, over the years frustration concerning the ever denser regulative thicket and the lack of transparency and predictability was growing. The boundary between acts of general and acts of special application was not always well defined. The problem was exacerbated by the fact that many of the directives were based on a minimum harmonisation approach, leaving in particular cross-border business operators in a state of uncertainty as to the applicable national regulative standards.[25]

(c) In Search of a Unifying Conceptual Framework

The fragmentation of European commercial practices law was never really accepted as a satisfactory state of affairs. The 1984 Misleading Advertising Directive in its preamble committed the Community to continue the effort to find common ground for the harmonisation of unfair advertising.[26] The need for harmonisation and consolidation was likewise demonstrated by the abundant case law of the ECJ where divergent national advertising and marketing regulations were often scrutinised under the Community free movement provisions, and this even after the shift to greater judicial restraint marked by the seminal *Keck and Mithouard* judgment.[27]

---

[22] Directive 85/577/EEC [1985] OJ L 372/31 (Doorstep Selling Directive) and Directive 97/7/EC, [1997] OJ L 144/19 (Distance Selling Directive).

[23] Directive 89/552/EEC [1989] OJ L 298/23, amended by Directive 97/36/EC [1997] OJ L 202/60 (Television Directive) and Directive 2000/31/EC [2000] OJ L 178/1 (Electronic Commerce Directive).

[24] See for instance Directive 90/496/EEC of 24 Sept 1990 on nutrition labelling for foodstuffs, [1990] OJ L 276/40; Directive 2000/13/EC on the labelling, presentation and advertising of foodstuffs, [2000] OJ L 109/29; Directive 2001/83/EC on the Community code relating to medicinal products for human use [2001] OJ L 311/6; Directive 1999/45/EC on the classification, packaging and labelling of dangerous preparations [1999] OJ L 200/1; Directive 2003/33/EC on advertising and sponsorship of tobacco products [2003] OJ L 152/16 (Tobacco Advertising Directive).

[25] On these developments see A Bakardjieva Engelbrekt, *Fair Trading Law in Flux? National Legacies, Institutional Choice and the Process of Europeanisation* (Stockholm, dissertation, 2003).

[26] See Recital 6 of Directive 84/450/EEC [1984] OJ L 250/17.

[27] Joined Cases C–267 & C–268/91 *Keck and Mithouard* [1993] ECR I–6097.

Nevertheless agreeing on a new unifying conceptual framework did not prove easy. After the Community abandoned the unfair competition approach, harmonisation was initially organised around the concept of advertising. Obviously the attempt has been made to find a neutral 'functional' term to replace the term 'unfair competition', the latter being perceived as revealing a bias towards the classical competitor-oriented approach. Interestingly, the 'commercial practices' concept was used in the 1975 Preliminary Programme very broadly for practices other than advertising, including even standard contracts. It was then also employed in the early Door-step Selling Directive, but seems subsequently to have fallen into oblivion.

A Green Paper advanced by the Commission's Directorate General (DG) on the Internal Market in the mid-1990s introduced the modern economic notion of 'commercial communication'.[28] The concept was then employed in the E-Commerce Directive. In its main approach, however, the Green Paper remained conventional. It continued to rely on piecemeal and selective harmonisation, adding a de-regulative dimension. Comprehensive harmonisation and coherence were not the goal, which was instead levelling the playing field through minimum common standards and regulatory competition.[29]

A rich inventory of concepts was considered in the preparatory work to the UCPD. The Feasibility Study in 2000 built on a 'fair trading' approach opting for a positive terminology. Eventually 'unfair commercial practices' was selected as the preferred concept, interpreted in an unusually broad manner.[30] Needless to say, this conceptual disarray is reflected in the legislative acts that constitute the Community *acquis* in the area and have had serious repercussions on the national level as well.

(d) Between Consumer Empowerment and Public Intervention

One distinctive feature of the process of harmonisation of unfair commercial practices law has been its focus on substantive law aspects and its alleged procedural and institutional neutrality. This does not mean that

---

[28] Green Paper on Commercial Communication in the Internal Market, COM(96)192 final. The Green Paper was preceded by a study conducted by the Munich MPI on the advertising laws in the Member States: see G Schricker, *Recht der Werbung in Europa* (Baden-Baden, Nomos, 1995).

[29] On regulatory competition see JM Sun and J Pelkmans, 'Regulatory Competition in the Single Market' (1995) 33 *Journal of Common Market Studies* 67, C Barnard, 'Social Dumping and the Race to the Bottom: Some Lessons for the European Union from Delaware' (2000) 25 *European Law Review* 57.

[30] See Art 2(d) Directive 2005/29/EC [2005] OJ L 149/22.

the importance of enforcement mechanisms and institutional aspects has been denied. Already the Ulmer project stressed the crucial significance of establishing agreement on equivalent procedural safeguards of enforcement. In its procedural part the project contained a proposal envisaging private enforcement through injunctions and standing to sue for individual competitors and for business associations as a common standard. In addition, the pertinence of a speedy procedure, like preliminary injunctions, was underlined. The enforcement model familiar from German unfair competition law was thus advanced as the most appropriate option at the Community level as well.[31] Ulmer spoke passionately in defence of this model with broad procedural rights of business unions and associations for enforcement of collective interests.[32] At the same time, the prospects of arriving at a common understanding on the issue of enforcement of collective interests was pessimistically assessed, since in this respect even the laws of the original six Member States belonging to a common Roman/canonical law continental tradition varied widely.[33]

Once the efforts were redirected from a Convention to a Community instrument, namely a harmonisation directive, the ambitions to achieve a level playing field in the area of enforcement were rolled back. This was chiefly due to the inherent limitations on the Community's competence in the area of procedure. As in other areas, harmonisation in the domain of unfair commercial practices rested from the outset on the assumptions of procedural and institutional neutrality. In the face of the variety of institutional approaches to regulating the field in the Member States, the Misleading Advertising Directive presented administrative action and private litigation as equally acceptable options. This was subsequently reiterated in other consumer protection directives.

At the same time, with its very first steps as an actor in the consumer policy arena, the Community, and notably the Commission, actively engaged in promoting the role of national consumer organisations. In the literature this phenomenon has been explained on the one hand by a genuine concern for the power imbalance between consumers and producers in Community law and policy-making and, on the other hand, by the self-interest of the Commission in finding allies to support its growing involvement in the area. In this second account the creation of strong and viable consumer unions at the national level and the institutionalisation of their cooperation at the Community level are seen as bricks in the strategy of the Community towards expanding the scope of its powers.[34] A preference for consumer

---

[31] Ulmer, above n 13, 256.
[32] Ulmer emphasised in particular that it would be wrong to establish a strict requirement of connection between standing to sue and affected interests of union members: ibid, at 258.
[33] Ibid, at 241.
[34] Bourgoignie, above n 16 at 123.

organisations as main agents in law enforcement can be discerned also in legislative initiatives, such as the Injunctions Directive, which introduces a principle of 'mutual recognition' of entities authorised to bring injunction proceedings for the protection of collective consumer interests.[35] The Directive makes a decisive step away from the presumption of national procedural autonomy and into the domain of remedies and procedure. Although it applies only to cross-border proceedings, it gives important impetus to empowering consumer organisations also in purely internal situations.[36]

A substantial shift of attitude can be observed in the Regulation on Consumer Protection Cooperation that was negotiated in parallel to the UCPD.[37] This Regulation is at least as remarkable as the Directive in the boldness and novelty of the approach taken. In the explanatory memorandum to its original proposal, the Commission embarks on a daring comparative institutional analysis of the advantages and disadvantages of public versus private enforcement. Acknowledging the many merits of consumer organisations and private enforcement, the Commission still reveals a somewhat surprising penchant for public enforcement in the consumer protection field, including fair trading.[38] Although the Commission underlines the 'valuable role' to be played by consumer organisations in the process of enforcement, it does not appear ready to sustain the 'privileged position' provided to these organisations by Community law and especially by the Injunctions Directive.[39] Ostensibly, for the first time in Community documents some drawbacks of consumer organisations are brought to the fore. Thus the accountability of consumer associations is openly called into question.[40] On the basis of these assessments the Commission appears uncompromising in its resolve to require that Member States assign mutual assistance rights and obligations in the consumer protection field exclusively to public authorities.[41]

Summing up, the history of fair trading at the EC level has oscillated from grand ambitions of comprehensive harmonisation on the basis of an

---

[35] Directive 98/27/EC on Injunctions for the Protection of Consumers' Interests [1990] OJ L 166/51.

[36] For the mechanism of such spill-over effects see Bakardjieva Engelbrekt, above n 25, 429–31.

[37] Regulation (EC) 2006/2004 of the European Parliament and of the Council of 27 Oct 2004 on cooperation between national authorities responsible for the enforcement of consumer protection laws [2004] OJ L 364/1 (the Regulation on consumer protection cooperation).

[38] The advantages of public authorities are seen to lie in sufficient investigation powers; sufficient guarantee of confidentiality and professional secrecy; proven efficiency and effectiveness of a public dimension to enforcement in the Member States where such exists; impartiality and accountability: see COM(2003)443 final, Explanatory memorandum, para 34.

[39] See ibid, Explanatory memorandum, para 32.

[40] Private bodies are said to be 'not so accountable': ibid, para 34.

[41] Ibid, Explanatory memorandum, para 34.

unfair competition law approach, through a long period of 'identity crisis' and ensuing fragmentation, finally to arrive at a general concept of unfair commercial practices, this time under the hallmark of consumer protection. In terms of enforcement, despite the overall claim of procedural neutrality, the Community seems to have moved from reliance on competitors and competitors' associations, through promoting consumer empowerment and vesting trust in consumer organisations, to open acknowledgement of the virtues of public intervention for the protection of consumer interests.

4. UNFAIR COMMERCIAL PRACTICES LAW IN THE CEE COUNTRIES IN THE EARLY STAGE OF TRANSITION

Having traced the twists and turns of Community involvement in commercial practices law that eventually led to the UCP Directive, I will now turn to the situation in the EU Member States and candidate states from CEE.

(a) Legacies of the Past

The starting position of these states in the years immediately following the demise of state socialism as a political and economic system appears, at least at first glance, to have been the almost complete absence of legal rules framing the emerging market economy. Most of the CEE countries had some history of pre-World War II antitrust and unfair competition laws.[42] This legislation was, however, typically either abolished or dormant during the years of the command economy.[43]

Yet on a closer look deeper historical and ideological undercurrents can be identified under the seemingly uniform and monolithic surface of the Soviet-type economic system, accounting for not insignificant legislative and

---

[42] Bulgarian Act Against Unfair Competition of 22 Nov 1940; Act No 111 Against Unfair Competition of 1927 (Czech Republic); Hungarian Act Against Unfair Competition of 1923 (Act No V/1923); Polish Act on the Combat of Unfair Competition of 1926; Romanian Act Against Unfair Competition of 18 May 1932; Yugoslav Act Against Unfair Competition of 4 Apr 1930. Yugoslav developments are discussed here by reason of their relevance for Slovenia.

[43] In Bulgaria, for instance, the Unfair Competition Act from 1940 was repealed by the remarkable 1951 Law on the Abolition of All Laws Enacted Before 1944. A similar fate befell the Yugoslav Act (Yugoslav Act 1946 on the Non-Validity of Rules Enacted before 6 Apr 1941 and During the Enemy Occupation) and the Romanian Act (Decree Nr. 691/1973). In Hungary the Act Against Unfair Competition of 1923 (Act No V/1923) was declared by the Supreme Court to have lost its substance. In Poland the Act on Cartels of 1933 was not expressly repealed but had no noticeable influence on doctrine or practice. Cf T Várady, 'The Emergence of Competition Law in (Former) Socialist Countries' (1999) 47 *American Journal of Comparative Law* 229.

institutional differentiation. Three factors stand out as particularly important in this respect: the degree of continuity with the legal heritage of the past, the openness to Western legal developments and, at a later stage, economic and political reform efforts within the socialist system. Concerning the bonds with legal tradition, it deserves mention that in Hungary and in Poland major parts of the pre-World War II Unfair Competition Acts were never formally abolished and stirred some academic discussion in the 1960s and 1970s.[44] Similarly, contacts between legal scholars from the same countries and their Western colleagues were never fully interrupted. Intellectual exchange was taking place even in legal areas of no practical relevance in the East such as competition law.[45] More decisive were the intellectual isolation and the break with past legacies in the Baltic states, which lost their sovereignty by becoming part of the Soviet Union, as well as in Bulgaria where communism regime was practised more zealously.[46]

In the 1980s attempts at s(t)imluating a market-type economy were undertaken in a number of communist countries from CEE, triggering some legislative activity in the area of competition law. The trend was set with the 1974 Yugoslav Act on Suppression of Unfair Competition and Monopolistic Agreements.[47] Hungary followed suit with an Act on Prohibition of Unfair Economic Activity in 1984.[48] Both Acts were broadly conceived as market conduct acts, partly inspired by international developments, and partly due to ideological barriers to emphasising competition as an organising economic principle. In Poland an Act on Countering Monopolistic Practices in the National Economy was adopted in 1987. Unlike the Hungarian and the Yugoslav acts this was a purely anti-monopoly piece of legislation. It did not tackle unfair trade practices.

Although these Acts, predictably, remained with very limited practical application, their influence can still be traced in the modern market law statutes of the respective countries. More importantly, with the benefit of hindsight we may say that they (re)introduced the conceptual apparatus of competition law in legal discourse, a fact that facilitated the diffusion

---

[44] See decision of the Polish Constitutional Court of 1991 [1991] *GRuR Int* 654. Cf I Wiszniewska, 'Recht der Werbung in Polen' in G Schricker (ed), *Recht der Werbung in Europa* (Baden-Baden, Nomos, 1999) Nr 26. On continuity in Romania see Y Eminescu, 'Das Recht des unlauteren Wettbewerbs in Rumänien' [1994] *GRUR Int* 688.

[45] See on Romania, ibid.

[46] See A Dietz, 'Die Einführung von Gesetzen gegen den unlauteren Wettbewerb in ehemals sozialistischen Staaten Mittel- und Osteuropas' [1994] *GRUR Int* 649.

[47] On this act see J Straus, 'Die Entwicklung des jugoslawischen Wettbewerbsrechts und die Neuregelung von 1974' [1976] *GRUR Int* 426–37; Várady, above n 43.

[48] See HG Graf Lambsdorff, 'Das Recht des unlauteren Wettbewerbs in Ungarn' [1994] *GRuR Int* Teil 714; I Vörös, 'Das neue einheitliche Gesetz über den wirtschaftlichen Wettbewerb und das Recht der Wettbewerbsbeschränkungen in Ungarn' [1985] *GRUR Int* 550; K Cseres, 'The Hungarian Cocktail of Competition Law and Consumer Protection: Should it be Dissolved?' (2004) 27 *Journal of Consumer Policy* 43; cf Várady, above n 43.

of competition law and policy culture at the beginning of the 1990s.[49] This only comes to demonstrate that path dependence is a powerful explanatory model for legal and institutional change, even in a context of dramatic ideological and societal transformation.[50]

To conclude this admittedly sketchy review of past legacies, a word on the uneasy position of consumer protection in socialist legislation and legal scholarship is in order. It is patently obvious that the whole theory of consumer protection developed in the West builds on the premises of free market economy. It addresses situations of market failures and proposes different instruments to compensate for such failures. The socialist economy was by definition not a market economy, and it was ideologically difficult to admit that it had failed in any way. Against this backdrop, appeals for increased consumer protection could easily be perceived as politically incorrect. Moreover, consumer law and policy as they evolved in the West responded to the grievances of a highly developed 'affluent society'.[51] In contrast, the socialist economy has been pertinently characterised as an economy of shortage.[52] The concerns were consequently markedly different on the two sides of the Iron Curtain. Despite some scholarly discussion in the 1970s and 1980s no major legislative initiatives were undertaken in the field.[53]

(b) Unfair Commercial Practices Law as Part of the Broader Regulation of the Market

With the advance of the market economy at the beginning of the 1990s the need for more effective rules of economic conduct was invariably experienced by all CEE countries. The prospect of accession to the European Union was at this historical juncture pretty distant. Therefore 'chance and prestige' steered the search among alternative legislative and institutional models, in which European and also American and other foreign prototypes were considered and combined with local solutions.[54] A first generation of legislative acts devoted partly or entirely to the regulation of unfair commercial practices was introduced in the CEE countries as early as

---

[49] Cseres, above n 48; cf Várady, above n 43.

[50] On path dependence see D North, *Institutions, Institutional Change and Economic Performance* (Cambridge, Cambridge University Press, 1990).

[51] JK Galbraith, *The Affluent Society* (London, Hamish Hamilton, 1968).

[52] J Kornai, *Economics of Shortage* (Amsterdam, North-Holland, 1980), referred in A Kozminski, 'Consumers in Transition from a Centrally Planned to a Market Economy' (1991) 14 *Journal of Consumer Policy* 351.

[53] For an incisive analysis see E Łętowska, 'Consumer Protection as Public Interest Law' [1999] *Droit polonais contemporain* 39.

[54] G Adjani, 'By Chance and Prestige. Legal Transplants in Russia and Eastern Europe' (1995) 43 *American Journal of Comparative Law* 93.

the beginning of the 1990s. These acts revealed a surprisingly rich variety of regulative solutions.[55]

(i) Systemic Arrangements

One important question that emerged in the legislative process was that of defining the relationship of the law of unfair competition to antitrust law.[56] Two main systemic solutions emerged in regard to this particular policy question.

(1) Divided (dualistic) approach   Some CEE countries preferred to follow traditional continental models and treat antitrust law and unfair competition law separately. Thus Poland and Romania were obviously inspired by the German UWG, which had also served as a model to their pre-World War II law and practice.[57] In both countries separate Acts against unfair competition were thus adopted, where the interests of competitors, but also in particular in Poland the interests of consumers and the general public, were taken into account. A slightly different systemic solution was preferred in the Czech Republic and Slovakia, where rules on unfair competition were incorporated in the Commercial Code along with other commercial law matters such as company law, bankruptcy, etc.[58] Antitrust was subject to separate legislation in all countries from this group.[59]

(2) Integrated (monistic) approach   Another group of CEE countries opted for an integrated regulation of antitrust and unfair trade practices law. This approach is more unusual in the Continental context. It was first introduced by Hungary, which built on the experience with the 1984 Unfair Economic Activity Act. Subsequently, the model achieved a remarkable spread to Bulgaria, Estonia, Latvia and Lithuania.[60] Slovenia adopted a similar solution

---

[55] For a formidable comparative overview see Dietz, above n 46.

[56] Ibid.

[57] Poland: Act on Combating Unfair Competition of 16 Apr 1993, State Gazette (Dziennik Ustaw) No 47/1993 Pos. 211; Romania: Act on the Combat of Unfair Competition of 28 Jan 1991, State Gazette (Monitorul Oficial) I, No 24 of 30 Jan 1991, at 3. For a German translation of these earlier acts see U Schulze, *Die Wettbewerbs- und Kartellgesetze der osteuropäischen Staaten* (Berlin, Berlin Verlag, 1994).

[58] Czech Republic: First Part of the Commercial Code of 5 Nov 1991; Slovak Republic: First Part of the Commercial Code of 5 Nov 1991, State Gazette (Sbírka zákonů) No 513/1991. See Schulze, above n 57.

[59] Poland: Act Counteracting Monopolistic Practices of 24 Feb 1990, State Gazette (Dziennik Ustaw) No 89/1991, Pos 403: Czech Republic: Act on the Protection of Economic Competition of 30 Jan 1991, State Gazette (Sbírka zákonů) No 63/1991; Schulze, above n 57.

[60] Cf Bulgaria: Act on Protection of Competition of 1991, State Gazette (Darzaven Vestnik) No 39/1991; Estonia: Competition Act of 9 July 1993; Hungary: Act LXXXVI on the Prohibition of Unfair Trade Conduct of 20 Nov 1990, State Gazette (Magyar Közlöny) 1990, 2361; Latvia: Competition Act of 3 Dec 1991 State Gazette (Latvijas Republikas Augstākās Padomes un Valdības Ziņotājs), No 51/1991; Lithuania: Competition Act of 15 Sept 1992, State Gazette (Lietuvos Aidas) of 29 Sept 1992; Slovenia: Act on Protection of Competition of 25 Mar 1993, State Gazette No 18/1993 of 9 Apr 1993, 816.

corresponding to the 1974 Yugoslav Unfair Competition Act. Distinctive of this approach are comprehensive Competition or Market Conduct Acts regulating both freedom and fairness of competition. Also under this systemic arrangement the interests of competitors, consumers and the general public in fair competition are as a rule taken into consideration. Yet the approach is characterised by a holistic view on competition and relies on a different institutional framework, involving partly different actors.

The spread of the integrated model can be explained by a combination of factors, besides the obvious positive synergies that were expected from the joint regulation of free and fair competition. As indicated above, for some countries historical legacies, even short-term ones, apparently played a formative role. Recourse to legal borrowings was also used as a convenient short cut around 'reinventing the wheel'.[61] Interestingly, whereas there was a rich '*smorgasbord*' of Western models it seems that the Hungarian experience has revealed particular attraction for other CEE countries, probably because of its perceived suitability for the conditions of a transition economy.[62] The choice of a monistic approach was presumably confirmed by legal and policy advice offered within the framework of American legal aid initiatives. In the early 1990s experts from the US Federal Trade Commission (FTC) commented on legal drafts and subsequently offered technical assistance to newly built competition agencies in Bulgaria, Poland, Hungary and Czechoslovakia, arguably contributing to the emulation of the FTC model.[63] With its reliance on public intervention, the integrated approach was certainly in better harmony with old habits from the time of controlled economy. Finally, the choice was most likely prompted by the simple logic of legislative economy steering overloaded law-making institutions.

(ii) Substantive Rules

From a substantive law point of view, almost all of the legal acts mentioned above, irrespective of the underlying regulative model, built on some kind of general clause against unfair competition or unfair market conduct.[64] This is probably easy to explain since all CEE countries have a background

---

[61] TW Waelde and JL Gunderson, 'Legal Transplants as a Short Cut to Social Market' (1994) 43 International & Comparative Law Quarterly 347.

[62] On its influence over the drafting of the Bulgarian Competition Act see T Kamenova, 'First Steps Towards Competition Law in Bulgaria' [1989] International Review of Intellectual Property and Competition Law 180.

[63] See FTC Press Release 'FTC offers technical assistance to emerging democracies of Central and Eastern Europe', 28 May 1991; cf EM Fox, 'Competition Policy in Eastern Europe. The Bulgarian Project as a Case Study' (1991) 60 *Antitrust Law Journal* 243.

[64] Art 11 and 12 of the 1991 Bulgarian Competition Act prohibited as an act of unfair competition 'any action or omission in the carrying out of economic activity which is contrary to *bonos mores* in commerce and which impairs or is likely to impair the interests of com-

either in the French or in the German legal tradition, both of which are familiar with general clauses.

An additional technique that won recognition irrespective of the adopted regulative model was to complement the general clause with more or less detailed catalogues of examples clarifying and complementing it. Under this exemplification as a rule fell misleading advertising, disparagement, trade mark and trade name confusion, passing off, disclosure of trade secrets, etc.[65] These catalogues have not always been the best example of legal drafting, replete with overlaps and repetitions. Nevertheless, they have provided useful guidance to market actors and enforcement bodies alike in the interpretation of the law. In this sense the black lists proved to be of particular importance in the context of transition economies, where the rules of fair play were still not well established. Particularly receptive to modern developments has been the 1990 Hungarian Unfair Trade Conduct Act, which in its substantive rules stressed consumer fraud and included factors such as environmental protection and health protection in the assessment of the misleading nature of an advertising claim.[66]

(iii) Enforcement and Sanctions

Corresponding to the two different systemic approaches to unfair commercial practices outlined above there were, broadly speaking, two main enforcement techniques. In the countries pursuing the UWG approach, enforcement was predominantly entrusted to private actors, chiefly competitors and their associations, but also, explicitly in Poland, in the Czech Republic and in Slovakia, consumer associations.[67] The main decision-making institution was thus the judiciary, acting in a decentralised manner. Associated with this approach was also an emphasis on private law remedies (injunctions and damages).[68] The alternative integrated approach relied to a greater extent on public competition authorities with various sets

---

petitors in their mutual relations or in their relations with consumers'. The 1992 Lithuanian Competition Act laid down in Art 7 a general prohibition of activities of unfair competition. Art 3 of the Polish Act on Combating Unfair Competition of 1993 bans 'any act contrary to the law or to *bonos mores*, when it impairs or infringes the interests of another undertaking or the clients'. Art 13 of the 1993 Slovenian Act on Protection of Competition defined as an act of unfair competition 'any act of an undertaking in connection with its entry on the market which is contrary to bonos mores and which causes or is capable of causing damage to another participant on the market'.

[65] Dietz, above n 46.

[66] Cseres, above n 48.

[67] Cf S 19(1)(2) of the Polish Act on Combating Unfair Competition; Art 54 of the Czech and Slovak Commercial Code.

[68] These were, however, significantly complemented by penal sanctions with different degree of practical relevance and frequency of enforcement. See for Poland R Skubisz, 'Das Recht des unlauteren Wettbewerbs in Polen' [1994] GRUR Int 681; for Romania see Eminescu, above n 44.

of investigatory, monitoring, sanctioning and quasi-adjudicative powers. Emphasis was placed on administrative law remedies.[69]

Whereas drafting the substantive rules has been relatively unproblematic, designing an adequate institutional and enforcement framework has proved particularly challenging. Unfair commercial practices law is an area of regulation straddling private and public law, where a variety of disparate interests, both private and public, are potentially involved. This posed unconventional tasks in designing enforcement and in finding the right mix of public and private enforcement.

In the case of private enforcement the difficult question has been to accommodate the protection of non-individual, collective interests within a framework of a traditionally very narrow understanding of private rights and civil procedure. The low degree of organisation of collective interests in the context of a generally weak civil society is a much observed problem.[70] Another major concern has been the notorious inefficiency of the post-communist judiciary, which lacked experience of collective and public interest litigation and tended to stick grudgingly to familiar categorisations and classical civil law doctrines. Injunction as a remedy has been widely regarded with scepticism due to its limited deterrent effect

In the case of public enforcement, defining the exact scope of competition authorities' competences and the relationship between private and public enforcement proved to be among the most difficult aspects of the regulative reform. Within the mould of a legal tradition of strict doctrinal divide between private and public law[71] and of rigid administrative law, creating the new public agency that was expected to exercise novel facilitative function in economic exchange was a major challenge.

In this respect the 1990 Hungarian Act demonstrated a sophisticated vision of efficient institutional design. The Hungarian Office for Economic Competition (OEC) was set up as a strong, independent and at the same time accountable, public agency. It was entrusted with unconventional quasi-adjudicative functions not only in matters of antitrust but also in matters of consumer fraud. Conversely, acts of unfair competition affecting individual business interests were predominantly left to private litigation

---

[69] See, however, the example of the Slovenian Competition Act, which carried through in its original version a differentiation between the competence of the Competition Agency in antitrust matters and a private law enforcement of unfair competition law: Dietz, above n 46.

[70] See S Rose-Ackerman, *From Elections to Democracy, Building Accountable Government in Hungary and Poland* (Cambridge, Cambridge University Press, 2005); cf W Jacoby, *The Enlargement of the European Union and NATO: Ordering from the Menu in Central Europe* (Cambridge, Cambridge University Press, 2004) 41.

[71] R Mańko, 'The Culture of Private Law in Central and Eastern Europe After Enlargement: A Polish Perspective' (2005) 11 *European Law Journal* 527.

before ordinary courts.[72] Less successful was the distribution of competences under the 1991 Bulgarian Competition Act. Although the avenue
for private litigation remained open for all affected actors as a fully fledged
parallel to public enforcement, there were no functional limitations on the
competences of the Commission for Protection of Competition (CPC). This
design powerfully tilted complainants' preferences towards public enforcement. In the first annual reports of the CPC the unfair competition cases
clearly dominated the Commission's case load.[73] Another unfortunate
peculiarity of the Bulgarian institutional design was the fact that the competition authority could issue only temporary decisions, which were then to
be confirmed by an ordinary civil court. This procedure was unnecessarily
time-consuming, but, on the positive side, ensured some involvement of the
judiciary in the process of decision-making.[74] Yet another approach was
adopted by the Slovenian Competition Act, which distinguished strictly
between the areas of antitrust, requiring public enforcement, and unfair
competition, referring to private enforcement.

I cannot here address the complex question of the advantages and disadvantages of the integrated and the divided approach and of private and
public enforcement, respectively. For the purposes of this chapter it suffices
to note that in the countries where powers in unfair commercial practices
were vested in specialised competition agencies administrative practice was
rapidly accumulating and the interests affected were able more easily to
find expression in the decision-making process. Even a hasty comparison
of the number of cases decided by the competition offices in Bulgaria and
Hungary and the cases reported in court practice in Romania and Poland
gives evidence of this differential effect.[75]

---

[72] For the evolution of the law and initial attempt to use the quick and inexpensive avenue
of complaint before the OEC via an extensive interpretation of the general clause see Dietz,
above n 46, at 654.

[73] In 1993 the Bulgarian Competition Commission issued its first annual report. Within the
1½ year of activity the Commission had received 114 complaints, discussed 135 matters and
issued 135 decisions. Of all the decisions, 97 related to matters of unfair competition, including two cases of trade secrets and 45 cases of alleged unfair competition by former employees
(a provision which was of a dubious nature and was later repealed). Compared with the 30
cases related to abuse of monopoly position, the unfair competition cases clearly stood out as
the predominant category in the practice of the Commission: see Commission for Protection of
Competition, Bulgaria, *Annual Report 1992/93*, 36. Cf Dietz, above n 46, at 655. The preva-
lence of unfair competition matters in the statistics of the Commission was maintained in the
years to follow (231 out of 328 files in 1993; 122 out of 211 in 1994; 109 out of 196 in 1995
and 78 out of 129 in 1996). See the *Annual Reports* for 1994, 1995, 1996 and 1997.

[74] On the Bulgarian experience see A Bakardjieva, 'Das Recht des unlauteren Wettbewerbs in
Bulgarien' [1994] GRUR Int 671; A Bakardjieva, 'Das neue Wettbewerbsgesetz in Bulgarien'
[1999] GRUR Int 395.

[75] Compare the above reported practice of the Bulgarian CPC and the record of the competent Chambers of Commerce in Romania of 24 cases per year in 1992/3: cf Eminescu, above
n 44. In Poland despite a lively doctrinal debate, the number of cases in the early 1990s was
also very limited. Cf Skubisz, above n 68; Wiszniewska, above n 44.

(iv) Competition Law as Consumer Protection Law

A common characteristic of these initial efforts to 'furnish' a free market economy in an institutional sense[76] is the almost complete absence of direct rules of consumer protection. In only a few countries, such as Czechoslovakia, Romania and Latvia, were there some early legislative initiatives in the field. The resulting acts were, however, largely symbolic, offering hardly any instruments for enforcement and implementation.[77] As Łętowska explains, one reason for this may be the rapid supplanting of the 'central-plan' paradigm with the 'invisible-hand' paradigm. Almost ironically, consumer law has for the second time proved to be politically incorrect.[78]

At the expense of missing tools for direct consumer protection, however, the competition acts, in particular in the countries taking an integrated approach, have been unusually receptive to consumer interests. By way of example, one can note that already in the early 1990s the competition authorities in Bulgaria, Hungary and the Baltic States saw themselves actively engaged in dozens of unfair commercial practices disputes which ultimately had important consequences for consumers. Some statistics may illustrate the point. On the basis of annual reports of the Hungarian Competition Office in 1992 Ben Slay notes the numerical importance of 'consumer deception' rulings. He finds it 'instructive that of the 103,5 million forints collected in fines during 1992, 103,5 million came from consumer deception rulings'.[79]

(c) Interim Evaluation

Unsurprisingly, the first generation of Competition Acts suffered from a number of 'childhood diseases'. One way of dealing with the above-described difficulties of enforcement design has been quite simply to disregard them. Typically the acts contained few and often enigmatic provisions on enforcement referring to general provisions of administrative and civil procedure or leaving important institutional details to governmental decrees.[80] In outlining novel functions for public authorities they employed

[76] See J Elster, C Offe and U Preuss, *Institutional Design in Post-Communist Europe. Repairing the Ship at Sea* (Cambridge, Cambridge University Press, 1998)
[77] See the country reports in E Alexiev *et al*, *Consumer Protection in Bulgaria, Czech Republic, Estonia, Hungary, Latvia, Lithuania and Romania. National Reports and Comparative Analysis* (Louvain-la-Neuve, Centre de Droit de la Consommation, Université Catholique de Louvain, CICPP No. 4, 1996).
[78] Łętowska, above n 53.
[79] B Slay, 'Industrial Demonopolization and Competition Policy in Poland and Hungary' (1995) 3 Economics of Transition 479 at 491. In a similar sense and on the basis of broader statistical data see Cseres, above n 48.
[80] See 1991 Bulgarian Competition Act, 1993 Slovenian Competition Act.

terminology from existing general civil and administrative law, which the judiciary tended to interpret strictly. There were quite a number of examples of misconceptions and sheer blunders in the drafting, creating bottlenecks in the enforcement procedure and ensuing inefficiency.[81]

At the same time, despite their numerous imperfections the Competition Acts appear to have achieved an important task in the early phase of transition, namely highlighting the market-building function of competition law and regulation and defying perceptions of the market economy as an ungoverned economy. Despite differences in the chosen patterns of regulation, there has generally been an attempt to find a comprehensive framework approach to the problem of unfair competition/unfair commercial practices. Fair trading law was conceived and employed as a practical tool for regulating competition and the market, which in an indirect and reflexive manner was beneficial for the interests of consumers and for society at large. The market-building approach was clearly predominant, conceiving of unfair competition law as an important component of the institutional framework of emerging markets.

Institutionally, in countries taking the integrated approach unfair competition law rapidly gained in importance and provided a relatively accessible and smooth channel for giving voice to relevant individual and collective interests.[82] The availability of a single authority which, in a simplified procedure and at fairly low cost, would tackle everyday rows over passing-off, disparagement and consumer fraud obviously offered an attractive alternative for both businesses and consumers, in particular given the slow, complicated and uncertain proceedings of ordinary courts. Competence in market law matters was rapidly accumulating with the newly built competition agencies, the composition of which often sought to ensure economic and specialised legal expertise, where courts were still detached from the minutiae of market realities and lacked the necessary qualifications. Importantly, increasing awareness about the appropriate balance between public and private instruments of enforcement and the complex interplay between the two was slowly beginning to emerge.

5. THE IMPACT OF ENLARGEMENT

Law reform during the second half of the 1990s took a decisively different turn. As in all other areas, the prospect of accession to the European Union has been the overriding motivation behind legislative initiatives in the CEE

---

[81] On the trials and tribulations of the Bulgarian Competition Commission before the Bulgarian civil courts see Bakardjieva, 'Das Recht', above n 74; Bakardjieva, 'Das neue Wettbewerbsgesetz,' above n 74.

[82] Dietz, above n 46.

states, determining both the direction and the dynamics of change. Given the variety of regulative objectives pursued by unfair commercial practices law, its fragmented state and complex interfaces with various areas of Community law, it is not surprising that influence has come from different directions. Of most direct relevance has been the Community *acquis* in the area of consumer protection, where most of the Community legal instruments concerning commercial practices are now classified. Less apparent but, as we shall see, still palpable has been the effect of Community competition law.

(a) The Accession Process: a Chronological Record

Formal ground for approximation of legislation with Community law was initially provided by the Europe Agreements entered into by all candidate states from CEE during the first half of the 1990s.[83] Compliance with Community Competition law was set out as a clear requirement to all CEE states in all so-called Association and Europe Agreements. In contrast, consumer protection was introduced in the first Agreements only hesitantly. However, it acquired an ever more prominent position in parallel with the maturing and constitutional anchoring of consumer policy at the Community level. The first Association Agreements mentioned consumer protection as only one area where approximation of legislation should be achieved.[84] In subsequent Agreements the aim of full compatibility with the Community consumer protection policy was spelled out, adding several areas of cooperation.[85] Moreover, in special chapters on economic co-operation detailed steps for the approximation of consumer law and policy were outlined, including technical assistance for establishing the necessary institutional infrastructure (cf Article 92 of Europe Agreement with the Czech Republic, Article 95 of the Europe Agreement with Estonia).[86]

The Copenhagen European Council was the first clearly to offer the prospect of EU membership for the CEE states. At the same time, the Council defined in more demanding terms the conditions for membership,

---

[83] For a review of the accession process see Grabbe, above n 7.
[84] Cf Art 68 of the Europe Agreement with Hungary [1993] OJ L 348/1, Art 69 of the Europe Agreement with Poland [1993] OJ L 347/1.
[85] See Art 92 of the Agreements with Czech Republic [1994] OJ L 360/1 and Slovakia [1994] OJ L 359/1; Art 93 of the Agreements with Bulgaria, Slovenia, Romania at [1994] OJ L 358/1, [1999] OJ L 51/1 and [1994] OJ L 357/1 respectively.
[86] On this development see T Bourgoignie, 'The Approximation Process of Consumer Laws of Central and Eastern European Countries to EU Legislation: A Favourable Context but an Urgent Need for Clarification' in HW Micklitz (ed) *Rechtseinheit oder Rechtsvielfalt in Europa? Zur Rolle und Funktion des Verbraucherrechts in den MOE-Staaten und in der EG* (Baden-Baden, Nomos, 1996) 91, and the Europe Agreement with Estonia [1998] OJ L 68/1.

including not only formal legal transposition of the Community *acquis*, but also political and institutional requirements, notably concerning the administrative capacity of the candidate states to cope with EU membership.

In 1995 the Commission White Paper on the Preparation of the Associated Countries of CEE for Integration into the Internal Market of the Union exerted a catalysing effect on the harmonisation process.[87] The Annex to the White Paper amounted to more than 400 pages, in which the mammoth task of summarising the Community *acquis* and ordering it into chapters and into Key Stage I and Stage II measures was undertaken by the Commission. It supplied the accession states with a concrete plan of action and order of priorities. Echoing the conclusions of the Copenhagen European Council the White Paper stressed the importance of functioning institutions for breathing life into the incorporated normative *acquis*.[88]

In the Annex to the White Paper of 1995 the *acquis* concerning advertising and fair trading practices fell under Chapter 23, together with the rich and varied measures that comprise the Community's 'consumer protection' *acquis*. Alignment with the Misleading Advertising Directive was set out as a Key Stage I measure, whereas bringing legislation into conformity with the Comparative Advertising Directive and other marketing methods directives was placed in the category of Stage II measures. The *acquis* in the area of competition law and policy was summarised in Chapter 6 and compliance was set as a high priority.

Interestingly, whereas the Community *acquis* in the area of enforcement of consumer protection was almost non-existent in the mid-1990s, Chapter 23 of the White Paper provided an extensive list of conditions that had to be met in order to make consumer legislation operative. Among these conditions the setting up of an adequate institutional structure governing consumer affairs was emphasised. Additional elements of the institutional framework that were highlighted were the setting up of consultative procedures which should secure representation of the consumer interest and ensure consumer participation in the decision-making process, granting consumers efficient redress mechanisms and helping to ensure the development of non-governmental organisations.[89]

The challenge of transposing the notorious 80,000 (and by now allegedly over 100,000) pages of Community *acquis* into national legislation

---

[87] White Paper on the Preparation of the Associated Countries of CEE for Integration into the Internal Market of the Union, COM(1995)163 final.

[88] Cf '[t]he main challenge [for the association countries] in taking over Internal Market legislation lies not in the technical adaptation of their legal texts to make them identical to those of the Community but in adapting their administrative machinery and their societies to the framework conditions necessary to make the legislation work': ibid, at 2.

[89] See White Paper, COM(1995)186 final, JP Pritchard (ed), *Consumer Protection in Poland* (Louvain-la-Neuve, Centre du Droit de la consommation, Université Catholique de Louvain, CICPP No 23, 2000).

was recognised on both sides of the accession process. On the part of Community institutions a serious effort to provide guidance and assistance to the candidate countries was made under the auspices of the PHARE programme. In the first phase of the PHARE venture a huge number of Western advisors were mobilised to provide a detailed digest and analysis of the Community *acquis*. On this basis expert teams were deployed in the candidate countries to screen the relevant national legislation and to check compliance with the relevant Community *acquis*.[90]

In the area of consumer protection a comprehensive Consumer Institutions and Consumer Policy Programme (CICPP) funded by PHARE was set up as early as the early 1990s. The complex task of screening and assessing compliance of Candidate countries' legislation with the relevant Community *acquis* was entrusted to the reputed research and education centre in consumer law and policy in Louvain-la-Neuve (hereinafter, the Centre). The institutional part of the Programme was carried out in close cooperation with Consumers International.[91] During the 1990s the Centre produced more than 26 volumes of analyses and recommendations, including both country-by-country analyses and comparative evaluations. In the area of competition law, apart from Community institutions the OECD competition unit was actively involved, producing country analysis of competition law and institutions and suggesting priorities for the reform agenda.

Starting in 1997, the prospect of membership became ever more tangible. In the so-called Agenda 2000 the Commission announced its new enlargement strategy. It has been argued that in this document a turn to softer forms of advice (new modes of governance) was made, leaving greater autonomy to the candidate states to define their priorities and the source of advice and assistance. Cooperation between Member States and accession states was encouraged, in particular in areas where no clear *acquis* could be elicited.[92]

Powerful pressure on institutional and law reform was exerted through the Regular Reports from the Commission on the Candidate Countries' Progress toward Accession.[93] In their brief statements the Regular Reports synthesised a multitude of less visible and more detailed sets of recommen-

---

[90] On the role of PHARE, see Grabbe, above n 7.

[91] See Consumers International, 'Handbook of Consumer Policy and Consumer Organisations in Central and Eastern Europe' and 'Guidelines for consumer policy in Central and Eastern Europe', both available at www.consumersinternational.org.

[92] E Tulmets, 'The Management of New Forms of Governance by Former Accession Countries of the European Union: Institutional Twinning in Estonia and Hungary' (2005) 11 *European Law Journal* 657.

[93] Hereinafter, the Regular Progress Reports from the Commission will be referred to as: Regular Report, followed by country and year of publication. All Regular Reports can be found on the website of the Commission, DG Enlargement at http://ec.europa.en/enlargement/key_documents/index_en.htm.

dations contained in other official and semi-official documents produced
by experts, PHARE/TACIS assignees, partners in twinning projects, and
the like.

(b) Implementing the *Acquis*: a Horizontal View

The need to bring national legislation into line with the Community *acquis*
outlined above produced several waves of legislative activity in the CEE
candidate countries, following each other closely, which resulted in serious
reform and restructuring of unfair commercial practices legislation. Broadly
speaking the changes can be traced as taking three distinct directions:

(i) The Rise of Consumer Protection Law and Policy

A first wave of legislative activity of relevance for fair trading law, unleashed
chiefly by EU conditionality, could be observed in the area of consumer protection law and policy.[94] In a massive effort to raise consumer protection
standards in the CEE to the level of those in the Community, specific consumer protection acts were introduced in many of the applicant states.[95]

Some of these Acts, like, for instance, the Bulgarian, the Latvian
and the Lithuanian Consumer Protection Acts, are conceived as fairly
comprehensive framework legislation.[96] They follow by and large the
structure of the consumer rights catalogue proclaimed in the 1975 EEC
Preliminary programme and later on taken over by the Amsterdam Treaty
(Article 153 EC). The different categories of rights are then fleshed out
with more specific rights and obligations, thus conceiving consumer protection as a coherent regulatory area in its own right. In many respects

---

[94] On the term 'conditionality' see F Schimmelfennig and U Sedelmeier, 'Governance by
Conditionality: EU Rule Transfer to the Candidate Countries of Central and Eastern Europe'
[2004] *Journal of European Public Policy* 661; See Jacoby, above n 70.

[95] Bulgaria: Act on Protection of Consumers and on the Rules of Commerce of 18 Mar
1999, replaced by Consumer Protection Act of 24 Nov 2005; Czech Republic: Consumer
Protection Act of 16 Dec 1992, last amended 2004; Estonia: Consumer Protection Act of
1994, amended 1999 and 2004; Hungary: Act CLV of 1997 on Consumer Protection; Latvia:
Consumer Protection Act of 29 Oct 1992, replaced by Act on Protection of Consumer Rights
of 18 Mar 1999; Lithuania: Law on Consumer Protection of 10 Nov 1994, amended 19 Sept
2000; Poland: Act on Competition and Consumer Protection of 15 Dec 2000; Act on Certain
Rights of Consumers of 2 Mar 2000; Romania: Ordinance on Consumer Protection of 1992,
amended 1999; Slovak Republic: Consumer Protection Act of 16 Dec 1992, amended 1998
and 1999; Slovenia: Consumer Protection Act of Feb 1998, amended 2002.

[96] On the complex relationship between the Consumer Protection Acts in the Baltic States
and the Civil Law Codes dubbed a dualist, monist and parallel approach see N Reich,
'Transformation of Contract Law and Civil Justice in the New EU Member Countries:
The Example of the Baltic States, Hungary and Poland' in F Cafaggi (ed), *The Institutional
Framework of European Private Law* (Oxford, Oxford University Press, 2006) 271.

such ambitious consumer codes go far beyond the Community consumer protection *acquis*, revealing a general perception that 'overcompliance' will be positively assessed. Probably the most extreme example in terms of ambition and comprehensiveness is the recent Bulgarian Consumer Protection Act with 233 provisions. Comprehensive framework consumer protection Acts (Consumer Codes) seem to have been the legislative strategy preferred and recommended by experts within the CICCP programme.[97]

Other countries like Poland have opted for Consumer Protection Acts of more modest scope and ambition, consisting mainly of a selection of transposed EC directives, sometimes taking over the provisions of the respective directive verbatim. The reasons for resisting the Consumer Code idea appear to have been partly ideological, namely objections against strong consumer protection policy because it is perceived as paternalistic, and partly stemming from concerns for system coherence and attempts to integrate consumer protection into existing, resurrected or newly devised Civil Codes and legislation.[98] Thus in the Czech Republic, most directives on different selling methods have been incorporated in the Civil Code of 1964.[99]

Since regulation of misleading advertising in Community law falls under the heading of consumer protection policy, those applicant states which had opted for comprehensive Consumer Protection Acts have felt obliged to incorporate provisions on advertising and marketing practices in the new Consumer Acts despite the existence of similar rules in the (unfair) Competition Acts. This was also the advice coming from the CICCP experts.[100] Interestingly, occasionally the recommendation was also to place rules on comparative advertising in the Consumer Protection Act, although comparative advertising was already regulated in Competition Acts.[101]

Furthermore various provisions on unfair advertising were often formulated on the basis of rules from sector-specific directives, however

---

[97] See Bourgoignie, above n 86.

[98] For a detailed account of these legislative choices in Hungary, Poland and the Baltic States see Reich, above n 95, 271; for Poland see S Heidenhain, *Das Verbraucherschutzrecht in Polen und in der Europäischen Union* (Dordrecht, Springer, 2000).

[99] Civil Code No 40/1964 State Gazette (Sbírka zákonů); cf Act No 135/2002 Coll (time share); Act No 136/2002 Coll (sales of consumer goods and warranties).

[100] Thus Bulgaria was advised 'to concentrate the provisions regarding enforcement of the consumers' interests in the Law on Consumer Protection': V Cambier, *Comparative and Misleading Advertising Legislation in Central and Eastern Europe* (Louvain-la-Neuve, Centre de Droit de la Consommation, Université Catholique de Louvain, CICPP No 12, 1999) at 25. A similar recommendation was addressed to Slovenia, namely, 'to centralise provisions related to advertising in the Act on Consumer Protection': ibid, at 78.

[101] Bulgaria was urged 'to introduce explicitly the definition and the principle of the admissibility of comparative advertising under specific conditions within the Law on Consumer Protection, in order to comply with European Union requirement': ibid, at 25.

extending the application of such provisions across media and product sectors.[102] Although such rules did not have a counterpart at Community level, they were seen as largely unproblematic by the CICCP experts since they provided higher levels of protection to consumers. It seems that the compatibility of such rules with Community fundamental freedoms was not given serious consideration.

On the institutional plane, an important consequence of the emphasis on consumer protection policy as a policy in its own right has been the setting up of specialised governmental agencies with the sole or chief task of monitoring and implementing consumer policy. This was also an implicit requirement in the White Paper on Accession.[103] Most countries have established such consumer protection agencies. The only countries where no such office has been established are the Czech Republic and the Slovak Republic, where certain functions have been vested in the Ministries of Industry and Trade and of the Economy respectively.[104]

The Polish institutional set-up deserves special mention. The original Competition Office was in 1996 transformed into one mega-office for the protection of competition and consumers. This Office increasingly took over responsibility for the enforcement of all collective consumer interests, including those under the Unfair Competition Act of 1993.[105] In Lithuania initially a similar pattern was followed.[106] In 1996 the Lithuanian Price and Competition Office was transformed into the State Competition and Consumer Protection Office. With the revised Consumer Protection Act of 2000 (CPA), however, this solution was abandoned in favour of a divided approach, featuring a Competition Council and a separate Consumer Protection Board (see s 29 CPA).

---

[102] See for instance the prohibitions on discriminatory advertising and on advertising offending human dignity, in s 16 Polish Unfair Competition Act 1993, s 6 Czech Consumer Protection Act 1992 and s 39 Bulgarian Consumer Protection Act 2005.

[103] See White Paper COM(1995)186 final. Bulgaria: Commission for (Trade and) Consumer Protection; Estonia: State Consumer Protection Board; Hungary: General Inspectorate for Consumer Protection; Latvia: Consumers' Rights Protection Board; Lithuania: Consumer Protection Board; Poland: Office for Protection of Competition and Consumers; Romania: National Authority for Consumer Protection, which replaced in 2001 the Office for the Protection of Consumers; Slovenia: Office for Consumer Protection (in the Ministry of Economic Relations and Development since 1998).

[104] See Consumers International, above n 91.

[105] See R Mańko, 'The Culture of Private Law in Central and Eastern Europe After Enlargement: A Polish Perspective' (2005) 11 European Law Journal 527; cf A Bakardjieva Engelbrekt, 'Grey Zones, Legitimacy Deficits and Boomerang Effects. On the Implications of Extending the Acquis to Central and Eastern Europe' in N Wahl and P Cramér (eds) Swedish Yearbook of European Law (Oxford, Hart Publishing, 2006), 1.

[106] See K Viitanen, 'Consumer Protection in Lithuania', in E Alexiev et al, *Consumer Protection in Bulgaria, Czech Republic, Estonia, Hungary, Latvia. Lithuania and Romania* (Louvain-la-Neuve, Centre de Droit de la Consommation, Université Catholique de Louvain, CICPP No 4, 1995) 173 at 176.

The setting up of specialised consumer protection agencies has been generally acclaimed by the Commission in the Regular Progress Reports.[107] At the same time the Reports suggest that in some countries the performance of these agencies has fallen short of expectations.[108] In individual reports there is even a talk of marginalisation of consumer policy.[109]

(ii) Strengthening Competition Law

In a parallel wave of legislative activism at the end of the 1990s the early Competition Acts were replaced by new or substantially revised Acts in almost all CEE countries. These acts reflect an attempt to streamline antitrust legislation and bring it closer to the Community requirements.[110] Further refinement of these Acts occurred in the New Member States following the Decentralisation of Enforcement Regulation 1/2003, vesting in national authorities the responsibility of enforcing Community law.[111]

For the countries following an integrated approach and tackling the regulation of unfair commercial practices as part of the broader concept of competition, the strengthening of the powers of competition authorities and their competence to impose more severe sanctions has had important repercussions for the enforcement of the rules on unfair competition. First, the new enforcement powers and stricter sanctions were extended also to acts of unfair competition, including consumer fraud and deception, where applicable. Secondly, in the Regular Reports the Commission repeatedly urged the competition agencies in the candidate states to streamline antitrust enforcement and to give priority 'to cases that concern the most serious distortions of competition'.[112] In the 2000 Regular Report on Hungary

---

[107] See eg Regular Report Latvia 2000, at 79; Regular Report Slovenia 1999.

[108] As regards the Latvian Centre for Consumers Protection the Commission notes, 'To date the Centre has not received any complaints concerning advertising'. See Regular Report Latvia 2001, at 91. A similar assessment is made in the Regular Report Bulgaria 2000; Regular Report Bulgaria 2001 at 79; Regular Report Bulgaria 2002, at 107.

[109] Regular Report Bulgaria 2004, at 114.

[110] Cf Bulgaria: Act on Protection of Competition of 1998; Estonia: Competition Act of 1998, replaced by Competition Act of 5 June 2001; Hungary: Act LVII of 1996 on the Prohibition of Unfair and Restrictive Market Practices, amended by Act No CXXXVIII of 2000; Latvia: Competition Act of 4 Oct 2001; Lithuania: Competition Act of 23 Mar 1999; Poland, Act on Competition and Consumer Protection of 15 Dec 2000, replacing the Act on Counteracting Monopolistic Practices and Protection of Consumer Interests of 24 Feb 1990; Slovakia: Amendment of 2000 of the 1993 Competition Act; Slovenia: Act on Prevention of the Restriction of Competition of 1999, Amendment of the 1993 Act on Protection of Competition; Romania: Competition Law No 21/1996.

[111] See K Cseres, *Competition Law and Consumer Protection* (The Hague, Kluwer Law International, 2005) 379.

[112] Regular Report Hungary 1998, at 42; Regular Report Hungary 1999, at 65; Regular Report Hungary 2000, at 41; Regular Report Estonia 2000, at 43; Regular Report Bulgaria, 2000, at 43: 'The main challenge is now to apply and enforce effectively the anti-trust rules, focusing on the most serious distortions of competition'; Regular Report Bulgaria 2002, at 61; Regular

the fact that 40 per cent of cases before the Office of Economic Competition were still devoted to consumer fraud was openly given a negative evaluation.[113] The attitude of the Commission to the activity of the Competition Council in Latvia is similar.[114] The Regular Report in 2001 offered an even more categorical judgement:

> The Latvian Competition Council appears to have a fair enforcement record, but further strengthening, as well as a much more deterrent sanctioning policy, are required. Priority should be given to cases that concern the most serious distortions of competition, and 'unfair competition' cases should not be allowed to divert scarce resources from the antitrust enforcement. To ensure this, the staff of the Competition Council needs to receive further training, as do those members of the judiciary that deal with anti-trust matters.[115]

Conversely, an increased portion of antitrust cases receives positive assessment.[116]

Recommendations coming from the OECD experts took very concrete shape and advised the candidate countries to shift concerns for consumer deception and unfair commercial practice to the Consumer Protection Acts.[117] At least some CEE countries followed this institutional advice to divest the competition authorities of their powers in the area of unfair competition. Thus in Estonia the 2001 Competition Act preserved a chapter on unfair competition but left enforcement exclusively to the private efforts of competitors and their associations.[118]

Report Bulgaria 2003, at 54: '[f]urther strengthening of the Commission for the Protection of Competition should be achieved through advanced training, as well as focusing on competition-related activities, rather than issues of 'unfair competition'. Regular Report Latvia 2000, at 46. Regular Report Lithuania 2000: 'many cases so far, and under the old legislation, tend to relate to less important breaches of competition law'. Regular Report Slovenia 2000, at 42.

[113] '[T]he Office of Economic Competition is well staffed but still about 40% of the cases dealt with concern consumer protection issues.' Regular Report Hungary 2000, at 41. The assessment of the Lithuanian Competition Council is similar: 'many cases so far, and under the old legislation, tend to relate to less important breaches of competition law': Regular Report Lithuania 2000, at 46.

[114] Noting that most of the cases (25 of a total of 48) concern unfair competition, the Commission's assessment is in the negative: '[a]t present, many cases concern less serious infringements': Regular Report Latvia 2000, at 46. The recommendation addressed to Bulgaria is along the same lines:' [f]urther strengthening of the Commission for the Protection of Competition-should be achieved through advanced training, as well as focusing on competition-related activities, rather than issues of 'unfair competition': Regular Report Bulgaria 2003 at 54.

[115] Regular Report Latvia 2001, at 55–6.

[116] Regular Report Bulgaria 2001, at 47: '[a]bout a third of the CPC's cases relate to anti-trust and two-thirds to unfair competition, though latest figures suggest an increasing proportion of antitrust cases'.

[117] OECD Report, *The Role of Competition Policy in Regulatory Reform, Hungary* (2000), available at www.oecd.org/countrylist/0,2578,en_2649_37421_1794487_1_1_1_37421,00.html.

[118] See s 54 of the Estonian Competition Act 2001, RT (Riigi Teataja) 56,332. Cf.

Other countries resisted such recommendations or followed them only partially. Thus, Hungary retained the powers of the Office of Economic Competition in consumer fraud cases. Likewise the Lithuanian Competition Council still has power to investigate acts of unfair competition where these acts violate the interests of a number of undertakings and consumers (Section 17(4) of the Competition Act). The Council is reported to be responsible for the major portion of enforcement of the prohibition against misleading advertising.[119] The Bulgarian Commission for Protection of Competition also remains competent to adjudicate cases and impose sanctions for acts of unfair competition. As a result of the (European) Commission recommendations, however, consumer protection objectives and fair trading concerns have been systematically downgraded in the priority order of enforcement agencies.[120]

Interestingly, in the Regular Reports the Commission did not seem to attach importance to the character of the competence of the competition authorities in unfair competition cases. As noted earlier, whereas in Hungary the Competition Act sets out sound premises for defining enforcement competences and empowers the OEC to intervene in cases of serious public interest (e.g. consumer fraud), the Bulgarian Commission for the Protection of Competition is competent in all cases of unfair competition, including those with little or no bearing on the public good. It seems that the Commission advice is convincing in the latter case, whereas in the former case, an interesting national institutional innovation is at stake, which should not be stifled but rather nurtured and carefully studied. Analysis of the practice of the OEC demonstrates that it applies solid economic reasoning for its decisions and makes active use of the synergies that flow from a holistic regulation of free and fair competition in the interests of consumers.[121]

(iii) Advertising as a Separate Regulative Area

Finally, it appears that in some countries where marketing issues remained in the sole domain of unfair competition law or were not integrated to a sufficient extent in new Consumer Protection Acts, separate Advertising Acts were adopted.[122] These Acts transpose into national law the Directives on Misleading and Comparative Advertising, the TV Directive and occasionally,

---

[119] 'From January 2001 to January 2002, 13 cases of misleading advertising were investigated. Since January 2002, the Competition Council has launched 11 cases related to misleading or comparative advertising. In 9 cases, companies were warned and obliged to cease immediately such advertising and to retract its claims publicly': Regular Report Lithuania 2002, at 111.

[120] See statistics as reflected in the Regular Reports on Hungary 2001, 2002, 2003 and on Bulgaria 2001.

[121] See Cseres, above n 48; Cseres, above n 111.

[122] Czech Republic: Law No 40/1995 regarding the regulation of advertising, amended 2002 by Act No 138/2002; Estonia: Advertising Act of 11 June 1997; Hungary: Advertising Act of 1997; Latvia: Law on Advertising of 20 Dec 1999; Lithuania: Law on Advertising of 2000; Slovakia: Act No 147/2001 on Advertisement and on Amendment to Certain Acts; Romania: Law on Advertising of 2000.

the more recent Electronic Commerce Directive or other product-specific directives. The reasons for the introduction of Advertising Acts appear to be two-fold. On the one hand, they represented an attempt, albeit an imperfect one, to introduce a certain degree of transparency into the regulative thicket of restrictions and prohibitions targeting different forms of advertising and marketing methods stemming from various sector-specific directives.

On the other hand, Community advisors in the CICPP studies insisted on strict transposition of the Misleading Advertising and Comparative Advertising Directives despite the existence of acts of more general application (such as Unfair Competition Acts and clauses on consumer fraud and deception in antitrust statutes). Thus, in the volume by V Cambier devoted to comparative and misleading advertising legislation in CEE, a recommendation to adopt the definitions and conditions for assessing the misleading nature of an advertisement from the Misleading Advertising Directive is invariably directed to all candidate states.[123] This indirectly also suggested that the best guarantee of receiving a 'passmark' in the accession process was a verbatim transposition of Community provisions. Concentration of advertising provisions in Advertising Acts was also a recommendation by the CICPP experts as a 'second best' to comprehensive Consumer Protection Acts.[124]

Given the rather weak normative status of the Misleading Advertising Directive the categorical tone of such recommendations is striking. Moreover, the analysis of the law in the candidate states is almost exclusively confined to 'black letter' law, devoting no attention whatsoever to administrative or judicial practice. The quality and reliability of compliance assessment on these premises have rightly been questioned in legal doctrine.[125]

(d) The combined effects on unfair commercial practices law

If we try to elicit the main direction of Community influence on fair trading law in CEE Member and candidate states, it appears to have been in

---

[123] Poland is advised 'to introduce definitions of advertising and comparative advertising; to develop the features to take into account for the assessment of the misleading nature of an advertising': see Camber, above n 100, at 60. The recommendation to Hungary is 'to define misleading advertising and to develop the features to evaluate the misleading character of the advertising': ibid, 45. In a similar vein are the recommendations ibid, to Bulgaria, at 25; Czech Republic, at 31; Estonia, at 39; Latvia, at 48; Lithuania, at 56; Poland, at 60; Slovakia, at 73; Slovenia, at 78.

[124] One of the recommendations to the Czech Republic is 'to centralize provisions related to advertising in the Act on Advertising': ibid, 31. Estonia is advised to deal with advertising in the Advertising Act': ibid, 39. The recommendation to Latvia is 'to define the notions . . . in the Draft (Advertising) Law which is in preparation': ibid, 48; and to Slovakia, 'to centralize provisions related to advertising in the Act on Advertising': ibid, 73.

[125] For general criticism in this respect see HW Micklitz, 'Verbraucherschutz West versus Ost—Kompatibilizierungsmöglichkeiten in der Europäischen Gemeinschaft—Einige Vorüberlegungen' in H Heiss (ed) Brückenschlag zwischen den Rechtskulturen des Ostseeraums (Tübingen, Mohr Siebeck, 2001) 137.

pushing institutional design towards drawing sharper boundaries between competition law and consumer protection law, and towards integrating the regulation of unfair commercial practices into the domain of consumer policy. This may not have been a directly expressed requirement or even an intention. However, it is the combined result of emphasising the need for strong competition authorities with a focus on antitrust enforcement, on the one hand, and the insistence on comprehensive consumer protection legislation and a corresponding central enforcement body, on the other.

At the same time, the pursued functional differentiation has been carried through in a highly imperfect manner. One common consequence is that the emerging regulative frameworks consist of *multiple layers* of rules anchored in different legal acts and domains of regulation. To the initial rules on fair trading incorporated in (unfair) Competition Acts was gradually added a consumer law layer in most countries, or alternatively a layer of specific advertising laws. Similar factual situations, eg misleading advertising, are thus addressed by different legal acts and through different remedies.[126]

Needless to say, such overlaps of regulative layers are apt to generate conceptual confusion. The norms forming the various strata of the institutional framework pursue transposition of different Community instruments, originating from different Community institutions representing divergent perspectives. Typically the relevant Community instruments have been conceived at different stages in the evolution of the Community's own policy in the respective area. Therefore they incorporate different and sometimes incongruent concepts and values. None of the law-makers in the CEE states, it seems, has truly succeeded in bringing these concepts into a coherent and practicable intellectual framework.

The admittedly cursory overview made above reveals a certain tendency towards *regulative overheat*, which is partly a consequence of the just-described multiple-layer framework. This can be seen on the one hand in setting unrealistically high standards that can hardly be upheld and enforced in practice and that are motivated chiefly by the zeal to demonstrate compliance. On the other hand, nothing in the process of extending the *acquis* seems to have emphasised the advantages of a lean and balanced regulative environment. The interrelation between consumer protection and market freedoms (including the fundamental Community freedoms as anchored in the EC Treaty) has not been sufficiently stressed.

---

[126] For instance the Czech 1992 Consumer Protection Act includes provisions on deception (s 8) that parallel the provisions in the Commercial Code and the provisions in the Advertising Act. The Estonian Consumer Protection Act in its s 8 (2) Nr 2 stipulates a prohibition for sellers to 'influence consumers by misleading advertising, disparagement of goods or services of other sellers, prohibited use of a firm name, trade mark or other characteristics, or in any other manner which is contrary to the general good ethics and practices of trade'. A similar general clause and a list of examples can be found in the Competition Act. In a similar manner the new Bulgarian Consumer Protection Act of 2005 contains a whole chapter on misleading and unfair advertising, despite the existence of similar provisions in the 1998 Competition Act.

Another common characteristic is the strong reliance on *public agencies* in the process of enforcement of fair trading rules. This tendency undoubtedly has its roots in the linking of fair trading regulation with antitrust law and consumer law respectively. The competition agencies in Bulgaria, Lithuania, Latvia, Hungary and also Poland under the amended Act on Competition and Consumer Protection of 2000 are all equipped with a right to act *ex officio* (alternatively to bring an action before the courts) in cases of violation of the relevant fair trading rules and are authorised to impose considerable penalties. Similar powers are assigned to consumer protection agencies.[127]

When it comes to the internal distribution of competences between various public bodies, accession seems to have influenced the institutional set up in the direction of shifting powers in consumer protection matters from competition to consumer protection agencies. The Commission has repeatedly insisted on the establishment of specialised consumer protection agencies, thereby raising considerable expectations as to the impact these public bodies can have on the level of consumer protection.[128] At the same time, once the bodies are in place, signs of anxiety are visible in respect of their capacity to cope with the rate of complaints.

In a similar vein the overlap in scope between Consumer Protection Acts, Unfair Trade Practices/Competition Acts and Advertising Acts may create significant risks of conflict of competencies or, even worse, of a legal vacuum. Evidence of duplicating enforcement before different public authorities is available for instance from Bulgaria, where the same matter may be brought before the Commission for Protection of Competition, the Commission for Consumer Protection and the Broadcasting Commission.[129] Generally, there the over-reliance on public institutions and administrative sanctions often comes at the expense of individual or group action of private actors.[130]

---

[127] Regular Report Poland 2001, at 84.

[128] Cf Regular Report Lithuania 2000, at 81; cf Regular Report Lithuania 2001, at 89; Regular Report Slovenia 1999.

[129] See Decision 46 of 9 Mar 2006, Commission for Protection of Competition; cf Decision No 19841 of 21 Oct 2005, Commission for Consumer Protection, concerning the misleading advertising of telecom services (as to the possibility of free of charge conversations), available at www. cpc.bg/system/storage/resh-46-06.RTF. The coordination between the two institutions is obviously not well defined in the relevant statutes and there are no established practices for dealing with such conflicts and overlaps. Particularly interesting is the litigation saga in the *Zagorka* line of cases, concerning allegedly sexually discriminatory advertising in an advertisement for beer. All three institutions mentioned above had been asked to rule on the matter, with sometimes conflicting outcomes. See E Millan and R Elliott, 'Offensive Advertising, Public Policy, and the Law: The Rulings on the Zagorka Case' (2004) 27 *Journal of Consumer Policy* 475.

[130] See for instance the reformed rules on standing under s 34 of the new Bulgarian Consumer Protection Act where the previously existing right of individual consumers to institute proceedings for protection of collective interests has been rescinded and substituted by a right of complaint to the Commission for Consumer Protection, probably as a result of the consumer activism demonstrated in the *Zagorka* cases discussed in n 129 above.

To sum up, the accession process has left the law of fair trading in the CEE candidate states in a fragmented and uncertain state. The initial centring of the rules on fair trading in the area of competition law has been disrupted. Additional layers of consumer protection and more specific advertising law have been added. Somewhat poignantly, it could probably be said that the fragmentation and the ambiguities in the Community's own approach to fair trading have produced spill-over effects on the law in the candidate states and have there been exacerbated by local institutional idiosyncracies.

At the same time, it would not be far-fetched to suggest that the direction of Community leverage could be regarded as indicative of the shape which Community fair trading law will take in the future. Thus, the insistence on comprehensive Consumer Protection Acts and on treating advertising regulation as part of the framework of consumer protection foreshadows the approach taken in the UCPD. Likewise the endorsement of centralised consumer protection agencies as best equipped to shoulder the monitoring and enforcement of the consumer protection *acquis* foreshadows the approach taken in the Consumer Protection Cooperation Regulation.[131]

6. DISENTANGLING THE LOGIC OF COMMUNITY INFLUENCE

It is not the place here to engage in a full-blown discussion of the vices and virtues of the enlargement process practised as a form of 'external governance'.[132] The legitimacy concerns raised by certain aspects of this methodology have been discussed elsewhere.[133] What appears important, however, is to try and disentangle the logic of Community influence, since similar logic may be dictating the interaction between the Community and its Member States in other areas of integration.

(a) The Joint Interest of the Rational 'Accession-seeker' and the Rational 'Accession-provider'

Given the limited time period within which the enlargement of the EU was supposed to take place and the enormous strain on scarce resources it exerted on both sides of the Union threshold, certain awkward features of the process of incorporation of the *acquis* are not surprising. To a large extent they can be explained by what could be dubbed the joint interest of the rational 'accession-seeker' and the rational 'accession-provider'.

---

[131] On the boomerang effects of enlargement see Bakardjieva Engelbrekt, above n 104.
[132] Schimmelfennig and Sedelmeier, above n 7.
[133] See Bakardjieva Engelbrekt, above n 104.

Whereas politicians and public officials of the candidate countries seek rapid accession and want to demonstrate visible progress, politicians and officials of the Community institutions (notably the Commission) require palpable results that are easy to identify, measure and monitor. Seen in this light the preference for discrete interventions in the form of specific legislative acts corresponding more neatly to Community legislative compartments is well understood. Such interventions are easy to manage and to observe. Perplexing issues of grappling with system complexity and ensuring coherence are avoided. The costs of penetrating the deeply engrained multiple social and cultural layers of legal system are not incurred.[134]

Similarly understandable is the preference for building regulative agencies for each area of EU law and policy. The agency provides a 'high visibility' arena, which allows the candidate countries to point to its existence in progress reports and when criticised for insufficient administrative capacity. For the EU institutions the agency is a partner that can be monitored and held accountable for possible failures in the transposition and enforcement process on a more continuous basis than changing governments and Parliamentary majorities. At the same time, the availability of an agency is a practical response to the general aversion to dealing with the minutiae of enforcement design. The notoriously mind-boggling task of linking enforcement and sanctions with the existing system of administrative, criminal and civil procedure can then be dealt with only in passing.

The logic of accession probably also explains an obvious differentiation among the candidate states. The process of implementation of the consumer protection *acquis* demonstrates that the more eager the accession-seeker, the greater the propensity has been to resort to specialised acts and regulative agencies. A growing self-confidence of a candidate country is, conversely, associated with intensified attempts to search for internal coherence and to integrate the Community *acquis* in a more meaningful way within the texture and architecture of domestic legal and institutional system.[135] Thus, the greater the success of rule-transfer on the surface, the greater the suspicion of a rubber-stamp law-making with limited participation of and influence by domestic groups.

---

[134] In a similar sense D Smilov, 'EU Enlargement and the Constitutional Principle of Judicial Independence' in W Sadurski, A Czarnota and M Krygier (eds), *Spreading Democracy and the Rule of Law? Implications of EU Enlargement for the Rule of Law, Democracy and Constitutionalism in Post-Communist Legal Orders* (Dordrecht, Springer, 2006) 313–34.

[135] For similar patterns in the area of civil service reform see A Dimitrova, 'Europeanisation and Civil Service Reform in Central and Eastern Europe' in Schimmelfennig and Sedelmeier (eds), above n 7, 84; B Bugarič, 'The Europeanisation of National Administration in Central and Eastern Europe' in W Sadurski, J Ziller and K Zurek (eds), *Après Enlargement. Legal and Political Responses in Central and Eastern Europe* (San Domenico di Fiesole, Robert Schumann Centre for Advanced Studies, EUI, 2006) 201.

(b) The Uncharacteristic Role of the Acquis as Model Legislation

Another factor that may help explain the puzzle of Community influence on fair trading law in CEE is the highly uncharacteristic role that the *acquis* was charged to play in the process of eastward enlargement. As in other areas, the Community instruments in the field of commercial practices were never intended to serve as model legislation. They are largely selective, provide minimum standards and leave enforcement and institutional design to the Member States. In the course of enlargement, however, the Community institutions often saw themselves involved in a larger process of law- and institution-building, where accession countries needed holistic advice and assistance in exactly those areas where no Community *acquis* was on offer. The missing bits and pieces of the jigsaw had then to be provided by way of 'induction'.[136] Filling of gaps was needed on at least two levels: between the demand for coherent models and the reality of the fragmented *acquis* and between the demand for institutional guidance and the alleged institutional neutrality.

(c) Institutional Bias

Finally, the institutional division of competencies at the level of the Commission has certainly played an important role in the particular outcome of Community influence in the accession process. Given the fact that experts and officials involved in consumer policy often develop a proactive attitude to consumer protection, the tendency to interpret the *acquis* in an extensive and more protective manner is not surprising.

Whereas it is true that some of the factors described above are intrinsic to the enlargement process, they are in no way limited to it. Thus, resource limitation, deference to dealing with system complexity and institutional bias certainly have explanatory power when applied to traditional harmonisation processes as well. Enlargement only makes these factors visible in a more condensed and graphic way.

7. THE UCPD AND ITS PROSPECTIVE EFFECTS ON CEE UNFAIR COMMERCIAL PRACTICES LAW: COHERENCE AT LAST?

As stated at the beginning of this chapter, the UCP Directive was politically marketed as a move towards simplification and improved coherence in Community consumer law. Indeed the UCPD takes a number of steps on the way to the promised coherence. (i) The Directive revives the attempt to

---

[136] On the legitimacy deficits in this process see Bakardjieva Engelbrekt, above n 104.

get a comprehensive regulative grip and operates with a concept of commercial practices which is broader than the more technical 'advertising'. It is even broader than the conventional concept of commercial or marketing practices used in Member States with comprehensive market law statutes.[137] (ii) The UCPD was conceived as a framework directive, which at least in theory, implies using Community legislation to provide only the main regulatory guidelines and leaving the detail to other institutional processes. (iii) In the same line of coherence enhancement is found the most distinctive feature of the Directive, namely the use of a general-clause approach. This is a major break-through given the staunch resistance on the part of the UK to such an approach and the perceived uncertainty it entails.

On a closer look, however, the Directive reveals a number of features that raise serious doubts about its potential to fulfil the promise of coherence and simplification. (i) The Directive unequivocally places consumers at the centre of attention. It draws a rather strict dividing line between B2B and B2C relations.[138] In this the Directive confirms and even deepens the already visible fissure between a market-building and a market-correcting view of the regulation of commercial practices. (ii) In a similar vein, partly due to inherent limitations on Community law-making powers, the Directive leaves outside its scope consumers' non-economic interests as well as regulation based on taste and decency. While this is a politically sound solution, it definitely does not contribute to regulatory clarity and simplicity. (iii) Despite the widely advertised simplification, the three-tier structure of the Directive opens a number of questions as to the relations between the various levels. Moreover, the black list, which initially was intended to outline only a few straightforward and central situations of unfairness, gradually turned into a long scroll of sometimes esoteric and sometimes fuzzy examples. Whatever one may think of simplification, the list in any case does not seem to support claims of deregulation. (iv) Another concession to the pledge to achieve simplification and deregulation is the persistence of a number of legislative acts regulating commercial practices in specific sectors, eg product-specific and media-specific directives and regulations. The relationship of these instruments with the directive is not always clear.[139] It is further complicated by a complex scheme of transition periods and proportionality checks.[140]

In a way, what the Community lawmaker gives with one hand it takes with the other. The flexibility and openness of the general clause is offset

---

[137] See e.g. the Swedish Marketing practices law. Cf Bakardjieva Engelbrekt, above n 5.
[138] In the Preamble, the UCPD acknowledges, however, the indirect positive effects of the regulation of unfair business-to-consumer practices for fairness of competition and the close links between unfairness in B2C and B2B relations. The Commission commits itself to investigating the possibility for a second phase of harmonisation in B2B commercial practices.
[139] See for instance the exception of health and safety in Art 3(1) UCPD, above n 30.
[140] See Bakardjieva Engelbrekt, above n 5.

by the exacting detail of the black list. The alleged 'framework' character of the Directive is thwarted by the insistence on total harmonisation. The claim to simplification is effectively defied by the perseverance of a legion of sector-specific directives and regulations with a not always clear relationship with the Directive. The reasons for the outlined disintegrative elements lie partly in limitations inherent in the constitutional and institutional framework of the European integration process and partly in the inevitable institutional bias stemming from the Directive's responsible directorate, DG Sanco, as the chief institutional actor.

In this light, the future effect of the Directive on the framework of unfair commercial practices in the CEE states is not easy to gauge. It may not be surprising that the implementation process in many of these states is just in its initial phase. Showing all the signs of 'legislative fatigue' as a consequence of enlargement,[141] national institutions have not been particularly eager to embark on the next implementation project.

A recent study by the British Institute of International and Comparative Law (BIICL) on the existing national laws on unfair commercial practices in the new EU Member States ventures a preliminary assessment of the expected difficulties with implementation of the Directive in national law. The tone of the study is on the whole optimistic.[142] In the new Member States the general view is reported to be that there are no major obstacles that might complicate the process of transposition of the Directive into national law. Yet a look at the more specific questions of implementation detail reveals a slightly different picture. A number of aspects of systemic arrangements, conceptual consistency and institutional design do not have a clear answer and may pose substantial difficulties.

(a) Systemic Arrangements

First, the emphasis on consumer protection in the UCPD and the decision to leave B2B commercial practices outside the scope of the Directive can be expected to give yet another push towards anchoring unfair commercial practices law in the domain of consumer protection and towards a divided approach. Certainly in the BIICL study most countries point to more than

---

[141] See C Dupré, 'Anticipating EU Membership: Importing the Law of the West', Paper presented at the Workshop: Implications of Enlargement for the Rule of Law and Constitutionalism in Post-Communist Legal Orders, EUI, 28–29 Nov 2003.

[142] British Institute of International and Comparative Law, 'Unfair Commercial Practices. An Analysis of the Existing National Laws on Unfair Commercial Practices between Business and Consumers in the New Member States' British Institute of International and Comparative Law (2005), available at http://ec.europa.eu/consumers/cons-int/safe_shop/fair_bus_pract/analysis_national_laws_en_htm (hereinafter the BIICL Report).

one avenue for transposing the Directive into national law. Yet Consumer Protection Acts are almost invariably indicated as one logical place for transposition (cf Latvia, Slovenia, Estonia, Lithuania). In Poland the Directive is even seen to offer a suitable occasion for introduction of a comprehensive Consumer Protection Act.[143] And whereas the reports on the Czech and Slovak Republics in the BIICL study suggest that implementation will proceed by amendment of a number of legislative acts, the recently adopted Consumer Policy Programme of the Czech Ministry of Industry and Trade indicates that implementation of the UCPD will rather enhance the concentration of provisions on marketing practices in the Consumer Protection Act.[144]

In particular in countries where fair trading rules have been divided between Competition Acts and Consumer Protection Acts there will be strong pressure to centralise all substantive rules implementing the new Directive in the recently adopted Consumer Protection Acts. Lithuania is a case in point. According to the assessment of the national rapporteur in the BIICL study the Directive will deeply influence the national legal system and cannot be implemented without systematic structural changes in Lithuanian civil law. As possible places for implementation of the Directive the Civil Code, the Consumer Protection Law, and the Competition Law are all indicated. However, implementation in the Competition Law is seen as problematic, since an additional adjustment of its scope—normally concerning only business-to-business relations—will have to be made. Similar considerations may influence the choices of the Latvian and Slovenian legislators. Likewise, in Bulgaria, in particular after the entry into force of the new Consumer Protection Act, the 'natural' place for the new provisions appears to be in this Act, an option that may affect the rules on unfair competition in the Competition Act.

Another consequence in terms of systemic arrangements concerns the Advertising Acts. Although of relatively recent date, these Acts may now appear as fossils with an uncertain position. The functional concept of advertising in these laws differs from the broader one of commercial practice, but at the same time is not confined to B2C relations. Consequently, they will either be transformed into comprehensive Unfair Commercial Practices Acts, or be retained, but then limited to only product-, media- and other sector specific advertising regulations. The relationship of such acts to the general regulation of unfair commercial practices will have to be carefully defined.

(b) Substantive Provisions

One of the main promises of the UCPD has been to consolidate existing legislation and to increase conceptual clarity and consistency. However,

---

[143] See ibid, at 78.
[144] See Consumer Policy Programme, 2006–2010, available at http://download.mpo.cz/get/26603/28977/315454/priloha001.pdf, at 3.

the BIICL study reveals a general concern in the process of transposition about how to reconcile with the Directive the existing detailed legislation in relation to business-to-consumer practices. One of the main difficulties in implementation of the Directive will, according to national rapporteurs, be to accommodate the new conceptual framework (average consumer, professional diligence and material distortion of the economic behaviour of consumers) into the already established concepts which the Directive does not replace or make obsolete.

Interestingly, the BIICL report does not signal any problems with regard to materially adjacent legislation protecting small and medium-sized enterprises or regulating taste and decency. Such legislation is, however, present in some of the new Member States. For instance the Polish Unfair Competition Act contains detailed prohibitions on sale at a loss or other selling arrangements with the explicit intention of protecting small and medium-sized enterprises. Statutory restrictions and prohibitions on marketing for reasons of taste, decency and morals are also abundant in the CEE states, as hinted above. Although such legislation may in most cases be outside the scope of the Directive, a more serious check of its compatibility with fundamental market freedoms appears pertinent. The reassuring statement in the BIICL report seems somewhat sweeping and premature.[145]

(c) Enforcement

Parallel to the dislocation of unfair commercial practices law from the domain of competition law to the domain of consumer protection, a corresponding reshaping of supervision and enforcement competences is to be projected. The centre of gravity of enforcement will in the future most probably shift even more perceptibly from competition authorities to consumer protection agencies. Thus, the Slovenian report in the BIICL study notes that the right of an individual consumer under Articles 26 and 27 of the Slovenian Competition Act to commence proceedings for compensation for breach of unfair commercial practices should be inserted in the Consumer Protection Act instead in order to avoid overlap or inconsistency.[146] In countries like Lithuania the competition agency's competence in the sphere of fair trading will be seriously undermined, for what is envisaged is mainly enforcement competences for the consumer protection agency. Also in Hungary institutional tugs of war between the OEC with long-term experience in the area of consumer fraud and unfairness, and the more recently founded General Inspectorate on Consumer Protection are not excluded.

---

[145] See *BIICL Report 2005*, above n 142, at 103.
[146] Ibid, at 95.

Whereas for instance dividing up the regime of fair trading practices into business-to-business and business-to-consumer sub-fields may be practicable and cause no problems in the present Community Member States, it may create distortions in the institutional framework in some CEE countries and produce bias toward public regulation of the classical command and control type at the expense of decentralised private enforcement and modern regulatory approaches.

On a positive note, a number of CEE countries seem to find in the Directive a chance to review comprehensively their national consumer protection legislation as well as its interfaces with adjacent legal areas. From the perspective of the Estonian reporter, the Directive could provide an impetus for the review of the whole system of regulation of commercial practices to bring it into a more cohesive form.[147]

8. CONCLUDING REMARKS: COHERENCE AT WHAT TIME, AT WHAT LEVEL AND AT WHAT COST?

Coming back to the Green Paper on Consumer Protection and its promise of simple and predictable rules for the accession states, one can first of all regret that the resulting Directive, in itself a commendable move, was badly timed from the point of view of the CEE states. As noted above, the period of accession negotiations required a substantial effort on the part of the accession states to penetrate the complexity of the European regulatory framework and to rearrange their domestic institutions accordingly. Even if short, this period was sufficient to set in motion a major process of law-making and institution-building, and to produce several layers of legislation and a web of interconnected national institutions. In most respects the complexity and the fragmentation characteristic of consumer protection regulation at the Community level was simply transferred to the national level, in turn triggering a quest for system coherence on the part of national law-making and law enforcement institutions. However, exactly at the time when this flurry of activity began to settle down and institutions were engaged in a comprehensive learning process, the UPCD suddenly required a new round of reshuffling and re-regulation.

In substantive terms, with its firm positioning in the consumer protection policy area, the UCPD has reinforced the preference for public regulation and law enforcement over private law and private litigation, visible in the pre-accession process and described above. It again challenges unconventional institutional solutions, for instance that of seeking to provide an integrated approach to antitrust and consumer protection or to integrate consumer-friendly reasoning in competitor-oriented unfair competition law.

---

[147] Ibid.

Positive cross-fertilisation between these interrelated spheres of regulation may be frustrated by the new Directive.

One of the main insights gained from enlargement concerns the intimate link between substantive rules, enforcement mechanisms and the institutional framework. Despite the often proclaimed intention of Community harmonisation endeavours to remain neutral to questions of enforcement and procedure, there are a number of direct and indirect ways in which the implementation of Community measures affects national institutional choices. Even when no institutional consequences are pursued or intended, changes in substantive rules and in classification and definition may precipitate institutional reform in the national legal systems of the Member States. Such influences may occasionally have the positive result of providing an opportunity for rethinking national institutional frameworks and finding a better balance of affected interests. They may, however, also have the effect of unsettling freshly achieved institutional equilibria and they may create unwanted institutional overlaps or conflicts. It is suggested that the Community institutions should develop greater sensitivity to identifying such effects and that Member States shoud be awarded greater margin of freedom and flexibility to mitigate such (often unintended) side effects in the implementation process.

The Commission has indeed been right to describe consumer protection law at the Community level as a highly fragmented field. The question is nevertheless at what level coherence can and should be pursued. Ensuring coherence means inevitably making choices as to the centre of gravity in the regulative framework, its relation to pertaining legal and policy areas and the respective conceptual apparatus. The Community preference for harmonising the law of unfair business-to-consumer commercial practices reveals institutional biases that reflect the Commission's own institutional structure and division of competences with clear separation between DG SANCO, DG Internal Market and DG Competition. However, what the Commission promotes as a separate and functionally closed area (consumer protection) is often already embedded in national law and connected to a number of surrounding areas, each with its own legislative history, conceptual legacy, economic and political context and institutional and organisational framework. The pull towards coherence at the European level could thus have unpredictable and disruptive effects on national legal and institutional frameworks. Such effects may, in turn, produce a push towards new harmonisation initiatives by national governments, thus lifting new areas up to the Community level.

It has been noted in other accounts of Europeanisation that there is an inherent tension between the logic of national (private) law systems and the logic of European integration.[148] The 'internal' logic of fair trading law

---

[148] See C Joerges and G Brüggemeier, 'Europäisierung des Vertrags- und Haftungsrechts' in PC Müller-Graff (ed), *Gemeinsames Privatrecht in der Europäischen Gemeinschaft* (Baden-Baden, Nomos, 1993).

as a legal discipline requires that any Community intervention, either in the form of harmonised rules on fair trading or in the form of suspended national regulation, be scrutinised through the endogenously produced criteria of systemic coherence and 'good' substantive outcome. At the same time the 'external' logic of European integration gives priority to the accomplishment of the Common Market.

The UCP Directive is arguably introducing a third kind of logic which complicates the picture. Despite what is claimed in the Preamble, the Directive can hardly be justified solely by reference to market integration. With its aspirations for comprehensiveness, coherence and clear rules, the Directive apparently tries to reinforce and follow the internal logic of fair trading law (including unfair commercial practices law), this time conceived as a Community-wide legal discipline. The kaleidoscopic picture of fair trading law in the new Member States in CEE has hopefully demonstrated that such ambitions would be highly unrealistic and, indeed, unnecessary. The diversity of national systems of substantive law and of law enforcement and institutional design will certainly persist even after implementation of the Directive. Such heterogeneity, however, should not exclusively be a reason for concern for Community institutions, but also be seen as a constant source of institutional innovation and learning, and, thus, an important asset of European integration.

5

The Unfair Commercial Practices Directive in Context

IDA OTKEN ERIKSSON AND ULF ÖBERG

1. INTRODUCTION

THE ADOPTION OF the Unfair Commercial Practices Directive[1] (hereinafter 'the UCPD') presents a new and intriguing development in European Union law. The purpose of this chapter is to situate the UCPD in a wider context and address four issues that the Directive gives raise to, namely:

(1) The question of the legal basis of the UCPD;
(2) The general character of the EC consumer protection rules;
(3) The possible impact of the proposal for a Directive on Services in the Internal Market; and
(4) The question of the future approach of the EC Court of Justice when interpreting the UCPD.

2. LEGAL BASIS

The UCPD is adopted under Article 95 EC, a legal basis which allows approximation of Member States' provisions that have as their object the establishment and functioning of the internal market. Article 95 EC refers to the definition in Article 14 EC, which in turn indirectly refers to the specific free movement Articles on goods, workers, services, establishment and capital.

---

[1] Directive 2005/29/EC of the European Parliament and of the Council of 11 May 2005 concerning unfair business-to-consumer commercial practices in the internal market and amending Council Directive 84/450/EEC, Directives 97/7/EC, 98/27/EC and 2002/65/EC of the European Parliament and of the Council and Regulation (EC) No 2006/2004 of the European Parliament and of the Council [2005] OJ L 149/22.

Since the publication of the Commission's Green Paper on Consumer Protection,[2] it has been widely discussed whether there is a sufficient legal basis in the Treaty to pursue further harmonisation of certain consumer and advertising rules.[3] We do not share the view that the UCPD lacks a proper legal basis simply on the ground that the Court has excluded certain selling arrangements from the scope of application of Article 28 EC in its landmark *Keck and Mithouard* case from 1993.[4]

Admittedly, in this judgment the Court stated that certain selling arrangements which affect domestic products and imported products in the same manner are not covered by the prohibition in Article 28 EC. However, there is no indication in the Treaty that the notion of measures having equivalent effect in Article 28 EC should necessarily be interpreted in exactly the same manner as the measures which can be adopted under Article 95 EC. For example, so-called internal situations that lack a transborder element do not fall within the scope of application of Article 28 EC.[5] They are nevertheless without doubt covered by the general nature of harmonisation measures under Article 95 EC. This would seem to rule out that Articles 28 and 95 EC should necessarily be interpreted in exactly the same manner.

Moreover, such an interpretation would create significant problems of definition and would be highly impractical. The UCPD, for example, affects both typical *Keck* 'selling arrangements'—eg false information in advertising about the quality of a product—and classical product-related measures which without doubt fall within the scope of Article 28 EC. An example taken from case law is the *Mars* case, where a product wrapper was marked '+10%'.[6] Furthermore, the Court has to date never admitted any *Keck* exception in the area of free movement of services.[7] And here again, the UCPD applies to both goods and services.[8]

However, this does not mean that there are no limits as to what can be the object of harmonisation measures under Article 95 in line with the principle of attributed competence.[9] As the Court stated in the first *Tobacco*

---

[2] COM(2001)531.

[3] See, for one of the latest contributions to the discussions, G Davies, 'Can Selling Arrangements be harmonised?' [2005] *European Law Review* 370, with further references; see in particular n 23.

[4] Joined Cases C–267 & 268/91 *Keck and Mithouard* [1993] ECR I–6097.

[5] See eg Case 286/81 *Criminal proceedings aginst Ooesthoek's Uitgeversmaatschappij BV* [1982] ECR I–4575. This, however, does not mean that a request for a preliminary reference concerning an internal situation may not be answered by the Court: see eg Case C–448/98 *Criminal proceedings against Jean-Pierre Guimont* [2000] ECR I–10663.

[6] Case C–470/93 *Verein gegen Unwesen in Handel und Gewerbe Köln eV v Mars GmbH* [1995] ECR I–1923.

[7] See eg Case C–384/93 *Alpine Investments BV v Minister van Financiën* [1995] ECR I–01141.

[8] Art 2(c) UCPD, above n 1.

[9] Stated expressly in Art 5 EC.

Advertising case, a measure adopted under Article 95 EC must genuinely have as its object the improvement of the conditions for the establishment and functioning of the internal market, a 'mere finding of disparities between national rules' or 'abstract risk of obstacles to the exercise of fundamental freedoms or of distortions of competition' is not sufficient.[10] Even if there may be good reason for questioning the legal basis of certain older consumer measures such as the Door-step Selling Directive,[11] there is little doubt that these criteria are fulfilled when it comes to the regulation of the commercial practices covered by the UCPD.

As mentioned above, the UCPD covers measures that to a large extent would be caught by the 'obstacle'/'restriction' case law of the Court under Articles 28 and 49 EC. Moreover, national regulations at issue are widely differing and even scattered over different national areas of law. Obviously, with the UCPD, all traders will have the advantage of having to comply with only one set of rules in respect of unfair business-to-consumer commercial practices and can rely on the same marketing strategies throughout the Community. Thus, even the more 'quantitative' or *de minimis* criteria—ie that the distortion of competition be appreciable—seems to be fulfilled. Indeed, the UCPD is wholly different from the situation at hand in the *Tobacco Advertising* cases.[12]

In this analysis we—perhaps a bit naïvely—make the assumption that all Member States will faithfully transpose the UCPD and respect what appears to be the ambition behind it. According to its wording and face value, the UCPD seems to aim to accomplish a full and total harmonisation, meaning that the notions contained in the UCPD shall be applied in exactly the same manner throughout the whole of the Union.

Still, there seems to be some confusion about the actual scope of the UCPD. In the *travaux préparatoires*, the UCPD was described as a 'framework directive', and it certainly contains several general clauses that are usually understood as leaving national courts significant discretion. With the final outcome in hand, however, it is difficult to grasp what is left of the 'framework character'. The discretion given by the general clauses is carefully limited by the specification of quite a large number of particular situations. Furthermore, in its recitals, the UCPD talks about 'uniform rules'

---

[10] Case C–376/98 *Germany v Parliament and Council* [2000] ECR I–8419, para 84. See also Case C–491/01 *The Queen v Secretary of State for Health, ex parte British American Tobacco (Investments) Ltd and Imperial Tobacco Ltd* [2002] ECR I–11453.

[11] Council Directive 85/577/EEC of 20 Dec 1985 to protect the consumer in respect of contracts negotiated away from business premises [1985] OJ L 372/31.

[12] See also A Bakardjieva Engelbrekt, 'EG-Direktivet om otillbörliga affärsmetoder: En stundande omdaning av svensk marknadsrätt' [2005] *Europarättslig Tidskrift* 236 at 240–41 and A Bakardjieva Engelbrekt, *EU and Marketing Practices Law in the Nordic Countrie— Consequences of a Directive on Unfair Business-to-Consumer Commercial Practices*, Report for the Nordic Council of Ministers Committee on Consumer Affairs (2005) at 10–11, (available at www.norden.org/pub/sk/showpub.asp?pubnr=2005:424).

and 'clarifying of certain legal concepts at Community level' (recital 5), of a 'high level of convergence' and a 'high common level of consumer protection' (recital 11) as well as of 'increased legal certainty', 'a single regulatory framework' (recital 12), replacement of Member States' 'existing, divergent general clauses and legal principles' (recital 13) and a 'full harmonisation approach' (recital 14).

Even the partially deleted 'internal market clause' in Article 4 supports the understanding of the UCPD as a total harmonisation measure. The UCPD sets out a number of substantive criteria that commercial practices measures must comply with in order not to be unfair, and the moment they do comply, no Member State may hinder the commercial practice on these grounds. Thus, in our view, there can be no doubt that the UCPD seems to constitute a total or full harmonisation of unfair commercial practices. One cannot help wondering whether the talk of a framework directive has mostly been a psychological measure meant to help Member States and national consumer and market law specialists to swallow the bitter pill of harmonisation.

3. GENERAL CHARACTER OF EC CONSUMER PROTECTION RULES

EC consumer protection law constitutes a sensitive area, as many Member States feel very protective towards 'their' consumers. Consequently, the Community has for years not had a proper legal basis from which to regulate consumer matters.[13] It has been able to adopt consumer law measures only in so far as they qualify as internal market measures under Article 95 EC. As a consequence, harmonisation has to date been relatively rare, sector-specific and has been kept strictly on a minimum basis, meaning that Member States may keep in force rules that are more stringent to ensure a higher level of consumer protection.

All the same, over the years the Community has managed to form an impressive number of directives actually regulating consumer matters, to mention a few: the Door-step Directive, the Misleading Advertising Directive, the Timeshare Directive, the Unfair Terms Directive, the Package Travel Directive, the Distance Contracts Directive, the Indication of Prices Directive, the Injunctions Directive, the Comparative Advertising Directive, the Certain Aspects and Guarantees Directive as well as the Financial Services Directive.[14] As this list shows, EC consumer law has a high degree

---

[13] See now Art 153 EC.

[14] Directive 2002/65/EC of the European Parliament and of the Council of 23 Sept 2002 concerning the distance marketing of consumer financial services and amending Council Directive 90/619/EEC and Directives 97/7/EC and 98/27/EC [2002] OJ L 271/16, Directive 1999/44/EC of the European Parliament and of the Council of 25 May 1999 on certain aspects of the sale of consumer goods and associated guarantees [1999] OJ L 171/12, Directive 98/27/EC of the

of 'patchwork character'. It is extremely difficult to overview and assess, particularly as many of the later directives amend earlier ones, as for example the directives on misleading and comparative advertising.

Obviously, the UCPD is intended to bring at least some order to this fragmented and confusing patchwork. The question is whether the Community legislator has succeeded in this respect. The UCPD partially amends several previous directives and to a certain extent even aggravates the situation. Notably, the UCPD states that it applies only in so far as there are no specific Community law provisions regulating specific aspects of unfair commercial practices in accordance with the general *lex specialis* principle.[15] However, this interpretation does not apply when it comes to more protective Member State legislation adopted in accordance with minimum harmonisation clauses. Such measures may only be kept in force for a transitional period of six years.[16] In other words, the application of the *lex specialis* principle is strictly kept at the Community level. At national level, the horizontal approach is supposed to hit with full force and the UCPD will apply even to specific sector areas such as, for example, medical products.

It is no understatement to conclude that Member States and lawyers will have difficulties in assessing the whole extent of the scope of application of the UCPD. It is rather telling that not even the Commission dares to list exhaustively the *Community* law provisions setting out rules for advertising and commercial communication.[17] It is hardly likely that Member States will have more energy in identifying particular national provisions that will be affected by the UCPD, even though the Member States are subject to a notification requirement in this regard.[18]

European Parliament and of the Council of 19 May 1998 on injunctions for the protection of consumers' interests [1998] OJ L 166/51, Directive 98/6/EC of the European Parliament and of the Council of 16 Feb 1998 on consumer protection in the indication of the prices of products offered to consumers [1998] OJ L 80/27, Directive 97/55/EC of European Parliament and of the Council of 6 Oct 1997 amending Directive 84/450/EEC concerning misleading advertising so as to include comparative advertising [1997] OJ L 290/18, Directive 97/7/EC of the European Parliament and of the Council of 20 May 1997 on the protection of consumers in respect of distance contracts [1997] OJ L 144/19, Directive 94/47/EC of the European Parliament and the Council of 26 Oct 1994 on the protection of purchasers in respect of certain aspects of contracts relating to the purchase of the right to use immovable properties on a timeshare basis [1994] OJ L 280/83, Council Directive 93/13/EEC of 5 Apr 1993 on unfair terms in consumer contracts [1993] OJ L 95/29, Council Directive 90/314/EEC of 13 June 1990 on package travel, package holidays and package tours [1990] OJ L 158/59, Council Directive 85/577/EEC of 20 Dec 1985 to protect the consumer in respect of contracts negotiated away from business premise [1985] OJ L 372/31, Council Directive 84/450/EEC of 10 Sept 1984 relating to the approximation of the laws, regulations and administrative provisions of the Member States concerning misleading advertising [1984] OJ L 250/17.

[15] Recital 10, UCPD, above n 1.
[16] Art 3(5) of ibid.
[17] Annex II of ibid.
[18] Art 3(6) of ibid.

On the other hand, this horizontal approach is without doubt a very effective way to obtain common rules and full harmonisation. Still, the method is unorthodox and stealthy—if not rather brutal.

4. THE POSSIBLE IMPACT OF THE PROPOSAL FOR A DIRECTIVE ON SERVICES IN THE INTERNAL MARKET

The Commission's initial proposal for a Directive on Services in the Internal Market[19] (hereinafter 'the initial Service Proposal') instituted a hard-core country-of-origin principle applicable to all service providers established in one Member State and offering their services in other Member States.[20] The country-of-origin principle was supposed to apply in particular as regards 'the behaviour of the provider, the quality or content of the service, advertising, contracts and the provider's liability'. Thus, a service provider was supposed to comply only with the marketing rules of his country of establishment, even when providing services to or in other Member States.

Although the question is by now more or less academic, it can be questioned, in the light of the express wording of Articles 47 and 50 EC, whether the Commission's initial proposal to introduce such a hard-core country-of-origin principle through secondary legislation had a sufficient legal basis in the Treaty.[21]

It can also be discussed whether the country-of-origin principle in the initial Service Proposal would in reality reinstate what the Community legislator expressly threw out of the UCPD.[22] Admittedly, the Commission's initial Service Proposal stated that it should be without prejudice to any legislative Community measures in the field of consumer protection and thus also to the UCPD. It could certainly also be argued—as the Commission did when confronted with the decision of the Member States to delete the country of origin principle from the UCPD[23]—that a country-of-origin clause does not have any real effect, as the UCPD establishes total harmonisation. If total harmonisation is to work, the evaluation of a certain commercial practice under the UCPD must be the same, no matter in which Member

---

[19] Proposal for a Directive of the European Parliament and of the Council on services in the internal market, COM(2004)2, SEC(2004)21.

[20] Art 16 of ibid.

[21] I Otken Eriksson and U Öberg, 'Consumer Protection Aspects of the Commission's Proposal for a Directive on Services in the Internal Market', Legal Opinion presented at the Nordic Seminar held at the Swedish Konsumentverket on 1 June 2004, at 13, available at www.norden.org/pub/sk/showpub.asp?pubnr=2004:795.

[22] See also Bakardjieva Engelbrekt 'EG-Direktivet' above n 12, at 246 and Bakardjieva Engelbrekt, *EU and Marketing Practices Law*, above n 12 at 71–72.

[23] Political Agreement reached by the Competitiveness Council on 18 May 2004, see Annex Communication from the Commission to the European Parliament COM(2004) 0753 final–COD(2003) 0134.

State the evaluation takes place. The legislative technique based on a country-of-origin principle is from a theoretical point of view an alternative to full harmonisation.[24]

However, what is not expressly covered by the UCPD falls outside its scope of application and thus under the general Service Proposal. And here we find very important aspects of the actual functioning of the UCPD such as questions of jurisdiction and choices of law. In this regard, the UCPD itself only states that Member States shall ensure that adequate and effective means exist to combat unfair commercial practices for persons or organisations regarded under national law as having a legitimate interest in combating such unfair commercial practices.[25] This Article could be interpreted as meaning that any commercial practice can be attacked in any Member State where, according to national law, someone has a legitimate interest in combating it. But if this Article is not to be construed as an express rule on jurisdiction—and it does not appear very natural to do that—the UCPD is silent on the point in which Member State unfair commercial practices should be fought. This would mean that, under the initial Service Proposal, the country-of-origin principle should apply and that unfair commercial practices should mainly be supervised and evaluated in the country of establishment, ie the home country. This is precisely what the Member States wanted to avoid in the UCPD.

The Service Proposal has recently undergone its first reading in the European Parliament and, as expected, the proposal did not go through untouched (hereinafter 'the Service Proposal as amended by the EP').[26] Among many other modifications especially as to the scope of application of the Directive, the hard-core country-of-origin principle seems to have disappeared as regards free movement of services. Instead, the Service Proposal as amended by the EP states that Member States shall *respect* the right of providers to provide a service in a Member State other than that in which they are established, and that the Member States in which the service is provided shall *ensure free access to and free exercise* of a service activity within its territory.[27] Furthermore, Member States shall not make access to or exercise of a service activity in their territory subject to compliance with any requirements which are not non-discriminatory, necessary for reasons

---

[24] U Öberg, 'Principen om ömsesidigt erkännande och ursprungslandsprincipen i gemenskapsrätten—särskilt med hänsyn till marknadsföringsåtgärder, friheten att tillhandahålla tjänster och skyddet för konsumenter, Rapport for the Nordic Council of Ministers' Committee on Consumer Affairs (Tema Nord 2003:534), available at www.norden.org/pub/sk/showpub.asp?pubnr=2003:534.

[25] Art 11 of the UCPD, above n 1.

[26] Position of the European Parliament adopted at first reading on 16 Feb 2006 with a view to the adoption of Directive 2006/000/EC of the European Parliament and Council on services in the internal market, EP-PE_TC1-COD(2004)0001.

[27] The Service Proposal as amended by the EP, Art 21(1).

of public policy or public security or the protection of the health and the environment, as well as proportional.[28] Paragraph 3 confirms that Member States to which the provider moves may impose requirements with regard to the provision of a service activity, where they are justified for reasons of public policy, public security, environmental protection and public health, and adds that Member States may also apply, 'in conformity with Community law', their rules on employment conditions, including those laid down in collective agreements.

Thus, under the Service Proposal as amended by the EP, host Member States may impose on service providers from other Member States specific national requirements on the grounds of public policy, public security, health and environment (as well as certain employment conditions).[29] This seems to be an exhaustive list of this kind of derogations from service providers' rights to provide a service in another Member State. It is particularly noteworthy that protection of consumers is not as such included in these grounds. This was one of the vigorously discussed issues in the Parliamentary debate. Certain observers argue that protection of consumers could be covered by the ground of public policy, but, looking at previous case law of the Court, this seems hardly likely.

Thus, it would seem that if the Service Proposal as amended by the EP is adopted, Member States will not be able to force service providers established in other Member States to observe stricter national requirements on grounds of pure consumer protection. This is a stricter approach than current case law of the Court of Justice on Article 49 EC, where all 'imperative requirements in the general interest' are accepted as grounds for derogation as regards non-discriminatory obstacles.[30] This may in effect constitute a country-of-origin principle in a new disguise. At least, the initial country-of-origin principle has not been totally watered down to a mere recognition of the Court's existing case law.

However, another important amendment to the initial Service Proposal further limits the possible impact of this instrument in the area of the UCPD. Contrary to the idea of the country-of-origin principle where supervision is to take place only in the home country, the Service Proposal as amended by the EP clearly states that supervision shall take place in the Member State where the service is actually provided.[31] This solution seems to be better in line with the intention behind the removal of the country-of-origin principle from the UCPD. Furthermore, the Service Proposal as amended by the EP expressly states that it shall be without prejudice to private

---

[28] Ibid, Art 21(1).

[29] Obviously, provided the requirements are non-discriminatory and proportional.

[30] Obviously, provided the measure is proportional: Case C–55/94 *Reinhard Gebhard v Consiglio dell'Ordine degli Avvocati e Procuratori di Milano* [1995] ECR I–04165.

[31] The Service Proposal as amended by the EP, above n 26 Art 16–17.

international law, in particular private international law governing contractual and non-contractual obligations, and that this means that the
consumer in any case benefits from the protection granted to him by the
consumer legislation in force in his Member State.[32]

Unsurprisingly, the Commission has accepted most of the amendments
proposed by the Parliament. On 4 April 2006, the Commission presented
its amended proposal for a Directive on Services in the internal market[33]
and the provisions on the freedom to provide services as amended by the EP
appear to have undergone only minor drafting adjustments.[34] Also the rules
on supervision are in principle accepted by the Commission, even though
some differences may be detected here.[35] Moreover, the express exclusion
of rules of private international law on contractual and non-contractual
obligations appears to be accepted by the Commission with only minor
adjustments.[36]

In conclusion, the Service Proposal as amended after the first Parliamentary
reading no longer seems to have significant consequences for the UCPD.
The rules on supervision in the Service Proposal may become of relevance,
as it is not expressly stated in the UCPD in which Member State unfair
commercial practices should be fought. However, under the amended
Service Proposal, efforts have been made to guarantee the Member State of
destination certain powers of supervision. This seems better in line with the
Member States' intentions behind the UCPD than the initial country-of-origin principle. Still, if we look to consumer law *outside* the field harmonised
by the UCPD—for example in business-to-business relations—even the
amended Service Proposal may still mean that host Member States will have
to supervise service providers' marketing activities in accordance with rules
of the home Member States.

5. FUTURE APPROACH OF THE COURT OF JUSTICE

Whereas the destiny of the Service Proposal is still uncertain, there is no
doubt that the Court of Justice will be called upon to interpret the UCPD.
The Court of Justice has several choices to make when it is presented with

---

[32] Ibid, Art 3(2) and (3).
[33] Amended proposal for a Directive of the European Parliament and of the Council on
services in the internal market, COM(2006)0160 final.
[34] Art 16 in the Commission's proposal, above n 33.
[35] The Commission's description of the extent of the supervision to be carried out in the
country of destination appears more guarded than that of Parliament: see Arts 34–35 of the
Commission's amended proposal: cf in particular Art 17 of the Service Proposal as amended
by the Parliament, above n 26.
[36] Art 3(2) of the Commission's amended proposal, above n 33.

the first cases under the Directive. The main question is to what extent the Court will detail its answers to requests for preliminary references. As a full harmonisation measure, the UCPD seems to require the Court of Justice to rule in detail on what may constitute an unfair commercial practice.

This seems to be slightly at odds with the recent approach of the Court in leaving certain assessments to the referring national courts, taking account of all relevant circumstances. This trend in the case law is understandable, given the limited resources of the Court and the current state of development of Community law. It also fits well into the discussions of a revision of the *CILFIT* doctrine,[37] the *Köbler* ruling[38] and the increased responsibilities of national courts. Such an approach from the Court in this relatively new area of Community law—'burdened' not only with deeply rooted traditions in national law, but also with newly reformed legislation[39]—could still seriously threaten and undermine the full effectiveness of the UCPD. If the UCPD has to be interpreted in the same manner in all courts throughout the Community, this requires a certain degree of centralisation and 'hands-on' approach by the Court, giving rather detailed answers to preliminary references. If the Court leaves a significant margin of appreciation to referring courts, other national courts will hesitate to refer preliminary questions and instead decide cases under the UCPD themselves.

It is difficult to second-guess how the Court will react. Most comparable previous case law has concerned significantly different legislation. In *Freiburger Kommunalbauten*, the Court stated that it 'may interpret general criteria used by the Community legislature in order to define the concept of unfair terms', but that it 'should not rule on the application of these general criteria to a particular term, which must be considered in the light of the particular circumstances of the case in question'.[40]

However, this case concerned the Unfair Terms Directive which is only a minimum harmonisation measure, and the annex specifying what may be unfair terms is, according to the Court, only of indicative and illustrative value.[41] In our view it seems necessary for the Court—at least initially—to take a somewhat more detailed approach to the UCPD in order to ensure that the full harmonisation ambition carries through.

---

[37] Case 77/83 *Srl CILFIT and others and Lanificio di Gavardo SpA v. Ministero della sanità* [1984] ECR 1257.
[38] Case C–224/01 *Gerhard Köbler v Republik Österreich* [2003] ECR I–10239.
[39] Eg in Denmark and Germany.
[40] Case C–237/02 *Freiburger Kommunalbauten* [2004] ECR I–3403, para. 22.
[41] Case C–478/99 *Commission v Sweden* [2002] ECR I–4147, para 20.

This being the case, it may well be that national consumer agencies and/ or associations will have an interest in bringing cases to national courts and/or to the Court of Justice 'as quickly as possibly' after the entry into force of the UCPD in order to secure their 'national' understanding of the Directive. If the UCPD is to be understood as a full harmonisation measure, national courts' decisions will have the effect of more or less foreclosing other courts from coming to differing results in similar situations. Thus, national consumer agencies may have an interest in getting their 'pet issues' of interpretation submitted to and throughly argued before the Court of Justice, a phenomenon that could perhaps be called a 'Race to the Court'.

6. CONCLUSION

The UCPD is certainly not an uncomplicated piece of legislation.[42] Seen in a wider context, it raises certain problems concerning its legal basis in the Treaty, its scope of application, its relation to the proposal for a directive on services in the internal market and as regards the future approach of the Court of Justice. None of these difficulties, however, seem to be insurmountable, nor should they hinder us from seeing the UCPD as a pioneering new development in EU law. There is no doubt that the UCPD is a high-risk venture, having regard to the strong traditions in the Member States. But if all involved—including Member States, the Commission, practising lawyers and the Court of Justice—shoulder their responsibility and accept the full harmonisation at its face value, the UCPD has enormous potential and may indeed—with words borrowed from the Commission's initial proposal for a directive on Services in the internal market—contribute to realising a 'genuine' internal market.

---

[42] For a comprehensive examination of the UCPD and all its 'challenges' see J Stuyck, E Terryn and T van Dyck, 'Confidence through Fairness? The New Directive on Unfair Business-to-consumer Commercial Practices in the Internal Market' (2006) 43 CMLRev 107.

6

Unfair Commercial Practices Directive—A Missed Opportunity?

GERAINT HOWELLS[*]

1. INTRODUCTION

T HE UNFAIR COMMERCIAL Practices Directive (UCPD)[1] was a bold measure. The field it covers is broad and notoriously difficult to regulate. The introduction of a European general clause was the fulfilment of a long-term ambition for many in the consumer movement and was especially welcome in countries like the United Kingdom where there had been no previous general clause regulating fair trading. Why then do I describe it as a missed opportunity? This is because of the juxtaposition of two sets of factors. First, I will make some criticisms of the form of the European legislation. In and of themselves these would not be damning. This is a difficult area to legislate on even at the national level, but, given the need to find a European consensus the drafters of the Directive, can be considered to have made a good first effort. The problem is that the newcomer European legislators believe they have found the perfect solution and have imposed it on all Member States and prohibited any greater protection being offered. It is the option of maximal harmonisation that turns the spotlight on the quality of the drafting and makes this a missed opportunity. Along the way this may have an important impact on the form and style of enforcement as specific punctual laws give way to reliance on general clauses and injunctions take over from criminal sanctions as front line tools of consumer protection.

---

[*] This chapter draws upon work done by me for *European Fair Trading—The Unfair Commercial Practices Directive* (with Hans Micklitz and Thomas Wilhelmsson) (Aldershot, Ashgate, 2006) and the section on maximal harmonisation is taken from 'The Rise of European Consumer Law—Whither National Consumer Law?' (2006) 28 *Sydney Law Review* 63. The paper this chapter is based on was presented in Malta on 17 Mar 2006 at a regional conference of the International Association of Consumer Law on Promoting Consumer Interests.

[1] Directive 2005/29/EC concerning unfair business-to-consumer commercial practices in the internal market [2005] OJ L 149/22.

First some background. The prospect of a general directive on unfair commercial practices came on to the agenda with the Green Paper on EU Consumer Protection.[2] Despite its broad title it really focused in on trade practices law and canvassed opinion on whether future European interventions should continue to be by punctual specific regulations (like the ideas that were developing around sales promotions) or whether a framework directive should be adopted. Even at this early stage the tone made it obvious that the Commission had ambitions for a general directive and this was confirmed in the Follow–up Communication on EU Consumer Law.[3] This concentrated on the form such a general framework directive should adopt, and it was clear that it would be based on a general clause and limited to business-to-consumer contracts. Some Member States favoured extending it to allow businesses to challenge unfair practices of competitors, but the Commission did not want to go that far.

On 18 June 2003 the Commission adopted a proposal for a directive concerning unfair business-to-consumer practices in the Internal Market.[4] The structure of the final Directive closely resembles that of the Proposal. At the same time the Commission also proposed a Regulation on Sales Promotion,[5] which would have forced a greater liberalisation of the sales promotions allowed in Member States. It was strange for these two initiatives to have come forward at the same time from two different branches of the Commission. DG SANCO promoted the UCPD, whereas DG Markt is promoting the Sales Promotion Regulation as part of its services strategy. It was unfortunate in many respects that the two projects were not better co-ordinated, for whilst the Green Paper on Consumer Protection tried to open a debate on the nature of European regulation, the Regulation would dictate directly the form of regulation in a major area of European fair trading law.

The Sales Promotion Regulation has, however, proven to be very controversial and little progress has been made; it now looks likely to be abandoned. By contrast, given the broad ambitions of the Directive, the different national traditions in this field and the complex nature of the law and practice in this area, the proposal made relatively brisk progress through the political decision-making process. A political agreement was reached in Competitiveness Council on 18 May 2004 with a common position being agreed on 15 November 2004.[6] The Directive was adopted at the Competitiveness Council on 7 March 2005 and Directive 2005/29/

---

[2] COM(2001)531.
[3] COM(2002)531.
[4] COM(2003)356.
[5] COM(2001)546 and the revised proposal at COM(2002)585. This is likely to be abandoned.
[6] [2005] OJ C 38/E/1.

EC concerning business-to-consumer commercial practices in the internal market and amending Council Directive 84/450/EEC, Directives 97/7/EC, 98/27/EC and 2002/65/EC of the European Parliament and of the Council and Regulation (EC) No 2006/2004 of the European Parliament and of the Council (Unfair Commercial Practices Directive) was published in the Official Journal on 11 June 2005.[7]

The UCPD regulates unfair commercial practices harming consumers' economic interests (Article 1). Article 2 provides a raft of definitions, while Article 3 delimits the scope of the Directive. Article 4 is the internal market (maximal harmonisation) clause. The meat of the Directive lies in Articles 5–9. Article 5 sets out the general unfairness test, Article 6 specifies this for misleading actions, Article 7 for misleading omissions (with Annex II listing those Community provisions setting out rules for advertising and commercial communication which are regarded as material) and Articles 8–9 for aggressive commercial practices. These are supplemented by a list of practices that are always considered unfair in Annex I. Codes of conduct are addressed in Article 10. Articles 11–13 deal with enforcement issues, including rules on the substantiation of claims. Articles 15–16 deals with consequential amendments to other directives. Articles 17–20 deal with some other procedural matters.

2. SOME CRITICISMS

Scholars from the continental tradition have been fairly complimentary about the drafting of the Directive; admiring its structure of general clause, clauses on misleading and aggressive practices and black list of prohibited practices. However, the common lawyer in me still feels uneasy about the many unanswered questions left by the drafting and the occasional difficulty in reconciling the rules with the stated policy objectives.

The Directive's reference point for judging the fairness of a practice is the average consumer, building on the jurisprudence of the European Court of Justice; although this standard is adapted to take the interests of vulnerable consumers into account as considered appropriate. The initial proposal had contained a definition of average consumer as meaning 'the consumer who is reasonably well informed and reasonably observant and circumspect'.[8] This was removed and the Common Position simply referred to the jurisprudence of the European Court of Justice in the recitals. This was expanded on in the final version to include in the recital wording lifted from the jurisprudence—namely that the average consumer is 'reasonably

---

[7] [2005] OJ L 149/22.
[8] Art 2(b), of the UCPD, above n 1.

well-informed and reasonably observant and circumspect, taking into account social, cultural and linguistic factors, as interpreted by the Court of Justice'.[9] There was a desire not to include a precise definition so as to allow jurisprudence to develop. Equally consumer advocates were keen to include references to social, cultural and linguistic factors to reflect the nuanced approach of the Court and to prevent the impression that European law uncritically assumed that everyone was always able to process information correctly and not be misled. It is therefore still a matter for debate whether European law will follow the hard-nosed European Court approach or allow (perhaps at the level of national application) more consumer friendly interpretations of the average consumer.[10]

Article 5 attempts to vary the average consumer standard to take account of the average member of a group that is particularly targeted. Moreover when a practice is aimed at the general public, but it is foreseeable that it is likely materially to distort the economic behaviour of only a clearly identifiable group which is particularly vulnerable to the practice or underlying product because of their mental or physical infirmity, age or credulity, then the practice is judged by the average member of that group. Especially the introduction of credulity risks undermining the general policy of judging practices by the average consumer standard. Moreover it is not clear whether these variations on the average consumer standard apply only to Article 5 or also the provisions on misleading and aggressive practices. This also turns on whether Article 5 should be viewed as the central provision or merely a fall-back clause.

A transactional decision requirement was built into the unfairness standard to underline that the test related to economic considerations, but has led to concerns about how much it limits the impact of the Directive. Consumer groups had concerns about the impact of this requirement on the need to establish causation between the practice and consumer detriment and also because there were difficulties in applying it to some situations where either unfair practices did not affect a transactional decision (for instance, when consumers ignored aggressive practices) or there was no opportunity for consumers to make a transactional decision (such as post-contractual removal of services by a trader). These concerns were not so much addressed as said not to be real concerns in practice. The transactional decision test is thought not to be a very high hurdle for consumers; we wait to see if the courts take a similar approach.

Annex I contains a list of commercial practices which are considered unfair in all circumstances. The original proposal listed 28 practices, which in the final version was extended to 31. Whereas some of these are

---

[9] Recital 18 ibid.
[10] See T Wilhelmsson, 'The Informed Consumer v the Vulnerable Consumer in European Commercial Practices Law—a Comment' (2006) 1 *Yearbook of Consumer Law* 211.

straightforward, others touch complex issues such as pyramid selling,[11] and one might wonder whether there is a need for more detailed rules than are found in the Annex I. Also the matters listed appear to be a rather rag bag collection of unfair practices. Although they are listed under two headings dealing with misleading and aggressive practices it is not even clear that all the practices are listed under the appropriate heading, and in some cases one might question whether they all are indeed examples of misleading and aggressive practices. Some seem to be simply objectionable practices that have been listed with little attention being paid to defining the underlying policy for the prohibition.

This reveals a more fundamental problem of aligning the underlying philosophy of the Directive with some of its provisions. This is especially true of aggressive practices. Aggressive practice must have two causal effects. They must impair the consumer's freedom of choice or conduct, and in turn this lack of freedom must cause her to take a transactional decision that she would not otherwise have taken. The requirement that the aggressive practice must significantly impair or be likely to impair the average consumer's freedom of choice or conduct with regard to the product encapsulates the core mischief the rules on aggressive practices are aimed at. However, this highlights a more fundamental flaw in a test based on impairment of choice. This may work with many examples concerning coercion and undue influence. Even if a particular individual is able to withstand such pressure in appropriate cases it will be possible to argue that the average consumer would have freedom of choice or conduct significantly impaired. Impact of freedom of choice is, however, not the objection to many practices considered to be harassing that also fall within the definition of aggressive practices. Many such practices concern protection of the consumer's private sphere rather than fears that they are forcing consumers into choices or conducts they would not normally make.[12] For instance, few people actually respond to unsolicited e-mails. It does not affect transactional decision-making for most consumers, but it does irritate many, and it is often considered anti-social and should fall for consideration as an aggressive practice. Likewise the making of persistent and unwanted solicitations by telephone is unlikely to impair the freedom of the average consumer.[13] One might even predict that it would have a negative effect on the average consumer and put him or her off trading with that business. But this is a practice that is always regarded as aggressive. It is hard to see a way of resolving this conundrum. One must conclude that the Article is badly drafted if the intention was, as it obviously was, to include such practices.

---

[11] Item 14, Annex I to the Directive, above n 1.

[12] H Köhler and T Lettl, 'Das geltende europäische Lauterkeitsrecht, der Vorschlag für eine EG-Richtlinie über unlautere Geschäftpraktiken und die UWG-Reform' [2003] *Wettbewerb in Recht und Praxis* 1019.

[13] Item 26, Annex I to the Directive, above n 1.

3. POLICY DEBATES ON MAXIMAL HARMONISATION

As was mentioned earlier, these criticism of the Directive would be less damning but for the maximal harmonisation nature of the Directive. When the UCPD was being adopted one of the central debating points was the Commission's determination to make it a maximal harmonisation directive. In favour of maximal harmonisation, the Commission invoked the arguments about businesses needing confidence that they would not be confronted with more protective national laws in order to encourage them to trade on a European wide basis. Just as it has been argued that the Commission abused the notion of the confident consumer to promote consumer directives,[14] so too it abuses the notion of the underconfident business to justify maximal harmonisation.

Moreover they argued that any objections were irrational as all unfair practices would be caught by the general clause. However, at least two counter arguments can be made to this stance. First, substantively the Directive's standard may not cover all unfair practices; only those practices defined as unfair by the Directive are prohibited. Secondly, it underplays the value of laws providing for specific controls.

It is misleading to suggest that all unfair practices are caught by the Directive, at least, if by that one means all conceivable unfair practices. The Directive uses a very specific conception of unfairness, albeit in many respects a fairly broad one. Practices are unfair if, contrary to the requirements of professional diligence, they materially distort the economic behaviour of the average consumer.[15] This is further refined to include misleading actions[16] and omissions[17] as well as aggressive practices.[18]

At least three elements risk making this a restrictive conception of unfairness. First, part of the definition of professional diligence in Article 2(h) refers to 'honest market practices'. There has been some, probably unwarranted, concern that this might allow traders to point to simple compliance with common industry practices as a defence. In any event this requirement is presumed to be satisfied for misleading and aggressive practices that will make up the bulk of unfair commercial practices. Secondly, the unfairness definition builds upon European Court of Justice jurisprudence[19] and uses an average consumer standard. However, the conception of the

---

[14] T Wilhelmsson, 'The Abuse of the "Confident Consumer" as a Justification for EC Consumer Law' (2004) 27 *Journal of Consumer Policy* 317.
[15] Art 5 of the Directive, above n 1.
[16] Art 6 of ibid.
[17] Art 7 of ibid.
[18] Arts 8–9 of ibid.
[19] See Cases C–315/1992 *Verband Sozialer Wettbewerb e V v Clinique Laboratoires SNC and Estee Lauder Cosmetics GmbH* [1994] ECR I–317 and C–210/96 *Gut Springenheide GmbH and Rudolf Tusky v OberKreisdirektor des Kreises Steinfurt—Amt für Lebensmittelüberwachung* [1998] ECR I–4657.

average consumer used by the Directive might be interpreted as assuming that this hypothetical person has abilities and ways of behaving which are superior to how the ordinary consumer actually behaves. Recital 18 echoes European Court of Justice jurisprudence by referring to the average consumer as someone who is 'reasonably well-informed and reasonably observant and circumspect'. Thankfully the other strand of the European Court of the Justice's jurisprudence was also eventually included to allow courts when making the assessment to take 'into account social, cultural and linguistic factors'. Thirdly, unfairness is limited to economic unfairness. The practice must have caused the consumer to take a transactional decision she would not otherwise have taken. This transactional decision test is an express part of the misleading and aggressive practices standard and is found in the general unfairness test as part of the definition of material distortion of the consumer's economic behaviour.[20] It is unclear how strict a causal test this will be. Although one could imagine courts taking fine points on this, the working assumption is that this will be a fairly easy threshold to pass. However, it does cause problems when the unfair practice occurs post-contractually and the consumer does not have to take a transactional decision, such as when a post-sales advice service is withdrawn. Furthermore it is hard to apply to aggressive practices that do not affect the average consumer. For instance, most consumers simply ignore spam e-mail, but that does not mean it should not be prohibited.[21]

In most legal systems there is usually a mass of detailed rules regulating particular practices. This is certainly the case for common law countries which have relied on punctual specific regulation of trade practices.[22] But such detailed rules exist even in systems with general fair trading clauses. They can be valuable in targeting particular practices and providing clear guidance on what is acceptable. Ideally one senses that the drafters of the Directive would like these swept away. That seems inconceivable, but they will all have to be reviewed to be brought into line with the Directive's standard. Some may be repealed, but most will probably be modified, and in the process a layer of complication will be added to national laws.

Therefore the maximal harmonisation approach of the UCPD gives rise to two sets of concerns. First, consumers may be left vulnerable to some unfair practices that Member States might wish to control. Secondly, a technical set of problems arises requiring the revision of numerous specific forms of regulation and possibly the removal of some traditional forms of protection.

---

[20] See Art 2(e) of the Directive, above n 1.

[21] See Annex I, item 26 to ibid.

[22] C Twigg-Flensen, D Parry, G Howells and A Nordhausen, *An Analysis of the Application and Scope of the UCP Directive* (London, DTI, 2005), available at www.dti.gov.uk/ccp/consultpdf/final_report180505.pdf.

4. THE INTERNAL MARKET CLAUSE

Article 4 of the Directive is the internal market clause. It simply states:

> Member States shall neither restrict the freedom to provide services nor restrict the free movement of goods for reasons falling within the field approximated by this Directive.

The original proposal had preceded this with a clause providing that traders shall only comply with the national provisions, falling within the field approximated by this Directive, of the Member States in which they are established. Member States in which the trader was established were to ensure such compliance. This was even more explicit in its intentions than previous consumer directives such as the Television without Frontiers Directive[23] and the E-Commerce Directive,[24] which had invoked a country of origin principle. These had simply preceded a clause similar to the one now found in Article 4, by a clause about Member States' obligations to ensure compliance by businesses established in their territory or jurisdiction. The effect was of course under all versions that traders only have to comply with the rules of the state in which they are established. The UCPD was simply more transparent in its original wording in making it clear to traders that they had to concern themselves with only one set of national rules.

The country of origin principle found in the first paragraph of Article 4 of the proposal on Unfair Commercial Practices was removed, apparently as a concession to those with concerns about the maximal harmonisation approach. However, this was a rather pyrrhic victory, for it was removed only on the understanding that it was not needed to achieve maximal harmonisation. Nevertheless, it does leave the receiving state as the state responsible for control. This can be very important for, due to limited resources, home states' regulatory authorities may be tempted to give low priority to protection of consumers in other states. It is unclear what control the receiving state can exercise. Can it only apply the rules of the Directive or, as has been suggested by at least one state, does Article 4 now permit it to continue to rely on the mandatory requirements set out in *Cassis de Dijon*?[25] This interpretation would be surprising, not least to

---

[23] Directive 89/552/EEC concerning the pursuit of television broadcasting activities [1989] OJ L 298/23, as amended by Directive 97/36/EC [1997] OJ L 202/60.

[24] Directive 2000/31/EC on certain legal aspects of information society services, in particular electronic commerce, in the Internal Market [2000] OJ L 178/1.

[25] Hans Micklitz suggests that Germany views Art 4 as mirroring *Cassis de Dijon* and therefore allowing national rules to be justified on the basis of mandatory requirements: see G Howells, H Micklitz and T Wilhelmsson, *European Fair Trading Law—The Unfair Commercial Practices Directive* (Ashgate, Aldershot, 2006).

the Commission, which certainly would not expect Article 4 to serve as a safeguard clause in disguise. It would run counter to their whole line of argumentation and their reluctant acceptance of the removal of the country of origin clause, but only on the basis that it was not needed to achieve maximal harmonisation.

The Commission refused to debate the maximal harmonisation principle during the implementation process. To do so risked being considered a wrecker who wanted to go over old ground, rather than assist in fine tuning the Commission's proposals. What is particularly surprising is the Commission's refusal even to consider introducing a safeguard clause that would allow Member States to react to practices that might develop outside the control of the Directive. Traders employ legions of lawyers and consultants and have every incentive to steal a march on their competitors by pushing legal rules to the limits.[26] It seems rash of the EC to place such faith in its general clause, especially before it has been interpreted by the courts. A parachute to safety in terms of a safeguard clause, as provided for in the General Product Safety Directive,[27] the E-Commerce Directive,[28] would have seemed a sensible precaution, at least in the early years of the Directive's existence. Even though such safeguard clauses build in close supervision of Member States' exercise of their discretion, the Commission was having none of it. It is confident its law can cover all eventualities.

The Commission's efforts to establish maximal harmonisation of all aspects covered by its directives are becoming a familiar feature of legislative procedures at the European level. Although it is winning many battles, the principle still meets some resistance, and this often leads to exceptions and derogations being slipped into the legislation. Even the Directive on the Distance Marketing of Consumer Financial Services[29] that strove so hard for maximal harmonisation, in the end and despite the long list of information requirements included in the Directive, reserved to Member States the right (pending further harmonisation) to add additional information requirements.

The UCPD includes its own limitations on the maximal hamonisation principle. A major limitation on the scope of the harmonised rules is that they apply only to business-to-consumer commercial practices.[30] Business-to-business and even consumer-to-consumer practices are excluded, although it is hard to imagine that these should logically be more heavily regulated than business-to-consumer rules. Rules concerning the certification and

---

[26] J Hanson and D Kysar, 'Taking Behaviouralism Seriously: The Problem of Market Manipulation' (1999) 74 *New York University Law Review* 630.
[27] Directive 2001/95/EC [2002] OJ L 11/4.
[28] Directive 2000/31/EC [2000] OJ L 178/1.
[29] [2002] OJ L 271/16.
[30] Art 3(1) of the Directive, above n 1.

indication of the standard of fineness of articles of precious metal are also excluded.[31]

Financial services are within the scope of the Directive but, as is customary in EC consumer law, receive special treatment. Member States remain free to impose more restrictive or prescriptive requirements with respect to financial services.[32] The same applies to immovables. A major concession was the introduction of a six-year stay of execution for rules more protective than the Directive which were introduced when implementing directives with minimal harmonisation clauses.[33] This concession in itself concedes that the Commission must foresee some recently enacted consumer protection rules might need to be repealed or modified because of the maximal character of the Directive.

The Directive is said to be without prejudice to rules on contract law,[34] health and safety,[35] rules determining jurisdiction[36] and rules relating to the integrity of the regulated professions.[37] Furthermore recital 7 makes it clear that the Directive does not address legal requirements relating to taste and decency and Member States can continue to ban practices for such grounds even if they do not limit consumers' freedom of choice. The exact scope of this exception is unclear, for the recital gives the example of banning commercial solicitations in the street, which suggests a broader understanding of taste and decency than usual.

5. CONCLUSION

Commercial practices cover a broad spectrum. Some clearly need to be harmonised or they will affect the ability to trade across borders. For example, a national rule which requires a particular warning in an advertisement might impede the ability of a company to have a pan-European advertising campaign. The difficulty of ascertaining which rules impede market access lies at the heart of the *Keck* decision,[38] and the problems in determining whether selling arrangements in practice impede imports is obvious from the subsequent case law.[39]

---

[31] Art 3(10) ibid.
[32] Art 3(9) ibid.
[33] Art 3(5) ibid.
[34] Art 3(2) ibid.
[35] Art 3(3) ibid.
[36] Art 3(7) ibid.
[37] Art 3(8) ibid.
[38] Joined Cases C–267/91 & C–268/91 *Criminal proceedings against Bernard Keck and Daniel Mithouard* [1993] ECR I–6097; see S Weatherill, 'After *Keck*: Some Thoughts on how to Clarify the Clarification' (1996) 33 *CMLRev* 885.
[39] Eg Case C–368/95 *Vereinigte Familiapress Zeitungsverlags-und vertriebs GmbH v Heinrich Bauer Verlag* [1997] ECR I–3689; Case C–34–36/95 *Konsumentombudsmannen (KO) v De Agostini (Svenska) Forlag AB and TV-Shop i Sverige AB* [1997] ECR I-3483 Case C–254/98 *Schutzverband gegen unlauteren Wettbewerb v TK-Heimdienst Sass Gmbh* [2000] ECR I–151; Case C–322/01 *Deutscher Apothekerverband eV v 0800 Doc Morris NV and Jacques Waterval* [2003] ECR I–14887.

From an internal market perspective one can see that harmonisation of some commercial practices is necessary, and that for many commercial practices harmonisation will be desirable. However, this needs to be weighed against the undesirability of removing traditional national protection in favour of the Directive's general clause. Although most of the non-common law Member States had general clauses prior to the enactment of the Directive, they varied in content and also there were many specific legal controls in all Member States.[40] The United Kingdom and Ireland of course did not have a general clause. Moreover, the substance of trade practices controls still seems very bound to national cultures. Germany (because of the controls by competitors) and the Nordic states (because of the supervision of the Ombudsmen) have traditionally been very protective of consumers. By contrast the United Kingdom has been more liberal, especially as regards advertising, especially comparative advertising,[41] and sales promotions.[42] The Directive actually adopts the form of the continental general clauses, but has the policy perspective of the United Kingdom. European jurisprudence under the Misleading Advertising Directive had already been moving in this direction.[43] But differences in culture persist as to what are acceptable commercial practices. In sum, it seems far too early for Europe to move towards a harmonised regime. The Directive would have been better advised to create a common framework so that the legal regimes evolved towards a common conceptualisation of fairness.

Again one perceives maximal harmonisation is more of a political than legal necessity. This becomes even more apparent when attention is focused on the possibility of harmonisation being brought about in practice. Leaving to one side the very real differences in enforcement apparatus, one can predict that the goal of simply being able to follow one set of rules and then happily marketing in all states will be illusionary. The implementation process may well give rise to some problems. States with general clauses may be tempted to keep with their own formula rather than moving over

---

[40] See VIEW, 'The Feasibility of a General Legislative Framework on Fair Trading', available at http://europa.eu.int/comm/consumers/cons_int/safe_shop/fair_bus_pract/green_pap_comm/studies/sur21_sum_en.pdf; R Schulze and H Schulte-Nölke, 'Analysis of National Fairness Laws Aimed at Protecting Consumers in Relation to Commercial Practices', available at http://europa.eu.int/comm/consumers/cons_int/safe_shop/fair_bus_pract/green_pap_comm/studies/unfair_practices_en.pdf. A study of the new Member States was carried out by British Institute of International and Comparative Law, 'Unfair Commercial Practices—An analysis of the existing national rules, including case law, on unfair commercial practices between business and consumers in the New Member States and the possible resulting internal market barrier'. See also Howells, Micklitz and Wilhelmsson, above n 25.

[41] Now covered by Directive 97/55/EC amending Directive 84/450/EEC concerning misleading advertising so as to include comparative advertising [1997] OJ L 290/18.

[42] As noted above, a European Regulation on Sales Promotions has been proposed but no agreement can be reached on it, underlining the different traditions in this area.

[43] Case C–373/90 *Criminal proceedings against X ('Nissan')* [1992] ECR I–13; Case C–112/99 *Toshiba Europe GmbH v Katun Germany GmbH* [2001] ECR I–7945; and Case C–44/01 *Pippig Augenoptik GmbH v Hartlauer Handelsgesellschaft mbH* [2003] ECR I–3095.

to the Directive's standard. Assuming the United Kingdom tries to some extent to retain its specific regulations alongside the new general clause, it will be a mammoth task to trawl through the mass of relevant legislation and modify it,[44] and an even more difficult task for the Commission to check this has been done properly. The best that can be expected is a good effort. When it comes to applying the general standard, national traditions and social understandings or fairness are bound to come to the fore. The European Court of Justice has already in the context of unfair terms backed off imposing a European application of the general test and indicated it is for national courts to decide.[45] This is perhaps inevitable, given that on a preliminary reference the European Court of Justice can interpret European law, but cannot apply it to the facts of the case. That is the function of national courts. Of course the European Court of Justice can give fairly detailed interpretations, which can sometimes seem to leave little room for national courts' discretion. Even when detailed instructions are given, it seems that on occasions national courts are willing to use their ingenuity to deviate from the sometimes pretty strong hints from the European Court of Justice.[46]

Maximal harmonisation of some commercial practices law might be necessary or at least in many cases desirable, but complete harmonisation of the whole field has come too soon. The introduction of a common general clause on fair trading is to be welcomed as creating a common base level of protection and being a mechanism for the creation of a European conception of fair trading. However, the field is too broad and complex for all problems to be resolved by a simple general clause. Complete uniformity does not appear to be an obtainable objective for now. The future, at least in the short to medium term, is likely to be one of increased legal complexity rather that the simplification that Brussels was trying to introduce. It is hard to find simple solutions to complex problems. In attempting to impose a common universal standard the Commission has missed an opportunity to promote the gradual evolution of a common European fair trading policy and risks making the position worse by imposing a standard that has flaws and which will in some cases be difficult to integrate with national systems. It has placed European politics and perpetuation of the myth of a common European consumer market ahead of developing a sound consumer policy.

---

[44] See Twigg-Flesner *et al*, above n 22.
[45] Case C–237/02 *Freiburger Kommunalbauten v Hofstetter* [2004] ECR I–3403.
[46] This is hard to establish as national follow-up judgments are often less well reported outside the state concerned.

7

Who is the 'Average Consumer'?

STEPHEN WEATHERILL

1. INTRODUCTION

CENTRAL TO THE regime envisaged by the Directive on Unfair Commercial Practices (UCPD)[1] is the notion of consumer as potential victim. It is intended that a harmonised standard of protection will be introduced which will shelter consumers across the European Union from business practices that fall below the chosen level of fairness. But consumers are not uniform in taste, outlook, education or sophistication. Moreover, consumer expectations about the honesty of traders and the utility of public intervention should things go wrong vary enormously across Europe. There may be an 'average consumer'—but in practice few, if any, consumers will be rated average across the wide range of characteristics that serve to define the consumer. If a commercial practice is banned because some consumers are likely to be its victim because they will be misled by it, is there not a risk that other more alert consumers will be deprived of exposure to a practice that may be helpful or informative? If a commercial practice is allowed because some consumers are likely to see through its potential vices and benefit from its virtues, is there not a risk that other less astute consumers will suffer only vice? Choosing the identity of the benchmark consumer-as-victim is clearly of vital importance to the practical implications of a regime designed to control commercial practices which will not have a uniform impact on consumers precisely because consumers themselves do not form a homogenous group.

The UCPD (2005/29) addresses this issue in Article 5. This provides in Article 5(2) that a commercial practice shall be unfair, and accordingly prohibited, if (a) it is contrary to the requirements of professional diligence and (b) it materially distorts or is likely materially to distort the economic behaviour with regard to the product of the average consumer whom it reaches or to whom it is addressed, or of the average member of the group when a commercial practice is directed to a particular group of consumers.

[1] Directive 2005/29 [2005] OJ L 149/22.

Here, then, the benchmark consumer is the 'average consumer', which leaves the legislation vulnerable to the accusation that it sacrifices the less able consumer, who will be exposed as victim of practices that may distort his or her economic behaviour, in order to enhance the position of the average (and above-average) consumer who can cope with the practices in question. However, Article 5 of the Directive does not stop here. This concern is addressed by Article 5(3) of the Directive, which provides that '[c]ommercial practices which are likely to materially distort [*sic*] the economic behaviour only of a clearly identifiable group of consumers who are particularly vulnerable to the practice or the underlying product because of their mental or physical infirmity, age or credulity in a way which the trader could reasonably be expected to foresee, shall be assessed from the perspective of the average member of that group. This is without prejudice to the common and legitimate advertising practice of making exaggerated statements or statements which are not meant to be taken literally'. So here the average consumer is to be considered not in the abstract but rather in its appropriate regulatory context. The purpose of Article 5(3) is to allow scope for the suppression of practices that would not harm the average consumer in the general population but would have a particular impact within a clearly identifiable group of consumers. Accordingly, at least where the pre-conditions of Article 5(3) are met, the Directive does not prohibit targeted protection of particular groups of vulnerable consumers.

So does the UCPD reveal an adequate appreciation of the heterogeneous qualities of consumers? Does it open up the possibility that protection of particularly vulnerable groups of consumers will be ruled incompatible with the requirements of EC law because of the Directive's focus on the 'average consumer' as its regulatory benchmark? The purpose of this chapter is to situate the scheme of Article 5 within the wider context of EC consumer law. It argues that it is conceivable that the Directive may lead to the abandonment of some aspects of national consumer protection, but that such regulatory reform is an inevitable and normal part of the process of market integration in the European Community—a process which itself is designed to bring considerable benefits to the consumer as a result of the prompts of more efficient competition. It also makes the case that the Directive does not exclude the possibility of protecting particularly vulnerable consumers from particularly harmful practices, but rather that the Directive forces national regulators to demonstrate just why they have chosen targeted approaches that treat some consumers as victims, and to show the aptitude of those approaches to achieve their ends. So, it will be argued, the Directive confines national choices about how to protect consumers, but it does not go so far as to eliminate the scope for national action to address particular problems affecting particular groups of consumers. And therefore the chapter's—optimistic—conclusion is that although hardly any consumer really is an 'average consumer', nonetheless the Directive's reliance on the benchmark 'average consumer' should not lead to a homogenised pattern of consumer protection in the EU which ignores the reality that some groups of consumers are peculiarly vulnerable to the status of victim.

2. THE VISION OF THE CONSUMER IN EC LAW—CONSTITUTIONAL INHIBITIONS TO THE DISCOVERY OF REGULATORY COHERENCE

What is the vision of the consumer which emerges from an examination of EC law? There is no consistent narrative. The EC Treaty in its original form contained only five explicit references to the consumer, all of them peripheral.[2] The principal benefits envisaged from the consumer perspective were those derived from the creation of a more competitive market consequent on the elimination of protectionist national practices, but the general economic law provisions of the Treaty do not make explicit the consumer interest in their effective functioning. Only with effect from 1993, and the entry into force of the Maastricht Treaty, has consumer protection been an explicit legislative competence conferred on the EC by its Treaty, but even that provision is relatively weak. Article 153(3)(b) provides that the Community may adopt measures which support, supplement and monitor the policy pursued by the Member States in order to promote the interests of consumers and to ensure a high level of consumer protection. It places the EC in a position subordinate to that of its Member States in matters of consumer protection and it has been the source of relatively few legislative acts.

Most of what is today conventionally labelled 'EC consumer law' is the product of Articles 94 and 95 EC (ex 100 and 100a respectively)—that is, it is harmonisation legislation ostensibly dedicated to the integration of markets in the EC. In so far as national laws governing consumer protection vary, the argument has typically proceeded that the construction of a unified trading space within the EU was hindered. Therefore harmonisation of such laws at EC level was required—'common rules for a common market'. So the strict constitutional purpose of harmonisation was rule-making designed to make an integrated market, but its effect was to allocate to Community level (albeit, by virtue of the commonly used minimum formula, typically not exclusively) the competence to decide on the substance of the relevant rules of consumer protection. So harmonising consumer law is not simply a technical process. It unavoidably means the shaping of a species of European consumer law.

The list of measures which subject national consumer law to the discipline of harmonisation and thereby transfer to EC level the responsibility

---

[2] The evolution of consumer policy in the EC is tracked in chapter 1 of S Weatherill, *EU Consumer Law and Policy* (Cheltenham, Elgar Publishing, 2005).

to shape a common European consumer law to underpin the European economic space is relatively long and conspicuously varied. It includes measures affecting contract law, such as Directive 90/314 on package travel,[3] Directive 93/13 on unfair terms in consumer contracts,[4] Directive 85/577 to protect the consumer in respect of contracts negotiated away from business premises,[5] Directive 87/102 concerning consumer credit, as amended by Directive 90/88 and Directive 98/7,[6] Directive 94/47 on timeshare basis,[7] Directive 97/7 on the protection of consumers in respect of distance contracts,[8] Directive 99/44 on certain aspects of the sale of consumer goods and associated guarantees,[9] and Directive 2002/65 concerning the distance marketing of consumer financial services.[10] Its has a less extensive though far from insignificant coverage in the field of non-contractual liability: Directive 85/374 is the 'Product Liability Directive', harmonising provisions concerning liability for defective products.[11] And the programme of legislative harmonisation also touches what one may conveniently label public or administrative law of consumer protection, concerning for example the establishment of common rules governing product safety[12] and advertising, a group of measures which includes regulation of misleading and comparative advertising,[13] aspects of advertising on television[14] and into which category the UCPD itself comfortably fits.

In some circumstances the perception that diversity among national consumer laws hindered the establishment of a single market may have been genuinely held and justified. In some cases, however, the political reality underpinning the quest for harmonisation was that the Member States were committed to the development of an EC consumer policy and, in the absence of any more appropriate legal basis in the Treaty, chose to 'borrow' the competence to harmonise laws in pursuit of economic integration to put it in place. The question whether such consumer law-making dressed up in the clothes of harmonisation was truly constitutionally valid was not addressed in any practically significant manner.[15] So some EC Directives

---

[3] [1990] OJ L 158/59.

[4] [1993] OJ L 95/29.

[5] [1985] OJ L 372/31.

[6] [1987] OJ L 42/48, amended by Directive 90/88 [1990] OJ L 61/14 and by Directive 98/7 [1998] OJ L 101/17.

[7] [1994] OJ L 280/83.

[8] [1997] OJ L 144/19.

[9] [1999] OJ L 171/12.

[10] [2002] OJ L 271/16.

[11] [1985] OJ L 210/29, amended by Directive 99/34 [1999] OJ L 141/20.

[12] Directive 2001/95 [2002] OJ L 11/4.

[13] Directive 84/450 on misleading advertising [1984] OJ L 250/17, amended by Directive 97/55 on comparative advertising [1997] OJ L 290/18.

[14] Directive 89/552 [1989] OJ L 298/23, amended by Directive 97/36 [1997] OJ L 202/60; Weatherill, above n 1, surveys EC advertising law in ch 8.

[15] But see G Close, 'Harmonisation of Laws: Use or Abuse of Powers under the EEC Treaty?' (1978) 3 *European Law Review* 461, for an early example of 'competence anxiety'.

that harmonise national consumer law and thereby create a species of European consumer law were the product of a political consensus about the desirability of such a development, and were not always blessed with a constitutionally pure 'market-driven' pedigree. Such legislative practice is troublingly inconsistent with the assertion found in Article 5(1) EC that the EC possesses only the competences attributed to it by its Treaty, and it was checked by the European Court's deservedly famous *Tobacco Advertising* ruling, which injects doubt about the constitutional validity of some of the legislative *acquis* in the field of consumer protection.[16] This inquiry into 'competence sensitivity' is of broad interest today in EC law and policy.[17] However, intriguing though it certainly is, it extends beyond the ambitions of this chapter. Suffice to say for present purposes that the Treaty confers no competence to harmonise per se: the competence is more limited than that and is, in short, tied to the process of market-building. Accordingly the UCPD depends for its constitutional validity on a demonstration that it actually contributes to eliminating obstacles to the free movement of goods or to the freedom to provide services, or to removing appreciable distortions of competition. The case in favour of this Directive being validly based on Article 95 EC seems reasonably sturdy.[18]

What is of particular present concern is not so much legal validity, but rather what this package of legislation, developed in this constitutionally ambiguous context, reveals about the 'vision of the consumer' in EC law. Most of all: what might this reveal about the likely shaping of the regulatory technique of the benchmark 'average consumer' favoured by the UCPD? The most prominent feature of the legislative *acquis* is its patchwork character. This is not a systematic programme of consumer law of the

---

[16] Case C–376/98 *Germany v Parliament and Council* [2000] ECR I–8419. See eg J Usher, 'Annotation' (2001) 38 *CMLRev* 1519 and, with particular reference to consumer law, S Weatherill, 'European Private Law and the Constitutional Dimension' in F Cafaggi (ed), *The Institutional Framework of European Private Law* (Oxford, Oxford University Press, 2006) 79. For subsequent case law see eg Case C–491/01 *R v Secretary of State for Health ex parte British American Tobacco (Investments) Ltd and Imperial Tobacco Ltd* [2002] ECR I–11543; Cases C–154/04 & C–155/04 *Alliance for Natural Health* [2005] ECR I–6451.

[17] Eg I Katsirea, 'Why the European Broadcasting Quota should be Abolished' (2003) 28 *European Law Review* 190; N Moloney, 'New Frontiers in EC Capital Markets Law: From Market Construction to Market Regulation' (2003) 40 *CMLRev* 809. See also S Weatherill, 'Why Harmonise?' in P Tridimas and P Nebbia (eds), *European Union Law for the Twenty-First Century: Rethinking the New Legal Order* (Oxford, Hart Publishing, 2004), ii.

[18] See the chs by I Otken Eriksson and U Öberg and by G Abbamonte in this book; J Stuyck, E Terryn and T Van Dyck, 'Confidence through Fairness? The New Directive on Unfair Business-to-Consumer Commercial Practices in the Internal Market' (2006) 43 *CMLRev* 107 at 113–15. For exploration of varying patterns of national regulation see eg R Schulze and H Schulte-Nölke, 'Analysis of National Fairness Laws Aimed at Protecting Consumers in Relation to Commercial Practices', available at http://europa.eu.int/comm/consumers/cons_int/safe_shop/fair_bus_pract/green_pap_comm/studies/unfair_practices_en.pdf; also A Bakardjieva Engelbrekt, *Fair Trading Law in Flux? National Legacies, Institutional Choice and the Process of Europeanisation* (Stockholm, US-AB, 2003).

type that one might hope to be able to identify in a national legal order. Instead it is the product of a rather complex and in part confused combination of influences from the EC's project of market-making pursued through common rule-making mixed with a dose of the political commitment to an EC consumer policy that was pioneered in the 1970s.

3. THE VISION OF THE CONSUMER IN THE EC'S LEGISLATIVE *ACQUIS*

The reality is that there is a European consumer law, albeit in patchwork and constitutionally ambiguous form. Harmonisation causes the EC unavoidably to assume the function of setting its own—common—rules. Community laws come into existence in order to integrate the market, but their incidental effect is additionally to regulate it—or more pertinently to 're-regulate' it in the sense that the Community is not acting as a *de novo* regulator but rather is responding to the pre-existing diverse regulatory choices among the Member States. So harmonisation sets common rules for the European market but it also involves a *choice* of the appropriate common standard of (re-)regulatory protection. Indeed the *quality* of the 're-regulatory' environment established at EC level is constitutionally relevant, as is made clear by the associations between market integration and regulatory protection on which provisions such as Articles 95(3), 6 and 153(2) EC insist.[19] Accordingly harmonisation breaks open traditional national regulatory structures but also stimulates a search for understanding of its 'Europeanising' character. So are built academic sub-disciplines—European environmental law, European sports law, European labour law, European healthcare law, and so on—which typically attempt to bring a degree of order and understanding to this complex background of overlapping sources of legal authority.[20] And, in the field of harmonised consumer law, these phenomena demand inquiry into the 'vision of the consumer' who is the beneficiary of legal protection granted by the EC.

---

[19] See also Art 38 EU Charter. This is non-binding, though this would change in the improbable event that the Treaty establishing a Constitution entered into force, when it would become Art. II–98. This would not, however, alter the admittedly aspirational character which weakens its likely legal force: cf A Kiss, 'Environmental and Consumer Protection' in S Peers and A Ward (eds), *The EU Charter of Fundamental Rights: Politics, Law and Policy* (Oxford, Hart Publishing, 2004).

[20] On environmental law see eg J Jans, *European Environmental Law* (Groningen, Europa Law Publishing, 2000); on labour market regulation and social policy more generally see eg J Kenner, *EU Employment Law: From Rome to Amsterdam and Beyond* (Oxford, Hart Publishing, 2003), C Barnard, *EC Employment Law* (Oxford, Oxford University Press, 2000); on family law see E Caracciolo di Torella and A Masselot, 'Under Construction: EU Family Law' (2004) 29 *European Law Review* 32; on health care law see T Hervey and J McHale, *Health Law and the European Union* (Cambridge, Cambridge University Press, 2004); on sports law see S Weatherill, 'Fair Play Please!: Recent Developments in the Application of EC Law to Sport' (2003) 40 *CMLRev* 51.

This has generated interest in making sense of the thematic connections that bind together the EC's interventions into private law generally and consumer law in particular. Commentators have debated the weight and merits of principles and techniques that pervade the *acquis,* such as information disclosure, respect for party autonomy and inquiry into substantive unfairness.[21] Community consumer law reflects perceptions of market failure which rob the consumer of an efficiently operating market. Intransparency in the market, for example, prompts a legislative response in the shape of mandatory information disclosure, which has become a *Leitmotif* of legislative policy in relation to the protection of economic interests of consumers.[22] In a number of the measures the EC legislative vision of the consumer involves an individual able to take care of him- or herself in the market by digesting and acting upon information that is mandatorily supplied and, if necessary, withdrawing from a deal on reflection after 'cooling-off'. Marketing practices subject to control in this manner are not banned. They are regulated. So for example the vision of the consumer protected by the Door-step Selling Directive is, according to its Preamble, the consumer who is 'unprepared', susceptible to a 'surprise element' in the case of contracts concluded by the trader away from his business premises. But the practice is not forbidden; instead it is regulated. Admittedly there are regrettable differences of detail between the different measures. There is, for example, no uniform length set for the cooling-off period. It varies for no obvious reason beyond inattentive law-making.[23]

---

[21] Eg—and by no means adopting the same outlook—J Stuyck, 'European Consumer Law after the Treaty of Amsterdam: Consumer Policy in or beyond the Internal Market?' (2000) 37 *CMLRev* 367; G Howells and T Wilhelmsson, 'EC Consumer Law: has it Come of Age?' (2003) 28 *European Law Review* 370; S Grundmann, 'Information, Party Autonomy and Economic Agents in European Contract Law' (2002) 39 *CMLRev* 269; S Grundmann, 'European Contract Law(s) of What Colour?' (2005) 1 *European Review of Contract Law* 184; Study Group on Social Justice in European Private Law, 'Social Justice in European Contract Law: a Manifesto' (2004) 10 *European Law Journal* 653; C Joerges, 'Europeanisation as Process: Thoughts on the Europeanisation of Private Law' (2005) 11 *European Public Law* 63; HW Micklitz, 'De la Nécessité d'une Nouvelle Conception pour le Développement du Droit de la Consommation dans la Communauté Européenne' in J Calais-Auloy (ed), *Liber amicorum Jean Calais-Auloy, Etudes de droit de la consommation* (Paris, Dalloz, 2004); N Reich and HW Micklitz, *Europäisches Verbraucherrecht* (Baden-Baden, Nomos, 2003); Rösler, *Europäisches Konsumentenvertragsrecht* (Munich, CH Beck, 2004); K Riesenhuber, *Europäisches Vertragsrecht* (Berlin, de Gruyter, 2003); Weatherill, above n 7.

[22] Cf G Howells, A Janssen and R Schulze (eds), *Information Rights and Obligations: a Challenge for Party Autonomy and Transactional Fairness* (Aldershot, Ashgate Publishing, 2005); W Kerber, S Grundmann and S Weatherill (eds), *Party Autonomy and the Role of Information in the Internal Market* (Berlin, Walter De Gruyter, 2002).

[23] Cf P Rekaiti and R Van den Bergh, 'Cooling-off Periods in the Consumer Laws of the EC Member States: a Comparative Law and Economics Approach' (2001) 23 *Journal of Consumer Policy* 371. Improving the quality of the regulatory environment is a current preoccupation of the Commission; for examination see S Vogenauer and S Weatherill (eds), *The Harmonisation of European Contract Law: Implications for European Private Laws, Business and Legal Practice* (Oxford, Hart Publishing, 2006).

But ex ante information disclosure coupled to ex post right of withdrawal after 'cooling-off' serves as a technique that illuminates broad themes based on the promotion of a 'well-informed consumer' that in turn help to make good the claim that the legislative *acquis* is, at least in part, systematic and coherent. However, this is no free-for-all, nor even a well-informed free-for-all. Concern for the possible exploitation of the economically weaker party is visible in some directives. The EC chooses to ban some practices. Misleading advertising is a long-standing example, prohibited by Directive 84/450. Unfair terms in consumer contracts are prohibited pursuant to Directive 93/13, offering an example of the EC's readiness to assert direct regulation of the *content* of the bargain, not simply the way in which it is made. This, certainly, stands as an important landmark in the shaping of a 'European contract law'.[24] The Preamble to Directive 93/13 draws on the 'soft law' programmes on consumer protection agreed at EC level to assert that 'acquirers of goods and services should be protected against the abuse of power by the seller or supplier, in particular against one-sided standard contracts and the unfair exclusion of essential rights in contracts'. The Court, interpreting the Directive, has hammered home the point: its system of protection 'is based on the idea that the consumer is in a weak position via-a-vis the seller or supplier, as regards both his bargaining power and his level of knowledge'.[25] Here, then, the vision is of a consumer who suffers as a result of structural imbalance in the market place. And the law strikes at unfair terms to which he or she may fall victim.

Do these measures seek to protect the 'average consumer'? It seems that they do. There is no suggestion that these measures are aimed at the protection of particular types of vulnerable consumers. Rather the assumption seems to be that an average consumer is liable to be taken by surprise if confronted by a sales pitch on his or her doorstep; and that any consumer can find him- or herself on the wrong end of a one-sided bargain containing unfair terms. Similarly, any consumer, including the 'average consumer', is entitled to protection when buying package travel or timeshare or credit, all of which are matters regulated at EC level (albeit not exclusively). The vision is therefore of an 'average consumer' who is no superman or superwoman. Rather, the market can operate to the detriment of the average consumer and may therefore need correction.

Therefore the lesson for the proper interpretation of the UCPD is that the legislative *acquis* offers no support for the view that the 'average consumer' is so robust as to need no more than a bare minimum of legal protection.

---

[24] See eg L Niglia, *The Transformation of Contract in Europe* (The Hague, Kluwer Law International, 2003); P Nebbia, 'Law as Tradition and the Europeanization of Contract Law: a Case Study' (2004) 23 *Yearbook of European Law* 363.

[25] Cases C–240/98 C–244/98 *Oceano Grupo Editorial SA v Rocio Murciano Quintero* [2000] ECR I–4941.

Quite the contrary. The 'average consumer' envisaged by the legislative *acquis* is smart enough to (for example) process disclosed information, but he or she is no perfect rational actor. He or she is recognised to be in need of protective rules (admittedly of a patchwork nature).

There is more to the legislative *acquis* that is of interest in understanding the vision of the consumer that should guide the proper interpretation of the benchmark 'average consumer' on which the UCPD is based. The *acquis* does not reveal a homogenous notion of the consumer. There is in particular measures apparent concern for the interests of groups of vulnerable consumers. For example, the position of minors is explicitly recognised in the Distance Selling Directives; so too, in the Television without Frontiers Directive, special provision is made for the impact of advertising on minors.[26] The recognition in Article 5 of the UCPD that vulnerable consumers are capable of forming a defined group the particular characteristics of which should determine the assessment of the relevant regime therefore fits a pre-existing pattern of readiness to take seriously group-specific consumer protection. And, it is submitted, the relevant provisions of the Directive should be read not as a grudging acceptance of an exceptional possibility to act in defence of vulnerable or disadvantaged groups of consumers, but rather as a thematically consistent expression of the proper place in EC consumer law of targeted action to protect particular identified groups or to deal with particular problems. Accordingly the critical Article 5 of the UCPD invites interpretation in the light of a legislative *acquis* which embraces the need for some regulatory protection for the average consumer—and even more regulatory protection for some particularly vulnerable consumers.

4. THE VISION OF THE CONSUMER IN THE COURT'S CASE LAW ON FREE MOVEMENT

What of the 'average consumer' in the Court's case law concerning free movement? Is this where the Directive draws its most visible inspiration? And does this import into the Directive a notion of the robust, commercially astute 'market citizen' who needs little protection? The risk is plain. And yet I argue that this need not follow. In fact—although it is necessary to make due allowance for the different context in which the vision of the consumer is developed in EC free movement law as opposed to the growth of harmonisation legislation—I submit that one can view the 'average consumer' as a generally applicable paradigm which is *not* properly associated with a ruthless deregulatory approach to the construction of the EC's

---

[26] Directive 89/552 as amended, above n 14; see Arts 15, 16 and 22.

internal market. Both the 'average consumer' and, in some cases, particular niche groups of consumer deserve and receive protection under the EC's harmonisation programme, and so too the 'average consumer' and particular niche groups of consumer can be protected by the national regulator even where such intervention impedes cross-border trade, provided a sound justification for such measures is shown. The same approach should apply to the UCPD. It should not be read as a measure intolerant of genuinely justifiable measures of group-specific consumer protection, for that would be inconsistent with the thematic core of EC consumer policy.

My claim that the average—and rather self-aware—consumer is not invariably used in the free movement case law as a lever to deregulate national markets requires closer attention, not least because I freely concede that the majority of the Court's decisions involves findings that national measures of alleged consumer protection are incompatible with the EC Treaty rules governing free movement of goods and services.

4(a) Free Movement Law as an Arena for Judging Competing Visions of the Consumer Interest

It is well known and straightforward that the pursuit of economic integration through law requires a framework for controlling and, where appropriate, prohibiting national rules which obstruct free trade. Several core provisions of the EC Treaty accordingly operate as restrictions on national measures which may have an effect hostile to cross–border trade. These provisions are conventionally termed 'negative', in that their effect is to strike down national measures where they conflict with the 'greater good' of market integration, subject only to narrowly defined exceptions.

Article 28 EC is the principal provision designed to achieve the free movement of goods. It provides that '[q]uantitative restrictions on imports and all measures having equivalent effect shall, without prejudice to the following provisions, be prohibited between Member States'. More helpfully and more broadly, Article 28 has been interpreted by the European Court to prohibit 'all trading rules enacted by Member States which are capable of hindering, directly or indirectly, actually or potentially, intra-Community trade'.[27] So Article 28 operates as a vigorous control over national measures that are hostile to market integration.[28] Article 28's application in the

---

[27] Case 8/74 *Dassonville* [1974] ECR 837.

[28] There is no call here to explore the *Keck* line of case law: its relevance is in short simply to insist on a careful analysis of whether a national rule damages the quest for market integration (in which case it must be justified), or whether it simply limits commercial freedom without impacting on cross-border trade in particular (in which case the rule is an expression of local regulatory autonomy): Cases C–267 & C–268/91 *Keck and Mithouard* [1993] ECR I–6097, analysed by S Enchelmaier, 'The Awkward Selling of a Good Idea, or a Traditionalist Interpretation of Keck' (2003) 22 *Yearbook of European Law* 249.

area of goods has a parallel in Article 49 in the area of services, which has also been interpreted by the European Court as an instrument for controlling national measures that inhibit suppliers of services from treating the wider market as integrated. The core idea—admittedly left inexplicit in the Treaty itself—is that an integrated European market achieves a superior degree of competitiveness and efficiency than is delivered by fragmented national markets, and that this better serves the consumer interest. The Treaty contains a narrow list of exceptions to Article 28 in Article 30, and to Article 49 in Articles 55 and 46, envisaging trade barriers justified on grounds including public policy, public security or public health, but the Court has followed a consistent line whereby the scope of derogation from the basic principle of free movement is construed narrowly. This approach serves to advance the overall cause of welding national markets into a single European market.

An example of what is at stake in the law of free movement is provided by litigation involving *Cassis de Dijon*, an undeservedly famous French blackcurrant liqueur.[29] This case provided the European Court with the opportunity to establish how Article 28 applies to national technical rules governing product composition which do not discriminate according to nationality, but which nevertheless have an effect hostile to market integration. German law imposed restrictions on the marketing of weak alcoholic drink, supposedly as an aspect of consumer health protection. This kept French-made products out of the German market, simply because in France the rules were different—in France weaker drink was allowed than German law would tolerate. So it was a barrier to inter-state trade. The European Court was unable to identify in this measure any coherent policy serving the consumer interest. The German measure simply denied the German consumer the opportunity to try a product made according to a different tradition. The national rule fell foul of Article 28 as unlawful state suppression of consumer choice. German law could therefore not be applied to exclude French-made imports.

Similarly in *Walter Rau v De Smedt*[30] the Court addressed the compatibility with Article 28 of a Belgian law requiring margarine to be marketed in cube–shaped blocks. The Court accepted that such a rule impeded the importation into Belgium of margarine marketed in different ways in other Member States. Consumer choice in Belgium was hampered and, as the Court observed and as economic theory dictates, margarine cost more in Belgium under this regime than in neighbouring states. The Belgian law was presented as a measure of consumer protection: the packaging requirement allegedly made margarine readily identifiable on the shelf and distinct from

---

[29] *Cassis de Dijon* is more formally known as Case 120/78 *Rewe Zentrale v Bundesmonopolverwaltung für Branntwein* [1979] ECR 649.
[30] Case 261/81 *Walter Rau v De Smedt* [1982] ECR 3961.

butter. The Court was unpersuaded that this consideration should override the consumer interest in a competitive cross–border market and enhanced choice. It did not exclude the possibility of national initiatives taken to protect consumers, but the rule at issue was too rigid. 'Consumers may in fact be protected just as effectively by other measures, for example by rules on labelling, which hinder the free movement of goods less.'

At heart the *Cassis de Dijon* ruling, and the Court's general interpretation of the EC Treaty rules governing free movement of goods and services, provides a strong impetus in favour of free trade between Member States in traditional products. It enshrines a principle of (non-absolute) 'mutual recognition'. This holds that if a product is fit for the market of one Member State, then it should normally be considered fit for the markets of all other Member States. Only exceptionally, where a good reason is shown, may products which are satisfactory in their country of origin be excluded from the market of the state to which they are exported.

In seeking to identify the 'vision of the consumer' on which EC consumer law is built, it is of central importance that in the *Cassis de Dijon* ruling the Court was dealing with two competing aspects of the consumer interest. On the one hand, Article 28 represented the consumer interest in market integration and enhanced choice. On the other hand, the challenged German measure was itself presented as a means of consumer protection; it therefore represented the consumer interest in regulation at national level. The Court was choosing in effect between different perceptions of where the consumer interest lay. In *Cassis de Dijon* itself, the resolution was quite straightforward because the German law was a thoroughly unmeritorious method of (alleged) consumer protection. In fact, the real protection enjoyed under the German law was that of German producers able to monopolise consumer choice. In other cases, the balance between consumer choice in the wider market and consumer protection at national level may be finer. This balancing task projects EC trade law into the realms of difficult decisions about what is best for the consumer. And it is here that the 'vision of the consumer' adopted by EC law is most revealing. And these cases merit investigation in an attempt to understand the role of the 'average consumer' under the UCPD.

Schutzverband gegen Unwesen in der Wirtschaft v Yves Rocher GmbH[31] addressed German law prohibiting advertisements in which individual prices were compared, except where the comparison was not eyecatching. Rocher showed that the rule inhibited its ability to construct an integrated marketing strategy because it could not export to Germany techniques used elsewhere in states with more liberal laws. The European Court focussed on

---

[31] Case C–126/91 *Schutzverband gegen Unwesen in der Wirtschaft v Yves Rocher GmbH* [1993] ECR I–2361.

the fact that the German law controlled eyecatching advertisements whether or not they were true. The law suppressed the supply of accurate information to the consumer. The Court's ruling leaves no room for doubt that such a restriction cannot find justification under Community law. And its vision of the consumer is one of the consumer able to process and act on proffered information. *Verband Sozialer Wettbewerb eV v Clinique Laboratories SNC*[32] concerned a German law prohibiting the use of the name 'Clinique' for cosmetics, because of an alleged risk that consumers would be misled into believing the products had medicinal properties. Klinik is the German word for hospital. This ban was held to impede trade in goods marketed in other Member States under the Clinique name. It fell to Germany to show justification for the rule, but it was unable to do this to the Court's satisfaction. The Court was not persuaded that there was sufficient likelihood of consumer confusion for a barrier to trade to be justified. It noted that cosmetics were not sold in outlets specialising in pharmaceutical products. It treated German law as 'over-regulatory'.

The Court's vision of the smart consumer is especially crisply stated in its ruling in *Verein gegen Unwesen in Handel und Gewerbe Köln eV v Mars GmbH*.[33] Mars found that its ambitions to create a pan-European marketing strategy for its ice-cream bars were undermined in Germany. A 'flash' on the wrapper advertised the bar as 10 per cent larger in size for the period of a short publicity campaign. This was accurate. The bar was 10 per cent bigger. But the 'flash' on the wrapper covered a surface area of more than 10 per cent and court proceedings were initiated in Germany with a view to preventing Mars using this device. It was alleged that it would mislead consumers about the size of the bar. Germany was called on to justify its intervention. It could not do so. The Court stated tersely that 'reasonably circumspect consumers' are aware that there is no necessary link between publicity markings relating to the size of increase in a product and the size of the increase itself. Here, then, is the benchmark consumer deployed by the Court to assess the compatibility of national measures with Article 28. The Court does not deny that *some* consumers may be fooled by the marketing practice in question. It contends, however, that the reasonably circumspect consumer would not be. And by implication it concludes that its reading of Article 28 entitles it, in judging the compatibility of the German measure with that provision, to prioritise the advantages of market integration enjoyed by the bulk of consumers over the disadvantages that German law seemed to think would be felt by the stupid few.

---

[32] Case C–315/92 *Verband Sozialer Wettbewerb eV v Clinique Laboratories SNC* [1994] ECR I–317.

[33] Case C–470/93 *Verein gegen Unwesen in Handel und Gewerbe Köln eV v Mars GmbH* [1995] ECR I–1923.

The 'reasonably circumspect' consumer has become a regular visitor to the Court's judgments. It plainly acts as an inspiration for the benchmark 'average consumer' envisaged by the UCPD. A recent example is available from *Commission v Spain*[34], which concerned rules setting a minimum chlorine content for bleach. Spain argued that its consumers expected bleach to be no weaker than the Spanish norm—and that they would be confused to find imported bleach containing less chlorine appearing on the market. This offered an amusing echo of the argument that German consumers expected drinks of the *Cassis de Dijon* type to be stronger than those originating in France. And, 25 years later, the Spanish submissions met the same fate as Germany's in *Cassis de Dijon*. In the Court's view '[t]he reference consumer is an average consumer who is reasonably well informed and reasonably observant and circumspect'.[35] This consumer can adapt to new products. The Spanish rules were not compatible with Article 28.

(b) Critical Examination of the Case Law—what 'Vision of the Consumer'?

This is the material on which one can construct an allegation that the Court has a vision of the consumer as a remarkably self-aware individual who is able to take care of him- or herself adequately in the integrating market without the need for often (longstanding) national measures of consumer protection. One can readily be sceptical of this vision. The literature that questions the ability of consumers to act rationally in a complex market place plays no evident role in these decisions. Can a consumer realistically be expected to absorb and assess disclosed information? Should we impose such an unrealistically conscientious rational model on the vision of the consumer when most consumers, straining to cope with the dauntingly rich diversity of everyday life, have a lot more on their minds than the small print they might find on bottles, packages and contracts if they look hard enough?[36] Such 'behavioural' insights would provide a basis for

---

[34] Case C–358/01 *Commission v Spain* [2003] ECR I–13143.

[35] Para 53 of the judgment. This benchmark consumer also appears in eg Case C–210/96 *Gut Springenheide* [1998] ECR I–4657; Case C–99/01 *Gottfried Linhart & Hans Biffl* [2002] ECR I–9375; Case C–44/01 *Pippig Augenoptik* [2003] ECR I–3095. It is regularly used in assessing confusion for the purposes of trade mark law: see eg J Davies, 'Locating the Average Consumer: His Judicial Origins, Intellectual Influences and Current Role in European Trade Mark Law' (2005) 2 *Intellectual Property Quarterly* 183; also more broadly C Twigg-Flesner, D Parry and G Howells, *An Analysis of the Application and Scope of the Unfair Commercial Practices Directive* (London, DTI, 2005).

[36] Eg J Hanson and D Kysar, 'Taking Behavioralism Seriously' (1999) 112 *Harvard Law Review* 1420; C Sunstein (ed), *Behavioral Law and Economics* (Cambridge, Cambridge University Press, 2000). Cf including adaptation to the European context G Howells, 'The Potential and Limits of Consumer Empowerment by Information' (2005) 32 *Journal of Law and Society* 349.

complaint that the Court expects too much of its 'average consumer' and that it therefore underestimates the harm that may be done to the consumer interest by elimination of national measures and the consequent release on to the market of novel cross-border practices and products. Is the Court concerned with theory not practice? The critique is vividly captured by Monique Goyens: '[h]as any judge or advocate-general ever shopped in a supermarket?'.[37] The Court's rulings are based on an implied and arguably exaggerated expectation that a consumer acquires available information and acts wisely on it.

The anxiety of those who view the Court as too quick to use its vision of the average, reasonably observant consumer to dismiss attempts to justify national rules is that it grants a strong deregulatory momentum to the interpretation of Article 28, which may undermine particular local choices about regulatory intervention.[38] And—such critics would warn—if this approach is transposed to the interpretation of the 'average consumer' criterion in the UCPD then the result will be that all too many practices that are currently suppressed at national level will be permitted on the spurious basis that the 'average consumer' is not harmed by them.[39] Yet—the criticism runs—the average consumer is in fact not so smart!

I understand the risk. But I protest against this reading of the case law. I do not think the Court's case law justifies such a deregulatory interpretation. And I do not believe the Directive should be read in such a fashion.

It is certainly true that in most cases the Court is unimpressed by the arguments advanced in support of national measures of consumer protection. But is this so surprising? *Cassis de Dijon*, along with many of its subsequent applications, illustrates the confrontation between the development of European market integration and the dead wood of centuries of regulatory tradition in the Member States. The Court's formula stands for the need to place the regulatory autonomy of the Member States under a control exercised by EC trade law, and to insist that a justification recognised by EC law be shown for public intervention in the market. As a general observation, the case law offers the Court the opportunity to

---

[37] M Goyens, 'Where There's a Will, There's a Way! A Practitioner's View' (1993) 16 *Journal of Consumer Policy* 375 at 385. In fact, an Advocate General certainly has, but the Court disagreed with his conclusions: see the treatment of Italian rules governing pasta composition in Case 407/85 *Drei Glocken v USL Centro-Sud* [1988] ECR 4233.

[38] Eg Howells and Wilhelmsson, above n 21; C Schmid, 'The Instrumentalist Conception of the Acquis Communautaire in Consumer Law and its Implications on a European Contract Law Code' (2005) 1 *European Review of Contract Law* 211.

[39] Eg T Wilhelmsson, 'The Informed Consumer v the Vulnerable Consumer in European Commercial Practices Law—a Comment' (2006) 1 *Yearbook of Consumer Law* 211; J Pegado Liz, 'The Total Harmonization Trickery: Special Reference to Directive 2005/29/CE and R Incardona and C Poncibo, 'The Average Consumer Test in the Unfair Commercial Practices Directive: Liberal and Anti-Paternalistic or Simply Approximate?', papers delivered at IACL Conference, Malta, Mar 2006, available at www.mcmp.gov.mt/consumer_affairs_sem01.asp.

weed out unrepresentative and outdated manifestations of national-level decision making that are hostile to, and inappropriate in, an integrating European market of the type to which the Member States have committed themselves under the EC Treaty. How could one really defend rules such as those challenged in *Cassis* and in *Walter Rau*? Even in *Mars* the German government presented no serious defence of its claim that German consumers needed protection of a type considered wholly unnecessary elsewhere in the EU. That Germany wishes to assert its autonomy to have different consumer protection rules from those prevailing elsewhere is an inadequate justification, for the very core of EC trade law is to put national measures to the test—to balance their advantages against disadvantages felt by out-of-state traders excluded from the regulated market and disadvantages felt by affected in-state parties, most obviously consumers denied wider choice. That the state's political processes have (at some point in the past) generated such a law is not of itself enough to legitimate it. One might, of course, object to the values that the Court attaches to particular interests when it makes these decisions, or doubt whether, say, trade integration and the interest in, for example, maintaining press diversity [40] or a viable public health care system[41] can truly be weighed on the same scale; additionally, one might wish to reflect on whether a judicial forum is the appropriate place to make such choices.[42] The deeper such case law intrudes into national practices that reflect sensitive cultural, moral and social choices the more acute such anxieties become: *Cassis de Dijon* was after all a relatively easy case! But—in my view—most of the cases involving measures of alleged national consumer protection are easy too. The rules in *Mars* were, seen in this light, simply indefensible on the basis of the case advanced so feebly by Germany. In other words, I agree with the Court's assessment based on the material available to it that the 'average consumer' benefits more from choice in the wider market than from 'protection' from the bold wrappers used by Mars. I make a similar assessment of the Court's insistence in *Procureur de la République v X*,[43] a reference from France, that a

[40] Eg Case C–368/95 *Vereinigte Familiapress Zeitungsverlags- und vertriebs GmbH v Heinrich Bauer Verlag* [1997] ECR I–3689.

[41] Eg Case C–157/99 *B S M Geraets-Smits v Stichting Ziekenfonds VGZ, H T M Peerbooms v Stichting CZ Groep Zorgverzekeringen* [2001] ECR I–5473; Case C–372/04 *Ex parte Watts*, judgment of 16 May 2006.

[42] Cf M Poiares Maduro, 'Striking the Elusive Balance between Economic Freedom and Social Rights in the EU' in P Alston (ed), *The EU and Human Rights* (Oxford, Oxford University Press, 1999); R Craufurd Smith, 'Community Intervention in the Cultural Field' in R Craufurd Smith (ed), *Culture and European Law* (Oxford: Oxford University Press, 2004); P Oliver, 'Competition and Free Movement: Their Place in the Treaty' in P Tridimas and P Nebbia (eds), *European Union Law for the 21st Century—Rethinking the New Legal Order* (Oxford, Hart Publishing, 2005).

[43] Case C–373/90 *Procureur de la Republique v X* [1992] ECR I–131. See Weatherill, above n 2, at 173–5.

practice be judged misleading only if a significant number of consumers fall victim to it. At stake was an opportunity to promote integration and competition in the market for cars, which is notoriously fragmented and poor at serving the consumer interest. The matter would have been different had Germany or France shown just why its consumers—or, more pertinently, a particular group of vulnerable consumers—were exposed to particular risks. They failed to do so.

AXA Royale Belge is a ruling that has attracted particular criticism for perceived preference for market integration over 'contractual justice among the parties'.[44] True, the Court ruled against Belgian rules requiring disclosure of information by suppliers of life assurance. But this conclusion was reached in circumstances in which the EC legislature itself had in Directive 92/96 chosen to confine the scope for stricter national rules as part of an overall legislative bargain which involves mandatory common rules of information disclosure. In other words, the case was largely concerned with legislative pre-emption,[45] and I consider that it provides very thin support for a case that the Court neglects the merits of information disclosure as a technique of market regulation favouring vulnerable consumers.

Note too that the Court has on occasion been persuaded of the worth of national measures of consumer protection, even where they are restrictive of cross-border trade. National rules which restricted the marketing of strong alcoholic drink were ruled compatible with Article 28 (ex Article 30) in *Aragonesa de Publicidad Exterior SA (APESA) v Departamento de Sanidad y Seguridad Social de la Generalitat de Cataluna (DSSC)*.[46] Even though such rules affected the sales of such drink from other Member States, the Court was persuaded that the benefits of consumer choice should not prevail over the consumer interest in public health protection set by the regulating body at national level. Thus EC law does not create a wholly deregulated 'free for all' in the market.[47] This ruling provides a neat contrast to the Court's entirely understandable scepticism in *Cassis de Dijon* that controlling the supply of *weak* alcoholic drink could form part of a coherent policy of public health protection.

The protection of the economic interests of consumers was found to be an acceptable basis for a trade-restrictive national rule in *Ministère Public v Buet*.[48] The Court held that a French law which prohibited 'doorstep selling'

---

[44] Schmid, above n 38, at 222; cf S Grundmann, 'European Contract Law(s) of What Colour?' (2005) 1 *European Review of Contract Law* 184 at 189–190.

[45] The Opinion of AG Jacobs is fuller on this point than the judgment of the Court.

[46] Cases C–1, C–176/90 *Aragonesa de Publicidad Exterior SA (APESA) v Departamento de Sanidad y Seguridad Social de la Generalitat de Cataluna (DSSC)* [1991] ECR I–4151.

[47] On the broader issues involved in the balance between free(d) trade and national-level regulation see S Weatherill, 'The Internal Market' in S Peers and A Ward (eds), *The EU Charter of Fundamental Rights: Politics, Law and Policy* (Oxford, Hart Publishing, 2004) 183–210.

[48] Case 382/87 *Ministére Public v Buet* [1989] ECR 1235.

of educational material was not incompatible with Article 28 in view of its contribution to the protection of consumers from pressure selling tactics. It was of significance that the national law was designed to protect consumers behind with their education and wishing to improve it. So the Court, in assessing the compatibility of the measure with EC trade law, took into account the national regulator's concern to protect a particular group of vulnerable consumers. So too in *A-Punkt Schmuckhandels v Claudia Schmidt*.[49] In considering Austrian rules restraining the sales achieved through the organisation of 'jewellery parties' in private homes, the Court was prepared to accept the relevance in justifying such restrictions of the potentially higher risk to consumers of being cheated by lack of information, impossibility of comparing prices and exposure to psychological pressure to buying in such a private setting. This was context-specific consumer protection—and it was treated as such by the European Court. By contrast, in *Yves Rocher* for example,[50] there were no such special considerations: the national rule simply prevented *all* consumers finding out (accurate) information. The Court did not find this a compelling justification.

In *Estee Lauder Cosmetics*[51] the Court re-deployed its formula based on 'the presumed expectations of an average consumer who is reasonably well informed and reasonably observant and circumspect' in judging whether a challenged state measure could survive the application of Article 28, but it added that 'social, cultural or linguistic factors' may justify special local anxiety about particular practices tolerated elsewhere.[52] Consumers are different across Europe, and so are consumer laws: but Articles 28 and 49 EC do not automatically sweep aside diverse national choices on a destructive tide of homogenisation. Instead they put those national rules to the test of justification. The Court invites national regulators to show it what are the special concerns underpinning a challenged trade-restrictive measure: it routinely insists that 'the fact that one Member State imposes less strict rules than another Member State does not mean that the latter's rules are disproportionate and hence incompatible with Community law'.[53] The problem is that regulating authorities rarely accept the Court's invitation by advancing worthwhile arguments. Instead they irritate the Court with lazy submissions of the type found in cases such as *Cassis de Dijon*, *Walter*

---

[49] Case C–441/04 *A-Punkt Schmuckhandels v Claudia Schmidt* judgment of 23 Feb 2006.
[50] Case C–126/91 *Schutzverband gegen Unwesen in der Wirtschaft v Yves Rocher GmbH* [1993] ECR I–2361.
[51] Case C–220/98 *Estee Lauder Cosmetics* [2000] ECR I–117.
[52] AG Fennelly's Opinion in the case explores factors that may lead to variation state by state. Cf on linguistic factors Case C–313/94 *Graffione Snc v Ditta Fransa* [1996] ECR I–6039.
[53] Eg in connection with the free movement of goods, Case C–294/00 *Deutsche Paracelsus Schulen* [2002] ECR I–6515, and in connection with the free movement of services Case C–3/95 *Reisebüro Broede v Gerd Sanker* [1996] ECR I–6511.

Rau v de Smedt and *Mars.* In fact, these feeble attempts to justify absurd protectionist rules probably simply reflect the lingering over-representation of local trading interests in national political processes against which EC trade law is directed. Articles 28 and 49 serve to challenge the Member States' persistent failure to engage constructively in consideration of what degree of regulatory protection a consumer requires in an integrating European market.

(c) The Court is not so Unrealistic! (but National Authorities Are)

I take very seriously the argument that one must take a realistic view of the capabilities of the consumer when one devises a programme of regulatory protection. As a general observation, if one over-estimates the ability of the consumer to act rationally in response to (inter alia) a programme of information disclosure, then one will adopt an unduly positive view of the correctability of the market, and the result will be the exposure of consumers, acting foreseeably irrationally, to market imperfections and/or injustice. However, my assessment is that once one considers the weak arguments that contaminate national justifications for trade-restrictive rules of alleged consumer protection, combined with the important perception that the consumer benefits from choice and competition flowing from a well-managed programme of market integration, it is hard to make good the case that in practice the Court is guilty of sweeping aside worthwhile measures of national consumer protection. In particular, targeted measures designed to protect particular groups of vulnerable or disadvantaged consumers are not imperiled provided their nature and purpose are properly defined and justified. My conclusion is that the Court's case law is built on the notion of an average, reasonably circumspect consumer who possesses a degree of self-reliance, but that it is receptive to seriously presented arguments about the limits of consumer capability and the reality that some consumers are peculiarly vulnerable. The main theme of the case law is that national regulators typically come empty-handed to Luxembourg.[54]

5. THE 'AVERAGE CONSUMER' UNDER THE UCPD

Let us dissect Article 5 of the UCPD in the light of the EC's legislative *acquis* and the Court's case law on free movement. Article 5(2) of the Directive refers to the 'average consumer' as the benchmark in assessing the impact of

---

[54] The argument here follows Weatherill, above n 2, ch 2. For a thorough investigation see M Radeideh, *Fair Trading in EC Law: Information and Choice in the Internal Market* (Groningen, Europa Law Publishing, 2005).

a particular commercial practice. One may readily suppose that this should and will be read with reference to the Court's case law under (in particular) Article 28 EC. The intent is that a practice which will distort the behaviour only of the unusually inattentive consumer should be allowed—just as the Court's case law reveals that national measures that are of value only to the exceptionally unobservant consumer cannot normally be successfully defended if shown to act as barriers to inter-state trade. Recital 18 of the Directive makes the link explicit. It refers to examination of 'the effect on a notional, typical consumer' in the Court's case law on advertising cases under Directive 84/450. Accordingly the Directive, via its Recitals if not its provisions, 'takes as a benchmark the average consumer, who is reasonably well-informed and reasonably observant and circumspect, taking into account social, cultural and linguistic factors'.[55] The Recital also refers to another matter that has caused some anguish in the case law by insisting that the 'average consumer test is not a statistical test. National courts and authorities will have to exercise their own faculty of judgement, having regard to the case-law of the Court of Justice, to determine the typical reaction of the average consumer in a given case.'

Article 5(3) of the Directive addresses the anxiety that this approach may damage a consumer protection policy dedicated to the interests of the vulnerable. It providers that '[c]ommercial practices which are likely to materially distort the economic behaviour only of a clearly identifiable group of consumers who are particularly vulnerable to the practice or the underlying product because of their mental or physical infirmity, age or credulity in a way which the trader could reasonably be expected to foresee, shall be assessed from the perspective of the average member of that group. This is without prejudice to the common and legitimate advertising practice of making exaggerated statements or statements which are not meant to be taken literally.' Recital 18 amplifies what is at stake in the Directive's recognition of the special case of vulnerable consumers. It states that '[w]here a commercial practice is specifically aimed at a particular group of consumers, such as children, it is desirable that the impact of the commercial practice be assessed from the perspective of the average member of that group. It is therefore appropriate to include in the list of practices which are in all circumstances unfair a provision which, without imposing an outright ban on advertising directed at children, protects them from direct exhortations to purchase.' And this duly appears in Annex I. It is unfair to include in an advertisement 'a direct exhortation to children to buy advertised products or persuade their parents or other adults to buy advertised products for them. This provision is without prejudice to

---

[55] Early drafts included the Court's terminology in the Directive proper, but in the finally agreed text it is confined to the Recitals.

Article 16 of Directive 89/552/EEC on television broadcasting.' Recital 19 adds that '[w]here certain characteristics such as age, physical or mental infirmity or credulity make consumers particularly susceptible to a commercial practice or to the underlying product and the economic behaviour only of such consumers is likely to be distorted by the practice in a way that the trader can reasonably foresee, it is appropriate to ensure that they are adequately protected by assessing the practice from the perspective of the average member of that group'.

More generally the Directive, according to its Recital 7, 'does not address legal requirements related to taste and decency which vary widely among the Member States. Commercial practices such as, for example, commercial solicitation in the streets, may be undesirable in Member States for cultural reasons. Member States should accordingly be able to continue to ban commercial practices in their territory, in conformity with Community law, for reasons of taste and decency even where such practices do not limit consumers' freedom of choice. Full account should be taken of the context of the individual case concerned in applying this Directive, in particular the general clauses thereof.' This is a distinct point, but falls within the general assessment of the scope of the Directive's concessions to local regulatory preference.[56]

How to judge this? There is, of course, no pretence here that there is an actual 'average consumer' on whom to rely: this is an attempt to navigate a course between the rich diversity of actual consumer behaviour and the need for an operational regulatory benchmark. That may be artificial, but in devising a harmonised system of regulation to underpin an integrated European market it is unavoidable.[57] It is much the same game that the Court plays in applying the Treaty rules on free movement. In my opinion Article 5(3) should be read with reference to the Court's case law under Article 28 EC which accepts that a system of consumer protection which can be shown to target protection of a particular group of consumers should be assessed on its own terms, and should not be swept aside on an unthinking application of the broad 'average consumer' test. That is to say, if the law is not designed to deal with a problem which would concern the average consumer, it must not be assessed as if it were so designed. This, of course, does not mean that the Court will not look hard at the claims made in support of the law. Frequently, as the case law examined above reveals, the claimed advantages of national measures do not stand up to close scrutiny. But in principle a regulator can advance arguments designed to show the inappropriateness of the 'average consumer' test as a basis for reviewing

---

[56] Stuyck, Terryn and Van Dyck, above n 18, at 122–123; Wilhelmsson, above n 39, at 222–5.
[57] Cf on regulatory technique F Gomez, 'The Unfair Commercial Practices Directive: A Law and Economics Perspective' (2006) 2 *European Review of Contract Law* 4.

a particular challenged measure, and the Court will in principle be receptive to such contextual arguments. This, I submit, is how Article 5(3) should be read. It serves as an invitation to the regulator to demonstrate just how and why a particular practice should be suppressed as incompatible with the Directive's control even though it is a practice that would not distort the behaviour of the 'average consumer' in the general population. So the Directive—as EC consumer law generally, in both legislative and judicial practice—is not blind to the needs of particular disadvantaged or vulnerable groups. Quite the contrary: it accepts the place of such targeted measures of consumer protection. It requires only that choice made by regulators be properly explained and justified, under an assumption which holds that national measures which restrict cross-border trade require such justification because, by impeding market integration, they damage the consumer interest in a more efficiently functioning market which delivers wider choice and competition on price and quality. But, it is submitted, if there are good reasons for asserting that particular practices harm a clearly identifiable group of vulnerable or disadvantaged consumers, then the pattern of EC law—in the case law of the Court and in the legislative practice considered above—amply supports the view that it is that group which should form the focus of assessment, not an abstract 'average consumer'. And in this way the Directive would not be used to slice away legitimate consumer protection in niche areas.

So far, so optimistic. But does Article 5(3) *really* lend itself to this interpretation? The features of vulnerability to which it chooses to draw attention are 'mental or physical infirmity, age or credulity'. What of educational attainment? Income? Ethnicity? There is a considerable amount of empirical research into patterns of consumer deception and the list in Article 5(3) has convincingly been described as 'quite arbitrary' in its restrictive approach by Stuyck, Terryn and Van Dyck, who call for empirical inquiry into the correlation between the characteristics of certain groups of consumers and the likelihood of vulnerability to particular practices.[58] I agree with this. Evidence of the particular effect of a practice will have to be advanced.[59] But it is important that the Directive be interpreted in a way that is receptive to the whole range of possible vulnerabilities and disadvantages with which particular groups of consumers are burdened. As a matter of detailed interpretation, the way to achieve this under Article 5(3) of the Directive is to take a broad view of what may be regarded as 'credulity'. This should be taken to cover, for example, consumers' 'emotional' foibles.[60] More

---

[58] Stuyck, Terryn and Van Dyck, above n 18, at 121–2.

[59] Cf discussion of the absence of such evidence in the *Duchesne* case initiated by the UK's Office of Fair Trading before the courts in Belgium, discussed by HW Micklitz 'Transborder Law Enforcement—Does it Exist?' in this book.

[60] Cf Incardona and Poncibò, above n 38.

generally, one should appreciate that—as this chapter has made abundantly clear—the vision of the consumer in EC judicial and legislative practice is sophisticated enough to take account of a broad sweep of possible vulnerabilities and disadvantages. Moreover, the Court has shown no hesitation in interpreting harmonised measures affecting consumer protection in a manner apt to achieve effective protection of the consumer, recognising the consumer's relatively weak position relative to the supplier.[61] No less is needed in the case of the UCPD. After all, the promotion of a high level of consumer protection in the EC is given constitutional force by Articles 95(3) and 153 EC. This is enough to justify a reading of Article 5(3) which insists on full account being taken of the need for genuine measures of targeted consumer protection, whatever the particular detailed aspect of vulnerability that may be at stake. Similarly the phrase in Article 5(3) which requires that 'the trader could reasonably be expected to foresee' the vulnerability of a particular group should be interpreted in a manner which is fully consistent with the need to promote space for genuine initiatives of consumer protection designed to protect particular vulnerable or disadvantaged groups from practices harmful to them. In particular if a regulator could reasonably be expected to foresee such an impact then it should be concluded that so could a trader! To conclude by re-connecting this examination of the Directive to the Court's existing case law under Article 28 EC, the important feature of a typical decision such as *Mars* is that Germany failed to demonstrate the existence of a particular vulnerable group of consumers likely to be damaged by the marketing practice in question. The ruling does *not* rule out properly crafted and properly explained control of practices aimed at consumers generally but evidently designed to exploit and likely to exploit only the vulnerable. This is how Article 5(3) of the Directive should be understood too.

6. CONCLUSION

The EC's internal market programme constitutes an exercise in deregulation but also an exercise in re-regulation. Harmonisation of laws deregulates the market by eliminating legislative diversity across the EU in favour of a common regime, but choices must be made about the content and quality of that single re-regulatory standard. This 'dual function' claimed by harmonisation is the key to understanding how the pattern of 'EC consumer law' has taken ever more intricate shape, despite the relative absence of explicit treatment of consumer interest in the Treaty itself. The UCPD fits comfortably into this trend. Agreeing a common rule brings with it an

---

[61] Eg Cases C–240/98–C–244/98 *Oceano Grupo Editorial SA v Rocio Murciano Quintero* [2000] ECR I–4941.

inevitable debate about the content and quality of that common rule. And that debate is by no means terminated once the legislative institutions of the EC have had their say, because inevitably points of interpretative ambiguity are delegated for resolution by the Court. The purpose of this chapter has been to situate that task of judicial interpretation in the wider context of EC law's 'vision of the consumer'. Most of all I have attempted to show that the Directive need not and should not be read in way that damages the protection of vulnerable or disadvantaged groups of consumers. Instead the Directive should be read with proper awareness of the empirically verifiable consumer who may not behave in a perfectly rational manner because he or she is poor at digesting or assessing information and/or because he or she simply chooses not to allocate scarce resources to intense examination of available information. EC law—in both legislative and judicial practice— does not deny the existence of such a consumer. And therefore the Directive should be applied with respect for the reality of consumer behaviour. Nor does EC law exclude an appreciation that the average consumer is different across Europe. It may normally prove to be the case that common assessments of the presence or absence of unfairness prevail across the EU, but it remains conceivable that a practice may be harmless in state X but harmful, and therefore unlawful, in state Y because consumers in state Y have different tastes, abilities or expectations. This would not be the application of a different legal standard in state Y when contrasted with state X: instead it would be the application of the same legal standard, but taking account of different conditions prevailing in the two markets.

My view is that the case law of the Court does not exclude these interpretations—quite the contrary, it supports them. And the EC's legislative *acquis* buttresses the argument that consumers are not always smart and self-reliant and that they may require regulatory protection. The issue, however, is that where regulatory intervention occurs, the explanations advanced must be a good deal more sophisticated than those which litter the Court's case law under Article 28, from *Cassis* to *Mars*. EC law generally, and this Directive in particular, is built on an assumption that the integration of markets benefits consumers, and this is frequently a benefit that exceeds the costs of diminished regulatory protection at national level—if, indeed, such diminution is a cost at all, which it surely was not in a case such as *Cassis*. But the law leaves space for the national regulator to present seriously considered justification for rules aimed at protecting the consumer interest. This is true of Article 28 EC, and it is true of Article 5 of the UCPD.

Am I too optimistic? There is of course a risk that this Directive will be used to attack legitimate initiatives of consumer protection. Let us try to counter that risk, while also appreciating the value to the consumer of a well-functioning integrated European market. The way to achieve this has been set out in this chapter.

8

The Relationship of the Unfair Commercial Practices Directive to European and National Contract Laws

SIMON WHITTAKER

1. INTRODUCTION

THE ENACTMENT OF the Unfair Commercial Practices Directive of 2005 (UCPD)[1] marks two radical departures in the evolution of the consumer *acquis*. First, it sets a very broad standard of commercial behaviour in relation to consumers in a 'general clause' which prohibits practices which, contrary to 'professional diligence', 'materially distort the economic behaviour' of an average consumer,[2] rather than following the previous approach of European legislation which has targeted particular types of unfair commercial practices, such as 'doorstep selling',[3] the operation of timeshares,[4] and package travel.[5] This general standard frames particular protections given to consumers by existing directives (though these special provisions prevail over the UCPD where they conflict[6]), and is fleshed out

---

[1] Directive 2005/29/EC of the European Parliament and of the Council of 11 May 2005 concerning unfair business-to-consumer commercial practices in the internal market and amending Council Directive 84/450/EEC, Directives 97/7/EC, 98/27/EC and 2002/65/EC of the European Parliament and of the Council and Regulation (EC) No 2006/2004 of the European Parliament and of the Council [2005] OJ L 149/22 ('UCPD' or '2005 Directive').

[2] Ibid, art. 5.

[3] Council Directive 85/577/EEC of 20 Dec 1985 to protect the consumer in respect of contracts negotiated away from business premises [1985] OJ L 372/31.

[4] Directive 94/47/EC of the European Parliament and of the Council of 26 Oct 1994 on the protection of purchasers in respect of certain aspects of contracts relating to the purchase of the right to use immovable properties on a timeshare basis [1994] OJ L 280/83.

[5] Coussncil Directive 90/314/EEC of 13 June 1990 on package travel, package holidays and package tours [1990] OJ L 158/59.

[6] UCPD, above n 1, Art 3(4).

by the 2005 Directive itself by the setting of two main examples of unfair commercial practices: misleading actions[7] and misleading omissions.[8] The 2005 Directive also provides a black list of particular commercial practices which 'are in all circumstances [to be] considered unfair'.[9]

Secondly, the UCPD broke away from the established pattern of earlier consumer protection directives by setting (in general) a maximum as well as a minimum legislative regulation to be implemented by Member States: it requires 'uniform rules'[10] and 'full harmonisation'.[11] So, apart from the exceptional situations provided for by Article 3 of the 2005 Directive,[12] Article 4 declares that Member States 'shall neither restrict the freedom to provide services nor restrict the free movement of goods for reasons falling within the field approximated by [the] Directive', that is, 'unfair commercial practices harming consumers' economic interests'.[13] This change in the nature of the legislative consumer protection required by Member States is inspired by internal market considerations, as Article 4's heading ('Internal market') and the Directive's own recitals make very clear.[14]

However, there is a third, less obvious way in which the 2005 Directive innovates when compared with a good deal of the consumer *acquis*, for it seeks to establish a clear distinction between its own form of consumer protection (which is concerned with 'laws, regulations and administrative provisions of the Member States on unfair commercial practices harming consumers' economic interests'[15]) and 'contract law'. This appears from Article 3(2) which provides that '[t]his Directive is without prejudice to contract law and, in particular, to the rules on the validity, formation or effect of a contract' and from Recital 9 which clarifies that this 'without prejudice' clause applies equally to 'Community and national rules on contract law'. This provision rests, therefore, on a distinction between the protection of consumers through administrative rules, criminal penalties and the like on the one hand and through regulating the legal (contractual) relationship between businesses and consumers themselves on the other. While such a distinction may easily be recognised by national lawyers,

---

[7] Ibid, Art. 6.

[8] Art 7 of the UCPD, above n 1.

[9] Ibid, Art 5(5) referring to Annex I.

[10] Recital 5 of the UCPD, above n 1.

[11] Recital 15 of ibid.

[12] Notably, as regards national rules relating to the health and safety aspects of products, ibid, (Art 3(3)) 'rules determining the jurisdiction of the courts' (Art 3(7)), 'conditions of establishment of or authorisation regimes, the deontological codes of conduct and other special rules governing regulated professions (Art 3(8)), requirements for financial services and immovable property (Art 3(9)) and rules relating to the certification and indication of the standard of fineness of articles of precious metal (Art 3(10)).

[13] Ibid, Art 1.

[14] Ibid, recitals 1 to 6.

[15] Ibid, Art 1. This also appears from the Directive's enforcement provisions, Arts 11–13.

broadly reflecting, perhaps, divisions between public law and criminal law on the one hand and private law on the other, it is striking that a good deal of the consumer *acquis* has rather sought to tie these two forms of consumer protection together. By contrast, the purpose of Article 3(2) is apparently to divorce these two forms of consumer protection, whether at a national or a European level.

In this chapter, I wish to consider the force of Article 3(2)'s 'without prejudice' clause. I will argue that while it saves 'contract law' (as specially and quite broadly understood for these purposes) from the 'fully harmonising' impact of the 2005 Directive, it does not preclude the Directive's provisions from influencing the development of both European and national contract law. However, as regards national laws, the extent to which and the way in which it will do so will depend to a considerable extent on the nature of national contract law rules and the interpretative attitudes of national courts.

2. DISTINGUISHING REGULATORY CONSUMER PROTECTION AND 'CONTRACT LAW'

I have earlier suggested that a good deal of European legislation enacted for the protection of consumers has sought to tie in new laws governing the legal rights and duties of parties to consumer contracts and administrative or regulatory intervention aimed at consumer protection. I think that this can be seen in two ways.

First, some European initiatives have combined the two sorts of protection in the same directive. So, for example, the Unfair Terms in Consumer Contracts Directive of 1993[16] requires Member States to make provision for the judicial review of unfair contract terms (as it defines them), both as between the parties to contracts and in proceedings brought by public authorities or consumers' associations ('persons or organizations having a legitimate interest under national law in protecting consumers') aimed at the cessation of the use or recommendation for use of unfair contract terms.[17] In this way, a consumer can rely on the 1993 Directive's protections in a dispute as to the rights and obligations arising from the contract itself (given that any unfair contract terms falling within the requirement of fairness are 'not binding' on consumers[18]), but Member States must also authorise consumer protection bodies (whether public or private) to intervene in the interests of preventing the use of unfair terms in consumer contracts. So, the

---

[16] Council Directive 93/13/EC of 5 Apr 1993 on unfair terms in consumer contracts ('Unfair Terms in Consumer Contracts Directive' or '1993 Directive') [1993] OJ L 95/29.
[17] Ibid, Arts 2–7.
[18] Ibid, Art 6(1).

1993 Directive is clearly directed to the alteration of consumer contract law (as it governs the validity of most contract terms and can sometimes even affect the validity of the whole contract[19]), but sometimes concerned instead with controlling the unfair commercial practice of using or recommending for use unfair terms in consumer contracts through preventive measures.

Moreover, the European Court of Justice has treated these two types of control as complementary. For example, in *Océano Grupo Editorial SA v Murciano Quintero*[20] the European Court was asked whether a national court had the power under the 1993 Directive to assess the fairness of a term of a consumer contract of its own motion. In holding that it did possess such a power, the European Court relied on the risk to the effectiveness of the protections given to consumers if they were themselves obliged to raise the unfair nature of such terms, given their likely legal ignorance and lack of legal advice.[21] But the European Court supported this view by reference to the aim sought by the preventive measures 'since if the court undertakes . . . an examination [of a term of its own motion], that may act as a deterrent and contribute to preventing unfair terms in contracts concluded between consumers and sellers or suppliers'.[22] In this way, the aim of this 'regulatory' aspect of the 1993 Directive was seen as helpful in the interpretation of an aspect of its 'contractual' aspect.

Secondly, the enactment of the Consumer Injunctions Directive in 1998[23] created a more general link between regulatory intervention of this sort (actions for injunctions brought before judicial or administrative bodies aimed at the protection of the collective interests of consumers) and the protections put in place by directives to govern the relative rights and duties of parties to consumer contracts, for the 1998 Directive's requirements as to actions for injunctions were applied to a number of directives which (at least in part) are concerned with the parties' contractual relations, as in the case of the Distance Contracts Directive[24] and the Timeshare Directive (both of which give a brief general right of withdrawal from the contract to the consumer and a longer right if specified information is not supplied)[25] and the Consumer Credit Directive (which entitles a consumer

---

[19] Ibid, Art 6(1) provides that 'that the contract shall continue to bind the parties upon those terms if it is capable of continuing in existence without the unfair terms' and so assumes that sometimes the contract itself will cease to bind the parties.

[20] Joined Cases C–240/98–C–244/98 *Océano Grupo Editorial SA v Murciano Quintero* [2000] ECR I–4942.

[21] Ibid, para 26.

[22] Ibid, para 28.

[23] Directive 98/27/EC of the European Parliament and of the Council of 19 May 1998 on injunctions for the protection of consumers' interests [1998] OJ L 166/51.

[24] Directive 97/7/EC of the European Parliament and of the Council of 20 May 1997 on the protection of consumers in respect of distance contracts [1997] OJ L 144/19, art 6.

[25] Directive 94/47/EC of the European Parliament and of the Council of 26 Oct 1994 on the protection of purchasers in respect of certain aspects of contracts relating to the purchase of the right to use immovable properties on a timeshare basis [1994] OJ L 280/83, Art 5.

borrower to pay off the loan early)[26]. And, subsequently, the Consumer Guarantees Directive of 1999 (which requires the introduction of certain rights in respect of 'contractual non-conformity' against sellers in contracts of consumer sales) was added to the list of directives the infringement of which harming the collective interest of consumers attracts an action for an injunction under the 1998 Directive.[27] In this way, therefore, an overall strategy of linking the controls put in place governing the contracting parties' relative rights with wider, preventive controls aimed at the policing of the market in the interests of consumer protection is promoted.

How, therefore, did the change in thinking reflected in Article 3(2) of the UCPD take place? This change is apparently explicable by the development by the European Commission of two parallel processes of review of European law affecting consumers which were initiated within a few months of each other in 2001, the one focussed on the development of a 'general clause' governing unfair commercial practices in the interests of the internal market,[28] the other on the possible harmonisation of European private law, and especially of contract law.[29] Nevertheless, to start with, the *travaux préparatoires* of the UCPD appeared to reflect a degree of joined-up thinking as to the way in which consumer protection should develop. So, in putting forward the idea of a 'framework directive' for the regulation of unfair commercial practices, the Green Paper on European Union Consumer Protection of 2001[30] compared the 'general test' which this would require to the approach found in the Unfair Contract Terms Directive, where a very open test of evaluation is used and an 'indicative list' of terms which may be unfair is provided.[31] And while the Green Paper considered that 'national contract law requirements would be excluded' from the proposed directive,[32] the latter would draw on:

ECJ jurisprudence and existing EU legal concepts, notably on misleading advertising and unfair contract terms tests, and;
National examples on issues such as misleading and deceptive practices, undue influence or pressure, disclosure, vulnerable consumers, equitable bargains and good faith[33].

---

[26] Council Directive 87/102/EEC of 22 Dec 1986 for the approximation of the laws, regulations and administrative provisions of the Member States concerning consumer credit [1987] OJ L 42/48, Art 8, as last amended by Directive 98/7/EC [1998] OJ L 101/17.

[27] Directive 1999/44/EC of the European Parliament and of the Council of 25 May 1999 on certain aspects of the sale of consumer goods and associated guarantees [1999] OJ L 171/12, Art 10.

[28] EC Commission, Green Paper on European Union Consumer Protection, COM(2001)531 final of 2 Oct 2001.

[29] Communication from the Commission to the Council and the European Parliament on European Contract Law, COM(2001)398 final.

[30] Above n 28.

[31] Ibid, para 4(1); 1993 Directive, above n 16, Art. 3(3) and Annex.

[32] Ibid.

[33] Ibid.

So, the provisions of the UCPD were themselves intended to draw (in part) on both European and national laws of contract, the latter being understood in the sense of the law governing the relative rights and duties of contracting parties, as the examples given in the second part of the above passage indicate.

However, by the time of the 2002 'Follow up Communication to the Green Paper on EU Consumer Protection',[34] the review of the 'contract law' aspects of the consumer *acquis* had been clearly separated from the proposed new 'framework directive' which was later enacted as the UCPD, as it notes that:

> the possibilities for reform of the contract law provisions in existing directives that have proved problematic would be examined in the context of the follow-up to the communication on European contract law.[35]

So, Article 3(2) of the UCPD puts 'contract law' on one side, so as to prevent the enactment of its own framework provisions from being delayed by the further and wider consideration of the future of European contract law. In this respect, it is to be noted that the earlier, very broad possibilities mooted by the Commission in 2001 as to the development of European private law (including contract law) appear to have been very much watered down.[36] So, in its most recent communication of September 2005,[37] the Commission's emphasis here was very much on the review of the contractual consumer *acquis* and a possible role of a Common Frame of Reference to be put in place in order to improve the quality and consistency of the *acquis* in the area of contract law.[38] At the time of writing, the precise nature of any future EC action in relation to the review of the contractual (consumer) *acquis* remains unclear, as do the content, status and role of any Common Frame of Reference.

In my view, the existence of this continuing and wide-ranging debate on European contract law explains the 2005 Directive's stipulation that its provisions are 'without prejudice' to national or European contract law. But does this mean that the 2005 Directive's provisions cannot and will not affect the development of European or national contract law?

In this respect, it is helpful to note the use of the phrase 'without prejudice' at other points in Article 3 of 2005 Directive: thus, the Directive is

[34] COM(2002)289 final.

[35] Ibid, para 27.

[36] Communication, above n 29; Communication from the Commission to the European Parliament and the Council, 'A More Coherent European Contract Law—An Action Plan', COM(2003)68 final; Communication from the Commission to the European Parliament and the Council, 'European Contract Law and the revision of the *acquis*: the way forward,' COM(2004)651 final.

[37] EC Commission, First Annual Progress Report on European Contract Law and the Acquis Review, COM(2005)456 final

[38] Ibid, para 2.6.1. and para 3.

said to be 'without prejudice to Community or national rules relating to the health and safety aspects of products'; 'to the rules determining the jurisdiction of the courts'; and to 'conditions of establishment of or authorisation regimes, the deontological codes of conduct' and other special rules governing regulated professions.[39] These other examples of the phrase confirm, first, that the Community and national rules in these areas *may* continue unaffected by the provisions of the Directive, this being particularly significant given the full harmonisation which the Directive generally requires.[40] Indeed, this way of thinking is specifically confirmed in the case of Article 3(2)'s 'without prejudice' provision as regards contract law by Recital 15 which is concerned with the impact of Directive's requirements of information for consumers under Article 7 (any failure to provide the information in question being capable of being a 'misleading omission'). Recital 15 provides that:

> Member States will be able to retain or add information requirements *relating to contract law and having contract law consequences* where this is allowed by the minimum clauses in the existing Community law instruments. Given the full harmonisation introduced by this Directive only the information required in Community law is considered as material for the purpose of article 7(5) thereof. Where Member States have introduced information requirements over and above what is specified in Community law, on the basis of minimum clauses, the omission of that extra information will *not* constitute a misleading omission under this Directive.[41]

So, while Member States cannot maintain or introduce more stringent information requirements than those set out by Article 7 of the 2005 Directive for the purposes of the regulatory controls which the Directive itself requires,[42] they may do so in areas of consumer *contract* law either where the circumstances are unaffected by Community legislation or where the Community legislation in question is minimal in its nature. This illustrates very nicely the significance of Article 3(2): it preserves the freedom of Member States to govern the rights and duties of parties to a consumer contract despite the fully harmonising nature of the 2005 Directive, even if the substantive content of this 'contract law' overlaps with the substantive content of the requirements put in place by the 2005 Directive. However, in my view, this does not mean that the provisions of the UCPD *must not and cannot* have any effect on the development or interpretation of Community or national contract laws, as such a required negative effect could be equally prejudicial to their development. Rather, Article 3(2) leaves it to EC

---

[39] UCPD, above n 1, Art 3(3), 3(7) and 3(8) respectively.
[40] Ibid, Art 4 and see above. Cf also the contribution of Howells to this book.
[41] Ibid, extract (emphasis added).
[42] These are found in the 'Final Provisions' of Ibid, Ch 4, Arts. 11–14.

law (either the legislator or the Court) and to national law (again, the legislator or the courts) to decide whether or not to use the UCPD as a source for the development of their 'contract laws' in the sense of the law governing the rights and duties of the parties to contracts. As has earlier been suggested, such a development may take the form of a legislative change of 'contract law' by a Member State on the basis of the 2005 Directive or some of its provisions, but even more significant is likely to be the question whether either the European Court of Justice or national courts would see this Directive as helpful in the interpretation of existing legal rules, whether legislative or otherwise.

Before looking at these possibilities, however, there is a further point relating to what is meant by 'contract law' for these purposes. Article 3(2) refers to 'contract law and, in particular, to the rules on the validity, formation or effect of a contract'. The particular emphasis of this provision on 'validity' and 'formation' of contracts within contract law is explicable by the substantive content of the requirements of the 2005 Directive, for the two broad limbs of unfair legislative practices which it sets out[43] concern the provision or failure to provide information and the use of improper pressure, practices the traditional contractual expressions of which (such as misrepresentation, undue influence and duress in English law[44] or *dol* and *violence* in French law[45]) go to the validity of the contract.[46] Moreover, the Directive is also concerned with commercial practices which concern the exercise by a consumer of rights which he or she enjoys under the contract. This appears from the general definition of prohibited commercial practices, which includes a condition that the practice 'material distorts or is likely to materially distort the economic behaviour with regard to the product of the average consumer',[47] this notion being defined to mean 'using a commercial practice to appreciably impair the consumer's ability to make an informed decision, thereby causing the consumer to take a transactional decision that he would not have taken otherwise'.[48] Finally, 'transactional decision' is defined as:

> any decision taken by a consumer concerning whether, how and on what terms to purchase, make payment in whole or in part for, retain or dispose of a product *or*

---

[43] Ibid, Arts 6–9. The unfair practices in the Annex are also divided between 'misleading commercial practices' and 'aggressive commercial practices'.

[44] GH Treitel, *The Law of Contract* (London, Sweet & Maxwell, 2003) ch 9 and 10.

[45] Art 1108 Code civil (the general provision as to invalidity); Art 1116 Code civil (*dol*); Arts 1111–1115 Code civil (*violence*).

[46] 'Validity' may, of course, be differently understood in different legal systems. So, in English law, misrepresentation and duress give rise to a unilateral right of rescission in the contracting party affected (*Redgrave v Hurd* (1881) 20 Ch D 1 (misrepresentation); *Pao On v Lau Liu Long* [1980] AC 614, 634 (duress), whereas in French law, *dol* and *violence* give rise to 'relative nullity', which permits the party affected to apply to a court for the annulment of the contract: Art 1117 Code civil.

[47] 2005 Directive, above n 1, Art 5(2)(b).

[48] Ibid, Art 2(e).

to exercise a contractual right in relation to the product, whether the consumer decides to act or to refrain from acting.[49]

So, a consumer's exercise of his or her contractual right may be affected by misleading information or aggressive behaviour by the business so as to constitute an unfair commercial practice within the meaning of the 2005 Directive. In some national laws, this sort of situation would attract the application of contractual controls based, for example, on performance in good faith or a doctrine of the abuse (by the business) of rights.[50] And it is for this reason in particular that the Directive's provisions were expressed as having no prejudicial effect on Community or national law's rules on the effects of contracts.

However, these examples from national law again raise the question of the boundaries of what is meant by 'contract law', but in a different way. So far, I have understood 'consumer contract law' (as distinguished from the regulation of business behaviour in the interests of consumers) in terms of the relative rights and duties of the parties to the contract.[51] However, this leaves open the question whether Community law or (and especially) national law needs to classify those rights *as contractual*. For while the law governing the possible invalidity of a contract on the ground of fraud, misrepresentation or duress is likely to form part of 'contract law' in any sense of these words, the law governing any possible claim for damages as a result of these same 'practices' by the other party to a contract may be considered contractual, but may instead be considered tortious or extra-contractual. So, for example, in English law a person who is induced to enter a contract as a result of a false pre-contractual statement may be able to claim damages in tort[52] or on the basis of a contractual warranty,[53] whereas in French law 'pre-contractual liability' is in general considered as extra-contractual (and is usually based on the general law of liability for fault[54]), while in principle any liability arising after contract between the parties will *only* be contractual.[55] This sort of possible divergence among national laws in the conceptual classification of liabilities arising between parties to a contract by reason of the sorts of practices addressed by the

---

[49] Ibid, Art 2(k) (emphasis added).

[50] So, eg, in French law: P Malaurie, L Aynès and P Stoffel-Munck, *Droit civil—Les obligations* (Paris, Defrénois, 2004) 351–4.

[51] Above, p. 144 text accompanying n 43.

[52] There are three main bases for such a tort claim: the tort of deceit (*Derry v Peek* (1889) LR 14 App Cas 337); the tort of negligence (*Hedley Byrne & Co Ltd v Heller & Partners Ltd* [1964] AC 465) and the Misrepresentation Act 1967 s 2.

[53] *Esso Petroleum Ltd v Mardon* [1976] QB 801.

[54] Arts. 1382–1383 Code civil and see J Bell, S Boyron and S Whittaker, *Principles of French Law* (Oxford, Oxford University Press, 1998) 313–4.

[55] This results from the rule of *non-cumul des responsabilités contractuelle et délictuelle*: ibid, 331–2.

2005 Directive[56] is, in my view, a good reason for interpreting 'contract law' for the purposes of Article 3(2) in a way which includes *any* laws which govern the relative rights, duties or liabilities of the parties to a consumer contract, whatever the formal classification as a matter of national law, since such an autonomous interpretation of 'contract law' for the purposes of the Directive avoids disparities in the application of the 'without prejudice' clause as between different national laws.

3. POSSIBLE INFLUENCES OF THE UCPD ON 'CONTRACT LAW'

Broadly speaking, there are three ways in which the UCPD may influence the development of 'contract law' in the sense in which I have just described it: it may be used as a basis of legislative change; its way of thinking may infiltrate porous European or national legal norms or concepts; and its paradigm of fair commercial behaviour may challenge contrasting national legal approaches. Interestingly, the same *substantive* influence of the Directive may take effect in different ways in the different national laws.

(a) Using the 2005 Directive as a Basis for Wider Legislative Changes

Having raised this as a possibility, it does not, however, seem very likely to me that the UCPD will be used by national legislatures as the basis for reform of contract law in the sense of the specific rules of validity of contracts or the exercise of contractual rights. These are matters which may well overlap with and, to an extent, echo the concerns of this Directive, but its scheme is fundamentally concerned with providing a proper basis for the preventive measures which it requires (whether actions of cessation or criminal sanctions) rather than with the effects on the relative rights and duties of the contracting parties: to use the one as the basis for the other risks an inappropriate private law regulation, at least without considerable adaptation. However, given the extended sense of 'contract law' which I have argued is necessary for the proper interpretation of Article 3(2),[57] the UCPD may well influence the development of extra-contractual

---

[56] Apart from differences between contractual and tortious liabilities in damages, laws of Member States may treat the restitutionary consequences of invalidity of a contract differently, some treating these very firmly as part of contract law (because they are seen as part of the effects of contractual nullity), whereas others may treat them as restitutionary, reflecting the application of a principle of unjustified enrichment. So, in French law these consequences are treated as part of contract law, specifically the so-called '*théorie des nullités*' (see Malaurie, Aynès and Stoffel-Munck, above n 50, 305ff), whereas many English lawyers see them as being restitutionary even if arising within a contractual context.

[57] See above pp. 146–7.

liability owed by one party to a contract (the business) to the other (the consumer). So, for example, in its consultation exercise the UK government asked whether breach of the duties (or some of the duties) to be imposed on implementation of the Directive should give rise to 'civil redress' and, if so, what form this civil redress should take.[58] The government expressed the view that 'sometimes, going to court is the only way for consumers to obtain justice. And giving consumers rights which are directly enforceable in the civil courts may encourage traders to try and resolve problems through other means first.'[59] The Office of Fair Trading has responded by arguing for the imposition of civil liability in respect of *all* breaches of the UCPD,[60] and proposing that the most appropriate form for this to take would be the creation of a private right of action in the tort of breach of statutory duty, principally aimed at the imposition of damages but making provision for judicial discretion as to the most appropriate remedy for the consumer.[61] If this approach were adopted by the legislation implementing the 2005 Directive, this would form a very nice example of the legislative adoption of its scheme of control for the development of 'contract law' in the wider sense which I have identified.

(b) The Infiltration of Underdeveloped Concepts or Porous Norms

A potentially much broader influence of the UCPD is likely to be in relation to the interpretation of wider European and national laws, particularly where they use porous norms or underdeveloped concepts.

(i) EC Law: Interpretative Integrity in the Consumer Acquis

As I have earlier explained, the UCPD provides the framework for the existing consumer *acquis* in relation to unfair commercial practices as well as making new specific provision, but it nevertheless itself forms part of a much wider legislative expression of the EU's wider consumer protection policy, the consumer *acquis*. One of the effects of this belonging to the consumer *acquis communautaire* is that the European Court of Justice draws on its case law in relation to one directive in interpreting the provisions of another directive, while taking proper account of any distinct and, at times,

---

[58] DTI, *The Unfair Commercial Practices (UCP)Directive: Consultation on implementing the EU Directive on Unfair Commercial Practices and Amending Existing Consumer Legislation* (London, DTI, December, 2005), questions 23–26, ch 10.

[59] Ibid, para 179.

[60] Office of Fair Trading, *Implementing the EU Directive on Unfair Commercial Practices and Amending Existing Consumer Legislation, A Consultation Response by the Office of Fair Trading* (London, OFT 839, Mar 2006), para. 3.59.

[61] Ibid, paras 3.60–3.61.

different wording or purposes of the two or more different instruments. To take just one example, in *Cape Snc v Idealservice Srl*[62] the European Court interpreted the definition of 'consumer' for the purposes of the Unfair Contract Terms Directive which refers to 'acting for purposes which are outside his trade, business or profession'[63] in the light of its earlier decision in *Di Pinto*,[64] which concerned the notion of consumer for the purposes of the Door-step Selling Directive.[65]

In this respect, the UCPD furnishes a very nice example of the European *legislator* drawing on the case law of the European Court of Justice but also developing its notions in order to define one of the elements of its regulation. Recital 18 explains that:

> It is appropriate to protect all consumers from unfair commercial practices: however the Court of Justice has found it necessary in adjudicating on advertising cases since the enactment of Directive 84/450/EEC[[66]] to examine the effect on a notional, typical consumer. In line with the principle of proportionality, and to permit the effective application of the protection contained in it, this Directive takes as a benchmark the average consumer, who is reasonably well-informed and reasonably observant and circumspect, taking into account social, cultural and linguistic factors, as interpreted by the Court of Justice, but also contains provisions aimed at preventing the exploitation of consumers whose characteristics make them particularly vulnerable to unfair commercial practices. Where a commercial practice is specifically aimed at a particular group of consumers, such as children, it is desirable that the impact of the commercial practice be assessed from the perspective of the average member of that group.[67]

Article 5 of the Directive itself therefore draws a triple distinction: (i) the average consumer; (ii) the average member of the group where a commercial

---

[62] Joined Cases C–541/99 & C–542/99 *Cape Snc v Idealservice Srl* [2001] ECR I–09049, paras. [23]–[28].

[63] 1993 Directive, above n 16, Art 2(b).

[64] Case 361/89 *France v Di Pinto* [1991] ECR I–1189.

[65] Council Directive 85/577/EEC of 20 Dec 1985 to protect the consumer in respect of contracts negotiated away from business premises, Art 2 [1985] OJ L 372/31.

[66] Council Directive 84/450/EEC of 10 Sep 1984 relating to the approximation of the laws, regulations and administrative provisions of the Member States concerning misleading advertising [1984] OJ L 250/17. For the case law see: Case C–44/01 *Pippig Augenoptik GmbH & Co. KG v Hartlauer Handelsgesellschaft mbH* [2003] ECR I–3095, para 55. The Court has referred to the notion of 'average consumer' in other contexts: Case C–210/96 *Gut Springenheide GmbH and Rudolf Trusky v Oberkreisdirektor des Kreises Steinfurt—AMT für Lebensmittelüberwachung* [1998] ECR I–04657 (marketing standards for eggs); Case C–220/98 *Estée Lauder Cosmetics GmbH & Co OHG v Lancaster Group GmbH* [2000] ECR I–00117 (marketing of cosmetics). For an extensive discussion in the context of the 2005 Directive, see C Twigg-Flesner *et al*, *An Analysis of the Application and Scope of the Unfair Commercial Practices Directive, A Report for the Department of Trade and Industry* (May 2005), available at www.dti.gov.uk/ccp/topics1/unfair.htm, at 15–30; also the contribution of Weatherill to this book.

[67] UCPD, above n 1, extract.

practice is directed to a particular group of consumers; and (iii) the average member of a clearly identifiable group of consumers who are particularly vulnerable to the practice or the underlying product because of their mental or physical infirmity, age or credulity in a way which the trader could reasonably be expected to foresee.[68] Now this legislative use of the European Court's case law is, of course, extremely interesting in itself—but it is also significant for present purposes as it suggests that the European Court is likely to draw on these refinements of its own notion of 'average consumer' as regards *other* directives within the consumer *acquis*. Again, the Unfair Terms in Consumer Contracts Directive comes to mind, as one could well see it as appropriate for a court to distinguish in determining the fairness or the 'plainness and intelligibility' of a contract term for the purposes of this Directive according to the *type* of consumer at whom the contract terms were aimed. So, for example, where a business aims a complex financial service at a target group of sophisticated consumers, the intelligibility of its contract terms should be assessed by reference to a standard of 'average consumer' of this group, taking into account their likely ability to understand more complex terms and concepts. Conversely, where a business markets its goods or services to a particularly vulnerable group of consumers, perhaps even one whose members he knows or can foresee will not understand the language type in which the terms are drawn, the standard of 'average consumer' should be adjusted taking into account their likely lack of understanding of language of the contract terms.[69] In this way, enactment of the UCPD can be seen as introducing a new and quite elaborate piece into the jigsaw puzzle of provisions which form the consumer *acquis*, both regulatory and 'contractual'. And while European legislative intervention in this area has sometimes been criticised as being piecemeal ('pointillist'[70]), the European Court certainly strives to ensure a degree of integrity in its interpretation of the various directives.[71]

(ii) Reception in National Laws through the Porous Nature of Certain Legal Norms or Concepts?

There is a second way in which the 2005 Directive may influence the interpretation of legal concepts, but this time at a national level. For, where national laws use open concepts or norms, such as a principle of good faith in contract or a principle of extra-contractual liability for harm caused by

---

[68] Ibid, Art 5(2) and (3).

[69] The question of the impact of the 1993 and 2005 Directives on the language types of consumer contracts is discussed further in S Whittaker, 'The Language or Languages of Consumer Contracts' (2007) 8 *Cambridge Yearbook of European Legal Studies* (forthcoming).

[70] WH Roth, 'Transposing "Pointillist" EC Guidelines into Systematic National Codes—Problems and Consequences' (2002) 10 *European Review of Private Law* 761.

[71] Above text accompanying nn 63 ff.

fault, then the particular provisions of the Directive's own more specific requirements may infiltrate these porous elements in the national laws of 'contract'. Here, I will provide a few examples from French law of how this could occur.[72]

First, under the French Civil Code, contracts may be invalidated on the ground of *dol*, and at first this notion drawn from Roman law was interpreted as requiring positive action (such as a false statement), really very much like the English law of fraud.[73] However, in the course of the later twentieth century, French writers and courts extended the impact of *dol* so as to allow the invalidation of contracts on the ground of failure to speak in circumstances where they thought that a party to a contract should have spoken (this being termed *dol par réticence*).[74] This includes cases where a would-be party to a contract owes the other a legal duty to speak (*une obligation d'information* or *une obligation de renseignement*).[75] What this means is that the setting of legal duties of information by legislation implementing the UCPD[76] in France will have an indirect effect on invalidity of the contract under the Civil Code where a business's failure to inform was deliberate, as it will set the circumstances where the business ought to have provided information.

However, secondly, an even broader likely indirect effect will be on the imposition of liability in damages. By Articles 1382 and 1383 of its Civil Code, French law imposes a notoriously broad basis for the imposition of extra-contractual (or 'delictual') liability, so that any fault causing harm of any type will in principle attract liability.[77] For this purpose, 'fault' has been interpreted very broadly and can include breach of any duty, legislative, regulatory or even customary.[78] This means that in French law the breach of the duties of information which the UCPD imposes on businesses will give rise to civil liability in damages for any harm caused as a result,

---

[72] Others could be seen as regards English law, eg, use of one of the commercial practices listed in the Annex to the Directive which 'shall in all circumstances be regarded as unfair' could be seen as in itself satisfying the 'illegitimacy' required by the common law of duress. More controversially, perhaps, the duties of information required by the Directive could be seen as overcoming the general absence of any duty of disclosure for the purposes of the validity of the contract. For a comparison of the rules at common law and those provided by the Directive, see Twigg-Flesner *et al*, above n 66 at 53–59, who also consider that the Directive does not require any change to existing domestic concepts, though 'this does not mean that, over time, there will not be some adjustment of domestic rules, eventually resulting in convergence between UCPD and domestic concepts': ibid, at 61.

[73] On French law, see Bell, Boyron and Whittaker, above n 54, 316–7. For English law see *Derry v Peek* (1889) LR 14 App Cas 337. In principle, a person who fails to inform another of a matter of which he knows does not commit fraud as there is no general duty of disclosure: *Smith v Hughes* (1871) LR 6 QB 597; *Bell v Lever Bros Ltd* [1932] AC 161.

[74] Bell, Boyron and Whittaker, above n 54, 316–7.

[75] Ibid, 317–8.

[76] The duties of information are set out in the 2005 Directive, above n 1, Art 7.

[77] Bell, Boyron and Whittaker, above n 54 357–60.

[78] Ibid.

without the need for any special legislative provision to this effect,[79] as has been mooted in the UK context.[80] French law's general principle of extra-contractual liability for fault could also provide a legal basis for the imposition of liability for financial losses or by upset (*dommages moraux*) caused by a business which commits those unfair commercial practices specifically banned by the Annex to the Directive, for example, false claims as to personal safety of consumer or family[81] or the various examples of threatening or abusive behaviour.[82]

Thirdly, French contract law recognises a general principle of good faith in the creation, performance and non-performance of contracts.[83] While expressed in the Civil Code only in relation to the performance and non-performance of contracts,[84] French writers later saw it as forming the basis for the imposition of pre-contractual duties of information[85] and of the imposition of liability for the abrupt breaking-off of pre-contractual negotiations.[86] Contractual good faith (and the related concept of the abuse of contractual rights) has certainly gained in importance in French law over the last 20 years or so, but its impact has become more controversial, reflecting in part a debate as to whether *general* contract law should itself be more 'social'.[87] The influence of the UCPD here would again be to provide more specific material on which a court could hold that a business party to a consumer contract had been acting in bad faith (or abusing its contractual powers). To take one example, Annex 1 to the Directive specifies the following commercial practice as one which will in all circumstances be considered unfair:

> requiring a consumer who wishes to claim on an insurance policy to produce documents which could not reasonably be considered relevant as to whether the claim was valid, or failing systematically to respond to pertinent correspondence, in order to dissuade a consumer from exercising his contractual rights.[88]

---

[79] In this respect the duties of information in the Directive are likely to be considered as 'pre-contractual' so as to avoid the impact of French law's rule of *non-cumul des responsabilités contractuelle et délictuelle* (on which see above n. 55).

[80] Above text at n 60.

[81] 2005 Directive, above n 1, Art 5(5), Annex 1, para 12.

[82] Ibid, paras 24–31.

[83] Bell, Boyron and Whittaker, above n 54 313–14, 335–6; R Zimmermann and S Whittaker, *Good Faith in European Contract Law* (Cambridge, Cambridge University Press, 2000) 32–9.

[84] Art 1134 al 3 Code civil (performance). The idea of good faith in non-performance can be seen in the aggravating of liability for deliberate non-performance ('*l'inexécution dolosive*'): Art 1150 Code civil.

[85] J Ghestin, 'The Pre-contractual Obligation to Disclose Information, French Report' in D Harris and D Tallon (eds), *Contract Law Today: Anglo-French Comparisons* (Oxford, Oxford University Press, 1989) 151, 153.

[86] Bell, Boyron and Whittaker, above n 54, 313.

[87] Malaurie, Aynès and Stoffel-Munck, above n 50, 351–4.

[88] UCPD, above n 1, Annex I, para 27.

So, where an insurance company acts in this way (and quite apart from any 'penalties' imposed by way of implementation of Article 13 of the Directive), it could be held to be acting in bad faith in the performance or non-performance of the contract so as (i) to deny the effectiveness of any purported exercise of a contractual right by the business and/or (ii) to give rise to contractual liability.

Of course, in this way the 2005 Directive does not change French law as such and a French court could well hold that the sort of commercial practice stigmatised as unfair by the 2005 Directive will constitute 'fault' for the purposes of liability under Articles 1382 and 1383 of the Civil Code or bad faith for the purposes of its law of contract without reference to the Directive's provisions, but implementation of the Directive in France will nevertheless crystallise what constitutes 'wrongfulness' for these purposes in a form from which the French courts can very easily draw. In this way, the introduction by an EC Directive of a new element of regulation in national law may have an indirect effect on the interpretation or the application of elements formally unaffected by it.

4. CHALLENGING THE PARADIGM OF (SOME) NATIONAL CONTRACT LAWS

Even given its limitation to consumer contracts, the UCPD's declaration of a very general prohibition on unfair commercial practices marks a very striking difference from the starting point of some national laws, of which English law is the obvious and key example.

As has been noted, the approach of the Directive is general, principled and based on a very open-textured standard of good practice. So, Article 5's 'general clause' defines the unfair commercial practices which it prohibits by reference to two key elements. The first element is that a commercial practice will be prohibited as unfair if it is 'contrary to the requirements of professional diligence', the latter being defined as:

> the standard of special skill and care which a trader may reasonably be expected to exercise towards consumers, commensurate with honest market practice and/or the general principle of good faith in the trader's field of activity.[89]

While this uses some language familiar to the English common lawyer ('the standard of special skill and care which a trader may reasonably be expected to exercise', which is reminiscent of the tort of negligence), it also refers (rather oddly, both cumulatively and in the alternative) to the 'general principle of good faith', a principle which English law formally denies, as I shall explain.[90]

[89] Ibid, Art 2(h).
[90] Below, text accompanying nn 93 ff.

Moreover, the ambit of this principle in the Directive is very wide, for the second element of Article 5(2)(b) refers to the 'material distortion' of the economic behaviour with regard to the product of the average consumer' which, as has been explained, can affect any aspect of a business's behaviour in relation to a transaction (and, therefore, a contract), whether at its formation, performance or non-performance.[91]

By contrast, the *general* approach taken by the English common law of contract denies a principle of good faith, fairness or the abuse of rights in relation to the creation, performance and non-performance of contracts.[92] For the majority of English lawyers, such a general principle is seen as having too much potential for interference with freedom of contract, the binding force of contracts and the certainty of contractual transactions, but it has not prevented English law from adopting a very considerable number of what Bingham LJ (as he then was) called 'piecemeal solutions' so as to deal with aspects of contractual fairness which in other legal systems would be dealt with by good faith.[93] These piecemeal solutions include the overt recognition of the relevance of good faith in particular circumstances (notably, in the regulation of terms in consumer contracts[94]) or as regards particular contracts, notably the implied term as to good faith and loyalty in contracts of employment,[95] fiduciary duties in certain types of contractual relations (for example, agency[96]) and legal duties 'of the utmost good faith' (*uberrimae fides*) in contracts of insurance.[97] Otherwise, English law employs a range of different techniques to deal with the sorts of qualification on a stark model of contract which in other legal systems are sometimes dealt with by reference to a principle of good faith, some at common law (notably, through use of 'reasonableness' in the construction of contracts, the implication of reasonable if 'necessary' contract terms, the law of frustration,[98] and unconscionability[99]), and some by statute (notably, through the control of unfair contract terms,[100] and the mandatory protection of consumers,[101] tenants[102] and employees[103]).

---

[91] Text at n 47.
[92] S Whittaker in H Beale (gen ed), *Chitty on Contracts* (London, Sweet & Maxwell, 2004) para 1–020 ff, where this established position and its qualifications are explained.
[93] *Interfoto Picture Library Ltd v Stilletto Visual Programmes Ltd* [1989] 1 QB 433 at 439.
[94] Unfair Terms in Consumer Contracts Regulations 1999, SI 1999/2083, implementing the 1993 Directive, above n 16.
[95] *Johnson v Unisys Ltd* [2001] UKHL 12; [2003] 1 AC 518, at para [24].
[96] FMB Reynolds in Beale (gen ed), above n 92, para 31–116 ff.
[97] PJS MacDonald Eggers in ibid, para 41–28 ff.; *Carter v Boehm* (1766) 3 Burr 1905 where Lord Mansfield went further, holding that good faith was required in all contracts.
[98] The leading authority is *Davis Contractors v Fareham UDC* [1956] AC 396.
[99] H Beale in Beale (gen ed), above n 92, para 7–111 ff.
[100] Unfair Contract Terms Act 1977.
[101] Eg Consumer Credit Act 1974.
[102] Formerly, the Rent Act 1977, and subsequently Housing Act 1988 (for private tenancies).
[103] The legislation here is particularly complex, but for an introduction see MR Freedland in Beale (gen ed), above n 92, ch 39.

As this list suggests, the range of techniques and their impact are very considerable, but the established position remains that these do not reflect a general principle of good faith in English contract law.

How could this position be affected by the 2005 Directive? A radical response by the courts to the new legislative paradigm of fair behaviour by businesses to consumers would be to reconsider the common law's denial of a principle of good faith *as regards consumer contracts*. Such a response would have the attraction of giving a substantive consistency to the law governing consumer contracts, whether 'contractual' or 'regulatory' and, as regards the 'contractual' side, would give a certain unity to the piecemeal interventions which the English courts and legislator have introduced. However, in my view, such a recognition of principle is unlikely for a number of reasons. First, where legislation has intervened for the protection of consumers, English judges are likely to see this intervention as defining the protection to be put in place, following their fundamental view of statutes as exceptions in the pattern of the common law: an English judges will not see statutory interventions as a ground for the drawing of a wider principle.[104] Secondly, and related to this, English courts are likely to see the enforcement mechanisms put in place by the UCPD and its UK implementing legislation as sufficient and, in some sense, defining of its consequences (this being supportable by Article 3(2)'s own 'without prejudice' provision). And, thirdly, English judges would find it difficult to develop (actually, to change) the common law so as to recognise a principle of good faith in relation solely to consumer contracts as the common law does not distinguish these as a distinct category. On the other hand, outside this category (and notably as regards commercial contracts), the courts may well consider that a principle of good faith should continue to play no role, not least because the UCPD does not seek to govern the behaviour of one commercial party to another.

Nevertheless, even if the courts do not see the UCPD as a reason for a radical change of principle, this still leaves the possibility that existing common law mechanisms which may be seen as giving effect to notions of contractual fairness or good faith may be used as a possible means of achieving at least something approaching the sort of shift in paradigm which the Directive suggests. However, care must be taken here. For example, an area which may be thought of at first as a particularly fruitful means of introducing good faith into the relationship of the parties after the conclusion of the contract is the interpretation of express terms and the finding of implied terms. Certainly, the courts have, on occasion, qualified express contractual powers (for example, to terminate the contract) by reference to reasonableness.[105] But there is a potentially difficult relationship here

---

[104] B Nicholas, 'The Pre-contractual Obligation to Disclose Information, English Report' in Harris and Tallon (eds), above n 85, 166 at 178.
[105] Eg *Rice v Great Yarmouth BC* (2001) 3 LGLR 4 (CA).

between contractual interpretation at common law and legislative regulation of unfair contract terms. For, where an express term in a consumer
contract gives a power to the business (notably, under a termination, cancellation or variation clause), the *potential* for its exercise unreasonably
would be a factor arguing for the unfairness of the term under the Unfair
Terms in Consumer Contracts Regulations, which implemented in the UK
the 1993 Directive.[106] It would be odd if a court were to interpret a wide
express contract term narrowly (perhaps qualifying it by reference to a condition of reasonableness) so that it avoided being held 'not binding' on the
consumer under the Regulations.[107] Here, therefore, the 2005 Directive's
acceptance of a substantive requirement of good faith should not render
another European Directive's protection less effective.

5. CONCLUSION

At first sight, the statement in Article 3(2) of the UCPD that its provisions
are 'without prejudice' to 'contract law' suggests that it will have no effect
on either national or Community contract laws. In this chapter, I have
argued that this Article should be given a more restrictive interpretation,
being concerned rather to ensure that national contract laws do not need
to be changed so as to conform to the fully harmonised pattern of regulation set out by the 2005 Directive. Moreover, I have suggested that the
Directive may indeed affect both European and national contract laws,
taking 'contract laws' for this purpose in the sense of the law governing the
relative rights and duties of parties to consumer contracts however these
are formally classified.

In this respect, it is one of the most interesting attributes of European
directives that, once implemented, their provisions belong to *two* sets of
legal norms: at the European level, the *acquis communautaire*; and at the
national level, whatever rules already exist to deal with the same or similar
circumstances. At the Community level, this means that the European Court
sees each directive—however 'sectoral' or particular its ambit—as forming
part of a wider legal picture, based on a wider European competence, reflec-
tive of and subject to European legal general principle and the object of its
own interpretative approaches. I have suggested that this belonging of the

---

[106] In the UK, this has been the consistent approach of the Office of Fair Trading: OFT, *Unfair
Contract Terms*, Bulletin No. 1 (London, OFT, May 1996) para. 1.2, at 5.

[107] In this respect, Art 5(2) of the Unfair Terms in Consumer Contracts Directive 1993, above
n 16, provides that its own requirement of interpretation most in favour of the consumer as
regards ambiguous contract terms will not apply to the preventive measures envisaged by Art
7. As the ECJ has held, this exception has the paradoxical effect of benefiting consumers: Case
C–70/03 *Commission v Spain* [2004] ECR I–07999 esp. at para 16 and see AG Geelhoed,
ibid, at para 13.

UCPD to the consumer *acquis* may well have significant consequences for the interpretation of other directives within the family, even though they concern 'contract law', giving the development of the notion of 'average consumer' by way of illustration.

At the national level, implementation of the UCPD will make a number of specific requirements but will also set a general approach to the regulation of business practices in relation to consumers. Both aspects may have an impact on the development and/or future application of national laws, the one by fulfilling the conditions for the application of national rules (such as the 'fault' element for civil liability or a duty for the invalidity of a contract on the grounds of a failure to inform), the other by challenging the very paradigm on which consumer contracting takes place. However, the force of the 'without prejudice' clause in Article 3(2) ensures that the extent to which they do so remains within the hands of Member States, whether as a matter of legislation or of judicial interpretation.

9

The Unfair Commercial Practices Directive and its Consequences for the Regulation of Sales Promotion and the Law of Unfair Competition

JULES STUYCK

1. INTRODUCTION

IN THIS CHAPTER I shall tackle three important failures of the Community legislature at the occasion of the adoption of the UCPD. First the Directive ignores the proposal for a Regulation on sales promotions in the internal market while achieving, probably unintentionally, some of its goals. Secondly, and contrary to the European Court of Justice, the Community legislature has failed to acknowledge the existence in a group of Member States of an integrated approach towards consumer protection against unfair commercial practices and the protection of competitors against acts of unfair competition. Finally the standard of consumer protection against unfair commercial practices is also affected by antitrust law. The Directive seems to ignore this. I shall advocate a more integrated approach to competition law in the broad sense, ie the law of unfair commercial practices, both in B2B and B2C relations and antitrust law.

2. THE DIRECTIVE IN CONTEXT

Until recently the European Community had no legislation in the field of commercial practices and/or unfair competition. Since national laws protecting consumers or competitors against commercial practices can form an obstacle to cross-border trade between Member States, these laws have often been challenged on the basis of the Treaty Articles on free movement, notably Article 28 EC (prohibiting quantitative restrictions on imports and all measures having equivalent effect) and Article 49 (prohibiting obstacles to the cross-border provision of services). Initially the case law of the European Court of Justice (ECJ) in this regard struck down a certain number of these laws.[1] However the ruling by the ECJ in *Keck & Mithouard* (1993) put an end to this line of cases. In that judgment the Court decided that national provisions on 'selling arrangements' remain outside the scope of Article 28 EC if they do not discriminate either between economic operators active on the national market or against imported products.[2]

With the adoption of Directive 2005/29 on B2C Unfair Commercial Practices in the Internal Market,[3] the regulation of commercial practices has gained momentum at the EC level. The Directive has to be implemented by the Member States before the end of 2007. It is an instrument of total harmonisation in the field of consumer protection against unfair commercial practices, but it leaves unaffected national laws protecting competitors against unfair commercial practices, ie unfair competition law.[4]

The relationship between consumer law in the area of trade practices and the law of unfair competition, as it exists in many a Member State, thus remains unsettled at the EC level. A comparison of the laws of the Member States shows great diversity in this respect.[5] In Member States where the law of consumer protection against unfair commercial practices is integrated with the law of unfair competition the implementation of the Directive will cause important problems. To mention just one: in certain Member States certain commercial practices (especially forms of sales promotion) are unfair in all circumstances, ie it is not necessary to examine whether in the case at hand they unduly influence the consumer's decision. If such practices are not included in the black list of the Directive Member States cannot, in B2C relations, continue to prohibit them in all circumstances.

Indeed, the Directive harmonises the law of 'commercial practices', in B2C relations only, defining 'commercial practice' as 'any act, omission,

---

[1] See eg Case C–362/88 *GB-INNO-BM v Confédération du commerce luxembourgeois* [1990] ECR I–668; Case C–126/91 *Yves Rocher* [1993] ECR I–2361.

[2] Joined Cases C–267/91 & 268/91 *Keck & Mithouard* [1993] ECR I–6097.

[3] Directive 2005/29 of 11 May 2005 concerning unfair business-to-consumer commercial practices in the interrnal market ('Unfair Commercial practices Directive') [2005] OJ L 149/22.

[4] On the directive see H Collins, 'The Unfair Commercial Practices Directive' [2005] *European Review of Contract Law* 417; J Kessler and HW Micklitz, 'Die Richtlinie unlautere Geschäftspraktiken im binnenmarktinternen Geschäftsverkehr zwischen Unternehmen und Verbrauchern' [2005] *Betriebsberater, BB Spezial* 1; J Stuyck, E Terryn and T Van Dyck, 'Confidence through Fairness? The New Directive on Unfair Business-to-Consumer Commercial Practices in the Internal Market' (2006) 43 *CMLRev* 107.

[5] H Harte-Bavendamm and F Henning-Bodewig, 'Gesetz gegen den unlauteren Wettbewerb' in H Harte-Bavendamm and F Henning-Bodewig, *Kommentar* (Munich, CH Beck, 2004).

course of conduct or representation, commercial communication including advertising and marketing, by a trader, directly connected with the promotion, sale or supply of a product to consumers'. On the other hand there is an amended Commission proposal for a European Parliament and Council Regulation concerning *sales promotions* in the Internal Market,[6] the objective of which is to establish rules concerning the use and commercial communication of sales promotions in order to ensure the proper functioning of the internal market and a high level of consumer protection (Article 1). Pursuant to Article 2(a) of this proposal 'commercial communication' means any form of communication designed to promote, directly or indirectly, the goods, services or image of a company, organisation or individual pursuing a commercial, industrial or craft activity or exercising a regulated profession.[7] 'Sales promotion' means the offer of a discount, a free gift, a premium or an opportunity to participate in a promotional contest or game (Article 2(b)). A means of sales promotion is also a 'commercial practice' within the meaning of the Directive, because it is an act of a trader directly connected with the promotion of a product to consumers. The debate which surrounded the adoption of the Directive and the now apparently frozen proposal for a Sales Promotion Regulation suggest that the Member States, while agreeing on the Directive, were not fully aware of the fact that the regulation of sales promotions in B2C relations has been captured by this (full harmonisation) Directive. This will be my second point of discussion.

Finally it is increasingly recognised that a system of effective competition is essential for the safeguard of the interest of consumers with regard to commercial practices. My third point of criticism of the Directive is that it fails properly to recognise the relationship between the law of commercial practices and antitrust law, in particular by the absence of reference, in the notion of fairness, of effective competition.

In the next section I would first like to recall briefly the case law of the ECJ concerning the fate of national regulations on commercial practices in the light of the Treaty provisions on free movement. It will appear that the Court does not, in the area of commercial practices, make a distinction between B2B and B2C and generally mentions 'fairness in commercial transactions' together with consumer protection.

---

[6] COM(2002)0585 final.
[7] However the following do not constitute commercial communications:
— information allowing direct access to the activity of the company, organisation or individual in particular a domain name or an electronic-mail address; and
— communications relating to the goods, services or image of the company, organisation or individual compiled in an independent manner, particularly when this is without financial consideration.

3. THE CASE LAW OF THE COURT OF JUSTICE ON FREE MOVEMENT IN THE AREA OF COMMERCIAL PRACTICES

In its seminal *Cassis de Dijon* judgment[8] the European Court of Justice accepted obstacles to the free movement of goods justified by mandatory requirements relating to, *inter alia,* fairness in commercial transactions and consumer protection. Other grounds of justification under this 'rule of reason' have been added in later cases (notably the protection of the environment and culture). The rule of reason applies only to measures which apply without distinction to domestic goods and goods imported from other Member States. Express grounds of justification for both import and export restrictions can be found in Article 30 EC (ie public morality, public policy, the protection of health and life of humans, the protection of national treasures possessing artistic, historical and archaeological value, the protection of health and life of animals and the protection of industrial and commercial property). Member States can also rely on the grounds mentioned in Article 30 EC to justify measures that are not applicable without distinction to imported and domestic goods (and therefore discriminate between these goods, at least formally), provided these measures do not constitute an arbitrary discrimination or a disguised protection for domestic goods (see Article 30(2) EC).

The 'rule of reason' of *Cassis de Dijon* was later extended to the other internal market freedoms: the freedom to provide services,[9] the freedom of establishment[10] and the free movement of capital.[11] In *Gebhard*[12] the Court summarised the 'rule of reason' as follows:

> It follows, however, from the Court's case-law that national measures liable to hinder or make less attractive the exercise of fundamental freedoms guaranteed by the Treaty must fulfil four conditions: they must be applied in a non-discriminatory manner; they must be justified by imperative requirements in the general interest; they must be suitable for securing the attainment of the objective which they pursue; and they must not go beyond what is necessary in order to attain it (see Case C–19/92 *Kraus v Land Baden-Wuerttemberg* [1993] ECR I–1663, paragraph 32).

Consumer protection has often been invoked—and indeed accepted by the Court—as a ground of justification for obstacles to the free movement of goods and the free provision of services.

---

[8] Case 120/78 *Rewe v Bundesmonopolverwaltung für Branntwein* ('*Cassis de Dijon*') [1979] ECR 649, para 8.
[9] Case C–76/90 *Säger v Dennemeyer* [1991] ECR I–4221.
[10] Case C–55/94 *Gebhard* [1995] ECR I–4165.
[11] Joined Cases C–163/94, C–165/94 & C–250/94 *Sanz de Lera and Others* [1995] ECR I–4821, para 23, and Case C–54/99 *Association Église de scientologie de Paris* [2000] ECR I–1335, para 18.
[12] Case C–55/94 *Gebhard* [1995] ECR I–1141, para 3.

In a certain number of cases the ECJ has mentioned fairness in commercial transactions (or the prevention of unfair competition), together with consumer protection, ie in the field of trade practices and sales promotions.[13] There are also a few cases, loosely connected to industrial and intellectual property (copyright, appellations of origin), where the Court examined separately whether a national measure could be justified to secure 'fairness in commercial transactions', 'fair trading' or 'fair competition'. It is noteworthy that these cases are not particularly recent. There are however, as far as I can see, no judgments in which a national measure restricting free movement of goods has been found to be justified solely on the ground of the protection of fairness in commercial transactions.[14] It is also noteworthy that Member States generally do not invoke the protection of fairness in commercial transactions as a justification for a restrictive measure, but rather argue that the measure is necessary to protect consumers, when it is obviously not,[15] or do not argue at all about the justification, but simply deny that the measure is restrictive.[16] In the field of unfair competition it should be mentioned that the ECJ recognised in several cases that the protection of competitors against the use of a confusingly similar trade name can be justified under Article 30 (the protection of industrial and commercial property).[17]

---

[13] See eg Case 120/78 '*Cassis de Dijon*' [1979] ECR 649, Case C–362/88 *GB-INNO-BM v Confédération du commerce luxembourgeois* [1990] ECR I–668 and Case C–126/91 *Yves Rocher* [1993] ECR I–2361. See further Case 56/80 *Dansk Supermarket* [1981] ECR 181, where the Court ruled that since agreements between individuals cannot derogate from the mandatory provisions of the Treaty on the free movement of goods, a party to an agreement is not allowed to classify the importation of goods legally marketed in another Member State as an 'improper or unfair commercial practice'.

[14] Even in a case concerning protection against imitation (of the design of goods) which is very close to IP law (Case 6/81 *Industrie Groep* [1982] ECR 707) the Court referred both to consumer protection and fairness in commercial transactions, although there did not seem to be a real consumer protection issue in that case (the Court rightly referred to Art 10*bis* of the Paris Union Convention, the *sedes materiae* of unfair competition). In Case 182/84 *Miro BV* [1982] ECR 3731 the Court examined separately whether a national measure (the prohibition on marketing, in the Netherlands jenever with an alcohol content of less than 30%) was justified on the basis of fairness in commercial transactions, but it found it was not. According to the Court the fixing of the minimum alcohol content of a traditional beverage to be complied with by products of the same kind imported from another Member State cannot be regarded as an essential requirement of fair trading if these goods are lawfully and traditionally manufactured under the same appellation in the Member State of origin and the purchaser is provided with proper information. In Case 16/83 *Prantl* (the '*Bocksbeutel*' case), and Case 179/85 *Commission v Germany* [1986] ECR 3879 ('*Petillant de raisin*'), the Court found that there were no reasons connected to fair trading (fair and traditional practices) for the Member State concerned (Germany) to refuse wine originating in another Member State in bottles of a certain shape traditionally reserved to wine makers on its own territory for a certain type of wine (Champagne).

[15] As in Case C–362/88 *GB-INNO-BM v Confédération du commerce luxembourgeois* [1990] ECR I–668 and Case C–126/91 *Yves Rocher* [1993] ECR I–2361.

[16] See eg Case C–84/00 *Commission v France* [2000] ECR I–4553, concerning rules on acceptable standards of fineness of precious metal.

[17] See eg Case C–255/97 *Pfeiffer Grosshandel* [1999] ECR I–9077.

The need to justify obstacles to the free movement of goods resulting from national rules on sales promotions and sales methods has been mitigated by the famous *Keck & Mithouard* case law.[18] This case law is well summarised in a recent judgment concerning the Belgian law on 'itinerant sale', the *Burnmanjer* judgment.[19] The law subjects the sale of goods outside the premises stated in the registration of the seller in the commercial register to a prior authorisation delivered by the competent Minister. Itinerant selling without authorisation is a criminal offence. Three people who had been charged with having sold, on the public highway in a Belgian city, subscriptions for periodicals for a German company, challenged the compatibility of that law with the EC Treaty. On Article 28 EC (free movement of goods) the ECJ recalled its previous case law in the following words:

> 23 To establish whether those rules come within the prohibition laid down by Article 28 EC, it is appropriate to note that, under settled case-law, all trading rules enacted by Member States which are capable of hindering, directly or indirectly, actually or potentially, intra-Community trade are to be regarded as measures having an effect equivalent to quantitative restrictions and thus prohibited by that article (see, in particular, Case 8/74 *Dassonville* [1974] ECR 837, paragraph 5; Case C–420/01 *Commission v Italy* [2003] ECR I–6445, paragraph 25, and Karner, paragraph 36).

> 24 The Court however stated, in paragraph 16 of *Keck and Mithouard*, cited above, that national provisions restricting or prohibiting certain selling arrangements which apply to all relevant traders operating within the national territory and affect in the same manner, in law and in fact, the marketing of domestic products and of those from other Member States are not such as to hinder directly or indirectly, actually or potentially, trade between Member States within the meaning of the line of case-law initiated by *Dassonville*.

> 25 The Court subsequently found that provisions concerning, in particular, certain marketing methods were selling arrangements within the meaning of *Keck and Mithouard* (see, in particular, Case C–292/92 *Hünermund and Others* [1993] ECR I–6787, paragraphs 21 and 22; Joined Cases C–401/92 and C–402/92 *Tankstation 't Heukske and Boermans* [1994] ECR I–2199, paragraphs 12 to 14, and TK-Heimdienst, paragraph 24).

The Court applied the *Keck* test to the case at hand.

National regulations on advertising, sales promotions and sales methods have thus been described as 'selling arrangements' giving these regulations immunity against application of Article 28 EC so long as they do not render the marketing of imported goods more difficult than that of domestic goods. A total ban on alcohol advertising in magazines (in Sweden) has been found

---

[18] See Joined Cases 267/91 & 268/91 *Keck & Mithouard* [1993] ECR I–6097 and numerous later cases.

[19] Case C–20/03 *Marcel Burnmanjer et al,* Judgment of 26 May 2005, not yet reported.

disproportionately to hinder imported goods (since domestic goods are generally made known to the public via other channels). The national court had thus to verify whether the ban could be justified on grounds of protection of public health[20] (the referring Swedish court eventually found it was not). A rule forbidding German consumers to buy pharmaceutical products on line was found to hinder the marketing of pharmaceuticals offered from other Member States more than those offered in Germany (where they can be purchased in pharmacies) and not to be justified for the protection of public health as it applies to over-the-counter pharmaceuticals.[21]

This case law freed Member States from the burden of justifying obstacles to the free movement of goods resulting from such regulations as being necessary to achieve a goal of general interest, such as fairness in commercial transactions and/or the protection of consumers, but only on condition that these regulations were not, in law or in fact, discriminatory vis-à-vis certain economic operators or vis-à-vis goods imported from other Member Sates.

Because of *Keck* there are relatively few cases in which the ECJ has scrutinised national regulations on sales promotions, advertising and sales methods on the ground of Article 30 EC or in the light of their (alleged) objective of protecting fair trade and/or the economic interests of consumers. These cases deal with 'selling arrangement' types of rules that either affect the conditions subject to which products can be put on the market (eg rules on advertising affecting the labelling of products) or have a discriminatory effect on imported goods (such as a ban on the use of a given medium for advertising purposes or a ban on the use of the internet for the sale of certain goods[22]).

4. THE UNFAIR COMMERCIAL PRACTICES DIRECTIVE: B2C ONLY

The state of play has dramatically changed with the adoption of the total harmonisation Directive 2005/29/EC of the European Parliament and of the Council of 11 May 2005 concerning unfair business-to-consumer commercial practices in the internal market.[23] In the harmonised field, ie commercial practices in the relationship between undertakings and consumers, all Member States have to adopt the same set of rules. 'Commercial practices' are defined by Article 2(d) as 'any act, omission, course of conduct or representation, commercial communication including advertising

---

[20] Case C–405/98 *Gourmet* [2001] ECR I–1795; see note by J Stuyck in [2001] *Cahiers de droit européen* 682.
[21] Case C–322/01 *Deutscher Apothekerverband* [2003] ECR I–14887.
[22] See *Gourmet* and *Deutscher Apothekerverband*, above in nn 20 and 21.
[23] Above n 3.

and marketing, by a trader, directly connected with the promotion, sale or supply of a product to consumers'. This is a very wide concept including sales methods, methods of sales promotion and advertising. The rules are the following. Unfair commercial practices shall be prohibited. A commercial practice shall be unfair if: (a) it is contrary to the requirements of professional diligence, and (b) it materially distorts or is likely materially to distort economic behaviour with regard to the product of the average consumer whom it reaches or to whom it is addressed, or of the average member of the group when a commercial practice is directed to a particular group of consumers. In particular, commercial practices shall be unfair where they are: (a) misleading, as set out in Articles 6 and 7, or (b) aggressive, as further set out in Articles 8 and 9, (Article 5). Annex I contains the list of those commercial practices which shall in all circumstances be regarded as unfair. The same single list shall apply in all Member States and may be modified only by revision of this Directive.

Consistently with the scope of application of the Directive (B2C only), Recital 8 states:

> This Directive directly protects consumer economic interests from unfair business-to-consumer commercial practices. Thereby, it also indirectly protects legitimate businesses from their competitors who do not play by the rules in this Directive and thus guarantees fair competition in fields coordinated by it. It is understood that there are other commercial practices which, although not harming consumers, may hurt competitors and business customers. The Commission should carefully examine the need for Community action in the field of unfair competition beyond the remit of this Directive and, if necessary, make a legislative proposal to cover these other aspects of unfair competition.

Although the Community legislator thus recognised the existence of a strong link between the law of unfair commercial practices in B2C relations and the law of unfair competition, it nevertheless adopted a directive that is limited to B2C relations and postponed *sine die* the harmonisation of the law of unfair competition.

5. THE LAW OF UNFAIR COMPETITION IN THE MEMBER STATES

In certain national legal systems (like those of the Nordic countries) the law on sales methods, advertising and unfair practices is often seen as one branch of the law with its specific system of legal protection (involving a Consumer Ombudsman or consumer organisations). In other countries, like Germany and Belgium, it is integrated with the law of unfair competition (the aim of which is historically the protection of competitors, but which has been enlarged so as to include the protection of consumers and even the public at large, the general interest).

The old German law on unfair competition dating from 1909 (see now the UWG 2004 discussed hereinafter) was the prototype of a private law approach to the regulation of fairness of commercial practices: protection of private interests (in particular the *Mittelstand* or small shop keepers) and private law enforcement. In a completely opposite approach to the German, the Scandinavian countries, Sweden being the first, started enacting a different type of legislation in this field as from 1970. The Scandinavian approach is one of public law (a Consumer Ombudsman) in the interest of consumers.[24]

The national systems in the EU show varying degrees of autonomy of the law on unfair competition and of integration of consumer law, competition law (in the broad sense) and unfair competition law, with ramifications on IP law.

Historically the law on unfair competition as it still exists in most of the Member States (though in a few, such as Germany, Austria and Greece, it is covered by a specific and separate Act) originates in the Paris Convention on Industrial Property of 1883 as amended in 1900 in Brussels. Article 10*bis* introduced the principle of domestic treatment of all citizens of Member States with regard to unfair competition. The Hague revision of the Convention additionally obliged the Member States to protect each other's citizens against unfair competition (*concurrence déloyale*).[25] At the same time unfair competition was defined as acts which are contrary to honest business practices (*actes contraires aux usages honnêtes en matière commerciale et industrielle*). The creation of confusion and misleading the public by false statements about competitors are listed as acts of unfair competition.[26] The law on unfair competition started as part of the law on industrial property, and in many countries the two are still closely linked.[27]

Germany was the first country to adopt legislation implementing the Paris Union Convention. A first Act on Unfair Competition (*Gesetz gegen den unlauteren Wettbewerb* or UWG) was adopted in 1896 and soon replaced by a more effective UWG in 1909. The 1909 UWG served as a model for several other countries. In 2004 it was replaced by a modern UWG. Section 1 of the new UWG sets out its objective: the protection of competitors, consumers and other market participants against unfair competition. It also protects the general interest in undistorted competition.

---

[24] See for an interesting comparison between the German and the Swedish models A Bakardjieva-Engelbrekt, *Fair Trading Law in Flux* (PhD thesis, Stockholm, 2003) at 13 ff.

[25] See above n 24.

[26] Harte-Bavendamm and Henning-Bodewig, above n 5, 46.

[27] The TRIPS Agreement contains a partial reference to unfair competition and to the Paris Convention. Pursuant to Art 39(1) Members shall, in the course of ensuring effective protection against unfair competition as provided in Article 10*bis* of the Paris Union Convention (1967), protect undisclosed information in accordance with para 2 and data submitted to governments or governmental agencies in accordance with para 3. Thus this provision only covers part of what is meant by unfair competition under the Paris Convention, i.e. the protection of undisclosed information.

The new German Unfair Competition Act (UWG) modernises and liber-alises this branch of the law. After the abrogation of the *Zugabeverordenung* (regulation on premium offers) and the *Rabattgesetz* (law on discounts) in 2001, the new UWG also abolishes the rules of the old UWG on special sales and clearance sales. It expressly recognises the consumer as beneficiary of the laws against unfair competition (following established case law) and it introduces a *de minimis* threshold (like in competition law).

While the new German UWG was enacted after due consideration of the proposal for a UCPD and was indeed inspired by that proposal, Germany has integrated the rules on commercial practices in an Act which also relates to B2B relations. The central provision, the *grosse Generalklausel* of sec-tion of the new UWG 3 prohibits unlawful acts of competition which are liable to affect not merely insignificantly competition to the disadvantage of competitors, consumers or other market participants. In other words the old standard of *gute Sitten* (honest business practices) has been replaced by a notion of fairness that directly relates to the requirements of effective com-petition and which grants market participants a market oriented freedom to act and make decisions.[28] In addition section 1 of the Act states that: '[t]he objective of the Act is to protect competitors, consumers and other market participants against unfair competition. It also protects the general interest in undistorted competition'.[29] This law integrates consumer protection, protec-tion of competitors and protection of competition. It remains to be seen how these new provisions will change the longstanding case law that has been developed on the basis of the traditional Unfair Competition Act of 1909, a law that did not mention the consumer or the general interest, but that was often applied taking into account these interests.[30]

The implementation of the Unfair Commercial Practices Directive (UCPD) is a complex matter. The three-tier structure of the Directive (a general clause, two more specific clauses and a black list) will necessitate important and varied adaptations of the national laws of the Member States. In some Member States, like the UK,[31] Ireland, Cyprus

---

[28] 'Unlautere Wettbewerbshandlungen, die geeignet sind, den Wettbewerb zum Nachteil der Mitbewerber, der Verbraucher oder der sonstigen Marktteilnehmer nicht nur unerheblich zu beeinträchtigen, sind unzulässig.' (free translation: "acts of unfair competition that are likely to impede not only insignificantly competiiton to the detriment of competitors, consumers or other market participants are prohibited")

[29] 'Dieses Gesetz dient dem Schutz der Mitbewerber, der Verbraucherinnen und der Verbraucher sowie der sonstigen Marktteilnehmer vor unlauterem Wettbewerb. Es schützt zugleich das Interesse der Allgemeinheit an einem unverfälschten Wettbewerb.' (free trans-lation: "this law aims at protecting competitors, consumers and other market participants against unfair competition. It also protects the general interest in undistorted competition").

[30] Harte-Bavendamm and Henning-Bodewig, above n 5

[31] See S Weatherill, 'National Report—United Kingdom' in R Schulze and H Schulte-Nölke, *Analysis of National Fairness Laws Aimed at Protecting Consumers in Relation to Commercial Practices* (June 2003), available at www.europa.eu.int./comm/consumers/cons_int/safe_shop/ fair_bus_pract/green_pap_com/studies/unfair_practices_en.

and Malta,[32] there is no general rule governing the fairness of commercial practices. In Sweden, the fairness of commercial practices is guaranteed by a statute (the Marketing Practices Act) the primary aim of which is to protect consumers and which consists of a general fairness clause supplemented by more specific provisions. Protection of business people against acts of unfair competition is a secondary aim of the Act.[33] Denmark has a similar approach.[34] Austria, Germany, Greece, Poland, Slovenia and Spain have laws on unfair competition.[35] Originally these laws aimed at business-to-business relations only. Nowadays at least some of their provisions also relate to fairness in business-to-consumer relations. Germany adopted a new Unfair Competition Act (UWG) in 2004; its aim is to protect competitors, consumers and other market participants against unfair competition as well as the general interest in undistorted competition. Poland amended its Law on Unfair Competition of 1993 very recently, on 15 June 2005: an act of unfair competition is conduct of an undertaking which violates a legal provision or *bonos mores* and damages or puts in jeopardy the interests of another undertaking or a consumer. The Czech provisions on unfair competition (including a general clause) are integrated in the Commercial Code.[36] In France[37] and the Netherlands fairness in commercial practices is guaranteed on the basis of tort law (Civil Code). Italy has a specific provision on unfair competition in its Civil Code. Belgium has one Trade Practices Act with a general clause on unfair competition and a general clause on fair practices vis-à-vis consumers (both clauses being based on the same notion of honest business practices derived from the Paris Union Convention).[38] Luxembourg has a comparable Act.[39] In Finnish law there are two separate statutes: a Consumer Protection Act and an Unfair Trade Practices Act.[40] Estonia, Latvia, Lithuania and Hungary have Competition Acts with a double aim: promoting effective as well as fair competition. In Portugal 'unfair competition' is part of the Code on Intellectual Property, but this country also has an Advertising Code and a Consumer Code which contain important provisions in the area covered by the UCPD.[41] Spain has a very complex system of national laws (a Competition Act and an Advertising Act, with civil sanctions) and laws of the autonomous regions.[42]

---

[32] Harte-Bavendamm and Henning-Bodewig, above n 5, 239, 271 and 344.
[33] See U Bernitz, 'National Report—Sweden' in Schulze and Schulte-Nölke, above n 30.
[34] Harte-Bavendamm and Henning-Bodewig, above n 5, 191.
[35] Ibid, at 180 ff and R Schulze and H Schulte Nölke, 'Comparative Overview' in Schulze and Schulte-Nölke, above n 30 at 11, for some of the countries.
[36] Harte-Bavendamm and Henning-Bodewig, above n 5, 331.
[37] Consumer law in France is grouped in a Code de la Consommation.
[38] J. Stuyck, *Handelspraktijken* (Mechelen, Kluwer, 2004).
[39] Harte-Bavendamm and Henning-Bodewig, above n 5, 264.
[40] Schulte Nölke, 'Comparative Overview', in Schulze and Schulte-Nölke, above n 30, at 11.
[41] Harte-Bavendamm and Henning-Bodewig, above n 5 299–300.
[42] Ibid, at 323–4.

The diversity in approaches towards unfair competition and trade practices between the Member States is in sharp contrast to the situation in the field of antitrust. As a consequence, inter alia, of the modernisation and decentralisation of EC competition law (in particular Regulation 1/2003[43] implementing Articles 81 and 82 EC), there is now a very high degree of convergence between the antitrust laws of the Member States. The same convergence also exists in the field of merger control (see now Regulation 139/2004). With regard to restrictive practices Article 3(1) of Regulation 1/2003 de facto forces the Member States to a (quasi absolute) convergence of their national antitrust laws, in that they are precluded from applying national provisions without at the same time applying the EC competition rules where a given practice affects trade between Member States. As they are under an obligation also to apply Article 81 or 82 EC in such a situation, maintaining national antitrust laws that differ substantially from Articles 81 and 82 would make enforcement at the national level very difficult. As to the relationship between antitrust law and unfair competition law attention should be drawn to Article 3(3) of Regulation 1/2003. Here it is expressly said that the principle of simultaneous application of EC and national competition law where a restrictive practice within the meaning of Articles 81–82 affects trade between Member States does not preclude the application of provisions of national law that predominantly pursue an objective different from that pursued by Articles 81 and 82 of the Treaty. The Community legislature had the law of unfair competition in mind whith this provision. The UCPD totally ignores this relationship between antitrust and unfair competition.

This brief overview of the law of the Member States suggests that the EC approach, consisting of harmonisation of the law of commercial practices in B2C relations, ignores the complexity of the legal situation before harmonisation and, in particular, the fact that the area of harmonised law is so closely intertwined with the law of unfair competition and antitrust law.

6. NATIONAL RULES ON SALES PROMOTIONS AFTER THE UCPD

As mentioned above the concept of 'commercial practices' in the UCPD is very broad, encompassing methods of sales promotion. Moreover the UCPD is a measure of total harmonisation of commercial practices in B2C relations. Practices that are not mentioned in the exhaustive black list of commercial practices annexed to the Directive can be prohibited in B2C relations only if either they are 'unfair' (ie they are contrary to professional diligence and are likely materially to distort the consumer's behaviour) within the meaning of Article 5 or misleading or aggressive within the meaning of Articles 6 and 7. Hence it is submitted that national rules

---

[43] [2003] OJ L 1/1.

which, in B2C relations, per se forbid certain methods of sales promotion, like sale at a loss, premium offers, coupons, prize competitions, clearance sales, etc, or regulate them in an abstract manner, ie without giving the judge power to appraise case by case whether the practice is unfair vis-à-vis consumers, can not longer be maintained.

This—unavoidable—consequence of the UCPD is surprising in the light of the proposal for a Regulation on Sales Promotion in the Internal Market,[44] the object of which is precisely to set the conditions under which Member States can regulate methods of sales promotion in both B2B and in B2C relations.

Article 3 of that proposal provides that the Member States shall not impose a general prohibition on the use or commercial communication of a sales promotion unless required by Community law, and that Member States' laws shall not provide for limitation of the value of a sales promotion, except for discounts on fixed-price products and sales below costs, for a prohibition on discounts preceding seasonal sales, or for a requirement to obtain prior authorisation, or any requirement having equivalent effect, for the use or communication of a sales promotion. 'Sales promotion' means the offer of a discount, a free gift, a premium or an opportunity to participate in a promotional contest or game.

The proposed Regulation thus allows the Member States to maintain, provided they respect the Treaty freedoms (see Article 3(2)), certain restrictions with regard to sales promotion, such as a prohibition or regulation of sales below costs and forms of sales promotion not mentioned in the list (eg the indication of discounts). It is however questionable whether such national rules can be maintained in the light of the maximum harmonisation character of the UCPD (except where the method of sales promotion fits in one of the items of the UCPD's black list or has to be considered 'unfair', 'misleading' or 'aggressive' within the meaning of the Directive).

7. THE INFLUENCE OF ANTITRUST LAW ON THE LAW OF CONSUMER PROTECTION AND UNFAIR COMPETITION

The law of commercial practices is not only intertwined with competition law in the broad sense, ie the law of unfair competition and antitrust law, but, as a separate branch of the law or as part of the law of unfair competition, the law of commercial practices is also influenced by antitrust law.

The importance of competition policy (antitrust and concentration control) for consumers is now generally recognised. Articles 81 and 82 EC, the Merger Regulation (Regulation 139/2004/EC[45]) and their domestic equiva-

---

[44] Amended proposal: COM(2002)585 final.
[45] [2004] OJ L 24/1.

lents are crucial for consumers. Consumers are the primary beneficiaries of a vigorous competition policy, in particular the effective enforcement of the prohibition of cartels and abuse of dominant positions and the prior control of concentrations. Competition policy guarantees that the consumer gets good quality and choice at a reasonable price.[46]

The protection of consumer interests requires additional measures, such as protection against unfair practices, including unfair contract terms, which may indeed also occur in situations where competition is effective. In addition it should be recognised that the consumer is not merely a *homo oeconomicus* who takes decisions on the basis of the quality and price of products, but he may want to know whether goods are produced according to fair trade principles (a decent revenue for the producer, no exploitation by multinational groups, no child labour, etc) and to buy accordingly. The debate on genetically modified organisms has also shown that at least some consumers want to take consumption decisions with due consideration for the environmental impact of these decisions.

Whatever the reality of the possibility of influencing fairness of trade or the environment by consumption decisions, one can agree that the consumer has the right to be informed about the environmental, social, societal and other non-economic consequences of his decision to buy a given product. The now generally accepted basic principle of consumer autonomy[47] also encompasses his right to be informed so as to enable him to decide according to his own principles and ethical values.

On the other hand it is possible for fairness rules to restrict competition in a way that is disadvantageous for consumers, whether these rules are (primarily) designed to protect competitors (the law of unfair competition) or indeed consumers (like the UCPD).

This has been increasingly recognised with the emergence of antitrust law. The law of unfair competition and commercial practices is much older than antitrust law. The function of 'honest business practices' was very often to protect existing positions on the market. New techniques of advertising and sales promotion, new sales methods and so on were described as being contrary to honest business practices, which meant contrary to what was usual. A good example is the prohibition of comparative advertising. Directive 97/55[48] has forced all the Member States to allow comparative advertising that fulfils certain conditions (of truthfulness and objectivity) so as to guarantee the proper information of consumers. Several Member States had

---

[46] See J Stuyck, 'EC Competition Law after Modernization: More than Ever in the Interest of Consumers' (2005) 28 *Journal of Consumer Policy* 1; K Cséres, *Competition Law and Consumer Protection* (The Hague, Kluwer, 2005).

[47] See J Drexl, *Die Wirtschaftliche Selbstbestimmung des Verbrauchers* (Tübingen, Mohr Siebeck, 1998).

[48] Amending Directive 84/450 and authorising comparative advertising, [1997] OJ L 290.

a long tradition of prohibiting comparative advertising, the aim or at least the effect of which was to protect incumbents against new entrants who want to position their products by reference to similar products offered by the incumbents. The 'honest business practices' were the practices that were considered to be honest by the incumbents.

Comparative advertising was thus liberalised through internal market harmonisation. Other practices that were traditionally qualified as unfair between competitors had to be accepted as normal under the pressure of antitrust actions. Since the early years of application of Articles 81 EC the ECJ has refused to accept the fight against unfair competition (eg under-bidding) as a justification for restrictive agreements between competitors.[49] On the other hand national courts had to define the relationship between antitrust law and unfair competition law, two branches of the law that may be complementary but are also to a certain extent incompatible. The question arises how one can protect market participants against 'unfair competition' without at the same time restricting effective competition? Interestingly in Belgium the Supreme Court (Hof van Cassatie, Cour de Cassation) has ruled that the conduct of an undertaking that restricts competition but that is authorised under antitrust law cannot be prohibited as an act of unfair competition when the alleged violation of honest business practices essentially consists of the restriction of competition.[50] This ruling overturned decisions of certain lower courts which (among other matters) qualified refusals to sell on the part of non-dominant undertakings that were not engaged in agreements appreciably restricting competition as acts of unfair competition.

Apart from clear examples where the Community courts or national courts cut back on the applicability of unfair competition law in cases where it restricted competition or prohibited as being 'unfair' a restrictive practice which did not adversely affect effective competition, it cannot be denied that in general the notion of honest business practices has been influenced by the development of antitrust law. In the pre-antitrust era aggressive competition or even innovative methods of competition could be considered unfair because they affected vested positions and existing goodwill. Nowadays it is generally accepted that undertakings have to put up with copying, imitation and other acts by competitors that affect the value of their businesses, unless they can prove an infringement of an intellectual property right recognised by law. Freedom of competition also means that undertakings basically have the right to poach clients from their competitors and that they should not be prevented from attracting consumers even

---

[49] Commission Decision of 15 May 1974, IFTRA [1974] OJ L 160/1; Commission Decision of 15 July 1975, IFTRA [1975] OJ L 228/3.

[50] Cass, 7 Jan 2000 [2001] *Revue Critique de Jurisprudence Belge* p. 256–269, annotation by J Stuyck.

with aggressive means of advertising or sales promotion, as long as they do not cause undue prejudice to their competitors (eg by denigrating them or, where they have the power to do so, by boycotting them) or to consumers, by misleading them or by exercising undue influence on them in such a way that their freedom of choice or conduct is impaired. Effective competition—the aim of antitrust law—assumes a certain degree of tolerance with regard to what has traditionally been considered unfair or aggressive.

8. PLEA FOR AN INTEGRATED APPROACH AT THE EC LEVEL

The UCPD completely fails to recognise the relationship between consumer law regarding commercial practices on the one hand and unfair competition law and antitrust law on the other.

The implementation of the UCPD promises to become an extremely difficult exercise in those Member States where the protection of consumers against unfair practices is part of a wider branch of the law including the protection of competitors against unfair practices.

The UCPD also fails to recognise the relationship between the law of commercial practices and antitrust law. Germany has set the example. The general clause of the new UWG from 2004 (section 3) prohibits acts in the course of competition which are likely to impede competition, not insignificantly, to the detriment of competitors, consumers or other market participants. The objective of the Act is to protect competitors, consumers and other market participants against unfair competition. It also protects the general interest in undistorted competition. This law integrates consumer protection, protection of competitors and protection of competition. It remains to be seen how these new provisions will change the longstanding case law that has been developed on the basis of the traditional Unfair Competition Act 1909, a law that did not mention the consumer or the general interest, although these were often taken into account when the law was interpreted.

It is the author's conviction that there can be no level playing field for undertakings, no genuine internal market and no effective and market-oriented but non-paternalistic protection of consumers until the law of competition, including unfair competition and the protection of consumers against unfair trade practices, is seen as whole. This will necessitate a real review of and a comparison of the basic aims, principles and concepts of these three areas of the law. The implementation of the UCPD could be a good start for such an exercise.

10

The Case for Reclaiming European Unfair Competition Law from Europe's Consumer Lawyers

CHRISTOPHER WADLOW*

1. THE UNFAIR COMMERCIAL PRACTICES DIRECTIVE AS WHAT KIND OF LEGISLATION?

A S ITS FULL title indicates, the Unfair Commercial Practices Directive[1] is principally concerned with consumer protection law. And as a passage in the middle of Recital 6 provides:

> It neither covers nor affects the national laws on unfair commercial practices which harm only competitors' economic interests or which relate to a transaction between traders; taking full account of the principle of subsidiarity, Member States will continue to be able to regulate such practices, in conformity with Community law, if they choose to do so.

This is consistent with the explanatory memorandum to the draft Directive published in 2003, which commented:[2]

> 40. It [the scope being confined to matters affecting consumers' interests] also means that acts which constitute unfair competition in some Member States but which do not harm the economic interests of consumers, such as slavish

---

* The present chapter is an exception to the majority in this volume in that it was not delivered to the Conference entitled The Regulation of Unfair Commercial Practices under EC Directive 2005/29: New Rules and New Techniques on 3 Mar 2006. It is based on a paper delivered to the Oxford Intellectual Property Research Centre on 7 Feb 2006, under the title 'Is it Time to Reclaim Unfair Competition Law from the Consumer Lawyers?', and is included here at the invitation of the Editors.
[1] Directive 2005/29/EC of the European Parliament and of the Council of 11 May 2005 concerning unfair business-to-consumer practices in the internal market ('the Unfair Commercial Practices Directive'); [2005] OJ L 149/22.
[2] Proposal for an Unfair Commercial Practices Directive, COM(2003)356 final, para 40.

imitation (i.e. copying independently of any likelihood of consumer confusion) and denigration of a competitor, are outside the scope of the Directive. Acts which are classed some Member States as unfair competition which do harm consumers economic interests, such as confusion marketing (which generates a danger of confusion among consumers with the distinctive signs and/or products of a competitor) are within scope.

So in the phraseology of the day it is concerned with business-to-consumer ('B2C') relationships rather than business-to-business ('B2B') ones. However, in almost the same breath the Directive acknowledges that it can hardly avoid affecting the latter as well. According to Recitals 6 and 8 (emphasis added):

(6) This Directive ... approximates the laws of the Member States on unfair commercial practices, including unfair advertising, which directly harm consumers' economic interests *and thereby indirectly harm the economic interests of legitimate competitors.*

(8) This Directive directly protects consumer economic interests from unfair business-to-consumer commercial practices. *Thereby, it also indirectly protects legitimate businesses from their competitors who do not play by the rules in this Directive and thus guarantees fair competition in fields co-ordinated by it.* It is understood that there are other commercial practices which, although not harming consumers, may hurt competitors and business customers. *The Commission should carefully examine the need for Community action in the field of unfair competition beyond the remit of this Directive and*, if necessary, *make a legislative proposal to cover these other aspects of unfair competition.*

It is this second aspect of the Directive which I propose to address. Given that the Directive acknowledges that it will have, at the very least, certain indirect effects on the law of unfair competition, then is it satisfactory for it to derive its policies and priorities entirely from the point of view of consumer protection, if that is indeed the case? Alternatively, might the Directive have gone too far in the opposite direction, so as to enact in the name of consumer protection a collection of principles and provisions which owe far more than is acknowledged to unfair competition law, and specifically to the legacy of the German *Gesetz gegen den unlauteren Wettbewerb* 1909 (the *UWG*)?[3] If these are taken as accusations rather than questions, then they may seem to be inconsistent with one another, but

---

[3] The UWG of 1909 has now been replaced by the similarly named Act of 2004, which claims to have pre-emptively incorporated most, if not all, of the requirements of the Directive. I shall refer principally to the 1909 Act because of its historical importance, and because it was still in force while the study led by Professor Micklitz (http://ec.europa.eu/comm/consumers/cons_int/safe_shop/fair_bus_pract/green_pap_comm/studies/sur21_vol#_en.pdf, considered more fully below) was taking place. (Replace '#' with '1', '2' or '3' for the relevant volume)

until the underlying questions are resolved both possibilities deserve to be taken seriously, and there is even a sense in which they might be reconciled, though it is rather a discouraging one. It is to suggest that the Directive may be at risk (either now or in the future) of being unconsciously over-influenced by a particular collectivist economic world-view which prevailed in Germany (and elsewhere) from the late nineteenth century to the advent of ordoliberalism after World War II, and which became entwined with the German UWG of 1909 and (especially) the enormous and hugely influential body of case law spawned by the latter. Conversely, it is suggested that those responsible for the Directive have not (so far) attempted to incorporate into it the results of any principled or scientific exercise balancing the legitimate rights and expectations of competitors inter se, or with respect to the public, as opposed to the rights of consumers vis-à-vis producers and suppliers.

All this does matter to consumers as well. The constitutional basis for the Directive is harmonisation within the internal market, but goods, persons, services and information neither know nor care whether legal barriers to their free movement are characterised as measures for consumer protection or come under a law of unfair competition. An immunity, incentive, disincentive or prohibition embodied in European consumer law may be vitiated or overridden by a contrary one in unharmonised national unfair competition law, at least until the discrepancy is acknowledged and European law is allowed to prevail. Fair and honest competitors who are disadvantaged by the 'unfair' and unrestrained competition of rivals, or by the action of 'unfair' laws, (perhaps even to the point of being driven out of business) will not be able to compete effectively, or at all, and the public will ultimately have no choice but to deal with those who have undeservedly supplanted them.

2. ENGLISH AND GERMAN ATTITUDES TO UNFAIR COMPETITION CONTRASTED

Since the late nineteenth or early twentieth century, English and German attitudes to unfair competition as a civil law tort have exhibited the polarity of irreconcilable opposites. To enumerate all the differences would easily fill the present volume and more. For present purposes, the point of difference on which I propose to dwell is the centrality of the consumer in English law, and his or her peripheral relevance in German law. English common law understands unfair competition almost entirely through the prism of the consumer: if the consumer is deceived by a competitor's misrepresentation or misconduct then there is (or may be) actionable passing-off or injurious falsehood; if not, there is likely to be a remedy only on the rare occasions on which one of the so-called 'economic torts' can be invoked. So English law equates 'fairness' with 'honesty', and 'honesty' with 'truthfulness', and makes the consumer the determinator of what is honest, and therefore of what is fair. Any business arguing that it subject to 'unfair' competitive conduct in any other sense must bring its complaint within one of the limited number of nominate torts. The *locus standi* of the competitor to sue is, so to speak, parasitic on the harm suffered by the consumer.

The same was at least formerly true of the United States,[4] and the *locus standi* of the competitor cannot be put better than it was by Judge Learned Hand in the Second Circuit Court of Appeals in a case in which a manufacturer of floor polish (Johnson's Wax) objected to the deceptive use of the same surname for a household textile cleaning compound. Learned Hand was prepared to describe the plaintiff as the 'vicarious champion' of the public against the deception practised on them, but quite strictly limited the ability of the plaintiff company to invoke this status to cases in which it suffered damage in its existing trading capacity (citations omitted):[5]

> It is true that a merchant who has sold one kind of goods, sometimes finds himself driven to add other 'lines' in order to hold or develop his existing market; in such cases he has a legitimate present interest in preserving his identity in the ancillary market, which he cannot do, if others make his name equivocal there. But if the new goods have no such relation to the old, and if the first user's interest in maintaining the significance of his name when applied to the new goods is nothing more than the desire to post the new market as a possible preserve which he may later choose to exploit, it is hard to see any basis for its protection. The public may be deceived, but he has no claim to be its vicarious champion; his remedy must be limited to his injury and by hypothesis he has none. There is always the danger that we may be merely granting a monopoly, based upon the notion that by advertising one can obtain some 'property' in a name. We are nearly sure to go astray in any phase of the whole subject, as soon as we lose sight of the underlying principle that the wrong involved is diverting trade from the first user by misleading customers who meant to deal with him.

German law historically took quite the opposite approach. The duty of fair trading imposed under the general clause of the UWG 1909 was primarily owed to one's competitors (interpreted in the broadest possible sense) and to the relevant business community at large, and was enforceable by them and by various trade associations dedicated to stamping out trade practices which their membership or their executive considered undesirable. Subsequently, consumers' organisations were added to the list of possible

---

[4] The present state of the law of unfair competition in the US is well beyond the scope of the present contribution.

[5] *S C Johnson & Son v Johnson*, 116 F 2d 427 (CA 2d Cir, 1940). Our hero had previously made an appearance (under the sobriquet of the 'vicarious avenger') in *Ely-Norris Safe Co v Mosler Safe Co*, 7 F 2d 603, (CA, 2d Cir, 1925).

plaintiffs. The principles governing *locus standi* under the UWG 1909 are summarised in the national report on Germany in the Micklitz survey:[6]

> The basic legal rule for fair-trading is §1 UWG which provides claims for injunctions and damages against everybody who acts contrary to honest business practice. Case Law shapes the contents of the general clause. The vast majority of the principles and values applied under the general clause to individual cases today have been laid down and developed by jurisdiction throughout the last 100 years. ... The original concept of the law against unfair competition is aimed at the protection of traders against the unfair acts of their competitors. Accordingly only competitors and business associations had been entitled to claim for injunctions and damages. But as not only competitors are concerned by unfair competition, but also consumers and the general public, the UWG now provides for a right of action by consumer associations as well and this has been the case since 1966.

Case law under section 1 of the UWG 1909 is by hallowed convention divided into five categories or *Fallgruppen*, of which it will be seen that only the first unambiguously corresponds to the scope and policy of the Directive (citations omitted):[7]

> The Act [the UWG 1909] contains specific provisions, and two general provisions of which section 1 UWG is the more important. It is a general expression of the principle that an injunction and a claim for damages are awarded in those cases in which someone in the course of business acts in conflict with *bonos mores*, good morals. The German courts have used this provision to build a comprehensive body of law governing the protection against unfair competition. Within this body of case law five categories of unfair acts can be distinguished, namely fishing for customers, obstructive practices, exploitation of reputation and achievement, breach of law, and disturbance of the market.[8]

Historically, and despite their many differences, English and German laws of unfair competition did have at least two things in common. First, that each expected businesses to foot the bill for suppressing conduct considered injurious to consumers. But businesses are not selfless. English law only works because (or to the extent that) their interests and resources are necessarily engaged on the same side as the consumer, and it is therefore extremely reluctant to allow businesses to invoke what purports to be concern for consumer welfare unless identity of interests is assured. No such invocation

---

[6] Micklitz Report, above n 3, volume 3, at 79. This should now be read subject to the repeal of the UWG 1909 and its replacement by the UWG 2004.

[7] A Kamperman Sanders, *Unfair Competition Law: The Protection of Intellectual and Industrial Creativity* (Oxford, Clarendon Press, 1997) 57. Practices under the first head ('*Kundenfang*') include both deceptive and aggressive marketing techniques.

[8] In German: *Kundenfang, Behinderung, Ausbeutung, Rechtsbruch* and *Marktstörung*.

of consumer welfare is necessary under German law, since aggrieved competitors may sue in their own capacity for breach of duties owed directly to them, but it is still assumed that the actions competitors take for their own protection or advantage will safeguard that abstract quality of 'fairness' in the market, and therefore benefit consumers as well.

Secondly, that each looked exclusively to a one-dimensional relationship to define 'fairness': in English law this was business-to-consumer (ie vertical); whereas in German law it was business-to-business (ie horizontal). English law asks: 'is this fair to your consumers?' (although its ideas of what is 'fair' to consumers are sometimes rather robust). German law asks: 'is this fair to your competitors?', and is altogether more solicitous. Each body of law seems to have taken it for granted that if conduct was 'fair' in the one dimension which it recognised, then it would also necessarily be 'fair' in the other. The assumption is beguiling, but on reflection it is self-evidently untrue as a general proposition, at least in the short term. To give two examples: charging below cost price (predatory pricing) can hardly be described as unfair to the consumer (who would think in terms of over-charging being unfair)—but it is certainly damaging to one's competitors, and it may be regarded as unfair to them. On the other hand, suborning a competitor's employees to divulge his trade secrets is as wrongful to him as it is self-evidently unethical (and there are effective common law remedies against it, though not under the name of unfair competition), but there is no immediate adverse effect on consumers. If anything, the latter stand to benefit from the cheaper, better, or more varied goods which the appropriator can now produce.

3. THE MICKLITZ STUDY AND THE PLACE OF UNFAIR COMPETITION

The immediate origins of the Directive lie in the monumental exercise undertaken for DG Health and Consumer Affairs by Professor Micklitz and his co-workers at the *Institut für Europäisches Wirtschafts- und Verbraucherrecht eV* (and elsewhere) under the title 'The Feasibility of a General Legislative Framework on Fair Trading'.[9] However, this exercise was in many respects the culmination of a programme which had begun with the attempted harmonisation of European unfair competition law in the period from 1965 to 1975, had continued with efforts to harmonise consumer protection law so far as advertising and 'commercial communications' were concerned, and

---

[9] Available at http://ec.europa.eu/comm/consumers/cons_int/safe_shop/fair_bus_pract/green_pap_comm/studies/sur21_vol#_en.pdf. (hereafter the 'Micklitz Report').

may now be within sight of returning full circle to the original project. As recital 8 to the Directive concludes:

(8) ... The Commission should carefully examine the need for Community action in the field of unfair competition beyond the remit of this Directive and, if necessary, make a legislative proposal to cover these other aspects of unfair competition.

One of the starting points for the Micklitz study was the survey of the unfair competition laws of the then Member States carried out for the Commission by the late Professor Eugen Ulmer and the Max Planck Institute for Foreign and International Patent, Copyright and Competition Law (Munich) in the 1960s.[10] That survey led to abortive attempts by the Commission to harmonise unfair competition law in the early 1970s;[11] and when these failed, the remnants of the programme formed the basis for the first exercises in harmonising the law of commercial communications: initially through the Misleading Advertising Directive[12] and subsequently through the Directive on Comparative Advertising[13] and the 1996 Green Paper on Commercial Communications[14]. The Micklitz survey itself was published in November 2000, and may be regarded as marking the point of transition between the end of the restrictive 'commercial communications' phase, and the 2001 Green Paper on Consumer Protection,[15] which led by way of drafts in 2003 and 2005,[16] to the present Directive. After much debate the latter is 'maximal' in the sense of leaving no scope for national law within what is now a wholly occupied field, but less than maximal in so far as that field is purportedly confined to consumer protection law.

As Professor Micklitz's acknowledgements of the Ulmer survey imply, there is a close connection between laws of consumer protection and those of unfair competition. This is partly historical. Consumer protection law as we know it today is a phenomenon of the late twentieth century, but laws of unfair competition go back to the second half of the nineteenth century,

---

[10] E Ulmer, *Das Recht des unlauteren Wettbewerbs in den Mitgliedstaaten der Europä-ischen Wirtschaftsgemeinschaft, Bd. 1, Vergleichende Darstellung mit Vorschlägen zur Rechtsangleichung* (Munich, CH Beck, 1965), with subsequent national volumes.

[11] For a critical commentary on these early developments, and their continuing relevance, see C Wadlow, 'Unfair Competition in Community Law' (Part I, 'The Age of the "Classical Model"') [2006] *European Intellectual Property Review* 433 and (Part II, 'Harmonisation Becomes Gridlocked') 468.

[12] Directive 84/450/EEC [1984] OJ L 250/17].

[13] Directive 97/55/EEC [1997] OJ L 290/18. See A Ohly and M Spence, *The Law of Comparative Advertising: Directive 97/55/EC in the United Kingdom and Germany* (Oxford, Hart Publishing, 1999).

[14] COM(96)192 final, updated by COM(98)121 final.

[15] COM(2001)531 final, with follow-up paper COM(2002)289 final.

[16] Proposal for an Unfair Commercial Practices Directive, COM(2003)356 final; Common Position [2005] OJ C 38E/1.

and to a considerable extent still embody modes of thought which were prevalent then. As the Micklitz Report notes (emphasis in original):[17]

> Originally—at the end of the 19th century—the law of 'Fair Trading' (or in other terms: the law of 'Unfair Competition') which developed as a result of industrialisation and the liberalisation from restrictive mercantilist trading rules, was relatively 'narrow minded'. There was one main purpose for competition law, whether it was based on the General Clauses of the civil code as in France or Italy, or on a specific statute directed against 'Unfair Competition' as in Germany—and its aim was: *to protect competitors—and that means traders—from each other and against unfair marketing practices*, in this way constructing the legal order of the (national) markets as a level playing field for enterprises. A by-product of this was a kind of consumer protection, e.g. as a result of the prohibition of misleading advertising, in other words a mere 'reflex' accepted by the lawmaker *but not intended*.

With the passage of time, the relationship of consumer protection law to unfair competition law became less one of parasitism and more one of equality, but always subject to tension, even to the point of antinomy. The story may be taken up by Professor Beier, summarising the outcome of the Ulmer survey of the unfair competition laws of the six original Member States in the 1960s (citations omitted):[18]

> Ulmer's comparative survey showed a clearly structured and coherent field of law despite national differences, namely the classical field of unfair competition or 'concurrence déloyale'. By the end of the 1950's this field had undoubtedly progressed considerably in Continental Europe from its beginnings as a concept developed by the French courts in the middle of the 19th century. It had evolved and gained considerable importance, but its development was a continuous and cautiously advancing achievement, based for more than a century on consistent concepts with regard to (a) the protected interests and (b) the overall objectives of unfair competition law.

> The protected interests were those of the honest trader in having the right to restrain his competitors from causing him injury by unfair conduct. The test was whether a competitor's conduct complied with the 'honest usages' of the trade, the 'usages honnêtes' (Article 10bis Paris Convention), the 'correttezza professionale' (Article 2598 Codice Civile) or the 'bonos mores ('gute Sitten') in the course of trade (Article 1, German Unfair Competition Act 1909).

However, all this is part of the history of the law of unfair competition, not consumer protection law. So far as the former was concerned, the Micklitz

---

[17] Micklitz Report, above n 9, ii, at 57.

[18] FK Beier, 'The Law of Unfair Competition in the European Community: Its Development and Present Status' [1985] *European Intellectual Property Review* 284. The article reproduces the Second Herschel Smith Lecture delivered in London in 1985, when Professor Beier was the Director of the Max Planck Institute for Foreign and International Patent, Trade Mark and Competition Law, Munich.

reporters agreed that the appropriateness of some sort of 'general clause' was widely accepted in national and international law (with the exception of the United Kingdom and Ireland, and subject to the unstated qualification that at least two types of 'general clause' were being treated as one[19]), but counselled that this was not to say that businesses should be allowed to define their own moral code (emphasis added, citations omitted):[20]

> At least in quantitative terms there seems to be a wide-spread agreement on the appropriateness of a general clause on fair trading. This is not only true for nation states, but also for international regulatory initiatives. ... The reference point ... however, is intellectual property rights and not so much fair trading as such. *Here, honest practice shall constitute the reference point. Eugen Ulmer had already emphasised the need to clarify that the final decision on honest practices should not remain in the hands of those who shape it. Otherwise business alone could decide over the degree of honesty to be guaranteed in industrial and commercial matters.*

So if we approach consumer protection law by way of unfair competition law (which in turn is almost universally accepted as a branch of intellectual property law[21]) then we should heed the warning:[22]

> The far-reaching disregard of consumers' interests in the field of Intellectual Property very often results in some kind of inappropriate 'extension' of the respective 'exclusive' right by interpreting the General Clauses on Fair Trading in a manner, which creates a 'supplementary function' widening the scope of protection given by the specific Rules of Intellectual Property Law. The reason for this anti-competitive approach lies mainly in tradition and the historic development of the concept of 'unfair competition', which is much more influenced by the interests of the supply side, being protected from one another against specific marketing activities, than by the spirit and philosophy of consumer protection.

But given the close connection in practice between laws of unfair competition and laws of consumer protection, and the historical dominance of the former, it is not surprising to see works on unfair competition cited as principal sources of reference in several of the mini-bibliographies which begin each national chapter of the Micklitz study, despite the fact that the latter is concerned in terms only with consumer protection law. The upshot of all this is that the United Kingdom's strong tradition of consumer

---

[19] There is a crucial difference between a general clause in a code or statute specifically dedicated to unfair competition (as in Germany); and a general clause which is not specific to any single field (as in France, where the 'general clause' in question is the general tort provision of Art 1382 of the Civil Code).

[20] Micklitz Report, above n 9, i, at 13.

[21] Art 10*bis* of the Paris Convention for the Protection of Industrial Property (Stockholm, 1967).

[22] Micklitz Report, above n 9, i, at 56.

protection by independent administrative authorities has been quite well
accounted for in the Survey and its recommendations;[23] but that the parallel tradition of minimal judicial interference with business competition at
the suit of competitors has not, nor has the common law action for passing-off received anything like the consideration it might have deserved in
comparison to the German UWG. This would not have mattered but for
the fact that the UWG has arguably been mischaracterised as a consumer
protection law at some point in the legislative process (in the absence of
any German law more to the point), and may have been given too much
influence as a result. This is not to say that the UWG was misunderstood
in the Micklitz exercise: on the contrary, its affinity to intellectual property
law and its attachment to the interests of traders, rather than consumers,
is fully recognised.[24] What is surprising is that the implementation of the
Micklitz proposals in the Directive sometimes gives the impression of taking the UWG as if it were a model consumer protection law, which it has
never been. This is particularly to be seen when it comes to the 'general
clause', and to enforcement mechanisms.

4. THE EXAMPLE OF LOOK-ALIKES

The self-imposed conceptual limitations of the Directive are well illustrated
by the issue of 'look-alike' or 'copycat' products in the fast-moving consumer goods industry.[25] These are not terms of art, but for present purposes
they denote that the packaging or get-up of products, typically but not
invariably supermarket 'private label' or 'own-brands', has been designed
so as to prompt a conscious or unconscious association with the brand
leader in the mind of the consumer, but with sufficiently prominent differences for it to be unlikely that any but a very careless consumer would actually mistake them for the brand leader. Own brand look-alikes are rarely
litigated in this country, partly because supermarkets and their suppliers are
well acquainted with the law and display excellent judgement in keeping
fractionally within its limits, and partly because brand owners are acutely
conscious of the commercial disadvantages of taking on a rival which is
also a major customer, unless the case is an open-and-shut one.

A judge faced with a reasonably close 'look-alike' for the first time can
react in a number of ways, and it is typical of the actual development of
the law in this field that this instinctive reaction in cases of first impression

---

[23] Presumably attributable at least in part to the presence iv the editorial team of Professor
Geraint Howells, a prominent British consumer lawyer.

[24] Eg Micklitz Report, above n 9, iii, at 96: 'Consumer protection and Intellectual Property
Rights: General Approach'.

[25] See the contribution of Vanessa Marsland to this book.

goes quite a long way to wards determining the actual outcome of that case and its successors, with rationalisation following. A judge, and especially an English judge, might well start from the proposition that what was complained of was entirely consistent with the normal cut-and-thrust of competition, and only be tempted to intervene if there were special factors on either the legal or moral plane to take the case out of the ordinary. Alternatively, a more sensitive judge might feel instinctively shocked, and might therefore be inclined to penalise the look-alike. But precisely what is it that the judge finds shocking? Once again, an essentially non-rational response is quite likely to come first, with rationalisation following.

Once either the judge or the commentator has begun to attempt to rationalise what was probably originally an instinctive and morally-driven response, we shall see that a number of quite different conceptual paths are open. First, the judge may have felt (or reasoned) that the look-alike was 'unfair' because it was likely to deceive or confuse. In context, this can only mean that customers would be deceived or confused: no one suggests deception of the brand owner is likely or relevant. Self-evidently deception is a bad thing and confusion not much better, but the first response of the judge may equally well have been driven either by concern for consumers for their own sakes; or by the thought that the deceptive look-alike was in some sense 'stealing' trade from its rightful owner, the brand-leader. So is it a case of the look-alike cheating the consumer, the competitor, or both? And does the answer to that question have any consequences either in fact or in legal analysis? At one extreme, the judge might deplore the fact that consumers were being deceived, but treat is as *res inter alios acta* so far as the brand-leader was concerned.[26] At the other extreme, the judge might reason that consumers actually suffered little or not at all from their mistakes or confusion (the look-alike perhaps being as good as or better than the brand-leader in terms of quality and value), but that the brand-owner suffered significantly, and that the latter was entitled to compel the look-alike to play by the rules of the game. So a rationale based on deception of consumers can be driven by concern for them, or by concern for competitors, or both, but even these variants do not exhaust all the possible rationales.

Secondly, the judge may have reacted on the basis that that the look-alike was an unauthorised copy. Its originator therefore took a short cut, and (mis)appropriated something of value to the brand-leader. At this point, a judge from the common law tradition would probably have said to himself that if no issue of statutory infringement arose, then it was not for him to invent new quasi-proprietary rights in a field which had been pre-empted by Parliament. There is much writing on the misappropriation of 'valuable

---

[26] This was the rationale of the old decision in *Webster v Webster* (1791) 36 ER 949 (Lord Thurlow LC), decided before the action for passing-off became accepted: '[t]he fraud on the public is no ground for the plaintiff's coming into this court.'

intangibles', but little or no case law.[27] The same judge would probably also be reluctant to interfere without statutory authority in a manner which would reduce freedom of competition, without having the excuse of suppressing falsehood. A judge from another tradition might have a very different response. He might regard it as self-evident that the promoter of the look-alike should not enrich himself at the expense of a fellow trader, and that to do so was not only morally wrong but *prima facie* unlawful as 'slavish' (or 'servile') imitation.[28] This train of thought finds a place in the doctrine of unfair competition in many Continental legal systems, including those of France and Germany:[29]

> German tort law on unfair competition provides a protection of commercial and industrial products against direct takeover, so-called 'slavish imitation'. The copying of a product, a characteristic product-line, a famous label or a well-known brand is regarded as an unfair trade practice when it is a 'free ride' by taking advantage of the competitor's investments of time, effort and money in research and marketing. Therefore, an exception to the general freedom of imitation is accepted under German law in addition to intellectual property rights. The reason for this is that the business person has been deprived of the possibility of recouping his or her costs of research, development and marketing by a simple one-to-one copy of the product or service. The competitor can offer the imitation for a much lower price than the original product or service and gains his market share by exploiting the achievement of the original producer.

At this point the argument can be pursued into at least two further sub-divisions: whether the matter appropriated was the *input* or *investment* of the brand-owner into the item copied (its quality, design, advertising expenditure, etc), or the composite *product* of these factors and others, namely the goodwill the brand-leader enjoyed and the willingness of the public to buy it in preference to its competitors, and possibly to pay more for it. At this point we may note that we have reached a rather similar end-point to one of those based on misrepresentation, but that we have reached it without invoking misrepresentation because it was the copying, rather than the deception, which provided the element of 'unfairness' which the law seeks to remedy. We could pursue further refinements of analysis according

---

[27] See M Spence, 'Passing Off and the Misappropriation of Valuable Intangibles' (1996) 112 *Law Quarterly Review* 472.

[28] See para 40 of the Explanatory Memorandum to the draft Directive (Proposal for an Unfair Commercial Practices Directive, COM(2003)356 final). The imitation need not be particularly close to count as 'slavish', the principal question generally being whether there was some valid reason (such as functionality) for copying, or whether the latter was gratuitous.

[29] The summary of the position in Germany is taken from B Steckler, 'Unfair Trade Practices Under German Law: "Slavish Imitation" of Commercial and Industrial Activities' [1996] *European Intellectual Property Review* 390 at 397. For France, see, eg, A Kamperman Sanders, *Unfair Competition Law: The Protection of Intellectual and Industrial Creativity* (Oxford, Clarendon Press, 1997) 24.

to whether we were dealing with what is effectively a branch of the law of unjust enrichment, or with innominate or emergent property rights as such, but in either event this entire chain of argument owes everything to the supermarket acting 'unfairly' vis-à-vis a competitor-cum-supplier, and nothing at all to its acting unfairly with respect to its own customers.

The issue of look-alikes poses few theoretical difficulties in English law, but that is at least partly because the common law is wholly attached to the misrepresentation model and has no place for 'parasitism' or 'slavish imitation', unless deception as well as misappropriation is involved. Of the two passing-off cases decided by the House of Lords in recent years, one concerned a (branded) look-alike rival to the *Jif* plastic lemon, and Jif won: *Reckitt & Colman v Borden*.[30] A rare but illuminating decision on supermarket own-brand or private label look-alikes is to be found in *United Biscuits v Asda Stores* (PENGUIN vs. PUFFIN biscuits).[31] In the course of his judgment for the plaintiffs Robert Walker J observed (citation omitted):

> These causes of action [passing-off and registered trade mark infringement] are the subject of a great deal of learning, some of which has been deployed in argument during the hearing, but their basic idea is quite simple. It is (and has been for a very long time) the policy of the law to permit and indeed encourage fair competition in trade but to discourage and indeed prevent unfair competition. ... The rules as to passing off and trade mark infringement are (in non-statutory and statutory form respectively) a very important part of the law preventing unfair competition. Their basic common principle is that a trader may not sell his goods under false pretences, either by deceptively passing them off as the goods of another trader so as to take unfair advantage of his reputation in his goods, or by using a trade sign the same as, or confusingly similar to, a registered trade mark.

After this lengthy introduction, can we say that supermarket look-alikes are 'unfair', in the case of those that do not actually deceive or confuse the average consumer? Not so according to the Directive, which recites (in part):

> (14) ... It is not the intention of this Directive to reduce consumer choice by prohibiting the promotion of products which look similar to other products unless this similarity confuses consumers as to the commercial origin of the product and is therefore misleading.

Likewise, paragraph 40 of the Explanatory Memorandum accompanying the draft Directive in 2003 singled out 'slavish imitation (i.e. copying independently of any likelihood of consumer confusion)' as an act frequently

---

[30] *Reckitt & Colman v Borden* [1990] 1 WLR 491; [1990] 1 All ER 873; [1990] RPC 340 (HL).
[31] *United Biscuits v Asda Stores* [1997] RPC 513 (Robert Walker J).

amounting to unfair competition under national laws, but outside the Directive's intended scope.[32]

And from the point of view of the consumer the answer is equally obviously 'no', unless the look-alike in question oversteps the line between legitimate and non-confusing copying of certain generic visual cues, into deceptive similarity or outright counterfeiting, or unless its quality is less than he or she had been led to expect from the implicit claim of parity with the brand leader. Brand-owners, on the other hand, tend to regard look-alikes as inherently unfair even if they are not confusing or deceptive. If the law allowed, they would follow the second line of argument above and assert that, deception aside, look-alikes are unethical and ought to be unlawful, because they are parasitic imitators. The supermarket reaps where it has not sown.

Despite the clarity of the Directive on this point, it is not surprising to find its general clause in danger of being misinterpreted (if not actually misappropriated) on behalf of brand owners to combat what is really, to their way of thinking, a case of unfair competition based on the 'misappropriation of valuable intangibles', and having little or nothing to do with misrepresentation. Just such a tendency may be seen from the following excerpts:[33]

> Even if the new law does not completely satisfy brand owners or provide guaranteed protection against lookalikes, it must be regarded as a step in the right direction.

> Brand owners will no doubt be watching this [transposition] with interest and may well wish to take the opportunity to ... maximise the benefits of the Directive in the UK for their specific purposes.

So in the name of 'fairness' towards consumers, we are being invited to suppress a practice which is, in most cases, perfectly innocuous from their point of view, and to impose a morality which (rightly or wrongly) can only draw its validity from a certain world-view of the rights of businesses inter se. If this is to be justified, it can only be on the basis of a properly thought-out law of unfair competition. But if this turns out to be the result of the Directive in practice, then we will have submitted ourselves to a de facto law of unfair competition which has not been thought out at all.

5. SUMMARY AND CONCLUSIONS

The thesis of the present contribution is that the legitimate interests of consumers and businesses do not routinely or necessarily coincide.

[32] Proposal for an Unfair Commercial Practices Directive, COM(2003)356 final, para 40.
[33] G Grassie, 'EU Directive on Unfair Commercial Practices—a UK Perspective' (2006) 1 *Journal of Intellectual Property Law and Practice* 107 at 111.

The expedient of the business claimant as the 'vicarious champion' of the consumer is a useful one, but it holds good only in limited circumstances. What is 'ethical' for one business vis-à-vis another business may not be ethical vis-à-vis the consumer, and vice versa. Laws of unfair competition and of consumer protection may impinge on the same conduct, but they pursue different agendas and reflect different moral values and economic priorities. They may be good neighbours, but they are unlikely to be happy bedfellows.

It follows that a consumer protection law based on what are in fact intra-business ethics will not appropriately protect consumers from unfair business practices in general, no matter how reasonable that law may appear to be in terms of its protection of business interests from unfair competition. Conversely, an unfair competition law based on what are in fact consumer-driven ethics is certain to be incomplete and is likely to be inappropriate. Incomplete, because the business-to-business dimension is ex hypothesi ignored or understated; inappropriate, because conduct which is neutral (or even beneficial) vis-à-vis the consumer may be 'unfair' to the point of being wrongful between competitors, once the latter's values and legitimate interests are taken into account. A law of either kind written by or for business incumbents is likely to be over-prescriptive, over-proscriptive, and over-protective of those who benefit from the status quo. Businesses tend to prefer collusion to competition (whatever they say to the contrary), and any law they write for themselves will reflect this. After all, the law they write is likely to be a collective, rather than a competitive, effort.

So does the Directive (and especially its general clause) take due but not excessive account of the legitimate interests of competitors (not to mention the public at large), or is it exclusively focussed on the interests of consumers as such? And to the extent that it does take account of the interests of competitors and the public, then how successful is it? These are big questions, but at the very least, we may all agree with Professor Micklitz when he recollected (citation omitted):[34]

> As early as 1965 Eugen Ulmer wrote, in his comparative analysis of the Member States' law on fair trading, that the range of interests which shall be protected— those of the competitors and/or those of consumers and/or the public at large—is of outstanding importance for each and every regulatory approach and may be of even greater importance than the actual wording of the general clause. Thirty-five years later there is nothing which lessens the relevance of this statement.

The case for reclaiming European unfair competition law from Europe's consumer protection lawyers, is that keeping the two separate is the only way to do justice to both sets of parties.

---

[34] Micklitz Report, above n 9, i, at 16.

11

Unfair Commercial Practices: Stamping out Misleading Packaging

1. INTRODUCTION—THE THESIS OF THIS PAPER

CONSUMERS ARE MISLED by copycat packaging, and measures to prevent this in the UK are overdue. The Unfair Commercial Practices Directive (UCPD) recognises that copycats are cases where consumers may be misled. It states that the problem must be addressed.

Enforcement through Trading Standards is unlikely to be an effective method of avoiding consumers being misled by copycat products, as consumers do not complain about occasional mistaken purchases. Meanwhile, there are no effective self-regulatory mechanisms for dealing with the copycat issue.

With respect to copycat products, passing off is not equivalent to unfair competition law and similar remedies in other countries. Even if a competitor brings an action for passing off, consumers do not enjoy equivalent protection in the UK to that in other Member States.

The UK government has an obligation under Article 11(1) of the UCPD to ensure that there are adequate remedies. To achieve equivalent protection for consumers across the EU as envisaged by the Directive, competitors should have the right to bring action in respect of misleading practices which involve consumers being misled by copycat products, regardless of whether this also amounts to passing off. To allow this is not to diverge from the consumer protection purpose of the Directive, but merely to facilitate its achievement, based on experience across Europe that enforcement by competitors whose packs are copied is likely to provide the most effective protection against consumers being misled.

---

[1] Vanessa Marsland, partner Clifford Chance LLP, assisted the British Brands Group in putting this chapter together. The British Brands Group represents the interests of branded manufactures in the UK. This chapter is published with their consent. The analysis of remedies in the UK contained in Annex 1 was prepared with significant input from Paul Walsh of Bristows.

2. BRANDS—WHY THEY ARE TARGETS

Brands rest in the minds of individual consumers and are built when a product (or service) delivers superior, differentiated performance consistently over time. As a consumer's expectations are continuously met (or exceeded), a strong reputation is created that leads to greater levels of consumer satisfaction and loyalty. To sustain this reputation against competitors requires continual investment, innovation and communication. Evidence supports this, showing that branded companies innovate significantly more than non-branded companies and deliver more economic value added.[2]

Concern for reputation drives brand manufacturers to sustain quality and avoid disappointment (and when things go wrong, to resolve problems quickly). Brands therefore provide a powerful mechanism for consumer protection. Brands only succeed if they meet consumer expectations; if they do not, consumers stop buying.

3. THE COPYCAT PROBLEM

Copycats mimic product designs and packaging created by others. With copycat packaging, a competitor deliberately adopts design features that are very similar to those of familiar branded products. Typically, the copycat does not copy the exact product name or pack design. Instead, copycats typically use a combination of similar colours and colour combinations, similar on-pack imagery and similar pack format to the brand leader. In some cases, the name of the copycat product may also be evocative of the branded product—eg ASDA's use of PUFFIN for its private label competitor to the PENGUIN bar.[3]

4. THE IMPACT ON CONSUMERS OF COPYCAT PRODUCTS

Copycats cause consumers to buy the copycat in the belief that they are buying the branded product. Research shows that consumers frequently buy the wrong product because of similar packaging. In this research,[4] around 17 per cent stated that they had purchased copycat products *by mistake* at some point in the preceding six months. Scaled up, this suggests that around 4–5 million UK consumers buy copycats by mistake in a six-month period.

---

[2] PIMS (Profit Impact of Market Strategy), of brands and growth (1988).
[3] *United Biscuits v ASDA Stores* [1997] RPC 513, one of the very few actions in the UK where passing off claims have been successful as regards copycats.
[4] NOP, for *Marketing Magazine*, Feb 1997.

Copycats cause consumers to believe the makers of the branded product make the copycat when they do not. Research evidence repeatedly confirms that UK consumers are much more ready to assume that products are made by the manufacturers of the brand leaders where the packaging design is very similar. At the lowest level in the research samples (32 per cent),[5] this suggests around 7.5 million shoppers in a six month period are misled by copycat packaging into assuming that products are made by the manufacturers of branded products, when they are not. Other research suggests that the number may be much larger.

Copycats cause consumers to believe the product is more similar to the branded product than they would otherwise have assumed (based on price, product description and less similar packaging). Research shows that, as well as increasing the likelihood that consumers will assume that products are made by the branded manufacturer, copycats increase consumer willingness to assume the product quality is as good as that of the branded product.[6] The consequence of the greater likelihood of assumption of equivalent quality is to increase the perception that the copycat is good value for money, and therefore worth trying. In fact, similarity of pack design gives no guarantee as to quality or value. This means that the risk of disappointment is much higher.

In the case of retailer private label copycats, the effect of pack similarity is often further accentuated by other factors at point of sale including:

positioning of the copycat on the shelf adjacent to the brand which it copies, encouraging comparison/connection with the branded product;
display material at point of sale inviting comparisons;
relative pricing of the brand leader and copycat;
other factors, such as stock availability.

5. THE UNFAIR COMMERCIAL PRACTICES DIRECTIVE

The UCPD seeks to deliver a high level of consumer protection and contribute to the proper functioning of the internal market. It seeks to achieve these objectives by establishing uniform rules at Community level and by clarifying certain legal concepts in order to provide legal certainty.

Copycats fall explicitly within the scope of the UCPD. Annex 1 to the Directive sets out a list of practices which shall in all circumstances be regarded as unfair. Clause 13 of Annex 1 specifically mentions 'promoting a product similar to a product made by a particular manufacturer in such

[5] RSGB, 'Study of Lookalikes', Mar 1998, for the British Brands Group.
[6] J-N Kapferer, 'Stealing Brand Equity: Measuring Perceptual Confusion between National Brands and "Copycat" Own-label Products', *Marketing and Research Today*, May 1995.

a manner as deliberately to mislead the consumer into believing that the product is made by the same manufacturer when it is not'. Recital 14 makes it express that similarity of packaging as a means to such misleadingness is within the scope of the Directive.

By Article 5, misleading actions are a category of unfair commercial practices, ie the acts prohibited under the Directive that materially distort consumer behaviour (and are contrary to the requirements of professional diligence). Article 6 addresses misleading actions. Misleading actions and practices include:

> False or deceptive information about the main characteristics of a product, including its commercial origin.[7]

> Marketing of a product which creates confusion with any products, trade marks, trade names or other distinguishing marks of a competitor.[8]

As the evidence in Annex 2 shows, copycats mislead consumers at both an explicit and a subliminal level, prompting many to make a purchase they would otherwise not make, and the UCPD clearly has the scope to address these consumer aspects.

Notwithstanding its consumer protection objectives, the Directive acknowledges that in respect of unfair commercial practices the interests of consumers and competitors converge, and that it is in the common interest of consumers and competitors that all traders in the market place respect the rules. Recital 8 states:

> *This Directive protects consumer economic interests from unfair business-to-consumer commercial practices. Thereby, it also indirectly protects legitimate businesses from their competitors who do not play by the rules in this Directive and thus guarantees fair competition in fields co-ordinated by it.*

6. EXISTING LEGAL REMEDIES AGAINST MISLEADING COPYCATS IN THE UK

6(a) Public Enforcement

Consumers do not complain about copycats. Where consumers have been misled on a one off purchase of a relatively inexpensive fast moving consumer goods item they may often 'put it down to experience' rather than go to the trouble of complaining. If they have been misled into thinking the brand manufacturer made the copycat, they may never realise the deception.

---

[7] Art 6.1(b) of the UCPD, Directive 2005/29 [2005] OJ L 149/22.
[8] Art 6.2(a) of ibid.

While Trading Standards have authority to act against copycats under the Trade Descriptions Act 1968, as amended,[9] it has not been possible to identify any instances where Trading Standards have pursued such a case. This is believed to be a reflection of the fact that they tend to focus their resources on acting on very clear-cut cases—such as infringement of registered trade marks by sale of blatant counterfeit products. One reason for this is that the tribunals in which Trading Standards prosecutions are typically brought are generalist tribunals covering a wide range of issues, and neither Trading Standards nor the Tribunals will have experience of dealing with the complex evidence that arises in copycat cases. Trading Standards' practice in non-identical copying cases and cases not involving registered rights is to encourage such cases to be dealt with by civil action, by affected competitors.

6(b) Self Regulation

There is no general self-regulatory mechanism for addressing copycat packaging[10] in the UK. That the copying and deception of consumers exemplified by copycat packaging is undesirable is recognised and addressed in The British Code of Advertising, Sales Promotion and Direct Marketing, administered by the Advertising Standards Authority.

Article 20.2, a provision against unfair advantage,[11] and Article 21.1, a provision against imitation,[12] would under normal circumstances provide some help in addressing copycats. However, while the code covers advertising, sales promotion and direct marketing, it does not cover packaging.

Packaging is arguably the most powerful of marketing tools, exerting its influence at point of sale where around 70 per cent of shoppers' purchasing decisions are made. However packaging is excluded from the scope of the

---

[9] By s 2, a trade description is an indication, direct or indirect, and by whatever means given, of any of a list of matters. The list includes composition, fitness for purpose or any other physical characteristics, and person by whom manufactured or approved. S3 confirms that a false trade description is a trade description which is false to a material degree.

[10] There is a voluntary system in the grocery sector known as the IGD Dispute Resolution Procedure. As the name suggests, this is more a dispute resolution procedure than a self-regulatory mechanism although it contains a provision calling on signatories not to use similar features to those of another product. Any such procedure is only as strong as its signatories and relies on the ability of the parties to agree. In this case, while some of the major supermarkets are signatories, most retailers are not and it is limited to the grocery sector. The procedure is shrouded in secrecy so it is impossible to know how often the procedure has been invoked. It is understood however, that it is rarely used.

[11] Marketers should not take unfair advantage of the reputation of trade marks, trade names or other distinguishing marks of organisations or of the designation of origin of competing products.

[12] No marketing communication should so closely resemble any other that it misleads, is likely to mislead or causes confusion.

CAP Code as there is no enforcement mechanism that can be applied by the self-regulatory authority.

6(c) Action by the Brand Owners

Factually, there is some overlap between the protection given to consumers by the UCPD and the protection given to brand manufacturers by virtue of their intellectual property rights, such as trade marks. However, securing trade mark registration of the kinds of design elements which are typically copied in copycat packaging, such as colours, colour combinations, graphic elements and pack shapes, is extremely time consuming, expensive and often impossible.[13] As a result, so far there have been relatively few registrations in the UK (or at the Community Trade Marks Office) for 'secondary' brand cues such as pure colours and pure colour combinations. In practice, copycat packaging often 'falls between the gaps' of the range of registered intellectual property protection in the UK.

In copycat cases where there is no infringement of registered rights, the main route to avoiding consumers being misled is for competitors whose packs are copied to bring an action for passing off. The cause of action in passing off is that a misrepresentation is being made to consumers which damages the competitor. Typically, the misrepresentation is said to be as to origin, though there have also been cases where clear misrepresentation as to product equivalence has been considered to fall within passing off. A more detailed study of the legislative and self-regulatory remedies available in the UK is provided in Annex 1.

This compares with the position in a number of other Member States, where 'unfair competition' laws are typically relied on by competitors to object to copycat packaging which is misleading consumers. These laws as applied in practice are often more flexible than the UK passing off action, in the way in which they address misleadingness of copycats.

Protection against misleading copycats tends to be more extensive and much less costly to obtain in other Member States under unfair competition laws than is the case in the UK under passing off. Reasons for this appear to include:

The approach taken by the UK courts to applying passing off to the facts of copycat cases—there is a perception of judicial scepticism about such cases, notwithstanding the repeated research findings about consumers being misled by packaging similarity. This compares with tribunals applying unfair competition doctrines in various other Member States, where there appears to be greater

---

[13] This is because of the requirement to prove that the elements have acquired distinctiveness as trade marks in relation to the product.

willingness to find unfairness/misleadingness based on pack-for-pack comparison rather than an unnecessarily high degree of pack similarity.

Practical difficulty in generating evidence of actual misleadingness of the products—competitors are forced to conduct surveys/witness interviews, which may then be challenged on the ground that the interviewees are being 'led' in providing the evidence.

Thus, consumers in many parts of the EU are better protected from misleading copycats than they are in the UK. The Directive is seeking to ensure a consistent level of protection throughout the EU and to overcome these discrepancies.

Similarly, members' experience has been that there is more effective protection against misleading copycats in Australia, which has what some consider a statutory form of unfair competition legislation under section 52 of the Trade Practices Act. More detailed analysis of the different laws in several of the larger Member States and in Australia, as applied to copycats, is in Annex 2.

The relatively limited protection available in the UK through passing off presents particular problems because of a unique combination of features of the UK retail market place. These features include:

High concentration in the retail market, with a small number of powerful retailers;
A particularly sophisticated own label offer by comparison with other European markets;
A large own label share—according to GFK/Worldpanel[14] (2005) the UK's share of own label is the second highest in Europe (after Switzerland) at 39.9 per cent.

7. THE INTERPLAY BETWEEN PUBLIC AND PRIVATE ENFORCEMENT UNDER THE DIRECTIVE

In the United Kingdom at present, it is only brand owners who in practice exercise any right of recourse against copycat products, and their rights are generally limited to the right to bring an action in tort for passing-off, the limitations of which have already been described. In a minority of cases the brand owner may be able to bring an action for trade mark or other intellectual property infringement. However, most copycat products are so designed that they do not usually infringe registered rights but use subtler means to mimic the attributes of branded products.

---

[14] Gfk/Worldpanel, 'Private Label Trends in Europe', *Planet Retail, June 2006,* available at www. competition-law.ox.ac.uk/lawvle/users/ezrachia/CCLP%20S.%2012-06.pdf.

Research indicates that when it comes to enforcement of national fairness laws aimed at protecting consumers in relation to consumer practices the United Kingdom differs from most other Member States by reason of the widespread reliance on self-regulatory codes.[15] The absence of a relevant self-regulatory code dealing with copycats and the practical absence of public enforcement means that, in order to fulfil the objective of the UCPD,

---

[15] *June 2003 report* "Analysis of National Fairness Laws Aimed at Protecting Consumers in Relation to Commercial Practices", coordinated by Prof Dr Reiner Schulze and Prof Dr Hans Schulte-Nolke, report commissioned by the Directorate-General Health and Consumer Protection of the European Commission (DG SANCO) (June 2003).

'Nearly all Member States apply a similar set of sanctions against unfair commercial practices (e.g. injunctions, damages, penal sanctions). In practice, the typically used sanctions may differ from the model laid down in the legal framework.*

Both aspects—enforcement system and applied sanctions —are of course influenced by the general approach to unfair commercial practices in the Member States.

The Consumer Ombudsman (CO) is the key enforcement institution in the Scandinavian countries. The independent position as a public watchdog on marketing practices seems to be one of the reasons for the success of this institution which is held in high reputation in the Scandinavian countries. Although the CO can initiate legal proceedings against unfair commercial practices, many cases can already be settled through measures taken by the CO.

A different approach is taken by countries like Austria, Belgium, Germany and Spain. In these countries legal actions against unfair commercial practices are taken by competitors or by associations of competitors or consumers. Interestingly, in countries such as Austria and Germany rules protecting consumers and those protecting competitors can both be enforced by competitors' associations. A clear delimitation in this field can be found in Belgium. Under Belgian law business associations can only bring an action against unfair practices violating Art. 93 LPC whereas consumer associations can only initiate proceedings against practices violating Art. 94 LPC.

Only in a few countries (e.g. Austria and France) can single consumers initiate legal proceedings against unfair commercial practices. Probably due to financial risks, consumers do not use this possibility very often.

The role of public authorities applying penal sanctions, especially fines, varies between the Member States. Due to the legal framework in this field, French authorities play a rather important role—several examples were outlined above—whereas in other Member States public authorities play a minor role. In this context the nulla poena sine lege principle sets strict limits to the application of penal sanctions for the violation of fairness rules, especially in cases where the commercial fairness provisions are formulated in a rather general way.

A completely different approach can be found in the United Kingdom. Due to widespread self-regulation in the field of unfair commercial practices many sanctions also derive from self-regulatory codes. Theoretically consumers and competitors can bring legal actions against unfair practices under common law or some statues in this field. In practice most of the cases can be settled through self-regulatory mechanisms, e.g. decisions of the Advertising Standards Authority leading to adverse publicity. The self-regulatory system is encouraged and guided by the Office of Fair Trading (OFT). In severe cases exhausting self-regulatory mechanisms the OFT can initiate legal proceedings against businesses using unfair practices.

As mentioned above, often a similar set of sanctions applies to unfair commercial practices. In all Member States an injunction or cease and desist order can be obtained, which is probably the most effective sanction as it stops the unfair behaviour. According to the Directive on injunctions for the protection of consumer's interests, registered consumer associations are entitled to obtain an injunction against misleading advertising. This Directive has been transposed in all Member States.

Additionally, in some Member States a court may order that the effects of unfair practices have to be removed (e.g. correction of misleading information) and that the judgment may be published.

it will be necessary to give both consumers and competitors enhanced enforcement rights.

The Directive requires that 'persons or organisations … having a legitimate interest in the matter *must* have legal remedies for initiating proceedings against unfair commercial practices'.[16] The DTI has suggested that enabling consumers to make complaints to the appropriate administrative authority will be adequate to satisfy the obligation in Article 11.1. However, as explained above, it is unlikely that complaints will be made or that Trading Standards Offices (TSOs) will treat copycat cases as priority cases for their limited resources. Therefore, in order to enforce compliance with the provisions of this UCPD in the interests of consumers, as provided for in Article 11.1 of the Directive, it will be necessary to extend enforcement rights to competitors.

It is also suggested by the DTI that the UK will comply with the UCPD if competitors are given the right to bring complaints before the TSOs (assuming they are the relevant administrative authority). However, based on the experience under the Trade Descriptions Act 1968, and from an understanding of Trading Standards' priorities and resources, it is unlikely that TSOs will devote resources to pursuing individual cases of copycats. Therefore, in order for consumers to be protected as required by the UCPD, it will be necessary for brand owners to take action against copycats directly relying on the UCPD provisions as implemented in English law.

Accordingly, in order to comply with the UCPD it will be necessary for the UK implementing legislation to give competitors the explicit right to bring an action in respect of copycat products under the UCPD. If that right were not to be granted the enforcement means referred to in Article 11.1 would be of no effect.

This will mean that in future a brand owner will have the option of bringing parallel actions, one for passing-off and the other for breach of the UCPD (in a similar manner to the situation in Australia, in respect of section 52 of the Trade Practices Act).

Empowering competitors to act in respect of all forms of unfair or misleading commercial practices covered by the Directive could risk cutting across existing effective mechanisms, such as self-regulatory regimes, and some types of practice are inherently unsuited to enforcement by a competitor. However, the copycat issue is a very specific example of misleadingness where the interests of consumers and competitors are the same, where there

In many countries, competitors and consumers are entitled to damages. Especially in cases harming consumers this may not be the most appropriate sanction as they often only suffer a small financial loss and may not find it attractive to start court proceedings.

Generally speaking, in all Member States severe cases of unfair commercial practices face severe penal sanctions such as fines or even imprisonment. A special fine can be found in Sweden, the so-called market disruption fee'. (ibid, at 82 and 83)

[16] See Recital 21, above n emphasis added.

is no effective self-regulatory mechanism, and where effective protection for consumers is most likely to be provided by enabling competitors to bring civil actions to prevent misleading practices.

ANNEX 1—AN ANALYSIS OF REMEDIES IN THE UK

Trade Mark Legislation

Registered trade marks are not designed to address copycat packaging and are ineffective in doing so. As Patrick McLoughlin MP stated in the House of Commons at the time of the Trade Marks Bill (1994),[17] 'the main characteristic of a look-alike product is that it does not copy a trade mark'.

Typically a copycat borrows a small amount from each of several aspects of the original product. It may reproduce part of the surface decoration, part of the shape, part of the colour and part of the brand name without reproducing any of these elements completely. In doing so, the copycat avoids infringing any single intellectual property right, but captures sufficient of the look and feel of the original to mislead shoppers. It therefore is able to avoid any trade mark infringement.

Trade marks are valuable of course in protecting against the use by a competitor of identical marks on identical goods, but many packaging features are simply not capable of registration if they are not deemed sufficiently distinctive. It would therefore be impossible (let alone enormously expensive) to register the full range of packaging features that might be used by a copycat.

To bring an infringement case against similar marks being used on identical or similar goods, it is necessary to prove likelihood of consumer confusion. In the case of copycats, similar marks are not often used and, even if they are, on a 'global appreciation' (the test set by the European Court of Justice in cases such as *Sabel v Puma* [18]) confusion may not arise.

A further limitation concerns the thorough registration process, which takes an impractical length of time in the context of fighting copycats. Where acquired distinctiveness has to be proved, typically three to five years' sales are required by the Registry, whilst a copycat can be (and often is) launched in a few months and could itself reduce the distinctiveness of the original.

The limitations of trade marks in fighting copycats are illustrated by the *Penguin v Puffin*[19] case in 1997. The survey evidence that sought to show consumer confusion was dismissed and the judge found no case of trade mark infringement, recognising that Puffins and Penguins are very different birds, being, literally, poles apart.

---

[17] Hc Debs, vol 000, col 299 (16 May 1994).
[18] Case C–251/95 [1997] ECR I–6191.
[19] ChD, 18 Mar 1997 not reported.

Registered Designs

Registered designs (both UK and Community) provide strong protection against counterfeits and provide a valuable means of protecting the shape of a product's packaging. Design registrations protect against substantial reproduction of a design, which in the context of packaging is defined as the shape, configuration, pattern or ornament applied to an article.

As a means of tackling copycats, however, registered designs have their shortcomings. The whole of the copy must not be substantially different from the whole of the registered design and an infringer must produce an article 'not substantially different' in order for a legal challenge to be successful. While copycats tend to borrow the essence of the original design, they tend not to use aspects which are subject to a registration or not to use substantial reproduction of these aspects. Furthermore, the rights cover the surface pattern but excludes 'printed matter primarily of … .artistic character, including …. Trade advertisements and similar articles'.

A registration-based system, as in the case of trade marks, has shortcomings in tackling copycats. These include the necessary time required to register, the difficulty in ascertaining what to register and the cost of registration (particularly of multiple registrations). Product packaging of fast-moving consumer goods (fmcg) changes frequently, compounding these shortcomings. Indeed, as designs must be new to be registrable, it is unlikely that later iterations of a pack's design will be eligible for this protection.

Unregistered Designs (Design Right)

Unregistered design protection has an advantage over registered designs in that it is an automatic right. However, protection is afforded only to the shape or configuration of a pack, not to its surface decoration (which would be covered by copyright). While substantial reproduction of any aspect of a design constitutes infringement, recent decisions suggest that the whole of an article must be considered, even if only a part has been copied.

A significant shortcoming in the context of copycats is the need to show copying. This is defined narrowly by the courts and tends to be avoided by the producers of copycats.

Copyright

While copyright has the advantage of being an automatic right rather than a registration-based system and protects the surface decoration of products, it provides no protection against those that copy the shape of articles. It is also necessary to show that the copying has been 'substantial', something that copycats avoid when designing surface decoration. Also in relation to copyright in pack designs, it is often difficult to track down the original author of the copyright work.

While unregistered designs protect the shape of the pack and copyright its surface decoration, these are independent rights, and the courts therefore do not look at them together. Instead, the court will consider whether the shape of a pack has been substantially reproduced and will then consider, separately, whether the surface decoration has been substantially reproduced. A copycat can clear both these tests individually while still achieving the look and feel of the original product.

Passing–Off

As the common law of passing-off is intended to prevent traders passing off themselves or their goods as those of another trader, to the extent that it causes that other trader damage, it could be deemed to be well suited to addressing copycats. However it has some significant disadvantages:

— obtaining factual evidence that consumers are being misled is very difficult. As copycats tend to be low value goods, consumers rarely complain. Some will blame themselves for their error or put it down to experience, while others will remain unaware that their assumptions about a product, induced by its packaging, are wrong. Furthermore, it is not practical to research in-store whether consumers are being misled as this would not be allowed by the retailer selling the copycat;
— proving that there is a risk of consumers being misled using evidence such as surveys (eg in the street or in mocked-up shops) is also fraught with difficulty as these must meet the rigorous standards set by UK courts.
— Obtaining interlocutory relief under passing-off is extremely risky and time consuming. It is necessary to show in affidavit evidence that there is an arguable case and evidence of irreparable harm. This is difficult to achieve quickly in the case of copycats. Furthermore, if the decision is reversed at full trial, the elaimant may (rightly) face punitive damages for the defendant's lost sales.

The *Penguin v Puffin*[20] case referred to above illustrates the potential but also the problems with passing-off. The judge found in favour of Penguin under passing–off and Asda was forced to change the packaging, but this outcome was uncertain and could not have been reasonably predicted (as the survey evidence was withdrawn, the judge relied on the persuasiveness of a few witnesses). Furthermore he did not specify how close to Penguin's packaging Puffin could go. As a result Puffin biscuits remain on the shelf today.

[20] Ibid.

The Relevant Designs for Penguin

Penguin – 1996

Puffin – 1996 (pre-court)

Puffin – 2004

(after United Biscuits (Penguin) had won its action for passing off)

Self Regulation: The CAP[21] Code

That the copying and deception of consumers exemplified by copycat packaging are undesirable is recognised and addressed in The British Code of Advertising, Sales Promotion and Direct Marketing,[22] administered by the Advertising Standards Authority. Article 20.2, a provision against unfair advantage,[23] and Article 21.1, a provision against imitation,[24] would under normal circumstances provide some help in addressing copycats. However, while the code covers advertising, sales promotion and direct marketing, it does not cover packaging.

Packaging is arguably the most powerful of marketing tools, exerting its influence at point of sale where around 70 per cent of shoppers' purchasing decisions are made. However packaging remains outside the scope of the CAP Code as there is no enforcement mechanism that can be applied by the self-regulatory authority.

The IGD[25] Dispute Resolution Procedure

As the name suggests, this is more a dispute resolution procedure than a self-regulatory mechanism although it calls on signatories not to use similar

---

[21] Committee of Advertising Practice.

[22] Available at www.cap.org.uk/cap/codes/cap_code/.

[23] Marketers should not take unfair advantage of the reputation of trade marks, trade names or other distinguishing marks of organisations or of the designation of origin of competing products.

[24] No marketing communication should so closely resemble any other that it misleads, is likely to mislead or causes confusion.

[25] Institute for Grocery Distribution.

features to those of another product.[26] Any such procedure is only as strong as its signatories, and relies on the ability of the parties to agree. In this case, while some of the major supermarkets are signatories, most retailers are not, and it is limited to the grocery sector. The procedure is shrouded in secrecy so it is impossible to know how often it has been invoked.

ANNEX 2—LEGAL MEASURES AVAILABLE IN DIFFERENT COUNTRIES

The Annex provides a brief survey of legal measures apart from intellectual property rights available to competitors in different Member States and in Australia to combat copycat packaging and get-up.

The Netherlands

The Dutch Unfair Competition Doctrine of 'Slavish Imitations'

Article 6:162 of the Dutch Civil Code provides for protection against unfair competition under the so-called doctrine of 'slavish imitations'. The protection against unfair competition stands side by side with the protection of registered trade marks and designs.

The Dutch courts have developed the doctrine of 'slavish imitations', which applies where a product copies elements of the packaging or get-up of another product so as to cause confusion amongst the public as to the commercial origin of the product or as to a connection of the copycat product with the maker of the original product. Competitors can take action under the relevant section to stop such acts of unfair competition.

Unlike the English passing off action, it is not a requirement under the 'slavish imitations' doctrine that the party making the complaint should prove that he acquired goodwill in the packaging being imitated or that the imitation causes damage to its business.

Examples from the Dutch Case Law

(1) In a decision of 6 July 2005, the District Court of Breda upheld a claim by Lego Systems A/S against Mega Bloks Inc[27] regarding the imitation of

---

[26] 'For the purpose of avoiding or resolving disputes, it is accepted that a product sold in the United Kingdom should avoid using any combination of the same or similar name, colour scheme, shape, typeface, design layout or portrayed images so as to convey significant visual features which are essentially similar to the those of another product. Exceptionally, a single feature may be sufficiently significant': IGD Dispute Resolution Procedure.
[27] *Lego Systems A/S v Mega Bloks Inc* (118470/HA ZA03-501).

toy building blocks. Despite the fact that LEGO'S registered intellectual property rights in relation to the building blocks had expired, the court held that it was possible for Mega Bloks to avoid confusion with LEGO blocks without impairing the functionality of the product. Mega Bloks failed to do so and its conduct was held to amount to unfair competition. Images of the Lego bricks and the Mega Bloks imitation bricks in question are provided below:

(2) In a decision of the District Court of Amsterdam of 15 April 2004,[28] Hasbro Inc was successful in a claim against *Simba Toys GmbH* in relation to the imitation of a toy kitten. Images of the original product (sold under the trade mark FUR REAL) and the imitation (sold under the trade mark LOVELY KITTEN) are provided below. The court held that Hasbro could assert no copyright in its product as the product lacked the necessary originality. No registered intellectual property rights were available either. The court held, however, that Simba Toys' LOVELY KITTEN product slavishly imitated Hasbro's product and that Simba failed to implement necessary differences in order to prevent the risk of avoidable confusion.

[28] *Hasbro Inc v Simbra Toys GmbH* (IER 2004/62).

Germany

The Provisions of the German Unfair Competition Act (the 'UWG')
relating to Misleading Trade Practices

In addition to the protection provided under German law to registered intellectual properties such as trade marks and design, the German Trade Marks Act provides protection to unregistered trade marks which have acquired reputation through use. Protection of unregistered trade marks in Germany is largely equivalent to the protection provided in passing-off in the UK where the imitation concerns unregistered marks. In addition, however, a broader scope of protection against unfair commercial practices is available in Germany under the Unfair Competition Act (known as the UWG).

In the area of copycat products, protection can be sought under the UWG under section. 4, No. 9(a), which prohibits acts in commerce which lead to a likelihood of confusion regarding the commercial source of a product. The elements of the claim are that the product or package being copied (ie the original branded product) incorporates competitively significant qualities, characteristics or features, and that the copycat, by imitating those elements, leads to a confusion of origin which would have otherwise been avoidable.

Under section. 8(3), No 1 UWG, a direct competitor can take action for breaches of the provisions of the UWG and may apply to the court for injunctions and orders for the recall of products and the destruction of goods and infringing advertising. Any person injured by unfair acts of competition (including competitors) can claim damages under section. 9 UWG where the offender has acted intentionally or negligently.

Unlike the passing off action in the UK, the claimant under the unfair competition provisions of the UWG does not need to show that he acquired goodwill in the packaging or get-up of the product being copied, and unless such claimant seeks to claim damages it is not necessary to show that the imitation caused damages to the claimant.

Examples from the German Case Law

(1) In a case of 15 September 2005[29] the German Supreme Court issued an injunction against the sale of copycat jeans on the ground that the stitching patterns, which were copied from the claimant's product, were likely to cause confusion regarding the origin of the copycat product. The Court ruled that the original product incorporated competitively significant features and that the copycat, having imitated those features, was likely to lead

---

[29] AZ/ZR 161/OZ, (Bech RS).

to avoidable confusion as to origin. The decision was based purely on the unfair competition provisions as the claimant did not allege an infringement of any intellectual property rights.

Representations of the stitching patterns of the original and copycat jeans are provided below:

Original Product → Look-alike

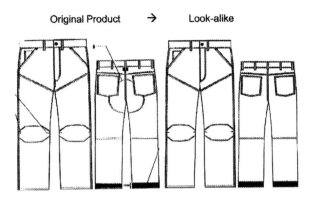

It is significant that the German Supreme Court rejected the argument raised by the defendant in this case that the unfair competition provisions did not apply on the ground that the stitching patterns enjoyed protection as unregistered designs under the Community Design Regulation.[30] The Supreme Court held that the Community Design Regulation did not preclude the application of unfair competition laws, and whereas its purpose was to protect the private work of the person who created the design, the provisions of the UWG were aimed at protecting consumers against misrepresentation.

The decision demonstrates the policy under the German unfair competition law to protect consumer interests by giving a right of action to competitors, on the basis that consumers and competitors alike have a mutual interest in preventing imitations which lead to confusion and deception. This, again, highlights the difference between the unfair competition laws in Germany and the passing off action in the UK, which protects the private interest of the claimant in its goodwill.

(2) On 24 November 2003, the Cologne Regional Court granted an injunction against the sale of OSCAR HUNDE-MENUE dog food cans under sections. 3 and 4, No 9 UWG (misrepresentation of origin)[31] on the ground that the product label was too similar to that of the well-known PEDIGREE brand for dog food.

---

[30] Council Regulation 6/2002 [2002] OJ.
[31] *Masterfoods GmbH v Plus Warenhandels GmbH* 33 0415/03.

The court held that significant elements of the original product packaging were copied, such as the yellow background and contrasting red border at the top of the label. The court held that these elements were likely to affect a consumer's perception of the source of the product and therefore their use constituted actionable unfair competition. Pictures of the two product labels are provided below:

Spain

The Provisions of the Spanish Unfair Competition Law relating to Misleading Conduct

Under Spanish law, protection is provided against unfair competition practices in addition to and side by side with the protection of specific intellectual property rights. The Spanish Unfair Competition Act[32] can be invoked in cases where there are no registered trade mark or other registered intellectual property rights, or where such rights are not infringed but where, nevertheless, a competitor takes unfair advantage of another trader's goodwill or reputation, or engages in conduct which might otherwise be considered as unfair.

The Spanish Unfair Competition Act prohibits, among others things:

— practices causing confusion as to the commercial source of goods or services;
— misleading or false indications or omissions as to the nature, characteristics, quality or quantity of the product; and
— imitation likely to cause confusion as to the commercial source of a product in order to take unfair advantage of the reputation or effort of another trader.

---

[32] Act 3/1991 of 10 Jan 1991.

Under Article 19 of the Spanish Unfair Competition Act, any trader whose economic interests are directly damaged or affected by an unfair act can take action before the Mercantile Court. In addition, consumer groups or associations can take action where the unfair conduct directly relates to their area of interest.

As in the case of Germany and The Netherlands, the unfair competition law in Spain is broader than the action of passing-off in the UK, as it is not a requirement to show that the original packaging or get-up of the product attracted goodwill or that the imitation caused damage to the competitor whose product is being imitated. It is sufficient to show that the imitation is likely to cause customer confusion.

Examples from Spanish Case Law

(1) *Warner Lambert Consumer Healthcare*,[33] which makes the pharmaceutical preparation ORALDINE, was successful in an unfair competition claim against the Spanish company *Laboratorios KIN SA* which sold a similarly looking product under the name ORALKIN. This was a pure unfair competition case and no claims were brought alleging trade mark infringement or asserting other intellectual property rights. The court held that due to the visual similarities between the products, there was a clear risk that consumers would confuse them or associate the defendant's product with the claimant's. The defendant's product, ORALKIN, like the claimant's ORALDINE, was sold without a box, in a rounded, transparent 200 ml container of a shape very similar to the claimant's ORALDINE product; in both cases, the liquid visible inside the bottle was a red-pink colour and the label combined blue, red-pink and white. The risk for consumers was particularly serious as Warner Lambert's ORALDINE was a medicine designed to treat minor infections of the mouth, whereas the imitation ORALKIN was simply a cosmetic oral hygiene product. Images of the two products are provided below:

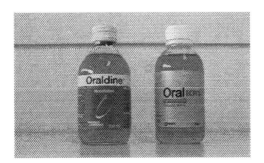

---

[33] *Warner Lambert Consumer v Laboratorios KINSA* (Oraldine/Oraklin), CFI No 4, Barcelona, not reported.

(2) *Mundipharma AG & Viatris Pharmaceuticals, SA v Laboratorios Betamadrileño, SL*[34] (BETADINE/BETAPOVIDONA) was another example where a claim of unfair competition was brought in respect of a copycat product. Again, the case involved no claims of infringement of intellectual property rights. The claimants brought the claim on the ground that the presentation of the defendant's antiseptic solution product BETAPOVIDONA was an imitation of the claimants' product BETADINE (combining a rounded shaped yellow bottle with a black cap, sold without a box with product information printed in black), encouraged confusion and constituted an act of unfair competition. The court held that the similar presentation of the product was likely to cause confusion and ordered that the defendant cease the manufacture and marketing of the offending product and that it remove the product from the market along with any promotional and advertising material. The defendant was also ordered to publish the decision in two nationally circulated newspapers in Spain. Images of the two products are provided below:

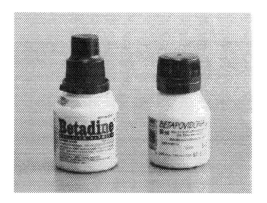

France

The Application of the French Unfair Competition Law to Copycat Packaging

In addition to and side by side with the protection of trade marks under French law, Article 1382 of the French Civil Code provides for protection against unfair competition. The provision applies where the similarity between products or their packaging creates a risk of confusion. For an action to succeed, there must be an imitation of the essential and specific elements of the product that are neither usual nor necessary nor commonly used in respect of such products. Competitors injured by an unfair competition practice can take action in court to stop such a practice.

---

[34] Not reported.

Again, as in the case of other unfair competition laws, it is not necessary for the trader who brings an action complaining that the defendant copied his product packaging or the appearance of his product to show that he has acquired goodwill in such packaging or get-up, as he would in a passing off action. It is sufficient that the packaging or get-up is not usual, necessary or commonly used.

Examples from the French Case Law

In a decision of 17 March 2004 in an action brought by Danone against Bridel,[35] the French Supreme Court found for the claimant in a case concerning the imitation of elements of the packaging. The Court held that '*the adoption by a competitor of a packaging which recaptures all the distinctive and recognised elements of a product packaging of another undertaking (and not providing the necessary product information to the prospective consumer) constitutes a civil wrong, even where the original packaging is not subject to protection by way of registered rights*'. Images of the original Danone product (ACTIMEL) and the copycat (B'A) are provided below:

Italy

The Application of the Italian Unfair Competition Law to 'Slavish Imitation'

In addition to protecting registered and unregistered trade marks, Italian law provides protection against unfair competition under section 2598, no 1 of the Italian Civil Code, which allows competitors to take action against 'slavish imitations' of their products or product packaging. Again, unlike the passing off action, the 'slavish imitations' doctrine focuses on protecting the consumer's interest in preventing imitations that are likely to cause confusion. It does not require a competitor who brings action to show that the packaging or get-up in question acquired goodwill in the market place.

Examples from the Italian Case Law

(1) In a decision of the Court of Naples of 17 July 2003,[36] the court found for the claimant in a case concerning a copycat packaging of a perfume

---

[35] *Danone v Bridel* court of cessation commercial chamber, 17 march 2004, No 02-13242 available at www.legifrance.gouvifr/WAspad/UnDocument?base= INCA &nod=1xcxcx2004x 03x04x00132x042.
[36] *Acqua di Parma Srl v Le Gioie Sas di Caiata Clandio and another*, No 19918/2001 [2003] *Giuris rudenza Napoletana* 353.

bottle. The Court of Naples stated in the decision that the likelihood of confusion arising from a 'slavish imitation' of the packaging was not excluded by the fact that the two products bore different trade marks. The judge stated that the packaging of the defendant's product was very similar to that of the claimant's. The court pointed out that the imitation of the shape of the packaging in itself was not unlawful as the shape was very common. On the other hand, the competitor was using an identical colour on the packaging which was not usual in the relevant market, and thus a very distinctive element of the packaging. This particular case did not turn purely on the packaging as the court also took into consideration that the defendant used a sign which was similar to the trade mark placed on the original packaging.

(2) In a decision of the Court of Verona of 21 September 1992[37], the court held that the packaging of the SINDRAMED toothpaste was confusingly similar to the packaging of the claimant's toothpaste CAPITANO amounting to unfair competition under section 2598, No 1 of the Civil Code. Images of the two packages are provided below:

(3) In a decision of the Court of Naples of July 14, 2005,[38] the court upheld a claim concerning the imitation of bedlinen packaging. The court stated that the strong similarity between the defendant's packaging and the claimant's showed the competitor's intention to reproduce all the elements of the original product. The court also pointed out that the presence of a different trade mark on the defendant's packaging did not exclude the likelihood of confusion. The court found similarities between the two products, in that the colour of the packaging was in both cases blue (albeit in different shades); the trade marks of each respective product (although different) were placed on the upper part of the packaging; the front of the packaging featured an open couch-shape through which the product was visible (this element also being crossed by a strip providing product information); the back

---

[37] *Lu Farmaceutici Dr Ciccarelli SpA v Lidl italia Srl*, not reported. For a short comment see [1992] *EIPR* D–238.

[38] *Frame Srl e Fratelli Ambrosio Srl v New Nagitex Srl* No 14712/2005, available at www.ip-italjuris.it.

of the packaging bore a picture of a yellow sofa; and another picture of a sofa appears on the side of the packaging.

Australia

The Application of Sections 52 and 53 of the Trade Practices Act 1974 to Copycat Products

Insofar as it concerns registered intellectual property rights, copyright and the tort of passing-off, the law in Australia is similar to that of the UK in relation to protection against copycat products. In addition, however, sections 52 and 53 of the Australian Trade Practices Act 1974 ('TPA') provide a more general protection against unfair competition and misleading advertising. Section 52 of the TPA provides that '*a corporation must not, in trade or commerce, engage in conduct that is misleading or deceptive or is likely to mislead or deceive*'.

A claim under section 52 of the TPA is not founded on the protection of goodwill or reputation (as is the case in passing-off); the focus rather is on public interest and consumer protection. Section 53 of the TPA prohibits specific forms of false, misleading or deceptive conduct. For example, it prohibits traders from representing that goods have sponsorship or approval which they do not have.

Under the TPA, any person can bring an action against a perpetrator. The conduct creates the jurisdiction, not the status of the complainant. Thus, any person can bring a court action against a company for breaches of sections 52 and 53 of the TPA, including competitors, consumers, consumer groups and a designated public authority, the Australian Competition and Consumer Commission. However, most actions are brought by competitors rather than consumers or the authorities. Further, the designated public authority tends not to pursue complaints brought by competitors, on the basis that they are free to do so independently.

The TPA empowers the Australian courts to issue a wide range of remedies in relation to unfair trade practices including (among others) injunctions, product recalls, orders to destroy offending products or packaging, orders for corrective advertising and awards of damages.

Examples from the Australian Case Law

(1) *In Pacific Publications Pty Limited v IPC Media Pty Limited*,[39] a claim by the publisher of '*HOME BEAUTIFUL*' magazine against the publication of a rival magazine '*25 BEAUTIFUL HOMES*' at the Australian

---

[39] (2003) *57 Intellectual Property Reports 28.*

Federal Court was successful under section 52 of the TPA, even though an additional claim for trade mark infringement had failed. Whilst the court found that the magazine title '*25 BEAUTIFUL HOMES*' was *not* deceptively similar and therefore *did not* infringe the trade mark '*HOME BEAUTIFUL*', it upheld the claim under section 52 of the TPA on the ground that the defendant's conduct was misleading and deceptive in that it instructed newsagents to place its magazine next to the *HOME BEAUTIFUL* magazine, using identical photos of homes previously featured in *HOME BEAUTIFUL* magazine, and not indicating the connection of the *25 BEAUTIFUL HOMES* magazine to its UK parent magazine.

(2) *In Sydneywide Distributors Pty Limited v Red Bull Australia Pty Limited*[40] the maker of the Red Bull energy drink was successful both in passing off and in a claim under section 52 of the TPA against an attempt by the defendant company, in the words of the court, to 'sail as close to the wind' as possible to take advantage of the market share that Red Bull had acquired through its substantial marketing. The court found that the defendant had intentionally adopted a get-up which appropriated part of the trade or reputation of Red Bull by copying the colour combination and general look of the can. The decision was upheld on appeal. Images of the claimant's and the defendant's products are set out below:

[40] (2002) 55 Intellectual Property Reports 354.

12

The Challenges Posed by the Implementation of the Directive into Domestic Law—a UK Perspective

CHRISTIAN TWIGG-FLESNER AND DEBORAH PARRY

1. INTRODUCTION

THE DIRECTIVE ON Unfair Commercial Practices (UCPD)[1] is, undoubtedly, a significant contribution to the developing field of European consumer law. However, as with all the other consumer law measures adopted at the European level, the success of the UCPD will depend on how it is implemented and applied by the Member States. The burden is therefore on the Member States to give effect to the UCPD in their national legal order as fully as possible. The purpose of this chapter is to consider some of the challenges which the Member States may face in the process of transposing the UCPD. It will start with a short overview of the key principles regarding the implementation of directives, as refined by the European Court of Justice (ECJ). It will then turn to specific aspects of the Directive which may cause particular difficulties, in particular the UCPD's status as a maximum harmonisation measure, and the use of a broad general clause[2] supplemented by two 'smaller' general clauses. These two aspects make it particularly challenging for a Member State such as the UK, which has not previously relied on a general clause to regulate unfair commercial practices, to implement the Directive effectively. This chapter does not attempt to provide any particular suggestions as to how the UK should implement the Directive, although it does attempt to identify a number of different possibilities regarding the general approach that could be adopted. It also does not offer an analysis of the UCPD itself.[3]

---

[1] Directive 2005/29/EC of the European Parliament and of the Council of 11 May 2005 concerning unfair business-to-consumer practices in the internal market ('the Unfair Commercial Practices Directive') [2005] OJ L 149/22.

[2] Art 5 of UCPD.

[3] See eg H Collins, 'The Unfair Commercial Practices Directive' [2005] *European Review of Contract Law* 417; J Stuyck, E Terryn and T van Dyck, 'Confidence through Fairness?

2. IMPLEMENTING DIRECTIVES—BASIC OBLIGATIONS

Before turning to an examination of the particular challenges thrown up by the UCPD, it is first appropriate, as a preliminary issue, to recall the requirements imposed by European Community (EC) law with regard to the obligation on the Member States when implementing a directive. The starting point is Article 249 EC, according to which a directive is 'binding, as to the result to be achieved, upon each Member State to which it is addressed, but shall leave to the national authorities the choice of form and methods'. A directive therefore specifies only a *result*, ie, the domestic laws of the Member States need to be adapted so as to ensure that their legal frameworks produce the same outcome as the directive would. The 'form and methods' by which this result can be achieved are a matter for the Member States. Undoubtedly, the easiest way of doing so is to adopt domestic legislation which incorporates the text of the directive verbatim, but this may not be the most attractive option. One reason for not wishing to do this may be that the terminology employed by a particular directive would be at odds with established notions in domestic law, and a different wording may be preferable to avoid causing terminological confusion. In addition, and irrespective of whether there are terminological problems, the provisions of a directive may not fit into the existing domestic framework without some adjustment of the latter. It is usually the case that a directive will deal with only selected aspects in respect of which there was a perceived need to adopt harmonising legislation, but related matters will not be covered. A verbatim transposition could make it much more difficult to apply existing domestic law and thereby undermine the objective pursued by a directive. A further reason for departing from the exact wording of a directive is that there may already be domestic legislation in place which corresponds in substance with that directive, making it unnecessary to take further steps to implement that directive.[4]

The rather general statement in Article 249 EC regarding the Member States' freedom of 'form and methods' has been given a sharper focus by the ECJ through a number of judgments handed down in the context of Article 226 proceedings.[5] From these cases, the scope of the phrase 'form and methods' in Article 249 EC can be defined more clearly. With regard to the use of terminology which differs from a directive, it seems that a terminological

---

The New Directive on Unfair Business-to-consumer Commercial Practices in the Internal Market' (2006) 43 *CMLRev* 107; G Howells, HW Micklitz and T Wilhelmsson, *European Fair Trading Law—The Unfair Commercial Practices Directive* (Aldershot, Ashgate, 2006).

[4] Cf Case 29/84 *Commission v Germany* [1985] ECR 1661.

[5] This is the provision which permits action to be taken against a Member State for failing to fulfil its obligations under the EC Treaty, and this includes not implementing a directive properly.

difference in the domestic provisions which does not produce a substantive departure from that directive is permissible.[6] Moreover, the ECJ has repeatedly confirmed the point made above that:

> the transposition of a directive into domestic law does not necessarily require that its provisions be incorporated formally and verbatim in express, specific legislation,[7]

but has also emphasised that domestic legislation must:

> guarantee the full application of the directive in a sufficiently clear and precise manner so that, where the directive is intended to create rights for individuals, the persons concerned can ascertain the full extent of their rights ...[8]

Not only may this not require a specific domestic measure, but it also seems unnecessary to adopt exactly the same words as are used in a directive; indeed, the 'general legal context' may suffice if the directive is applied in a sufficiently clear and precise manner.[9] This position has been repeated, confirmed and refined in many judgments, and over the last five years or so, there have been a string of rulings specifically in the field of consumer protection. The decision which had perhaps the biggest impact was *Commission v Netherlands*,[10] a case involving a shortcoming in the Dutch implementation of the Unfair Contract Terms Directive.[11] The Netherlands had argued that the relevant provisions of Dutch law were capable of interpretation in accordance with the Directive, and therefore not problematic. The ECJ gave this rather short shrift, holding that:

> even where the settled case-law of a Member State interprets the provisions of national law in a manner deemed to satisfy the requirements of a directive, that cannot achieve the clarity and precision needed to meet the requirement of legal certainty [which] is particularly true in the field of consumer protection.[12]

This judgment could be of particular concern to a Member State such as the UK, where case law and the doctrine of precedent (stare decisis) have a particularly strong position, because they appear to say that case law, even where this is settled, may not be enough to satisfy the requirements of a directive and that, as a result, legislation may be required.[13] This seems

---

[6] Case 363/85 *Commission v Italy* [1987] ECR 1733.

[7] Eg Case C–59/89 *Commission v Germany* [1991] ECR I–2607, para 18.

[8] Ibid.

[9] Case C–58/02 *Commission v Spain* [2004] ECR I–00621.

[10] Case C–144/99 *Commission v The Netherlands* [2001] ECR I–3541.

[11] Council Directive 93/13/EEC of 5 Apr 1993 on unfair terms in consumer contracts [1993] OJ L 95/29.

[12] Case C–144/99 *Commission v the Netherlands* [2001] ECR I–3541, para 21.

[13] See also H Beale, 'Unfair Terms in Contracts: Proposals for Reform in the UK' (2004) 27 *Journal of Consumer Policy* 289 at 302–3.

somewhat at odds with other judgments which have accepted that case law interpreting domestic legislation is relevant when considering whether that legislation complies with EC law,[14] and that a breach of EC law would only then exist where such case law was not unanimous or sufficiently well established to ensure an interpretation in conformity with EC law.[15] In an area such as consumer protection, it would appear that the demands of legal certainty set by the ECJ are such as to require legislation which is sufficiently clear and precise to give effect to a directive; however, this does not appear to entail that the terminology drawn from a directive needs to be transposed verbatim to achieve this, nor does it seem necessary to adopt specific legislation reflecting the requirements of a directive. To take a different view would be moving down the road of making the verbatim transposition of directives mandatory, effectively turning them into regulations. This view therefore seems unlikely to be in accordance with EC law.[16]

With regard to the specific question of transposing the UCPD, the short review of the demands of EC law suggests that it is *not* a requirement of EC law simply to copy out a directive verbatim, and to replace all the existing domestic measures with one single law in identical terms to the directive. Instead, the Member States are merely obliged to achieve a particular *result*, that is, the prohibition of unfair commercial practices in the manner prescribed by the UCPD. The Member States are free (to an extent) to choose how this will be achieved. This, for example, means that it should be perfectly possible to continue to use concepts familiar to domestic law, rather than unfamiliar notions introduced by a directive, if functionally equivalent notions can be identified in domestic law.[17] This point will be explored further below.

Of course, the jurisprudence of the European Court of Justice appears to have interpreted the freedom of choice and method given to the Member States under Article 249 EC rather strictly. There have certainly been instances where the ECJ has been critical of Member States which had not transposed consumer protection measures in a clearly identifiable manner, citing a lack of legal certainty as a main objection. It is submitted that in those particular instances the ECJ may have been entitled to conclude that the implementation in a particular Member State was deficient, but that these rulings do not have the effect of altering the fundamental character of directives, nor of the requirements imposed on the Member States by Article 249.

Having considered the basic obligations of the Member States under EC law, it is now appropriate to turn to the specific challenges thrown up by the UCPD.

---

[14] See, in particular, Case C–300/95 *Commission v UK* [1997] ECR I–2649.
[15] Case C–372/99 *Commission v Italy* [2002] ECR I–819.
[16] Cf Beale, above n 13.
[17] Cf Law Commission, LC 292, *Unfair Terms in Contracts* Cm 6464 (London, Law Commission, 2005).

3. IMPLEMENTING THE UCPD—MAIN CHALLENGES

The combination of two features of the UCPD poses the biggest challenge for its transposition: the fact that the Directive is a maximum harmonisation measure, and that it uses a general clause, designed to cover a multitude of commercial practices. The overall objective of the UCPD—to create a coherent framework for all unfair business-to-consumer commercial practices—may be attained through this approach, but this nevertheless raises interesting problems for the Member States, which are now faced with the need of implementing the Directive.

The vast majority of the EC directives in the field of consumer protection are so-called minimum harmonisation directives. This means that these directives contain a provision whereby Member States are permitted to introduce, or retain, more protective rules than those in the corresponding directive, provided that the minimum level of protection demanded by the directive is met. But even here, it should be noted that Member States were not left with total freedom to regulate; an ultimate ceiling is provided by the relevant provisions of the EC Treaty.

Minimum harmonisation directives are, on the whole, less difficult to implement than maximum harmonisation directives. Although EC law obliges the Member States to ensure that the provisions of such directives are transposed effectively,[18] this does not mean that domestic law must closely follow the text of the directive. In circumstances where a Member State already provides greater protection than that envisaged under a particular directive, a minimum harmonisation clause reduces the need to review thoroughly existing legislation for compliance with the directive. This is because any variations from a directive may be justified on the basis that these provide more protection for consumers, thereby obviating any need for greater reform of domestic law. In effect, a minimum harmonisation directive permitted a certain degree of laziness in the transposition of directives.

This is, of course, not possible with a maximum harmonisation measure, such as the UCPD. The UCPD prescribes the particular standard of protection which must be attained in all the Member States, and there is no room for departing from this (with the exception of the derogations/exclusions expressly stated in the Directive).[19] So it is clear that the domestic law in each Member State will have to contain provisions replicating exactly the standard set by the UCPD to ensure that the result demanded by the Directive can be achieved. In essence, this will require implementation of the general clause in Article 5 UCPD as well as the narrower tests for misleading and aggressive commercial practices in Articles 6–9 UCPD. Whilst

---

[18] See the cases discussed above.
[19] See Art 3 UCPD, above n 1.

this might instinctively suggest that a copy-out approach is the best way of achieving this, it need not inevitably be done in this way; for example, an adjustment to the language which has no immediate substantive impact remains possible.

It is, however, necessary to be much more systematic in dealing with the transposition of the UCPD. One obvious challenge is to identify what exactly the Directive's scope is. The freedom of the Member States to adopt legislation has only been pre-empted with regard to those aspects which fall within the scope of the Directive. In the case of minimum harmonisation measures, it has often not been necessary to worry quite as much about their precise scope, because any deviations were often justified with reference to the minimum clause. Some of these may have been rather dubious, but even the European Court of Justice accepted that variations from a directive could be explained on this basis, as long as the minimum level of protection had been achieved.[20]

However, determining the UCPD's scope seems more difficult than may be thought at first sight, particularly for a country such as the UK which has no significant prior experience of unfair competition law and, consequently, does not have in place a general clause of the kind found elsewhere. The UCPD is not a measure dealing with an isolated aspect of consumer protection, such as product liability, or package travel. Instead, it cuts across the entire spectrum of consumer transactions and seeks to regulate commercial behaviour in all of those. In order to achieve this, it relies on the general prohibition of unfair commercial practices, and a general clause,[21] supplemented by the more specific prohibitions of misleading[22] and aggressive[23] practices. It is not limited to specific consumer transactions, nor is it restricted to particular goods or services.

It is vital for each Member State to identify its existing legislation in the field occupied by the Directive, because all of this may, at the very least, have to be revised to ensure that it is in accordance with the UCPD. Alternatively, it may be preferred simply to repeal such existing legislation and replace it with a general measure modelled closely on the UCPD.

4. AFFECTED LEGISLATION

As already suggested, the twin factors of 'maximum harmonisation' and the 'broad general clause' necessitate a careful examination of existing domestic law in order to identify those measures which may have to be reviewed

---

[20] See eg Case 382/87 *Buet v Ministère Public* [1989] ECR 1235.
[21] Art 5 UCPD, above n 1.
[22] Art 6 of ibid.
[23] Art 8 of ibid.

during the implementation process. In a country such as the UK, which has traditionally eschewed general clauses in favour of more specific regulation, this will be a greater challenge than in a Member State which may already have relied on a broad framework (such as the UWG in Germany). This is a problem not previously encountered in this context: earlier consumer directives dealt with fairly specific matters, on which there was no previous legislation,[24] or a comparatively compact legal framework.[25] At worst, therefore, it was necessary to consider what changes may be necessary to three or four existing measures. This is not the case with the UCPD, which is much broader in scope.

The first task, therefore, is to figure out how many measures fall within the scope of the UCPD. Once these have been identified, it may further be necessary to consider whether it is feasible, or indeed permissible, to amend these to bring them into line with the UCPD, or whether some measures may simply have to be repealed.

In those Member States where there is already a framework similar to the UCPD, it may, in fact, be less difficult to transpose the Directive, because only changes to existing general rules may be required. As noted previously, identifying measures within the scope of the UCPD will be a particular challenge for the UK, which has a vast body of specific measures, and has not relied on a general clause to develop its legal framework on commercial practices.

A good starting point may be the overall objective of the UCPD, which is to protect the economic interests of consumers.[26] Therefore, it is necessary to identify legislation concerned with the protection of consumers' economic interests in domestic law. Not all of these will have to be considered for amendment or repeal—Article 3 UCPD contains a list of exclusions and derogations, which mean that measures in those areas are unaffected by the UCPD, *even if* they would otherwise contribute to the protection of consumers' economic interests.

A particular difficulty arises with regard to what might be called 'mixed measures'. This is domestic legislation which applies beyond the context of consumer transactions, and yet may deal with what could be regarded as unfair commercial practices. A good example is the Protection from Harassment Act 1997, sometimes referred to as the 'anti-stalking' law. This Act was adopted not for the protection of consumers' economic interests, but to deal with a form of behaviour which has been of more general concern. Nevertheless, the Act is drafted in such a way that it *could* be used

---

[24] See, eg, the Directives on Door-step Selling (85/577/EEC [1985] OJ L 372/31); Distance Selling (97/7/EC [1997] OJ L 144/19), or Package Travel (90/314/EEC [1990] OJ L 158/59).

[25] See, eg, the Directives on Consumer Sales and Associated Guarantees (99/44/EC [1999] OJ L 177/12), Unfair Contract Terms (93/13/EEC [1993] OJ L 95/29) or Timeshare (94/47/EC [1994] OJ L 280/83).

[26] Cf Art 1 UCPD, above n 1.

for the protection of consumers' economic interest,[27] ie, it could be used to prevent a trader from engaging in an aggressive commercial practice. So whilst the Act does not go far enough to meet all the requirements of Article 8 UCPD (on aggressive commercial practices), it certainly has the potential of overlapping with the UCPD. The simple answer might be to say that the Act did not pursue the protection of consumers as its primary objective, and any such effect is merely incidental—indeed, that is the view now taken by the UK's Department of Trade and Industry.[28] However, a different perspective is based on the fact that the UCPD, whilst clearly pursuing consumer protection as its objective, is ultimately an internal market measure and designed to create a level playing field for consumers and traders alike. If measures such as the Protection from Harassment Act 1997 *could* be used to deal with traders who are behaving in a manner contrary to the Act, but not to whichever provision will give effect to Article 8 UCPD, then that might suggest that domestic law has exceeded the standard set by the Directive. But amendments to such legislation, which has very different primary objectives, to bring it into line with the UCPD, is rather unattractive. With regard to such mixed measures, it may therefore be necessary to consider some sort of express disapplication of the legislation from circumstances which would amount to an unfair commercial practice. The point is, however, that 'mixed measures' cannot necessarily be ignored as part of the implementation process, but may have to be considered, and some adjustments may have to be made.

So the initial challenge is to identify all the measures which may be affected by the UCPD. The next step is then to consider what should be done with these measures.

5. TOWARDS IMPLEMENTING THE UCPD INTO UK LAW

It is now appropriate to consider how a Member State such as the UK might approach the task of implementing the UCPD. As the UK does not have an existing framework in this field which relies on broad clauses akin to Articles 5–9 UCPD, it will be essential that a measure is adopted which gives effect to the core requirements of the UCPD. This will have to feature both a general clause along the lines of Article 5 as well as the specific prohibitions in Articles 6–9. This will not only provide a 'visible implementation'

---

[27] See the Enterprise Act 2002 (Part 8 Domestic Infringements) Order 2003 (SI 2003/1593), the Schedule which includes the Protection from Harassment Act 1997. The Act is therefore regarded as one of the measures the contravention of which constitutes a 'domestic infringement' for the purposes of Part 8 of the Enterprise Act 2002.

[28] DTI, 'The Unfair Commercial Practices (UCP) Directive Consultation on Implementing the EU Directive on Unfair Commercial Practices and Amending Existing Consumer Legislation' (URN 05/1815 London, DTI, Dec 2005).

of the Directive, but it will also ensure that, if existing domestic measures with a narrower scope than the UCPD are retained, a safety-net is provided to ensure that those unfair commercial practices not covered by existing law will be so covered.

However, as explained earlier, a copy-out approach, whilst attractive to avoid any suggestion of incorrect transposition, is not required. In view of the somewhat unusual terminology employed in the UCPD, it may, in fact, be desirable to consider the use of language more familiar to a domestic lawyer. For example, the UCPD refers to the benchmark of the 'average consumer'. This is a concept not found in UK legislation. Instead, the objective benchmark is usually the 'reasonable person'. Would it not be easier to use this notion, rather than the less familiar 'average consumer'? It is certainly plausible to argue that the notion of the 'reasonable person' could be functionally equivalent to that of the 'average consumer'. If that were so, then there would be no need to adopt the latter concept in domestic law. However, such terminological familiarity might also be deceptive; the concept of the 'reasonable person', in particular, is used throughout domestic law and now carries with it a significant amount of 'case law baggage', which the courts would undoubtedly find difficult to abandon. It would also create the risk of confusion in respect of areas of law other than consumer law, where this notion should not be tainted by the need for an EC law conform interpretation.

What about the 'transactional decision' concept? Again, this concept is unfamiliar to domestic UK law, but it is central to the overall framework introduced by the UCPD. The 'transactional decision' requirement may have a two-fold function in this regard: on the one hand, it could simply be a kind of de minimis requirement, in the sense that the effect of any particular practice must be more than negligible. On the other, it could be the causative link between the practice and its effect on the average consumer. This might mean that a practice which is misleading, or aggressive, but which does not bring about a transactional decision a consumer would not have taken otherwise would not be unfair. It seems that there is a functional equivalent in the domestic law: the notion of 'reliance', be it detrimental reliance or any form of reliance. The 'transactional decision' concept has been defined in the UCPD as 'any decision taken by a consumer concerning whether, how, and on what terms to purchase, make payment in whole or in part for, retain or dispose of a product or to exercise a contractual right in relation to the product, whether the consumer decides to act, or to refrain from acting'.[29] This covers a very broad range of circumstances, and whilst it is possible that 'reliance' in domestic law would cover actions by a consumer not within the definition of a 'transactional decision' such instances are likely to be rare. 'Reliance' might therefore be an acceptable terminological substitute in domestic law,

---

[29] Art 2(k) UCPD, above n 1.

although, once again, the objection that the existing interpretation of 'reliance' might conflict with the definition of 'transactional decision' is relevant. The difficulty of finding appropriate 'domestic' terminology without running the risk of causing problems with the existing understanding of this in order to implement the UCPD might therefore point, on balance, towards a verbatim implementation. This would have the advantage of avoiding confusion with established case law on functionally equivalent domestic concepts, and it would emphasise the origins of the implementing legislation in EC law, thereby increasing the likelihood of EC law conforming interpretation.

If an existing domestic measure overlaps with one of the blacklisted commercial practices in the Annex, then it needs to be ensured that domestic law prohibits that commercial practice outright. It may then be possible to maintain the domestic rule if it already contains an outright prohibition of the same practice as that listed in the Annex to the UCPD, to modify it so as to convert it into an outright prohibition, or to repeal the domestic rule and transpose the Annex instead. To an extent, this will be a policy choice for the legislator. However, it has rightly been remarked that the Annex 'contains items which are not sufficiently precise and whose contents are as a result thereof subject to interpretation'.[30]

Matters become more complicated once the domestic measure is not subject to the Annex, but does, arguably, fall within the scope of Articles 6–9. These are the prohibitions of misleading or aggressive commercial practices. There clearly remains some discretion for the UK quite how far it will go in dealing with those existing measures now within the scope of the UCPD. The measures will generally be narrower in scope than the UCPD and deal only with particular aspects, sometimes providing for criminal sanctions in respect of any infringements. Crucially, such measures need not be repealed, if it is possible to amend them in such a way that they comply with the requirements of the Directive. It seems that there would are two broad options for the UK in this regard:

(i) A domestic measure within the scope of the UCPD could be repealed and the implementing measure, which essentially copies out the Directive itself, would take its place. This would create significant scope for simplifying existing domestic law.
(ii) A domestic measure within the scope of the UCPD could be retained, but amended to ensure that the standard it adopts does not deviate from that demanded by the UCPD.

Option (ii) is likely to be particularly attractive to the UK, with many separate pieces of legislation dealing with unfair commercial practices currently in force. It may seem preferable not to repeal all of these measures in one

---

[30] Stuyck, Terryn and van Dyck, above n 3, at 131.

go in order to maintain some continuity in domestic law after the implementation of the UCPD, particularly because some of the key measures are mature and familiar to enforcers, traders and consumers alike. The particular framework established in the Trade Descriptions Act 1968 (TDA) could, for example, be retained, albeit in amended form to ensure that it goes no further than the UCPD itself. It is worthwhile to consider what the impact of the UCPD on the TDA might be.

(a) Impact of UCPD on the Trade Descriptions Act 1968

There have been concerns expressed that the UCPD will have a major, and perhaps destructive impact on existing UK consumer protection measures using criminal law sanctions.[31] However, it may be that the TDA could be brought in line with the UCPD without major difficulty.

The TDA applies to both business-to-consumer and business-to-business transactions, which remains acceptable under the UCPD. The Directive is specifically concerned with business-to-consumer commercial practices;[32] however Recital 6 permits the retention of measures applying to business-to-business transactions. This means that the TDA could, therefore, remain in an unaltered form, for the purposes of prosecuting false trade descriptions in a business-to-business scenario. Similarly the possibility of prosecuting private individuals, under section 23 of the TDA 1968,[33] also would fall outside the scope of the UCPD. However, changes will, of course, be necessary where the TDA provides for offences in the business-to-consumer field, in particular in the light of the maximum harmonisation requirements of the UCPD.

A key omission from the principal offence sections under the TDA[34] is any requirement that a false statement 'causes or is likely to cause [a consumer] to take a transactional decision that he would not have taken otherwise', as required by UCPD, Article 6(1), under which most aspects of these offences appear to fall.[35] In the majority of situations this requirement

---

[31] See, eg, S Pudney, 'A Sheep in Wolves' Clothing?' (2005) 113 *Trading Standards Today* 29.

[32] '[A]ny act, omission, course of conduct or representation, commercial communication including advertising and marketing, by a trader, directly connected with the promotion, sale or supply of a product to consumers': Art 2(d) UCPD, above n 1.

[33] See *Olgeirsson v Kitching* [1986] 1 All ER 746.

[34] S 1 false trade descriptions of goods; s 12 false representations as to royal approval and Queen's Award to Industry; s 13 false representations regarding the supply of goods or services to anyone; s 14, false or misleading statements as to services, facilities or accommodation; and s 23 the by-pass provision.

[35] In one or two instances it is likely that the offence would be regarded as falling under UCPD Art 5(5), above n 1, and the 'black list' in Annex I, for example unauthorised use of devices or emblems signifying the Queen's Award to Industry, contrary to s 12(2) TDA 1968, which comes under UCPD Annex I, para (2) and is automatically unfair, without any need for a 'consumer transaction' test.

would, in fact, be satisfied, but case law under the TDA 1968 has, on occasions, made it clear that it is not a requirement to obtain a conviction that an average consumer has been or would be misled.[36] If, instead of an offence coming within the terms of misleading actions under the UCPD, Article 6(1), an unfair commercial practice under UCPD Article 5 is alleged, then it is 'unfair' if it 'materially distorts or is likely to materially distort the economic behaviour with regard to the product of the average consumer whom it reaches or to whom it is addressed, or of the average member of the group when a commercial practice is directed to a particular group of consumers'. This requirement is similarly absent from the existing offences under the TDA. To ensure compliance with the maximum harmonisation aspects of the UCPD it would, therefore, be necessary to introduce some form of 'transactional decision' test into each of the offences under the TDA.

Turning now to look at some specific provisions, section 1(1)(a) of the TDA creates an offence of applying a false trade description to goods. This covers the usual situation of a business seller supplying goods to a consumer, but it can also apply to a business buyer *purchasing* goods from a consumer.[37] A typical example would be an antique dealer understating the importance of a piece of furniture to obtain it cheaply. Selling goods to consumers will be covered under the UCPD. However, buying goods falls outside the definition of a 'commercial practice' is outside the scope of the UCPD and can, therefore, remain unaltered.

Section 2 of the TDA defines a 'trade description' for the purposes of offences under section 1 of the Act. Subsection (1) contains a finite list of matters which constitute 'trade descriptions'. These, when compared with Article 6(1)(a)–(g) of and Annex I to the UCPD, cover very similar ground. Although section 2(1) is narrower in scope than the matters covered in the UCPD, this is not a problem as it seems possible to retain specific domestic legislation which is more restrictive, provided that there is also a general measure implementing the UCPD covering all aspects of the Directive. Nothing contained in section 2 appears to conflict directly with the maximum harmonisation requirements of the UCPD. It could be argued that some important matters covered under section 2(1) are not specifically identified in Article 6(1) UCPD, for example false car mileages and false claims regarding the previous ownership of vehicles, both of which fall

---

[36] See, eg *Ashurst v Hayes and Benross Trading Co Ltd* (1974) unreported, where Widgery CJ stated: 'a defendant cannot escape responsibility merely because it is likely the average person would not be misled by the false trade description he has applied to the goods'. Also, in *Chidwick v Beer* [1974] RTR 415, Mackenna J said: 'it is a mitigating circumstance that the buyer was not deceived by the representation contained in the advertisement which is the basis of the charge. The matter may be taken into account by the justices in considering the penalty, but it is not a defence to the charge.'

[37] *Fletcher v Budgen* [1974] 2 All ER 1243.

under 'other history' under section 2(1)(j) of the TDA.[38] It is suggested that Article 6(1)(b) UCPD, in encompassing 'the main characteristics of the product', could be used for these situations. Even though the list of factors in Article 6(1)(b) UCPD, apart from 'usage', may not precisely equate with 'previous history', the inclusion of the words 'such as' before the specified list of features demonstrates that this is not a finite list of characteristics and so can cover additional matters not specifically mentioned.

The test for establishing whether a trade description is false is set out in section 3 of the TDA. Although largely compatible with the UCPD, the test for misleading trade descriptions, under subsection (2), does not specifically refer to the effect on the 'average consumer', as required by Article 6(1) UCPD. In *Dixons Ltd v Barnett*[39] Bingham LJ stated: 'it was for [the magistrates] to put themselves in the position of the ordinary high street shopper and decide as a matter of fact whether this trade description was misleading or not'. To ensure complete compatibility, it would be sensible to include reference to the 'average consumer' within the test.

Section 14 of the TDA 1968 creates offences for providing false statements about services, facilities and accommodation. The definition of 'product' within Article 2(c) of the UCPD covers 'any goods or service including immoveable property, rights and obligations' which encompasses 'services facilities and accommodation'. Similarly, an examination of the five subsections ((i)–(v)) of section 14(1), indicating the matters about which false statements must relate for an offence to arise, shows close compatibility with the requirements for a misleading action under UCPD, Article 6(1). An offence may arise under section 14 where there has been a post-contractual statement, as well as for pre-contractual statements.[40] This is also compatible with the UCPD, as Article 3(1) refers to the Directive applying to unfair business-to-consumer commercial practices 'before, during and after a commercial transaction in relation to the product'.

A particular feature of section 14 of the 1968 Act is that there are *mens rea* requirements: either knowing a statement is false, under subsection (1)(a), or recklessness, under subsection (1)(b). Article 11(2) of the UCPD does indicate that powers may be conferred upon courts or administrative authorities to take action 'even without proof (...) of intention or negligence on the part of the trader'. This does not, however, mean that *mens rea* cannot be retained for the purposes of section 14, if wished. Providing there is an implementing statutory instrument covering the requirements of the UCPD for situations where there is no *mens rea*, it is permissible to retain

---

[38] See, eg, *R v Hammerton Cars Ltd* [1976] 3 All ER 758 (false mileage recording) and *R v Southwestern Justices and Hallcrest Garages Ltd* (1983) 147 JP 212 (car subject to commercial leasing agreements described as having had 'one owner').
[39] *Dixons Ltd v Barnett* [1988] BTCL 311 at 315.
[40] See *Breed v Cluett* [1970] 2 QB 459.

more restrictive measures. The same arguments can be employed with respect to the due diligence defences in sections 24 and 25 of the TDA.

(b) General Implications of Option (ii)

The preceding section attempted to demonstrate by using the example of the TDA what might have to be done if the decision were taken to retain an existing domestic measure dealing with some of the matters now covered by the UCPD. If this approach were indeed to be the preferred one, then there would be a number of matters that would have to be reflected in all the domestic measures to be retained. Most significantly, it seems that the key benchmarks of the 'average consumer' and 'transactional decision' would have to be included in such existing domestic measures.

As is clear from the Directive itself, the 'average consumer' concept is borrowed from the jurisprudence of the ECJ,[41] which has developed this notion as a reference point for determining for example, whether advertising would be misleading for the purposes of the Misleading Advertising Directive. In the UK, domestic legislation does not generally refer to the notion of an 'average consumer'; however, courts applying the provisions of legislation such as the Trade Descriptions Act 1968 have developed their own concept of the reasonable, or ordinary, consumer which is, on the whole, compatible with the European 'average consumer'.[42] One might therefore suggest that there may be no need to amend existing domestic measures to be retained in this respect. Moreover, domestic courts would, in any event, be under an obligation to interpret any domestic concepts in legislation deemed to be transposing an EC directive in accordance with that directive under the doctrine of interpretation in compliance with EC law, or 'indirect effect'.[43] However, it should be emphasised that this doctrine has been developed as a remedial tool to minimise the impact of incomplete or inadequate transposition of a directive, rather than as an alternative to direct implementation, and the UK should therefore not rely on compliant interpretation as sufficient to give effect to (parts of) the UCPD. As already discussed above, on balance, an adjustment to the terminology of domestic legislation to be retained may be preferable.

---

[41] Eg Case C–210/96 *Gut Springenheide GmbH and Rudolf Tusky v Oberkreisdirektor des Kreises Steinfurt—Amt für Lebensmittelüberwachung* [1998] ECR I–4657, or Case C–220/98 *Estee Lauder Cosmetics GmbH & Co. OHG v Lancaster Group GmbH* [2000] ECR I–117.

[42] Eg *Dixons v Barnett* (1989) 153 JP 268 ('the ordinary High Street shopper'); *Janbo Trading Ltd v Dudley Metropolitan Borough Council* (1993) 157 JP 1056 ('the reasonable consumer'); *Doble v David Greig Ltd* [1972] 2 All ER 195 (if particular response is reasonable, then there is an infringement; even if other responses might also be reasonable); and *Bryan Roy Lewin v Purity Soft Drinks Limited* [2004] EWHC 3119 ('reasonable consumer').

[43] Case C–106/89 *Marleasing SA v La Comercial Internacional de Alimentación SA* [1990] ECR I–4135; Case C–334/92 *Wagner Miret v Fondo de Garantia Salaria* [1993] ECR I–6911.

Similarly, domestic measures within the scope of the UCPD which purely focus on, say, whether a statement is misleading per se, but do not require that at least the likelihood of a 'transactional decision' which the average consumer would not have taken otherwise be shown, would not correspond with the UCPD. Such legislation would therefore have to be amended by adding the 'transactional decision' concept to the relevant provisions. We may note, for example, that the DTI has indicated that it may be necessary to amend the Trade Descriptions Act to take into account these particular requirements of the UCPD.

(c) Enforcement

As well as dealing with the transposition of the substantive provisions of the UCPD, some thought will have to be given to the sanctions that could be introduced to deal with any infringements of the implementing legislation. The UCPD emphasises the use of administrative enforcement procedures, such as injunctions. In addition, there is reference, in Article 13, to penalties, which must be effective, proportionate and dissuasive. From the UK perspective, the use of the criminal law in particular areas of consumer protection is long-established, and there will be a desire to maintain this after the implementation of the Directive.

The preferred UK approach has been based around strict liability criminal offences, which are subject to a 'due diligence' defence.[44] Now, as noted, strict liability itself is not a problem by virtue of Article 11(2) UCPD. However, a variation from the current domestic scheme is that there are provisions imposing strict liability without consideration of the impact of the particular practice on a consumer—in other words, there is nothing that is akin to the 'transactional decision test'. As mentioned earlier, this test is essential under the UCPD, and existing domestic provisions would have to be modified.

Reference to 'effective, proportionate and dissuasive' penalties such as that in Article 13 UCPD encompasses the right to use the criminal law. So the use of the criminal law would not be problematic per se. It would certainly be desirable in respect of those practices which are to be outlawed outright. It may also be attractive in respect of the specific prohibition against misleading and aggressive commercial practices. When it comes to the general clause, however, it may be felt that this would be too vague to be capable of giving rise to a criminal sanction. It would clearly be necessary

---

[44] Although see the approach adopted in the context of reg 15 on 'consumer guarantees' in the Sale and Supply of Goods to Consumers Regulations 2002 (SI 3045/2002), which relies on an injunctive procedure for infringements of the provisions regarding guarantees on consumer goods.

to tread carefully. However, any major concerns here might be alleviated if a 'due diligence' defence were introduced. Such a defence would permit a trader to argue that he has taken all reasonable precautions and exercised due diligence to avoid committing the offence, and, if successful, he will not be criminally liable.

The benefit of being able to use criminal sanctions may be more relevant in respect of any domestic measures to be retained after the implementation of the UCPD. As stated earlier, such measures will generally be narrower in focus than the UCPD, dealing with more specific problems, and there seems no reason why such measures could not continue to impose criminal sanctions. It must be conceded that the inclusion of the 'transactional decision' requirement, and the 'average consumer' benchmark, would probably increase the risk of making it more difficult to secure a conviction, because including these provisions would add to the evidential burden for the enforcers.

(d) Individual Consumer Actions

A further question, and one which is not limited to the UK, is whether it may be appropriate to give individual consumers specific enforcement rights when they have been the victim of an unfair commercial practice. The UCPD itself does not envisage this, being more concerned with administrative enforcement.

The most obvious problem a consumer may have is that he/she has concluded a contract based on a misleading or aggressive commercial practice. This, in itself, will give the consumer no right to compensation or to terminate/avoid the contract. However, it will often be the case that there will be an overlap between the conditions for establishing that there has been an unfair commercial practice, and that there has been, eg, a misrepresentation, or duress. Nevertheless, there may be instances where domestic contract law, particularly in the UK, may not recognise an obvious right of action when there has been an unfair commercial practice. It may be that the common law of contract will evolve to absorb the conditions for unfair commercial practices within the scope of existing doctrines, but that is not guaranteed, and would, in any event, be a slow process.

Instead, it may be felt desirable to introduce a separate right of compensation for consumers who have been the victim of an unfair commercial practice and have no other private law cause of action available to them. There is ECJ jurisprudence, notably in *Courage v Crehan*[45] and *Antonio Munoz Cia SA v Frumar Limited*,[46] indicating a development in the effectiveness

---

[45] Case C–453/99 *Courage v Crehan* [2001] ECR I–6297.
[46] Case C–253/00 *Antonio Munoz Cia SA v Frumar Limited* [2002] ECR I–7289.

principle which points towards use of private actions—presumably for damages—to ensure the effective application of EC law. Although this case law has hitherto been concerned with directly applicable provisions, it would seem possible to extend this approach also to the present context. What this may mean, in effect, is the evolution of a new domestic remedy of breach of statutory duty for EC law inspired provisions.[47]

6. POST-IMPLEMENTATION ISSUES

The objective of this chapter so far has been to draw out what might be described as the technical challenges in implementing the UCPD, with a focus on key changes that might have to be made to legislation. However, ensuring that the formal legal framework of a directive is transposed correctly into domestic law is only part of the challenge; often, the real test of whether this has been successful is the practical application of the implementing legislation. In this regard, there is a question over the likely involvement of the European Court of Justice in interpreting Article 5, in particular. The experience in the context of the Unfair Contract Terms Directive[48] suggests that it is unlikely that the ECJ will pronounce on the unfairness of a particular commercial practice, referring the matter back to the domestic courts.[49] The main burden will fall on the enforcement agencies, in any event, and the early post-implementation period will undoubtedly be a challenging one.

It will be important for anybody applying the new law to be aware of its European origins, and the need to treat every key concept differently from comparable domestic ones. The main national legal measure implementing the UCPD (whether, in the UK, this will become the 'Unfair Commercial Practices Regulations 2007', or something else remains to be seen), which will probably closely resemble the UCPD itself both in form and in terminology, will presumably be more obviously applied in accordance with the UCPD itself and any judgments of the ECJ which will eventually be forthcoming. But if it is assumed that the UK will not simply replace all its existing measures with a single piece of legislation, then there will be some pre-existing measures which will remain in force, albeit in amended form. Therefore, there will be a challenge for the enforcement authorities and courts to accept that these domestic rules need to be interpreted and applied in a different light. These measures will then be implementing an EC directive, and must be interpreted accordingly. This may mean that older case

---

[47] See G Betlem, 'Torts, a European *Ius Commune* and the Private Enforcement of Community Law' (2005) 64 *Cambridge Law Journal* 126.
[48] [1993] OJ L 95/29.
[49] See Case C–237/02 *Freiburger Kommunalbauten v Hofstetter* [2004] ECR I–3403.

law can no longer be relied upon, unless it is not in open conflict with EC law. More importantly, even though the terminology in these measures may remain unaltered to some extent, it will nevertheless have to be applied and understood against the European backdrop now provided by the UCPD.

7. STEPS TAKEN TOWARDS IMPLEMENTATION BY THE UK

Before we conclude our thoughts, it is useful to consider, briefly, the steps which the UK has taken so far towards implementing the Directive. Even before the UCPD had been finalised, the DTI commissioned research from a group of scholars to analyse the scope of the UCPD and to identify domestic measures which fall within its scope and would therefore be affected by it. An indicative list drawn up in the final report identified a significant number of measures which may fall within the scope of the UCPD.[50] The DTI has since reviewed this list and has indicated which of these it does not believe are within the scope of the Directive in its first consultation document.[51]

In many instances, this is because the domestic measure is based on an existing EC measure, which, by virtue of Article 3(4) UCPD, takes precedence over the UCPD. To some extent, the DTI is side-stepping a conceptual difficulty here. Many of the domestic rules so excluded relate to EC-based labelling requirements. However, these do overlap, to some extent, with the UCPD in that a failure correctly to label goods could be regarded as a misleading omission. According to Article 3(4) UCPD, the 'specific aspects' of these sectoral measures prevail, but generally the question of sanctions is left to the Member States. This may, therefore, leave a gap in the law. This problem arose in *Bryan Roy Lewin v Purity Soft Drinks Limited*[52] in the context of the Food Labelling Regulations 1996 and the Trade Descriptions Act 1968, but was not resolved by the court. In any event, one may note in passing that whilst it may not be *necessary* to review these measures, it would nevertheless provide an opportunity to consider whether these separate measures still need to be kept, or if they could also be made subject to the legislation implementing the UCPD, thereby simplifying domestic law.

As far as the retention of existing measures is concerned, the DTI's Consultation Paper on implementing the UCPD indicates that consideration is being given to retaining the TDA 1968 in an amended form to include transactional decision tests, for business to consumer transactions and, maybe, for business-to-business transactions also. The possibility of

---

[50] C Twigg-Flesner, D Parry, G Howells and A Nordhausen, *An Analysis of the Application and Scope of the Unfair Commercial Practices Directive* (London, DTI, 2005).
[51] The Unfair Commercial Practices (UCP) Directive Consultation, above n 28, at 85.
[52] [2004] EWHC 3119.

removing the *mens rea* element from section 14 and extending that section to misleading statements is also being mooted. If this comes about, then the UCPD will not have had a destructive impact on the TDA 1968, but it may actually facilitate improvements to the Act, widening its scope in some situations, with only a very few situations having to be removed from its protection.

8. CONCLUSIONS

It does not seem appropriate to draw any particular conclusions from the preceding discussion. What is clear is that the implementation of the UCPD poses a much greater challenge than that of previous directives in the consumer law field. This task is especially difficult for the UK, with no previous experience in the field of unfair competition law and therefore no existing general legal framework in this area. Instead, there is a plethora of measures dealing with specific aspects of unfair commercial practice or unfair competition. The maximum harmonisation nature of the UCPD requires considerable care in identifying which domestic measures are affected. There will then have to be decisions, perhaps on a case-by-case basis, whether to retain and amend existing measures or to repeal them and let the general measure implementing the UCPD take their place. There is certainly scope for a 'clean slate' approach in this area, and a wide range of measures could be repealed. However, such a 'big bang' approach may appeal neither to business nor to enforcers, and a more gradual approach may be preferable.

13

Transborder Law Enforcement— Does it Exist?

HANS W MICKLITZ

1. NEW RULES AND NEW TECHNIQUES ON TRANSBORDER LAW ENFORCEMENT UNDER DIRECTIVE 2005/29?

STRICTLY SPEAKING THE Directive contains neither new rules nor new techniques on law enforcement. Article 11 largely reiterates the procedures already laid down in Directive 84/450/EEC. It is the overwhelming understanding that the Member States remain free to put enforcement into the hands of either public authorities or trade and consumer organisations.[1] The only remedy to be made available is the action for an injunction, backed by interim relief. Remedies beyond injunctive action, so heavily discussed in the Member States now under the heading of 'skimming off', 'ill-gotten gains' or 'disgorgement' procedures,[2] did not play a role in the legislative process. Individual consumers are excluded from the enforcement process, although the Commission seemed initially willing to take an individual action for compensation into consideration.[3]

The only 'new rule' is laid down in Article 13, which obliges Member States to lay down penalties for infringements of national provisions adopted in application of this Directive. Penalties are not to be understood

---

[1] For a different reading see HW Micklitz in N Reich and HW Micklitz, *Europäisches Verbraucherrecht* (Baden-Baden, Nomos, 2003), § 30. 11, in which I argue that the EC secondary law in combination with Art 153 EC Treaty requires the Member States to grant consumer organisations the power to file an action for an injunction, as a minimum standard. The background to the question comes from a reference of the High Court, which wanted to know whether the UK government is obliged to grant the Consumers' Association standing under Directive 93/13/EEC on unfair terms in consumer contracts. However, the reference was suspended and later withdrawn when the UK government decided to solve the issue in favour of the consumers' organisation: see for the UK background, J Dickie, 'Article 7 of the Unfair Terms in Consumer Contracts Directive' [1996] *Consumer Law Journal* 112.

[2] See for an overview of the Member States' legislation, HW Micklitz in *Münchener Kommentar zum UWG* (Munich, CH Beck, 2006), Teil UWG § 10 at 14–17.

[3] See COM(2002)289 final, 18.

in the sense of criminal sanctions. That is why Member States may provide for civil sanctions as well.[4] These penalties must be—and this has become a standard formula in consumer law directives—'effective, proportionate and dissuasive'. In short the body of law with regard to enforcement remains underdeveloped.[5] Particular rules on *transborder* enforcement do not exist.

However, this is not yet the end of the story. The subject is *transborder* enforcement of unfair commercial practices. Here at least two other pieces of EC legislation come into play, Directive 98/27/EC[6] on *injunctions* and Regulation 2006/2004 on consumer protection co-operation.[7] In taking these three pieces of EC legislation all together I will try to show first that the European Community tried to *privatise* transborder law enforcement by granting rights and remedies in particular to consumer organisations. This is Directive 98/27/EC. In the light of the nearly complete failure of this approach,[8] the European Commission now relies on statutory agencies. The Regulation on consumer protection co-operation *nationalises* (*verstaatlicht*) transborder law enforcement; private organisations are more or less excluded from law enforcement. Agencies have to handle transborder conflicts and solve them through conciliation or as a last resort through injunctive action. This is the second message. However, the question remains whether Regulation 2006/2004 will lead to the envisaged results. I start from the hypothesis that a third step is needed to make transborder enforcement work. Without *additional remedies*, such as collective claims for compensation and without integrating lawyers and law firms into collective transborder law enforcement, the system will be neither proportionate, nor effective, and certainly not dissuasive.

2. THE STORY BEGINS—*DISTANT SHOPPING* (SWEEPSTAKES I)

In the early 1990s the German Verbraucherschutzverein (now the Bundesverband Verbraucherzentrale) and the French Union Fédérale des Consommateurs (UFC) tried to get to grips with misleading cross-border advertising by German-based distance selling firms which addressed French

---

[4] See J Stuyck, E Terryn and T van Dyck, 'Confidence Through Fairness ? The New Directive on Unfair Business-To-Consumer Commercial Practices in the Internal Market' (2006) 43 *CMLRev* 107 at 136.

[5] See C Alexander, 'Die Sanktions- und Verfahrensvorschriften der Richtlinie 2005/29/EG über unlautere Geschäftspraktiken im Binnenmarkt, Umsetzungsbedarf für Deutschland' [2005] *GRUR Int* 809.

[6] [1998] OJ L 166/51.

[7] [2004] OJ L 364/1.

[8] U Docekal, P Kolba, HW Micklitz and P Rott, 'Die Umsetzung der Richtlinie 98/27/EG in den Mitgliedstaaten' Vienna, Republic of Austria, (forthcoming).

consumers, in French, by mailshots (so called sweepstakes) from German territory.[9] The French consumer organisations were quite successful in obtaining a favourable decision before French courts both under criminal law and under private law. The endless efforts to get these two French judgments executed in Germany are a story in itself. Despite the Brussels Convention, the consumer organisations met nearly insurmountable barriers and finally gave up.[10]

The German consumer organisations were approached by the French consumer organisations via the European consumer organisation (*Bureau Européen des Unions de Consommateurs*). The European Commission was willing to sponsor a test case. It wanted to know whether transborder law enforcement is possible and, if not, what the barriers are. I confess that the consumer organisations asked me to write the evaluation report addressed to the European Commission. The difficulties the German consumer organisations faced can be grouped around a number of issues:

— Correct address and jurisdiction: *Distant Shopping* had sent out the sweepstakes under a post box address. The German consumer organisation had to ask the then German *Bundespost* who was hiding behind the address. In the meantime consumer organisations were given a legal right to require that sort of information under the revised German law on unfair commercial practices. Then it had to be clarified whether German courts are competent under the Brussels Convention where the company consists of a post box.
— Translation: getting the French advertising translated into German. This was necessary as the action for an injuction had to be filed before a German court.
— Differences in the legal concept of misleading advertising: under the then French law misleading advertising had to be presumed to exist even if it remained an abstract danger, whereas the German concept required concrete evidence, ie the German consumer organisations had to convince the German court that the danger was real in the sense that consumers had ordered products as they wanted to win the prize.[11] French consumer organisations were obliged to provide evidence that French consumers had been misled and to make that information available to their German counterparts.
— Standing: do German consumer organisations have legal standing to protect French consumers?
— The applicable law: what is the applicable law where the infringement is felt in France but initiated in Germany? Does the so-called 'market

---

[9] See for a more complete analysis, HW Mickitz, 'Cross-Border Conflicts—A French–German Experience' (1993) 16 *Journal of Consumer Policy* 435.

[10] This part of the story is reported in ibid.

[11] The ECJ has made it clear in the meanwhile that abstract protection is not compatible with EC law: see Case 303/97 *Sektkellerei Kessler* [1999] ECR I–513.

rule' (*Marktwirkungsregel*) apply or should the law of the country of origin, ie where the advertising was initiated come to bear?[12]

The German *Verbraucherschutzverein* managed after all to bring the case before German courts, but lost after two years of litigation. The Federal Supreme Court confirmed German jurisdiction, left the issue of standing undecided but held that French law applied due to the fact that the mailouts were addressed to French consumers. The lesson to be learned can be summed up as follows: French consumer organisations failed to protect French consumers before French courts due to major problems in getting a favourable French judgment executed in Germany. German consumer organisations failed to protect French consumers. German courts were not willing to grant German consumer organisations standing in order to protect French consumers against misleading advertising emanating from German territory. This was done in a rather awkward way.[13] The Supreme Court opted for the application of French law. It applied the *Marktwirkungsregel*. The rules on standing under German unfair practices law, however, provided for standing only if German law was infringed. As the German consumer organisation had not referred to French law as the applicable law, the German court left the question open whether the German rules on standing cover violations of the French law on unfair commercial practices.

A year later the Supreme Court made it definitively clear that German consumer organisations have no standing to protect Irish consumers against advertising measures emanating from Germany. This loophole will be closed in the envisaged plans of the German government to implement Regulation 2006/2004.[14] The draft explicitly extends standing to protect foreign EC consumers as long as the company starts its activities from Germany. Another 10 years have passed.

3. DIRECTIVE 98/27/EC—PRIVATISATION OF TRANSBORDER LAW ENFORCEMENT

The experiences gained from *Distant Shopping* legitimated the European Commission's decision to take action to improve the enforcement of consumer law,[15] by this time against misleading advertising and nowadays

---

[12] See for an early discussion of the interrelationship between international private law and European law, N Reich, 'Rechtsprobleme grenzüberschreitender irreführender Werbung im Binnenmarkt' (1992) 56 *Rabels Zeitschrift für ausländisches und internationales Privatrecht* 444.

[13] BGH, 28 Nov 1997, Az I ZR 148/95—Gewinnspiel im Ausland [1998] *Neue Juristische Wochenschrift* 1227.

[14] Entwurf eines Gesetzes über die Durchsetzung der Verbraucherschutzgesetze bei innergemeinschaftlichen Verstößen vom Februar (2006, not yet published).

[15] See Recitals 3 and 4, above n 6.

against unfair commercial practices. Directive 98/27/EC on injunctions for the protection of consumers' interests pursues as an objective access to justice by consumers in the respective Member States and in *transborder* litigation before foreign Member States' courts, the free movement of injunction orders and the approximation of procedural law provisions. It relies heavily on consumer organisations, ie on the organisation of societal interests to overcome the territorial boundaries of jurisdiction.

(a) Mutual Recognition of Standing to Sue

Seen in the light of the experience with *Distant Shopping*, the Directive's major purpose is to enable so-called qualified entities registered on a Commission-run list to file actions for injunctions before Member States' courts. Therefore the Directive provides for the establishment of a register to which all Member States have to notify those entities which they regard as protecting the legitimate interests of consumers, be they statutory agencies and/or private consumers' organisations. Member States are then obliged mutually to recognise the standing to sue of the registered entities. Member States' courts retain residual powers to examine whether the qualified entities are acting in the interest of consumers in the concrete case at issue. Based on French law,[16] the Directive draws a distinction between the *qualité d'agir* (standing to sue)— which is presumed to exist to the benefit of the registered entities and the *intérêt pour agir* (*Rechtsschutzinteresse*, which means whether eg a consumer organisation which specialises in tenant protection can defend the interests of consumers in sales promotion techniques). The European Commission published a first list of qualified entities in 2003[17] which was updated in February 2006[18] and now covers the new Member States as well.

The Directive guarantees the protection of *national* consumer interests before courts in other EC Member States. It neither deals—at least not directly—with the protection of consumers in other EC member States by way of national consumer organisations, nor defines who is legitimately defending the consumer's interest, although legal doctrine deduces some minimum requirements from the existing body of EC directives granting standing to consumer/trade organisations and public agencies. The Directive affects matters of procedural law alone. It leaves the question of the applicable law to the Member States' international private law ie to the envisaged EC regulation on extra-contractual obligations (Rome II).[19]

---

[16] See J Calais-Auloy and F Steinmetz, *Droit de la Consommation* (Paris, Dalloz, 2003) 583.
[17] [2002] OJ C 30/2.
[18] [2006] OJ C 39/2.
[19] Com(2003)427 final.

Ingmar[20] which concerns the extra-territorial reach of mandatory rules in Directive 86/653/EEC on self-employed commercial agents allows one to raise the question whether mandatory EC rules, such as those enshrined in Directive 2005/29/EC on unfair commercial practices, may *generally* be taken as a legal platform within the European Community which set aside international private law rules. However, the ECJ has not yet had the opportunity to clarify the reach of *Ingmar*.

(b) Effects of Directive 98/27/EC on Transborder Law Enforcement

In 2005 the Austrian *Verein für Konsumenteninformation* and the Institut für Europäisches Wirtschafts- und Verbraucherrecht (VIEW) conducted a study on the implementation of Directive 98/27/EC into the Member States' legal orders and its practical importance in national and transborder law enforcement.[21] Whilst it was relatively easy to identify the legislative measures that the 15 old Member States took, the research turned out to be much more challenging in the 10 new Member States. Member States have to notify the relevant legislative measures to the European Commission, however, only in their own language. In most cases, there is an English translation available, but it is not officially approved and often suffers from numerous errors rendering it difficult to scrutinise the level of enforcement.

The vast majority of the Member States have taken *measures to implement* the Directive. There are a number of issues—it might be more appropriate to speak of *tendencies*—which deserve attention in our context. First, implementation measures tend to put law enforcement into the hands of consumer organisations. Territorial restrictions of jurisdiction shall be overcome in mobilising the societal powers enshrined in private organisations. That is why Member States have granted powers for *transborder* injunctive actions to consumer organisations even if a public authority is responsible for law enforcement in the national environment, thereby using relatively homogenous standards of what might constitute a legitimate representation of the consumer interest. Secondly, Member States do not necessarily apply the same standards to national and transborder enforcement. Wider powers granted under national law are usually not extended to transnational enforcement. If national law reaches beyond injunctive action as required by the Directive, these remedies are not granted to EC foreign entities. The same is true with regard to the scope of application. Member States either bind the scope of application to the requirements of the Directive 98/27/EC, or, if the scope is broader, they exclude its application from *transborder*

---

[20] Case C–381/98 *Ingmar* [2000] ECR I–9305.
[21] Docekal, *et al*, above n 8.

litigation. Thirdly, Member States have not used the Directive to establish a national list of qualified entities, although they are obliged to notify nationally qualified entities to the European Commission. Fourthly, Member States have not adopted particular procedural rules on how a collective action may be governed. So far they have ie relied on the feasibility of their national law on civil procedures.

The picture becomes blurred when one starts to evaluate the *practical* importance of injunctive actions. Here the VKI/VIEW project largely relied on a questionnaire which was sent to the Member States in order to disclose relevant case statistics as well as to explore the extra-legal environment in which the law enforcement was placed, such as the combination of public authorities and consumer organisations, available resources for law enforcement and in particular for transborder law enforcement.

The results are striking. Cross-border litigation within the European Community de facto plays no role. The proceedings having the most practical relevance were initiated by the Office of Fair Trading, details of which will be presented separately.[22] Also worth mentioning are activities initiated by German and Austrian consumers' associations which deal with the specific particularities of the German-Austrian economy. The same language, advertising strategies and business practices facilitate cross-border litigation. Similar experiences are to be reported from the Scandinavian countries which have been cooperating in cross-border legal enforcement for some time although they do not speak the same language.

No resources are made available for transborder law enforcement in particular. This may help one understand why the qualified entities do not engage in transborder law enforcement. However, the VKI study was not meant particularly to investigate non-court and out-of-court mediation and conciliation. This will be done in a study commissioned by the European Commission in 2005 which will be completed in August 2006 and which is run by the Centre for European Economic Law of the University of Leuven.

(c) *OFT v Duchesne*—the First and Sole Transborder Litigation (Sweepstakes II)

Duchesne is a Belgian company which is active in the mail order sales sector, by means of various catalogues for household, decorative, leisure and do-it-yourself products. To promote the products shown in its catalogue, *Duchesne* regularly includes with them a promotional game whose characteristics are, according to *Duchesne*, always the same. So just as in *Distant Shopping*, *Duchesne* deals with sweepstakes. It has to be recalled

---

[22] See the *Duchesne* case in the next sub-section below.

that promotional games were heavily discussed in the draft regulation on sales promotion; however, whether or not they are covered by Directive 2005/29/EEC is the subject of controversy.[23] So far a clear understanding is missing.

After having found out where *Duchesne* has its registered office—which was according to the OFT a hard job—the OFT sent a letter to Duchesne on 19 February 2004 informing it that it had received a series of complaints from consumers about advertising mail-outs in the United Kingdom. On 4 March, *Duchesne* was summoned to appear before the President of the Commercial Court of Brussels hearing an *urgent* application. In his judgment of 6 December 2004, the first judge held that the sales promotion measure violated the Control of Misleading Advertising Regulations 1988 and ordered cessation of the acts thus recorded and the advertising material in which those were contained, on pain of a fine of € 25,000 per contravention ascertained as from the date when the judgment was reported. On 9 December 2005 the Chamber of the Appeal Court of Brussels upheld the first decision. There are a number of points to be underlined:

(1) The plaintiff is a public agency and not a private organisation. *Distant Shopping* demonstrated that substantial resources are needed to prepare and to execute a transborder injunctive action. Consumer organisations are generally short of money. *Distant Shopping* was made possible through additional funds granted from the European Commission. The OFT acted on its own. However, it seems even a public agency is unable systematically to pursue transborder violations of consumer law due to scarce resources.[24]

(2) The OFT filed an action in Belgium and not in the UK, so it circumvented the problems faced by the German and French consumers' organisations in *Distant Shopping* which both intended to protect French consumers from their national home base. The French consumers' organisations wanted to protect French consumers against German-based unfair commercial practices. They did not consider filing an action for an injunction in Germany. German consumers' organisations were trying to strike down unfair commercial practices at their origin, ie in Germany. They argued in favour of a source responsibility (*Quellverantwortung*)[25] of the Member State in which the company was based and from which the commercial practices originated.

(3) The Belgian courts did not call into question the OFT's standing to sue a Belgian company. This might underline the need mutually to recognise

---

[23] See Stuyck, Terryn and van Dyck, above n 4, at 149.
[24] See Statement of M Haley, Office of Fair Trading, at the Vienna conference on collective redress, 24 Feb 2006 (papers to be made available by the Austrian presidency soon).
[25] Reich, above n 12.

standing as provided for under Directive 98/27/EC. However, one might wonder whether the Belgian courts would have confirmed the standing of a registered national consumers' organisation in the same way or whether they would have challenged the competence of the consumers' organisation to deal with transborder unfair commercial practices under Article 4(1) (3) of Directive 98/27/EC.[26]

(4) The Belgian courts regarded commercial practices as extra-contractual obligations, which is in line with the Rome II project.[27] According to Article 5 claims arising from unfair competition or other harmful marketing practices are assessed under the law of the country in which the unfair competition or other practice affects competitive relations or the collective interests of consumers. Rome II will therefore codify the so-called 'market rule' (*Marktwirkungsregel*), eg applicability of the law of the market where the competitive relations or collective consumer interests are affected.[28] Article 5 is very much in line with the general policy of Rome II as laid down in Article 3, which acknowledges the *lex loci delicti commissi,* ie where the damage arises or is likely to arise (usually the place of residence of the victim). Hitherto the Belgian courts would have had to apply UK law. Surprisingly the Court of Appeal decided to apply Belgian law instead. Contrary to the first instance it did not consider the country where the effects of the advertising are felt as the one which defined the applicable law, but instead chose the country of origin where the advertising measures come from. The judgment might be read as a late confirmation of efforts in legal doctrine to stop unfair commercial practices at their point of origin.[29]

(5) The Belgian courts did not differentiate between the average British and the average Belgian consumer. *Duchesne* argued British consumers are more robust than continental consumers, which may not be factually correct but which is very much in line with predominant cultural prejudices.[30] At the same time the Court of Appeal rejected the OFT's argument that the advertising measures were particularly dangerous to vulnerable consumers as the OFT did not manage to provide evidence of that. It is common ground that the distinction between the average and the vulnerable consumer as inserted in the

---

[26] See for a closer analysis of the meaning of Art 4(1)(3), HW Micklitz and P Rott in E Grabitz and M Hilf, *Kommentar zum europäischen Sekundärrecht* (Munich, CH Beck, 2006) Art 4 Rn 17 ff.

[27] COM(2003)427 final.

[28] See for a critical account of the market rule H Muir Watt, 'Integration and Diversity: The Conflict of Law as a Regulatory Tool' in F Cafaggi (ed), *The Institutional Framework of European Private Law* (Oxford, Oxford University Press, 2006) 191.

[29] See, for a deep analysis of the strange effects of the market rule, Ibid.

[30] See, for a legal analysis of the different consumer images, T Lettl, *Der lauterkeitsrechtliche Schutz vor irreführender Werbung in Europa* (Munich, CH Beck, 2004) 81 ff, 218 ff.

Directive 2005/29/EC, though politically sound, will produce uncertainties on the concrete yardstick to apply.[31] In the case at issue, the Belgian courts carefully analysed the sales promotion material and came to the conclusion that the general presentation was designed to convince consumers that they had definitely won the amount of the cheque mentioned. That means it went beyond mere attraction.

(6) The amount of the fine to be imposed on *Duchesne* remains a subject of controversy. The first instance court foresaw rather draconic measures where the company went on to send out folders in contravention of the cessation order. A fine of € 25,000 per folder sent out would be due. The Court of Appeal found such a fine excessive and reduced it to € 2,500 per folder sent out, thereby limiting the fine to a maximum of € 1,000,000 so as to avoid the possibility of its producing undesired effects, that is to say 'imperiling' *Duchesne*. EC law is not of much help here as it requires only sanctions that are 'effective, proportionate and deterrent'. Member States retain discretion in fixing the fine. EC law may step in only if the fine remains symbolic, which does not seem to be the case at issue.

(7) In practical terms it is very important who bears the preparatory costs of the litigation. The OFT spent substantial resources in the investigation, ie to find out who the correct plaintiff was and to translate the necessary documents. It wanted to be reimbursed of the translation costs by the defendant. However, the Court of Appeal rejected the OFT's claim for reimbursement of the translation costs and those incurred in obtaining a sworn translation of some of its documents without further discussion. The court simply stated that translation costs were 'not expenses essential to the proceedings'. Whether or not the Court of Appeal correctly applied Belgian law might be a subject for discussion. However, the reasoning demonstrates that the judges are far away from reality. Translation of the necessary documents is an indispensable prerequisite in transborder enforcement. The denial of reimbursement is indeed 'deterrent', but rather to the qualified entities which intend to pursue transborder violations of consumer law than to the wrongdoers!

4. REGULATION 2006/2004—NATIONALISATION (VERSTAATLICHUNG) OF LAW ENFORCEMENT

Before *Duchesne* could provide evidence on the degree to which the Injunction Directive is an appropriate means of improving transborder law

---

[31] See T Wilhelmsson in G Howells, HW Micklitz and T Wilhelmsson, *European Fair Trading Law—The Unfair Commercial Practices Directive* (Aldershot, Ashgate, forthcoming), chapter 5 (b) (iii).

enforcement, the European Commission was already preparing the next regulatory 'coup'. The Injunctions Directive aimed at strengthening private enforcement, mainly through consumer organisations. The Regulation on Consumer Protection Cooperation relies on cooperation between competent public authorities. 'Significantly [to] improve' the protection of the legal interests of the consumer in cross-border transactions and thus to increase the 'efficiency of the internal market' the Commission wants to have appointed central authorities in Member States which challenge cross-border infringements by way of mutual cooperation. This means that the European Commission is now trying to overcome territorial restrictions through enhanced cooperation of national administrations.

The International Marketing Supervision Network as founded by the OECD, which was recently renamed the International Consumer Protection Enforcement Network (ICPEN), served as a model for the Commission. For more than 20 years this informal body has been made up of representatives of public authorities consumers and organisations from the OECD countries. It meets twice a year to discuss problems which arise in connection with unfair commercial practices. The Commission seeks to respond to insufficient cross-border law enforcement. The idea had already been mentioned in the Green Book on Consumer Protection.[32] It passed smoothly through the legislative process. From the Austrian and the German points of view there is one notable exception. Austria and Germany have been opposed to the *nationalisation (Verstaatlichung)* of law enforcement. As a result, both countries may delegate the rights and duties under the Regulation to consumer and trade associations.

(a) The Objective and Contents of the Regulation

The Regulation came into effect in part on 29 December 2005. However, administrative cooperation has been postponed to 29 December 2006.

The Regulation does not purport to establish new authorities, or to replace controlling structures with new ones. Nor does it purport to take away the competence from Member States and to give it to the Commission. It relies on the possibility of further development of existing control structures in such a way that cooperation and transborder law enforcement can be improved. Therefore, the Regulation on Consumer Protection Cooperation is said not to interfere with the Consumer Injunctions Directive.[33]

The Regulation applies only to economic consumer protection as defined in Annex 1, which lists the relevant consumer law directives. Article 16

---

[32] J Glöckner in H Harte–Bavendamm and F Henning–Bodewig, *Gesetz gegen den unlauteren Wettbewerb* (Munich, CH Beck, 2004), Introduction B No 199 ff.
[33] COM(2001)531 final.

of the Unfair Commercial Practices Directive provides for an amendment of the Annex so as to include unfair commercial practices. The list is as exhaustive as that in the Consumer Injunctions Directive.

The Regulation is based on the concept that Member States denominate competent authorities which will cooperate in cases of a transborder violation of the law (Article 3(c)). This approach proceeds from the assumption that authorities exist which have the investigation and enforcement powers necessary for the application of the Regulation and shall exercise them in conformity with national law (Article 4(1)(3)). The Regulation establishes a number of minimum powers which Member States must grant to the competent authorities, such as access to documents, carrying out on-site inspections and action for an injunction. However, the Regulation does not provide for compensation claims.

The Regulation distinguishes between *exchange of information* with and without request in Articles 6 and 9 and a *request for enforcement measures*. Articles 8 to 15 regulate the details of the request for information or the request for enforcement measures which can be made by the authority, under what circumstances it may do so, which measures may be taken to keep data confidential and which measures can be taken by the requesting authority. Cooperation is based on the principle of confidentiality. The rules provided for are not meant to put the requesting authority in a position to compel the requested authority not even to provide information. For this reason there are no provisions in the event that the requested authority improperly declines to accede to a request to provide information or even to take appropriate measures to prevent violation of the law. The requesting authority may refer conflicts on the legitimacy of the request to the Commission, but is not obliged to do so.

Theoretically, the committee procedure in Article 19 is the focus of this interest. All possible conflicts between the Member States on how, by whom and by what means transborder litigation shall be executed are delegated to the committee procedure under Article 19. Despite the fact that the Regulation on Consumer Protection Cooperation uses 'comitology',[34] the crucial difference is that the committee procedure is not automatically triggered in case of conflict, but only if a Member State asks for a formal decision on the legitimacy of a request under Articles 5 and 7 of Decision 1999/468/EC.

Even if the Commission formally has no powers to intervene in transborder litigation, it is still the 'spider in the web'. Under Article 10, its task is to build up a database which saves all information and enforcement requests and their consequences. Every second year, Member States have to provide a report to the Commission in compliance with a detailed catalogue: Article

---

[34] There is an endless literature on the subject: see C Joerges *et al* (eds), *EU Committees: Social Regulation, Law and Politics* (Oxford, Hart Publishing, 2000).

21(3)(a) to (f). These reports will be made available to the public by the Commission.

(b) The Significance of the Regulation with regard to the Organisation of Transborder Law Enforcement

The Regulation covers the entire spectrum of contractually relevant consumer law directives, including the UCPD. The strong reliance on public control authorities heavily affects Austrian and German consumer and trade organisations to which the enforcement of the unfair commercial practices law is entrusted. It cannot be excluded that other countries face similar problems.[35]

The centre of the conflicts was Article 4(2) read together with Article 8(3), according to which Austria and Germany have to designate a competent authority. Given the compromise, these might be the established consumer and trade organisations. However, the Regulation does not release Member States from the obligation to designate one competent statutory body, which must supervise consumer and trade organisations to which the rights and duties under the regulation are delegated. To this end the designated Member State's authorities retain a residual control competence: Article 8(3). This authority must be given power to file an action for an injunction if consumer or trade organisations fail to take action for whatever reason—despite an explicit order to do so. That is why the ultimate responsibility remains in the hands of the designated national authorities in all Member States, including Germany and Austria.

(c) A Changing Outlook of Law Enforcement in the EU?

The Regulation profoundly changes the outlook of consumer law enforcement, not just in the fields of unfair commercial practices and transborder law enforcement.

A preliminary analysis reveals a whole set of changes. The impact of private organisations is reduced, if not rejected. Whether or not they are integrated into transborder law enforcement remains at the discretion of the Member States. The regulation reduces the role of private organisations—or more ambitiously of societal interests—and increases the role of statutory powers. The strong reliance on public agencies as law enforcers will greatly affect the role consumer and trade organisations are playing in the *national context*. It is hard to image a bifurcated concept of law enforcement in the

---

[35] See for a more detailed account of the situation in the Member States, Docekal, *et al*, above n 8.

sense of putting national enforcement into the hands of consumer organisa-tions and transborder enforcement into the hands of public agencies.

Soft law means will be substituted for hard law enforcement. One might argue that the more or less complete failure of the Injunction Directive legit-imises such a policy shift. This seems even truer if one takes into account the complex legal setting in transborder injunctive actions. However, the shift equally affects the sharing of tasks between consumer organisations and public agencies. Consumer as well as trade organisations have to go to court and request the cessation of unfair commercial practices. They may negotiate the cessation just as public agencies, but the difference in terms of legitimacy and regulatory powers persists. Consumer and trade organisa-tions are not acting on behalf of the state. In neither Austria nor Germany was the legislator willing formally to delegate statutory tasks to private organisations. This means they *may* get involved in law enforcement, but they are *not* legally *obliged* to take action.[36] The increased role and impor-tance of soft law is even strengthened by the lack of powers to oblige the requested agency to take action. As the comitology procedure enhances the regulatory role of the Commission, it may work as a deterrent and inhibit Member States from delegating decision-making to the European level. It fits into the down-grading of consumer organisations that, unlike the draft Regulation,[37] the adopted version no longer provides for the possibility of inviting so-called 'qualified bodies' under the Injunction Directive, which means authorised or competent organisations, to participate in the comitol-ogy procedure.

On reflection, one might raise the question whether the European Community acquires more of the shape of a traditional international organ-isation, ie fewer powers to the European Commission and more powers to the Member States, less hard law and more soft law, less judicial action and more administrative action.

5. THE FUTURE—COLLECTIVE ACTIONS TO RECOVER ILL-GOTTEN GAINS?

Whilst the European Community has frozen the set of available European remedies to injunctive action alone, the Member States go on develop-ing remedies beyond mere injunctions. Of particular interest are all those efforts which aim at skimming off profits which result from unfair com-mercial practices and which are said to be 'unjust'. Ill-gotten gains are hard to measure. *Duchesne v OFT* indicates that the company must make a lot

---

[36] The issue came up in the legislative process leading to Regulation 2006/2004: see the posi-tion paper of the European Consumer Law Group, The Regulation on Consumer Protection Co-operation ECLG/021/04 Apr 2004, available at www.europeanconsumerlawgroup.org.
[37] COM(2003)443 final.

of money out of its sales campaigns otherwise it would not fight so hard against the OFT's efforts to put a stop to these practices.

The Member States' initiatives are not limited to unfair competition law. More and more they are considering adopting skimming off procedures in cartel or antitrust law. The well-known *Ashurst* study[38] has revealed that the Member States' remedies securing private enforcement are still deficient. These findings have brought the European Commission to the fore, as discussed below. Any European initiative dealing with ill-gotten gains in antitrust law will certainly affect European remedies to fight unfair commercial practices.

(a) The German Model in Unfair Commercial Practices Law

The German legislator granted trade and consumer organisations the right to skim off 'unjust profits' (*Unrechtsgewinnabschöpfung*) in the new law on unfair commercial practices passed in 2004.[39] Consequently, in the case of wilful acts of unfair competition by virtue of which a profit is obtained to the detriment of a large number of customers, the party committing the infringement can be forced to hand over such profit to the Ministry of Finance under section 10 of the Unfair Competition Act (UWG). The infringing party is also obliged to hand over the profits made as a result of the violation in case of so-called 'widespread' damage, where the individual party concerned often shies away from taking legal action because of the high costs and risks associated with the proceedings—the aim being to stop unfair competition from 'always being worthwhile'. There is not much practice available to inspect. However, the two leading claimants have launched test cases in order to find out whether the new remedy is a feasible instrument. As the Supreme Court had not yet had the chance to decide the issue it is too early to assess the feasibility of the German approach—although lower court decisions are not at all promising.[40]

Similar rules exist in a number of Member States and the US.[41] However, in France and Spain the available remedies are not particularly designed to recover ill-gotten gains. In these countries collective compensation claims

---

[38] Above n 22. Available at the homepage of the DG Competition, available at http://ec.europa.eu/comm/competition/ antitrust/others/actions_for_damages/comparative_report_clean_en.pdf.

[39] See for a full account of the new law A Stadler and HW Micklitz, 'The Development of Collective Legal Action in Europe, especially in German Civil Procedure' [2006] *European Business Law Review* (forthcoming).

[40] See the statement of P von Braunmühl in Bundesministerium für Ernährung, Verbraucherschutz und Landwirtschaft (ed.), *Kollektive Rechtsdurchsetzung—Chancen und Risiken* (results of the second Bamberger Verbraucherrechtstage 20/21 Münster, Landwirtschaftsverlag, 2006, forthcoming).

[41] See A Stadler and HW Micklitz, *Das Verbandsklagerecht in der Informations- und Dienstleistungsgesellschaft* (Münster, Landwirtschaftsverlag, 2005).

equally apply to the type of law infringements at stake here. Sweden and the United States, however, have designed particular remedies in order to be able to skim off unjustified profits of the wrongdoer.

(b) A European Initiative on Private Enforcement against Antitrust Injuries?

The question of private enforcement has to be placed in context. With the adoption of Regulation 1/2003,[42] the European Commission introduced an extensive reorientation of its policy, characterised by two main points. First, the monitoring of antitrust law is to be decentralised, with the Commission relinquishing a number of areas of competence. Instead, the Member States' agencies are to be urged to accept greater responsibility in order to help European antitrust law gain acceptance, at the same time raising the supremacy claimed by antitrust law. Secondly, decentralisation is increasing the pressure to strengthen private enforcement, something expressly documented by the Commission in Recital 7.[43] Up to that time, private enforcement, understood as the activities that professional traders, entrepreneurs and consumers develop individually or collectively, played only a secondary role in most Member States. Traditionally, the idea of private legal entities able to help antitrust law to become more effective comes from the Anglo-American legal framework. Regulation 1/2003[44] can therefore also be embedded in a wider context of the reorientation of commercial law by the European Community.[45]

The Commission's policy shift comes at a time when the European Court has pointed the way ahead with the so-called 'Courage' doctrine. As long ago as 1993, Advocate General van Gerven raised in *Banks*[46] the question whether and to what extent an entitlement to compensation for professional traders could be derived from Article 81 of the EC Treaty. It took seven years for this problem to reach the European Court again. In *Courage*, Advocate General *Mischo*[47] not only supported the establishment of entitlement to compensation arising from Article 81; he also clearly emphasised that, in addition to entrepreneurs, consumers can, potentially, also be considered

---

[42] [2003] OJL 1/1.

[43] See the criticism of this with regard to the division of powers in H Weyer, 'Schadensersatzansprüche gegen Private kraft Gemeinschaftsrecht' [2003] *Zeitschrift für Europäisches Privatrecht* 318 at 323; amplified by AA Alvizou, 'Individual Tort Liability for Infringements of Community Law' (2002) 29 *Legal Issues of Economic Integration* 177.

[44] Above n 42.

[45] Cf J Keßler and HW Micklitz, *Anlegerschutz in Deutschland, Schweiz, Großbritannien, USA und der Europäischen Gemeinschaft*, Volume 15 of the VIEW series (Baden-Baden, Nomos 2004).

[46] Opinion of 27 Oct 1993, in Case 128/92 *Banks* [1994] ECR I–1209, paras. 36–45.

[47] Opinion of 22 Mar 2001, in Case C–453/99 *Courage v Crehan Ltd* [2001] ECR I–6314, para 38 .

as holders of compensation entitlements under antitrust law. The European Court's ruling was more cautious, in that it did not speak of consumers, referring to 'any individual' instead.[48] Since the adoption of '*Courage*', a discussion has flared up in the Member States which is also associated with the reorientation of European antitrust law in Regulation 1/2003. Private enforcement in antitrust law is the requirement of the moment; but there is considerable uncertainty as to how this process should be organised. This stems not least from the substantial legal uncertainty which is exacerbated further by diverging regulations in the Member States. The *Ashurst* Study[49] in its executive summary of the comparative report on the laws of the 25 Member States as delivered to the European Commission in August 2004 comes to the following conclusions: '[t]he picture that emerges from the present study on damage actions for breach for competition in the enlarged EU is of one of astonishing diversity and underdevelopment'.

The Green Paper on private enforcement in competition law adopted in December 2005[50] invites all parties interested in the field to comment on a series of questions which all aim at discovering whether additional means to secure private enforcement are needed and whether consumers and consumer organisations shall also be given the right to claim compensation for antitrust injuries. The Commission will probably come up with a proposal to take action in the field of antitrust law. Any solution will have effects well beyond cartel law and may very well spill over to unfair commercial practices.

(c) Skimming Off Remedies in the Transborder Context—to the Benefit of Private Persons, of Consumer and Trade Organisations and/or Statutory Agencies?

Introducing new remedies raises a whole series of very sensitive questions which can only be touched upon. They all focus around a pure national perspective. The transborder implications of a remedy that implies compensation are not even discussed. The reason may be that skimming off remedies at the national legal level is far from being well established.

The first question is whether the remedy is to be put into the hands of the competent agencies or whether trade and, in particular, consumers' organisations is also to be granted standing. There is no easy answer. It has been

---

[48] Judgment 20 Sept 2001, in Case C–453/99 *Courage v Crehan Ltd* [2001] ECR I–6314, paras 25–27, for comment see N Reich, 'The Courage Doctrine: Encouraging or Discouraging Compensation for Antitrust Injuries?' (2005) 42 *CMLRev* 35.

[49] Available at the homepage of DG Competition, http://ec.europa.eu/comm/competition/antitrust/others/actions_for_damages/comparative_report_clean_en.pdf.

[50] COM(2004)672 final.

argued that continental legal systems as well as common law systems start from the premise that where there are statutory agencies there is no need to grant equal powers to consumers' organisations. Private enforcement is said to be rooted in the United States' enforcement policy, which does not have specialised agencies to the same extent as Europe and where private enforcement serves to compensate for the lack of statutory control.[51]

The second issue concerns the question of who shall benefit from the money which is taken from the companies. There seems to be a growing trend in Europe towards using ill-gotten gains or cartel fines to establish a fund to be used to finance the work of consumers' organisations. Italy has taken the lead here,[52] whereas other Member States remain reluctant, although there is a certain temptation to solve the problem of public funding of consumers' organisations 'for ever'.

Once these major problems are solved the question remains what a transborder skimming off remedy should look like and who should take action, maybe not in support of the consumers of one country alone.

6. TRANSBORDER LAW ENFORCEMENT—A NEVER–ENDING STORY?

It seems that transborder law enforcement has not gained the importance it deserves, politically and legally. The European Commission has adopted two far reaching pieces of regulation in less than 10 years. So far, mainly various types of promotional games and even sales promotion measures have been the focus of interest, mostly all sorts of promotional games or even broader of sales promotion, measures have been the focus of interest. The network of European legislative measures has become ever more complicated, but the European Commission has failed to adopt a European fair trading law which fully covers sales promotion measures. Member States' laws differ considerably in the degree to which they allow or prohibit these sorts of commercial practices.[53]

But even if EC law was to bring about common standards on all sorts of unfair commercial practices a number of issues remain unsolved even

---

[51] FJ Säcker, *Die Einordnung der Verbandsklage in das System des Privatrechts* (Munich, CH Beck, 2006); M Andenas, B Hess and P Oberhammer (eds), *Enforcement Agency Practice in Europe* (London, British Institute of International and Comparative Law 2005).

[52] In Italy, fines resulting from antitrust injuries are put in a fund which serves to finance consumer organisations.

[53] See R Schulze and H Schulte-Nölke (eds), *Analysis of National Fairness Laws Aimed at Protecting Consumers in Relation to Precontractual Commercial Practices and the Handling of Consumer Complaints by Business* (Munster, June 2003, unpublished manuscript), a study undertaken on behalf of DG Sanco, European Commission, available at http://ec.europa.eu/consumers/cons_int/safe_shop/fair_bus_pract/green_pap_ comm/studies/unfair_practices_en.pdf.

under the regime of Regulation 2006/2004.[54] Unfair commercial practices are not confined to European territory. That is why international rather than European transborder law enforcement is needed. The International Consumer Protection and Enforcement Network (ICPEN) plays a certain role. However, it is not subject to public scrutiny.

No one seems to care about the extremely complicated legal questions which are raised at the substantial and procedural level of transborder European law enforcement. Currently it seems to be an area for legal doctrine ie for academia, whereas the enforcement authorities, be they private or public, largely refrain from getting involved, mainly because they lack resources in terms of money but also solid knowledge in that particular field of law. Soft law should not lead to the de-legalisation and de-judicialisation of law enforcement.

Two further problems of transborder law enforcement are equally neglected. What about language? Transborder law enforcement involves theoretically knowledge of more than 20 languages or (even harder) *legal* languages. It is common ground that lawyers, too, prefer to have documents translated into their native language even if they read and write legal texts in foreign languages. Translation may therefore be indispensable, and this is expensive and time consuming. Last but not least, judgments need to be executed. So far not a single collective action has ever reached the stage of being about to be executed. One might wonder whether the sad experiences gathered in the past along the lines of *Distant Shopping* really belong to the past.

Last but not least, it seems necessary to insert new remedies, such as skimming off procedures at the European level, thereby taking into account the transborder dimensions. The effects of unfair commercial practices or antitrust injuries are not confined to the territorial reach of Member States' law.

[54] Above n 7.

Appendix

Directive 2005/29/EC of the European Parliament and of the Council of 11 May 2005 concerning unfair business-to-consumer commercial practices in the internal market and amending Council Directive 84/450/EEC, Directives 97/7/EC, 98/27/EC and 2002/65/EC of the European Parliament and of the Council and Regulation (EC) No 2006/2004 of the European Parliament and of the Council ('Unfair Commercial Practices Directive')

Official Journal L 149, 11/06/2005 P. 0022–0039

THE EUROPEAN PARLIAMENT AND THE COUNCIL OF THE EUROPEAN UNION,

Having regard to the Treaty establishing the European Community, and in particular Article 95 thereof,

Having regard to the proposal from the Commission,

Having regard to the opinion of the European Economic and Social Committee [1],

Acting in accordance with the procedure laid down in Article 251 of the Treaty [2],

Whereas:

(1) Article 153(1) and (3)(a) of the Treaty provides that the Community is to contribute to the attainment of a high level of consumer protection by the measures it adopts pursuant to Article 95 thereof.

(2) In accordance with Article 14(2) of the Treaty, the internal market comprises an area without internal frontiers in which the free movement of goods and services and freedom of establishment are ensured. The development of fair commercial practices within the area without internal frontiers is vital for the promotion of the development of cross-border activities.

(3) The laws of the Member States relating to unfair commercial practices show marked differences which can generate appreciable distortions of competition and obstacles to the smooth functioning of the internal market. In the field of advertising, Council Directive 84/450/EEC of 10 September 1984 concerning misleading and comparative advertising [3] establishes minimum criteria for harmonising legislation on misleading advertising, but does not prevent the Member States from retaining or adopting measures which provide more extensive protection for consumers. As a result, Member States' provisions on misleading advertising diverge significantly.

(4) These disparities cause uncertainty as to which national rules apply to unfair commercial practices harming consumers' economic interests and create many barriers affecting business and consumers. These barriers increase the cost to business of exercising internal market freedoms, in particular when businesses wish to engage in cross border marketing, advertising campaigns and sales promotions. Such barriers also make consumers uncertain of their rights and undermine their confidence in the internal market.

(5) In the absence of uniform rules at Community level, obstacles to the free movement of services and goods across borders or the freedom of establishment could be justified in the light of the case-law of the Court of Justice of the European Communities as long as they seek to protect recognised public interest objectives and are proportionate to those objectives. In view of the Community's objectives, as set out in the provisions of the Treaty and in secondary Community law relating to freedom of movement, and in accordance with the Commission's policy on commercial communications as indicated in the Communication from the Commission entitled "The follow-up to the Green Paper on Commercial Communications in the Internal Market", such obstacles should be eliminated. These obstacles can only be eliminated by establishing uniform rules at Community level which establish a high level of consumer protection and by clarifying certain legal concepts at Community level to the extent necessary for the proper functioning of the internal market and to meet the requirement of legal certainty.

(6) This Directive therefore approximates the laws of the Member States on unfair commercial practices, including unfair advertising, which directly harm consumers' economic interests and thereby indirectly harm the economic interests of legitimate competitors. In line with the principle of proportionality, this Directive protects consumers from the consequences of such unfair commercial practices where they are material but recognises that in some cases the impact on consumers may be negligible. It neither covers nor affects the national laws on unfair commercial practices which harm only competitors' economic interests or which relate to a transaction between traders; taking full account of the principle of subsidiarity, Member States will continue to be able to regulate such practices, in conformity with Community law, if they choose to do so. Nor does this Directive cover or affect the provisions of Directive 84/450/EEC on advertising which misleads business but which is not misleading for consumers and on comparative advertising. Further, this Directive does not affect accepted advertising and marketing practices, such as legitimate product placement, brand differentiation or the offering of incentives which may legitimately affect consumers' perceptions of products and influence

their behaviour without impairing the consumer's ability to make an informed decision.

(7) This Directive addresses commercial practices directly related to influencing consumers' transactional decisions in relation to products. It does not address commercial practices carried out primarily for other purposes, including for example commercial communication aimed at investors, such as annual reports and corporate promotional literature. It does not address legal requirements related to taste and decency which vary widely among the Member States. Commercial practices such as, for example, commercial solicitation in the streets, may be undesirable in Member States for cultural reasons. Member States should accordingly be able to continue to ban commercial practices in their territory, in conformity with Community law, for reasons of taste and decency even where such practices do not limit consumers' freedom of choice. Full account should be taken of the context of the individual case concerned in applying this Directive, in particular the general clauses thereof.

(8) This Directive directly protects consumer economic interests from unfair business-to-consumer commercial practices. Thereby, it also indirectly protects legitimate businesses from their competitors who do not play by the rules in this Directive and thus guarantees fair competition in fields coordinated by it. It is understood that there are other commercial practices which, although not harming consumers, may hurt competitors and business customers. The Commission should carefully examine the need for Community action in the field of unfair competition beyond the remit of this Directive and, if necessary, make a legislative proposal to cover these other aspects of unfair competition.

(9) This Directive is without prejudice to individual actions brought by those who have been harmed by an unfair commercial practice. It is also without prejudice to Community and national rules on contract law, on intellectual property rights, on the health and safety aspects of products, on conditions of establishment and authorisation regimes, including those rules which, in conformity with Community law, relate to gambling activities, and to Community competition rules and the national provisions implementing them. The Member States will thus be able to retain or introduce restrictions and prohibitions of commercial practices on grounds of the protection of the health and safety of consumers in their territory wherever the trader is based, for example in relation to alcohol, tobacco or pharmaceuticals. Financial services and immovable property, by reason of their complexity and inherent serious risks, necessitate detailed requirements, including positive obligations on traders. For this reason, in the field of financial services and immovable property, this Directive is without prejudice

to the right of Member States to go beyond its provisions to protect the economic interests of consumers. It is not appropriate to regulate here the certification and indication of the standard of fineness of articles of precious metal.

(10) It is necessary to ensure that the relationship between this Directive and existing Community law is coherent, particularly where detailed provisions on unfair commercial practices apply to specific sectors. This Directive therefore amends Directive 84/450/EEC, Directive 97/7/EC of the European Parliament and of the Council of 20 May 1997 on the protection of consumers in respect of distance contracts [4], Directive 98/27/EC of the European Parliament and of the Council of 19 May 1998 on injunctions for the protection of consumers' interests [5] and Directive 2002/65/EC of the European Parliament and of the Council of 23 September 2002 concerning the distance marketing of consumer financial services [6]. This Directive accordingly applies only in so far as there are no specific Community law provisions regulating specific aspects of unfair commercial practices, such as information requirements and rules on the way the information is presented to the consumer. It provides protection for consumers where there is no specific sectoral legislation at Community level and prohibits traders from creating a false impression of the nature of products. This is particularly important for complex products with high levels of risk to consumers, such as certain financial services products. This Directive consequently complements the Community acquis, which is applicable to commercial practices harming consumers' economic interests.

(11) The high level of convergence achieved by the approximation of national provisions through this Directive creates a high common level of consumer protection. This Directive establishes a single general prohibition of those unfair commercial practices distorting consumers' economic behaviour. It also sets rules on aggressive commercial practices, which are currently not regulated at Community level.

(12) Harmonisation will considerably increase legal certainty for both consumers and business. Both consumers and business will be able to rely on a single regulatory framework based on clearly defined legal concepts regulating all aspects of unfair commercial practices across the EU. The effect will be to eliminate the barriers stemming from the fragmentation of the rules on unfair commercial practices harming consumer economic interests and to enable the internal market to be achieved in this area.

(13) In order to achieve the Community's objectives through the removal of internal market barriers, it is necessary to replace Member States' existing, divergent general clauses and legal principles. The single,

common general prohibition established by this Directive therefore covers unfair commercial practices distorting consumers' economic behaviour. In order to support consumer confidence the general prohibition should apply equally to unfair commercial practices which occur outside any contractual relationship between a trader and a consumer or following the conclusion of a contract and during its execution. The general prohibition is elaborated by rules on the two types of commercial practices which are by far the most common, namely misleading commercial practices and aggressive commercial practices.

(14) It is desirable that misleading commercial practices cover those practices, including misleading advertising, which by deceiving the consumer prevent him from making an informed and thus efficient choice. In conformity with the laws and practices of Member States on misleading advertising, this Directive classifies misleading practices into misleading actions and misleading omissions. In respect of omissions, this Directive sets out a limited number of key items of information which the consumer needs to make an informed transactional decision. Such information will not have to be disclosed in all advertisements, but only where the trader makes an invitation to purchase, which is a concept clearly defined in this Directive. The full harmonisation approach adopted in this Directive does not preclude the Member States from specifying in national law the main characteristics of particular products such as, for example, collectors' items or electrical goods, the omission of which would be material when an invitation to purchase is made. It is not the intention of this Directive to reduce consumer choice by prohibiting the promotion of products which look similar to other products unless this similarity confuses consumers as to the commercial origin of the product and is therefore misleading. This Directive should be without prejudice to existing Community law which expressly affords Member States the choice between several regulatory options for the protection of consumers in the field of commercial practices. In particular, this Directive should be without prejudice to Article 13(3) of Directive 2002/58/EC of the European Parliament and of the Council of 12 July 2002 concerning the processing of personal data and the protection of privacy in the electronic communications sector [7].

(15) Where Community law sets out information requirements in relation to commercial communication, advertising and marketing that information is considered as material under this Directive. Member States will be able to retain or add information requirements relating to contract law and having contract law consequences where this is allowed by the minimum clauses in the existing Community law instruments. A non-exhaustive list of such information requirements in the acquis

is contained in Annex II. Given the full harmonisation introduced by this Directive only the information required in Community law is considered as material for the purpose of Article 7(5) thereof. Where Member States have introduced information requirements over and above what is specified in Community law, on the basis of minimum clauses, the omission of that extra information will not constitute a misleading omission under this Directive. By contrast Member States will be able, when allowed by the minimum clauses in Community law, to maintain or introduce more stringent provisions in conformity with Community law so as to ensure a higher level of protection of consumers' individual contractual rights.

(16) The provisions on aggressive commercial practices should cover those practices which significantly impair the consumer's freedom of choice. Those are practices using harassment, coercion, including the use of physical force, and undue influence.

(17) It is desirable that those commercial practices which are in all circumstances unfair be identified to provide greater legal certainty. Annex I therefore contains the full list of all such practices. These are the only commercial practices which can be deemed to be unfair without a case-by-case assessment against the provisions of Articles 5 to 9. The list may only be modified by revision of the Directive.

(18) It is appropriate to protect all consumers from unfair commercial practices; however the Court of Justice has found it necessary in adjudicating on advertising cases since the enactment of Directive 84/450/EEC to examine the effect on a notional, typical consumer. In line with the principle of proportionality, and to permit the effective application of the protections contained in it, this Directive takes as a benchmark the average consumer, who is reasonably well-informed and reasonably observant and circumspect, taking into account social, cultural and linguistic factors, as interpreted by the Court of Justice, but also contains provisions aimed at preventing the exploitation of consumers whose characteristics make them particularly vulnerable to unfair commercial practices. Where a commercial practice is specifically aimed at a particular group of consumers, such as children, it is desirable that the impact of the commercial practice be assessed from the perspective of the average member of that group. It is therefore appropriate to include in the list of practices which are in all circumstances unfair a provision which, without imposing an outright ban on advertising directed at children, protects them from direct exhortations to purchase. The average consumer test is not a statistical test. National courts and authorities will have to exercise their own faculty of judgement, having regard to the case-law of the Court of Justice, to determine the typical reaction of the average consumer in a given case.

(19) Where certain characteristics such as age, physical or mental infirmity or credulity make consumers particularly susceptible to a commercial practice or to the underlying product and the economic behaviour only of such consumers is likely to be distorted by the practice in a way that the trader can reasonably foresee, it is appropriate to ensure that they are adequately protected by assessing the practice from the perspective of the average member of that group.

(20) It is appropriate to provide a role for codes of conduct, which enable traders to apply the principles of this Directive effectively in specific economic fields. In sectors where there are specific mandatory requirements regulating the behaviour of traders, it is appropriate that these will also provide evidence as to the requirements of professional diligence in that sector. The control exercised by code owners at national or Community level to eliminate unfair commercial practices may avoid the need for recourse to administrative or judicial action and should therefore be encouraged. With the aim of pursuing a high level of consumer protection, consumers' organisations could be informed and involved in the drafting of codes of conduct.

(21) Persons or organisations regarded under national law as having a legitimate interest in the matter must have legal remedies for initiating proceedings against unfair commercial practices, either before a court or before an administrative authority which is competent to decide upon complaints or to initiate appropriate legal proceedings. While it is for national law to determine the burden of proof, it is appropriate to enable courts and administrative authorities to require traders to produce evidence as to the accuracy of factual claims they have made.

(22) It is necessary that Member States lay down penalties for infringements of the provisions of this Directive and they must ensure that these are enforced. The penalties must be effective, proportionate and dissuasive.

(23) Since the objectives of this Directive, namely to eliminate the barriers to the functioning of the internal market represented by national laws on unfair commercial practices and to provide a high common level of consumer protection, by approximating the laws, regulations and administrative provisions of the Member States on unfair commercial practices, cannot be sufficiently achieved by the Member States and can therefore be better achieved at Community level, the Community may adopt measures, in accordance with the principle of subsidiarity as set out in Article 5 of the Treaty. In accordance with the principle of proportionality, as set out in that Article, this Directive does not go beyond what is necessary in order to eliminate the internal market barriers and achieve a high common level of consumer protection.

(24) It is appropriate to review this Directive to ensure that barriers to the internal market have been addressed and a high level of consumer protection achieved. The review could lead to a Commission proposal to amend this Directive, which may include a limited extension to the derogation in Article 3(5), and/or amendments to other consumer protection legislation reflecting the Commission's Consumer Policy Strategy commitment to review the existing acquis in order to achieve a high, common level of consumer protection.

(25) This Directive respects the fundamental rights and observes the principles recognised in particular by the Charter of Fundamental Rights of the European Union,

HAVE ADOPTED THIS DIRECTIVE:

CHAPTER 1

GENERAL PROVISIONS

Article 1

Purpose

The purpose of this Directive is to contribute to the proper functioning of the internal market and achieve a high level of consumer protection by approximating the laws, regulations and administrative provisions of the Member States on unfair commercial practices harming consumers' economic interests.

Article 2

Definitions

For the purposes of this Directive:
  (a) "consumer" means any natural person who, in commercial practices covered by this Directive, is acting for purposes which are outside his trade, business, craft or profession;
  (b) "trader" means any natural or legal person who, in commercial practices covered by this Directive, is acting for purposes relating to his trade, business, craft or profession and anyone acting in the name of or on behalf of a trader;
  (c) "product" means any goods or service including immovable property, rights and obligations;
  (d) "business-to-consumer commercial practices" (hereinafter also referred to as commercial practices) means any act, omission, course of conduct or representation, commercial communication including advertising and marketing, by a trader, directly connected with the promotion, sale or supply of a product to consumers;

(e) "to materially distort the economic behaviour of consumers" means using a commercial practice to appreciably impair the consumer's ability to make an informed decision, thereby causing the consumer to take a transactional decision that he would not have taken otherwise;

(f) "code of conduct" means an agreement or set of rules not imposed by law, regulation or administrative provision of a Member State which defines the behaviour of traders who undertake to be bound by the code in relation to one or more particular commercial practices or business sectors;

(g) "code owner" means any entity, including a trader or group of traders, which is responsible for the formulation and revision of a code of conduct and/or for monitoring compliance with the code by those who have undertaken to be bound by it;

(h) "professional diligence" means the standard of special skill and care which a trader may reasonably be expected to exercise towards consumers, commensurate with honest market practice and/or the general principle of good faith in the trader's field of activity;

(i) "invitation to purchase" means a commercial communication which indicates characteristics of the product and the price in a way appropriate to the means of the commercial communication used and thereby enables the consumer to make a purchase;

(j) "undue influence" means exploiting a position of power in relation to the consumer so as to apply pressure, even without using or threatening to use physical force, in a way which significantly limits the consumer's ability to make an informed decision;

(k) "transactional decision" means any decision taken by a consumer concerning whether, how and on what terms to purchase, make payment in whole or in part for, retain or dispose of a product or to exercise a contractual right in relation to the product, whether the consumer decides to act or to refrain from acting;

(l) "regulated profession" means a professional activity or a group of professional activities, access to which or the pursuit of which, or one of the modes of pursuing which, is conditional, directly or indirectly, upon possession of specific professional qualifications, pursuant to laws, regulations or administrative provisions.

Article 3

Scope

1. This Directive shall apply to unfair business-to-consumer commercial practices, as laid down in Article 5, before, during and after a commercial transaction in relation to a product.

2. This Directive is without prejudice to contract law and, in particular, to the rules on the validity, formation or effect of a contract.
3. This Directive is without prejudice to Community or national rules relating to the health and safety aspects of products.
4. In the case of conflict between the provisions of this Directive and other Community rules regulating specific aspects of unfair commercial practices, the latter shall prevail and apply to those specific aspects.
5. For a period of six years from 12 June 2007, Member States shall be able to continue to apply national provisions within the field approximated by this Directive which are more restrictive or prescriptive than this Directive and which implement directives containing minimum harmonisation clauses. These measures must be essential to ensure that consumers are adequately protected against unfair commercial practices and must be proportionate to the attainment of this objective. The review referred to in Article 18 may, if considered appropriate, include a proposal to prolong this derogation for a further limited period.
6. Member States shall notify the Commission without delay of any national provisions applied on the basis of paragraph 5.
7. This Directive is without prejudice to the rules determining the jurisdiction of the courts.
8. This Directive is without prejudice to any conditions of establishment or of authorisation regimes, or to the deontological codes of conduct or other specific rules governing regulated professions in order to uphold high standards of integrity on the part of the professional, which Member States may, in conformity with Community law, impose on professionals.
9. In relation to "financial services", as defined in Directive 2002/65/EC, and immovable property, Member States may impose requirements which are more restrictive or prescriptive than this Directive in the field which it approximates.
10. This Directive shall not apply to the application of the laws, regulations and administrative provisions of Member States relating to the certification and indication of the standard of fineness of articles of precious metal.

Article 4

Internal market

Member States shall neither restrict the freedom to provide services nor restrict the free movement of goods for reasons falling within the field approximated by this Directive.

CHAPTER 2

UNFAIR COMMERCIAL PRACTICES

Article 5

Prohibition of unfair commercial practices

1. Unfair commercial practices shall be prohibited.
2. A commercial practice shall be unfair if:
   (a) it is contrary to the requirements of professional diligence, and
   (b) it materially distorts or is likely to materially distort the economic behaviour with regard to the product of the average consumer whom it reaches or to whom it is addressed, or of the average member of the group when a commercial practice is directed to a particular group of consumers.
3. Commercial practices which are likely to materially distort the economic behaviour only of a clearly identifiable group of consumers who are particularly vulnerable to the practice or the underlying product because of their mental or physical infirmity, age or credulity in a way which the trader could reasonably be expected to foresee, shall be assessed from the perspective of the average member of that group. This is without prejudice to the common and legitimate advertising practice of making exaggerated statements or statements which are not meant to be taken literally.
4. In particular, commercial practices shall be unfair which:
   (a) are misleading as set out in Articles 6 and 7, or
   (b) are aggressive as set out in Articles 8 and 9.
5. Annex I contains the list of those commercial practices which shall in all circumstances be regarded as unfair. The same single list shall apply in all Member States and may only be modified by revision of this Directive.

Section 1

Misleading commercial practices

Article 6

Misleading actions

1 A commercial practice shall be regarded as misleading if it contains false information and is therefore untruthful or in any way, including overall presentation, deceives or is likely to deceive the average consumer, even

if the information is factually correct, in relation to one or more of the following elements, and in either case causes or is likely to cause him to take a transactional decision that he would not have taken otherwise:

(a)   the existence or nature of the product;

(b)   the main characteristics of the product, such as its availability, benefits, risks, execution, composition, accessories, after-sale customer assistance and complaint handling, method and date of manufacture or provision, delivery, fitness for purpose, usage, quantity, specification, geographical or commercial origin or the results to be expected from its use, or the results and material features of tests or checks carried out on the product;

(c)   the extent of the trader's commitments, the motives for the commercial practice and the nature of the sales process, any statement or symbol in relation to direct or indirect sponsorship or approval of the trader or the product;

(d)   the price or the manner in which the price is calculated, or the existence of a specific price advantage;

(e)   the need for a service, part, replacement or repair;

(f)   the nature, attributes and rights of the trader or his agent, such as his identity and assets, his qualifications, status, approval, affiliation or connection and ownership of industrial, commercial or intellectual property rights or his awards and distinctions;

(g)   the consumer's rights, including the right to replacement or reimbursement under Directive 1999/44/EC of the European Parliament and of the Council of 25 May 1999 on certain aspects of the sale of consumer goods and associated guarantees [8], or the risks he may face.

2. A commercial practice shall also be regarded as misleading if, in its factual context, taking account of all its features and circumstances, it causes or is likely to cause the average consumer to take a transactional decision that he would not have taken otherwise, and it involves:

(a)   any marketing of a product, including comparative advertising, which creates confusion with any products, trade marks, trade names or other distinguishing marks of a competitor;

(b)   non-compliance by the trader with commitments contained in codes of conduct by which the trader has undertaken to be bound, where:

(i)   the commitment is not aspirational but is firm and is capable of being verified,

and

(ii)   the trader indicates in a commercial practice that he is bound by the code.

Article 7

Misleading omissions

1. A commercial practice shall be regarded as misleading if, in its factual context, taking account of all its features and circumstances and the limitations of the communication medium, it omits material information that the average consumer needs, according to the context, to take an informed transactional decision and thereby causes or is likely to cause the average consumer to take a transactional decision that he would not have taken otherwise.

2. It shall also be regarded as a misleading omission when, taking account of the matters described in paragraph 1, a trader hides or provides in an unclear, unintelligible, ambiguous or untimely manner such material information as referred to in that paragraph or fails to identify the commercial intent of the commercial practice if not already apparent from the context, and where, in either case, this causes or is likely to cause the average consumer to take a transactional decision that he would not have taken otherwise.

3. Where the medium used to communicate the commercial practice imposes limitations of space or time, these limitations and any measures taken by the trader to make the information available to consumers by other means shall be taken into account in deciding whether information has been omitted.

4. In the case of an invitation to purchase, the following information shall be regarded as material, if not already apparent from the context:

   (a) the main characteristics of the product, to an extent appropriate to the medium and the product;

   (b) the geographical address and the identity of the trader, such as his trading name and, where applicable, the geographical address and the identity of the trader on whose behalf he is acting;

   (c) the price inclusive of taxes, or where the nature of the product means that the price cannot reasonably be calculated in advance, the manner in which the price is calculated, as well as, where appropriate, all additional freight, delivery or postal charges or, where these charges cannot reasonably be calculated in advance, the fact that such additional charges may be payable;

   (d) the arrangements for payment, delivery, performance and the complaint handling policy, if they depart from the requirements of professional diligence;

   (e) for products and transactions involving a right of withdrawal or cancellation, the existence of such a right.

5. Information requirements established by Community law in relation to commercial communication including advertising or marketing,

a non-exhaustive list of which is contained in Annex II, shall be regarded as material.

Section 2

Aggressive commercial practices

Article 8

Aggressive commercial practices

A commercial practice shall be regarded as aggressive if, in its factual context, taking account of all its features and circumstances, by harassment, coercion, including the use of physical force, or undue influence, it significantly impairs or is likely to significantly impair the average consumer's freedom of choice or conduct with regard to the product and thereby causes him or is likely to cause him to take a transactional decision that he would not have taken otherwise.

Article 9

Use of harassment, coercion and undue influence

In determining whether a commercial practice uses harassment, coercion, including the use of physical force, or undue influence, account shall be taken of:

(a) its timing, location, nature or persistence;
(b) the use of threatening or abusive language or behaviour;
(c) the exploitation by the trader of any specific misfortune or circumstance of such gravity as to impair the consumer's judgement, of which the trader is aware, to influence the consumer's decision with regard to the product;
(d) any onerous or disproportionate non-contractual barriers imposed by the trader where a consumer wishes to exercise rights under the contract, including rights to terminate a contract or to switch to another product or another trader;
(e) any threat to take any action that cannot legally be taken.

CHAPTER 3

CODES OF CONDUCT

Article 10

Codes of conduct

This Directive does not exclude the control, which Member States may encourage, of unfair commercial practices by code owners and recourse to such bodies by the persons or organisations referred to in Article 11 if proceedings before such bodies are in addition to the court or administrative proceedings referred to in that Article.

Recourse to such control bodies shall never be deemed the equivalent of foregoing a means of judicial or administrative recourse as provided for in Article 11.

CHAPTER 4

FINAL PROVISIONS

Article 11

Enforcement

1. Member States shall ensure that adequate and effective means exist to combat unfair commercial practices in order to enforce compliance with the provisions of this Directive in the interest of consumers.

   Such means shall include legal provisions under which persons or organisations regarded under national law as having a legitimate interest in combating unfair commercial practices, including competitors, may:

   (a) take legal action against such unfair commercial practices; and/or

   (b) bring such unfair commercial practices before an administrative authority competent either to decide on complaints or to initiate appropriate legal proceedings.

   It shall be for each Member State to decide which of these facilities shall be available and whether to enable the courts or administrative authorities to require prior recourse to other established means of dealing with complaints, including those referred to in Article 10. These facilities shall be available regardless of whether the consumers affected are in the territory of the Member State where the trader is located or in another Member State.

   It shall be for each Member State to decide:

   (a) whether these legal facilities may be directed separately or jointly against a number of traders from the same economic sector; and

   (b) whether these legal facilities may be directed against a code owner where the relevant code promotes non-compliance with legal requirements.

2. Under the legal provisions referred to in paragraph 1, Member States shall confer upon the courts or administrative authorities powers enabling them, in cases where they deem such measures to be neces-

sary taking into account all the interests involved and in particular the public interest:

(a) to order the cessation of, or to institute appropriate legal pro-ceedings for an order for the cessation of, unfair commercial practices;

or

(b) if the unfair commercial practice has not yet been carried out but is imminent, to order the prohibition of the practice, or to institute appropriate legal proceedings for an order for the prohi-bition of the practice,

even without proof of actual loss or damage or of intention or negli-gence on the part of the trader.

Member States shall also make provision for the measures referred to in the first subparagraph to be taken under an accelerated proce-dure:

- either with interim effect,

or

- with definitive effect,

on the understanding that it is for each Member State to decide which of the two options to select.

Furthermore, Member States may confer upon the courts or adminis-trative authorities powers enabling them, with a view to eliminating the continuing effects of unfair commercial practices the cessation of which has been ordered by a final decision:

(a) to require publication of that decision in full or in part and in such form as they deem adequate;

(b) to require in addition the publication of a corrective statement.

3. The administrative authorities referred to in paragraph 1 must:

(a) be composed so as not to cast doubt on their impartiality;

(b) have adequate powers, where they decide on complaints, to mon-itor and enforce the observance of their decisions effectively;

(c) normally give reasons for their decisions.

Where the powers referred to in paragraph 2 are exercised exclusively by an administrative authority, reasons for its decisions shall always be given. Furthermore, in this case, provision must be made for pro-cedures whereby improper or unreasonable exercise of its powers by the administrative authority or improper or unreasonable failure to exercise the said powers can be the subject of judicial review.

Article 12

Courts and administrative authorities: substantiation of claims

Member States shall confer upon the courts or administrative authorities powers enabling them in the civil or administrative proceedings provided for in Article 11:

(a) to require the trader to furnish evidence as to the accuracy of factual claims in relation to a commercial practice if, taking into account the legitimate interest of the trader and any other party to the proceedings, such a requirement appears appropriate on the basis of the circumstances of the particular case;
and
(b) to consider factual claims as inaccurate if the evidence demanded in accordance with (a) is not furnished or is deemed insufficient by the court or administrative authority.

Article 13

Penalties

Member States shall lay down penalties for infringements of national provisions adopted in application of this Directive and shall take all necessary measures to ensure that these are enforced. These penalties must be effective, proportionate and dissuasive.

Article 14

Amendments to Directive 84/450/EEC

Directive 84/450/EEC is hereby amended as follows:
1. Article 1 shall be replaced by the following:

"Article 1

The purpose of this Directive is to protect traders against misleading advertising and the unfair consequences thereof and to lay down the conditions under which comparative advertising is permitted."
2. in Article 2:
- point 3 shall be replaced by the following:
"3. "trader" means any natural or legal person who is acting for purposes relating to his trade, craft, business or profession and any one acting in the name of or on behalf of a trader."
the following point shall be added:
"4. "code owner" means any entity, including a trader or group of traders, which is responsible for the formulation and revision of a code of conduct and/or for monitoring compliance with the code by those who have undertaken to be bound by it."
3. Article 3a shall be replaced by the following:
"Article 3a
1. Comparative advertising shall, as far as the comparison is concerned, be permitted when the following conditions are met:
(a) it is not misleading within the meaning of Articles 2(2), 3 and 7(1) of this Directive or Articles 6 and 7 of Directive 2005/29/EC of the European Parliament and of the Council of 11 May 2005

concerning unfair business-to-consumer commercial practices in the internal market [9];

(b) it compares goods or services meeting the same needs or intended for the same purpose;

(c) it objectively compares one or more material, relevant, verifiable and representative features of those goods and services, which may include price;

(d) it does not discredit or denigrate the trade marks, trade names, other distinguishing marks, goods, services, activities, or circumstances of a competitor;

(e) for products with designation of origin, it relates in each case to products with the same designation;

(f) it does not take unfair advantage of the reputation of a trade mark, trade name or other distinguishing marks of a competitor or of the designation of origin of competing products;

(g) it does not present goods or services as imitations or replicas of goods or services bearing a protected trade mark or trade name;

(h) it does not create confusion among traders, between the advertiser and a competitor or between the advertiser's trade marks, trade names, other distinguishing marks, goods or services and those of a competitor.

4. Article 4(1) shall be replaced by the following:

"1.Member States shall ensure that adequate and effective means exist to combat misleading advertising in order to enforce compliance with the provisions on comparative advertising in the interest of traders and competitors. Such means shall include legal provisions under which persons or organisations regarded under national law as having a legitimate interest in combating misleading advertising or regulating comparative advertising may:

(a) take legal action against such advertising;

or

(b) bring such advertising before an administrative authority competent either to decide on complaints or to initiate appropriate legal proceedings.

It shall be for each Member State to decide which of these facilities shall be available and whether to enable the courts or administrative authorities to require prior recourse to other established means of dealing with complaints, including those referred to in Article 5.

It shall be for each Member State to decide:

(a) whether these legal facilities may be directed separately or jointly against a number of traders from the same economic sector;

and

(b) whether these legal facilities may be directed against a code owner where the relevant code promotes non-compliance with legal requirements."

5. Article 7(1) shall be replaced by the following:
"1. This Directive shall not preclude Member States from retaining or adopting provisions with a view to ensuring more extensive protection, with regard to misleading advertising, for traders and competitors."

Article 15

Amendments to Directives 97/7/EC and 2002/65/EC

1. Article 9 of Directive 97/7/EC shall be replaced by the following:

"Article 9

Inertia selling

Given the prohibition of inertia selling practices laid down in Directive 2005/29/EC of 11 May 2005of the European Parliament and of the Council concerning unfair business-to-consumer commercial practices in the internal market [10], Member States shall take the measures necessary to exempt the consumer from the provision of any consideration in cases of unsolicited supply, the absence of a response not constituting consent.

2. Article 9 of Directive 2002/65/EC shall be replaced by the following:

"Article 9

Given the prohibition of inertia selling practices laid down in Directive 2005/29/EC of 11 May 2005 of the European Parliament and of the Council concerning unfair business-to-consumer commercial practices in the internal market [11] and without prejudice to the provisions of Member States' legislation on the tacit renewal of distance contracts, when such rules permit tacit renewal, Member States shall take measures to exempt the consumer from any obligation in the event of unsolicited supplies, the absence of a reply not constituting consent.

Article 16

Amendments to Directive 98/27/EC and Regulation (EC) No 2006/2004

1. In the Annex to Directive 98/27/EC, point 1 shall be replaced by the following:
"1. Directive 2005/29/EC of the European Parliament and of the Council of 11 May 2005 concerning unfair business-to-consumer commercial practices in the internal market (OJ L 149, 11.6.2005, p. 22)."

2. In the Annex to Regulation (EC) No 2006/2004 of the European Parliament and of the Council of 27 October 2004 on cooperation between national authorities responsible for the enforcement of the consumer protection law (the Regulation on consumer protection cooperation) [12] the following point shall be added:
"16. Directive 2005/29/EC of the European Parliament and of the Council of 11 May 2005 concerning unfair business-to-consumer commercial practices in the internal market (OJ L 149, 11.6.2005, p. 22)."

Article 17

Information

Member States shall take appropriate measures to inform consumers of the national law transposing this Directive and shall, where appropriate, encourage traders and code owners to inform consumers of their codes of conduct.

Article 18

Review

1. By 12 June 2011 the Commission shall submit to the European Parliament and the Council a comprehensive report on the application of this Directive, in particular of Articles 3(9) and 4 and Annex I, on the scope for further harmonisation and simplification of Community law relating to consumer protection, and, having regard to Article 3(5), on any measures that need to be taken at Community level to ensure that appropriate levels of consumer protection are maintained. The report shall be accompanied, if necessary, by a proposal to revise this Directive or other relevant parts of Community law.
2. The European Parliament and the Council shall endeavour to act, in accordance with the Treaty, within two years of the presentation by the Commission of any proposal submitted under paragraph 1.

Article 19

Transposition

Member States shall adopt and publish the laws, regulations and administrative provisions necessary to comply with this Directive by 12 June 2007. They shall forthwith inform the Commission thereof and inform the Commission of any subsequent amendments without delay.

They shall apply those measures by 12 December 2007. When Member States adopt those measures, they shall contain a reference to this Directive or be accompanied by such a reference on the occasion of their official publication. Member States shall determine how such reference is to be made.

Article 20

Entry into force

This Directive shall enter into force on the day following its publication in the Official Journal of the European Union.

Article 21

Addressees

This Directive is addressed to the Member States.
Done at Strasbourg, 11 May 2005.

For the European Parliament
The President
J. P. Borrell Fontelles
For the Council
The President
N. Schmit

[1] OJ C 108, 30.4.2004, p. 81.
[2] Opinion of the European Parliament of 20 April 2004 (OJ C 104 E, 30.4.2004, p. 260), Council Common Position of 15 November 2004 (OJ C 38 E, 15.2.2005, p. 1), Position of the European Parliament of 24 February 2005 (not yet published in the Official Journal) and Council Decision of 12 April 2005.
[3] OJ L 250, 19.9.1984, p. 17. Directive as amended by Directive 97/55/EC of the European Parliament and of the Council (OJ L 290, 23.10.1997, p. 18).
[4] OJ L 144, 4.6.1997, p. 19. Directive as amended by Directive 2002/65/EC (OJ L 271, 9.10.2002, p. 16).
[5] OJ L 166, 11.6.1998, p. 51. Directive as last amended by Directive 2002/65/EC.
[6] OJ L 271, 9.10.2002, p. 16.
[7] OJ L 201, 31.7.2002, p. 37.
[8] OJ L 171, 7.7.1999, p. 12.
[9] OJ L 149, 11.6.2005, p. 22."
[10] OJ L 149, 11.6.2005, p. 22."
[11] OJ L 149, 11.6.2005, p. 22."
[12] OJ L 364, 9.12.2004, p. 1.

ANNEX I

COMMERCIAL PRACTICES WHICH ARE IN ALL CIRCUMSTANCES CONSIDERED UNFAIR

Misleading commercial practices

1. Claiming to be a signatory to a code of conduct when the trader is not.
2. Displaying a trust mark, quality mark or equivalent without having obtained the necessary authorisation.
3. Claiming that a code of conduct has an endorsement from a public or other body which it does not have.
4. Claiming that a trader (including his commercial practices) or a product has been approved, endorsed or authorised by a public or private body when he/it has not or making such a claim without complying with the terms of the approval, endorsement or authorisation.

5. Making an invitation to purchase products at a specified price without disclosing the existence of any reasonable grounds the trader may have for believing that he will not be able to offer for supply or to procure another trader to supply, those products or equivalent products at that price for a period that is, and in quantities that are, reasonable having regard to the product, the scale of advertising of the product and the price offered (bait advertising).

6. Making an invitation to purchase products at a specified price and then:
    (a) refusing to show the advertised item to consumers;
    or
    (b) refusing to take orders for it or deliver it within a reasonable time;
    or
    (c) demonstrating a defective sample of it,
with the intention of promoting a different product (bait and switch)

7. Falsely stating that a product will only be available for a very limited time, or that it will only be available on particular terms for a very limited time, in order to elicit an immediate decision and deprive consumers of sufficient opportunity or time to make an informed choice.

8. Undertaking to provide after-sales service to consumers with whom the trader has communicated prior to a transaction in a language which is not an official language of the Member State where the trader is located and then making such service available only in another language without clearly disclosing this to the consumer before the consumer is committed to the transaction.

9. Stating or otherwise creating the impression that a product can legally be sold when it cannot.

10. Presenting rights given to consumers in law as a distinctive feature of the trader's offer.

11. Using editorial content in the media to promote a product where a trader has paid for the promotion without making that clear in the content or by images or sounds clearly identifiable by the consumer (advertorial). This is without prejudice to Council Directive 89/552/EEC [1].

12. Making a materially inaccurate claim concerning the nature and extent of the risk to the personal security of the consumer or his family if the consumer does not purchase the product.

13. Promoting a product similar to a product made by a particular manufacturer in such a manner as deliberately to mislead the consumer into believing that the product is made by that same manufacturer when it is not.

14. Establishing, operating or promoting a pyramid promotional scheme where a consumer gives consideration for the opportunity to receive compensation that is derived primarily from the introduction of other consumers into the scheme rather than from the sale or consumption of products.

15. Claiming that the trader is about to cease trading or move premises when he is not.

16. Claiming that products are able to facilitate winning in games of chance.

17. Falsely claiming that a product is able to cure illnesses, dysfunction or malformations.

18. Passing on materially inaccurate information on market conditions or on the possibility of finding the product with the intention of inducing the consumer to acquire the product at conditions less favourable than normal market conditions.

19. Claiming in a commercial practice to offer a competition or prize promotion without awarding the prizes described or a reasonable equivalent.

20. Describing a product as "gratis", "free", "without charge" or similar if the consumer has to pay anything other than the unavoidable cost of responding to the commercial practice and collecting or paying for delivery of the item.

21. Including in marketing material an invoice or similar document seeking payment which gives the consumer the impression that he has already ordered the marketed product when he has not.

22. Falsely claiming or creating the impression that the trader is not acting for purposes relating to his trade, business, craft or profession, or falsely representing oneself as a consumer.

23. Creating the false impression that after-sales service in relation to a product is available in a Member State other than the one in which the product is sold.
    Aggressive commercial practices

24. Creating the impression that the consumer cannot leave the premises until a contract is formed.

25. Conducting personal visits to the consumer's home ignoring the consumer's request to leave or not to return except in circumstances and to the extent justified, under national law, to enforce a contractual obligation.

26. Making persistent and unwanted solicitations by telephone, fax, e-mail or other remote media except in circumstances and to the extent justified under national law to enforce a contractual obligation. This is without prejudice to Article 10 of Directive 97/7/EC and Directives 95/46/EC [2] and 2002/58/EC.

27. Requiring a consumer who wishes to claim on an insurance policy to produce documents which could not reasonably be considered relevant as to whether the claim was valid, or failing systematically to respond to pertinent correspondence, in order to dissuade a consumer from exercising his contractual rights.
28. Including in an advertisement a direct exhortation to children to buy advertised products or persuade their parents or other adults to buy advertised products for them. This provision is without prejudice to Article 16 of Directive 89/552/EEC on television broadcasting.
29. Demanding immediate or deferred payment for or the return or safe-keeping of products supplied by the trader, but not solicited by the consumer except where the product is a substitute supplied in conformity with Article 7(3) of Directive 97/7/EC (inertia selling).
30. Explicitly informing a consumer that if he does not buy the product or service, the trader's job or livelihood will be in jeopardy.
31. Creating the false impression that the consumer has already won, will win, or will on doing a particular act win, a prize or other equivalent benefit, when in fact either:
    - there is no prize or other equivalent benefit,
    or
    - taking any action in relation to claiming the prize or other equivalent benefit is subject to the consumer paying money or incurring a cost.

[1] Council Directive 89/552/EEC of 3 October 1989 on the coordination of certain provisions laid down by Law, Regulation or Administrative Action in Member States concerning the pursuit of television broadcasting activities (OJ L 298, 17.10.1989, p. 23). Directive as amended by Directive 97/36/EC of the European Parliament and of the Council (OJ L 202, 30.7.1997, p. 60).
[2] Directive 95/46/EC of the European Parliament and of the Council of 24 October 1995 on the protection of individuals with regard to the processing of personal data and on the free movement of such data (OJ L 281, 23.11.1995, p. 31). Directive as amended by Regulation (EC) No 1882/2003 (OJ L 284, 31.10.2003, p. 1).

ANNEX II

COMMUNITY LAW PROVISIONS SETTING OUT RULES FOR ADVERTISING AND COMMERCIAL COMMUNICATION

Articles 4 and 5 of Directive 97/7/EC
Article 3 of Council Directive 90/314/EEC of 13 June 1990 on package travel, package holidays and package tours [1]

Article 3(3) of Directive 94/47/EC of the European Parliament and of the Council of 26 October 1994 on the protection of purchasers in respect of certain aspects of contracts relating to the purchase of a right to use immovable properties on a timeshare basis [2]

Article 3(4) of Directive 98/6/EC of the European Parliament and of the Council of 16 February 1998 on consumer protection in the indication of the prices of products offered to consumers [3]

Articles 86 to 100 of Directive 2001/83/EC of the European Parliament and of the Council of 6 November 2001 on the Community code relating to medicinal products for human use [4]

Articles 5 and 6 of Directive 2000/31/EC of the European Parliament and of the Council of 8 June 2000 on certain legal aspects of information society services, in particular electronic commerce, in the Internal Market (Directive on electronic commerce) [5]

Article 1(d) of Directive 98/7/EC of the European Parliament and of the Council of 16 February 1998 amending Council Directive 87/102/EEC for the approximation of the laws, regulations and administrative provisions of the Member States concerning consumer credit [6]

Articles 3 and 4 of Directive 2002/65/EC

Article 1(9) of Directive 2001/107/EC of the European Parliament and of the Council of 21 January 2002 amending Council Directive 85/611/EEC on the coordination of laws, regulations and administrative provisions relating to undertakings for collective investment in transferable securities (UCITS) with a view to regulating management companies and simplified prospectuses [7]

Articles 12 and 13 of Directive 2002/92/EC of the European Parliament and of the Council of 9 December 2002 on insurance mediation [8]

Article 36 of Directive 2002/83/EC of the European Parliament and of the Council of 5 November 2002 concerning life assurance [9]

Article 19 of Directive 2004/39/EC of the European Parliament and of the Council of 21 April 2004 on markets in financial instruments [10]

Articles 31 and 43 of Council Directive 92/49/EEC of 18 June 1992 on the coordination of laws, regulations and administrative provisions relating to direct insurance other than life assurance [11] (third non-life insurance Directive)

Articles 5, 7 and 8 of Directive 2003/71/EC of the European Parliament and of the Council of 4 November 2003 on the prospectus to be published when securities are offered to the public or admitted to trading [12]

[1] OJ L 158, 23.6.1990, p. 59.
[2] OJ L 280, 29.10.1994, p. 83.
[3] OJ L 80, 18.3.1998, p. 27.
[4] OJ L 311, 28.11.2001, p. 67. Directive as last amended by Directive 2004/27/EC (OJ L 136, 30.4.2004, p. 34).

[5] OJ L 178, 17.7.2000, p. 1.
[6] OJ L 101, 1.4.1998, p. 17.
[7] OJ L 41, 13.2.2002, p. 20.
[8] OJ L 9, 15.1.2003, p. 3.
[9] OJ L 345, 19.12.2002, p. 1. Directive as amended by Council Directive 2004/66/EC. (OJ L 168, 1.5.2004, p. 35).
[10] OJ L 145, 30.4.2004, p. 1.
[11] OJ L 228, 11.8.1992, p. 1. Directive as last amended by Directive 2002/87/EC of the European Parliament and of the Council (OJ L 35, 11.2.2003, p. 1).
[12] OJ L 345, 31.12.2003, p. 64.

Index

acquis communautaire:
  CEE countries, 49, 70–1
    growth of consumer law, 72–5
    implementation, 72–8
    model legislation role, 83
  EC view of consumers, 120–3
  growth of consumer law, 1–3
  source of legal principle, 157
advertising:
  British Code, and copycat packaging,
    195–6, 203
  broadcasting, 3–4
  CEE countries, 77–8, 86
  comparative advertising, 3
    ECJ jurisprudence, 39
    national laws, 172–3
  EU regulation, 3–4
  exaggerated statements, 116
  harmonisation of laws, 55, 181
  misleading advertising, 3
    CEE countries, 70, 73–4
    cross-border selling, 236–8, 241–4
    Directive, 54, 78
    ECJ jurisprudence, 37–9, 113
    national standards, 12–13
    protection of competitors' interests,
      41
    sweepstakes, 236–8, 241–4
    types, 42–3
  pharmaceutical products, 44
  Sales Promotions Regulation, 104
  Sweden, 12, 164
  taste and decency, 9
  tobacco, 3, 44, 92–3, 119
Agenda 2000, 71
aggressive practices, effects, 107
appellations of origin, 43

artistic national treasures, 162
ASDA, 192, 202
Ashurst Study, 249, 251
Australia, copycat packaging, 197, 199,
    213–14
Austria, 167, 169, 198n15, 240, 245,
    247, 248
average consumers:
  acquis communautaire, 120–3
  Article 5, 24–7, 115–16
  asymmetric power, 122
  benchmark of unfair practices, 6,
    24–7, 105–6
  constitutional validity, 117–20
  credulity, 136
  ECJ free movement jurisprudence,
    109, 123–33
  meaning, 39, 108–9, 115–38
    infiltration, 150–1
  reasonably circumspect consumers,
    127–8, 132
  social and cultural context, 26–7
  UCPD, 133–7
  UK implementation, 223, 228
  vulnerable groups, 116, 123, 134–7

Beier, FK, 182
Belgium:
  itinerant sales, 164
  OFT v Duchesne, 241–4
  Trade Practices Act, 169
  unfair competition law, 166, 198n15
    v competition law, 173
black list of unfair practices:
  consistently unfair practices, 6
  copycat packaging, 193–4

defects, 84, 106–7
detail, 21, 85
omissions, 21, 160, 170–1
text (Annex 1), 275–8
UCPD structure, 36
UK implementation, 224
brands, copycat problem, 192
British Brands Group, 191n1
British Institute of International and
  Comparative Law, 85–6, 87
broadcasting, tobacco advertising, 3–4
Bulgaria:
  American technical assistance, 63
  Commission for Protection of
    Competition, 66, 77, 80
  communism, 60
  competition law
    as consumer protection, 67
    case law, 66
    v consumer enforcement, 80
    pre-EU membership, 62
  Consumer Protection Act, 72, 73
  enforcement mechanisms, 66
  UCPD transposition, 86
burden of proof, 40

Cambier, V, 78
Cassis de Dijon, 125, 126, 128, 129,
  130, 131, 132, 162
causation, 106
CEE countries:
  Association and Europe Agreements, 69
  EU membership impact, 68–81
    accession process, 69–72
    advertising, 77–8, 86
    coherence, 81–3
    competition law, 75–7
    consumer protection, 72–5
    unfair commercial practices, 78–81
  historical legacies, 48, 59–61
  post-communist judiciary, 65
  pre-EU unfair commercial practices
    American technical assistance, 63
    competition law as consumer pro-
      tection, 67
    enforcement techniques, 64–7
    legal legacies, 59–61

legal mechanisms, 59–68
  market regulation, 61–7
UCPD and
  coherence, 88–90
  enforcement, 87–8
  implementation, 86–7
  prospective effects, 9–10, 83–8
  taste and decency, 87
children:
  Swedish advertising, 12
  vulnerability, 134–5
choice of law, 18, 19, 97, 99
clearance sales, 171
codes of conduct:
  copycat packaging, 195–6, 203
  limitations, 28–30
  UCPD and, 105
coercion, 107
comitology, 246, 248
commercial agents, 240
commercial communications:
  1996 Green Paper, 181
  meaning, 161
commercial practices:
  antitrust law and, 161
  ECJ free movement case law, 162–5
  meaning, 35, 160–1, 165–6
  scope, 166, 170
commercial property, 162, 163
competition law
  see also unfair competition
  CEE countries
    competition agencies, 80
    competition as consumer protec-
      tion, 67
    legacies, 59, 60
    strengthening, 75–7
    unfair competition and antitrust,
      62–4
  commercial practices and, 161
  consumer protection and, 171–4
  Courage doctrine, 250–1
  ECJ pro-competition approach, 39,
    40
  harmonisation of laws, 170
  ill-gotten gains, 249, 250–1
  intellectual property and, 183

UCPD and, 17
unfair competition law and, 17, 62–4, 170, 171–4
confusing marketing, 17
consumer contracts
see also unfair terms in consumer contracts
English law, 155, 156
consumer credit, 142–3
consumer guarantees, 143
Consumer Ombudsmen, 166, 167
consumer organisations:
accountability, 58
CEE countries, 64
French-German sweepstakes, 237–8
Nordic countries, 166
privatisation of enforcement, 236, 238–44, 245
qualified entities, 239, 241
regulation v consumer empowerment, 57–8
unfair contract terms and, 141
consumer protection:
2001 Green Paper, 4, 11, 35, 49–50, 88, 104, 143, 181
antitrust law and, 171–4
CEE countries
accession process, 72–5
competition law as consumer protection, 67
Consumer Codes, 73
government agencies, 74–5
contract law and, 141–8
cross-border see cross-border consumer protection
Directorate, 53, 54
EC view of customers, 117–20
enforcement, 7, 30–1, 59
CEE countries, 64–7
EU regulation, 94–6
competence, 4, 91–4
fragmentation, 49–59
free movement principle and, 162
Green Book, 245
harmonisation see harmonisation of laws
national diversities, 12–13

Nordic countries, 166, 198n15
UCPD focus, 15, 33–5, 85–6, 88, 89, 160, 165–6, 175–7
unfair competition and, 181–4, 189
United Kingdom, 183–4, 198–9
Consumer Protection Cooperation Regulation, 6, 31, 58, 236, 244–8
consumers
see also average consumers
consumer autonomy, 172
meaning, 150
contract law
see also unfair terms in consumer contracts
consumer protection and, 141–8
harmonisation, 1–3, 122, 143, 144
meaning, 146–8
UCPD effect, 9, 16, 44, 113, 139–58
basis for wider changes, 148–9
English law, 154–7
infiltration of porous norms, 149–54
possible influences, 148–54
UK consumer contracts, 155, 156
validity, 146
cooperation, 6, 31, 58, 236, 244–8
copycat packaging:
Actimel-B'A case, 211
Australian remedies, 197, 199, 213–14
Betadine-Betapovidona case, 210
brands, importance, 192
Dutch remedies, 204–5
French remedies, 210–11
German remedies, 206–8
Hasbro-Simba Toys case, 205
Home Beautiful-25 Beautiful Homes case, 213–14
impact on consumers, 192–3
Italian remedies, 211–13
LEGO-Mega Blocks case, 204–5
Oraldine-Oralkin case, 209
Pedigree-Oscar Hunde Menue case, 207–8
Penguin-Puffin case, 192, 200, 202–3
point-of-sale practices, 193
problem, 192
Red Bull-Live Wire case, 214

Sindramed-Capitano case, 212
Spanish remedies, 208–10
UCPD and, 17, 42, 191, 193–4, 197–200
    public and private enforcement, 197–200
UK remedies, 194–7, 200–4
    actions by brand owners, 196–7
    copyright, 201–2
    design rights, 201
    IGD dispute resolution, 203–4
    passing-off, 196–7, 202
    public enforcement, 194–5
    registered designs, 201
    self-regulation, 195–6, 203
    trade marks, 200
unfair competition
    v consumer protection, 184–8
    remedies, 196–7
copyright, 201–2
cosmetics, labelling, 17
counterfeiting, 195
country of origin principle, 35, 45–6, 96, 98, 110
coupons, 171
Courage doctrine, 250–1
cross-border consumer protection:
    cooperation, 6, 31, 58, 236, 244–8
    French-German distance selling, 236–8
    future, 248–53
    Injunctions Directive, 238–44
    languages, 253
    nationalisation, 236, 244–8
    OFT v Duchesne, 19, 241–4, 248–9
    privatisation, 236, 238–44, 245
    qualified entities, 239, 241
    skimming off, 251–2
    statutory agencies, 31, 236
cultural context:
    average consumers, 26–7
    OFT v Duchesne, 243
    taste and decency, 135
Cyprus, 168–9
Czech Republic, 62, 64, 69, 73, 74, 86, 169
Czechoslovakia, 63, 67

damages:
    breach of UCPD, 149, 152–3
    misrepresentation, 147
delict:
    France, 152, 154, 169
    Netherlands, 169
denigration, 17, 43
Denmark, 37, 53, 169
design rights, 201
directives, implementation, 216–18
    see also implementation of UCPD
discounts, 171
discrimination, 27
disgorgement procedures, 235
distance selling, 55, 142–3, 236–8, 241–4
dol, 146, 152
door-step selling, 12, 26, 55, 121, 122, 131–2
due diligence defence, 228, 229, 230

e-commerce, Directive, 55
economic interests:
    ECJ protection, 131–2
    UCPD scope, 36, 84, 109, 194, 221
employment contracts, English law, 155
enforcement *see* cross-border consumer protection; UCPD remedies
enlargement *see* EU enlargement
environment, 53, 98, 172
Estonia, 62, 69, 76, 86, 88, 169
EU enlargement:
    1995 White Paper, 70, 74
    Agenda 2000, 71
    Community wide effect, 49
    effect on CEE countries, 68–81
        accession process, 69–72
        advertising, 77–8
        coherence, 81–3
        competition law, 75–7
        consumer protection, 72–5
        unfair commercial practices, 78–81
    justification for UCPD, 49–50
    power asymmetry, 49

fair trade principles, 172
false statements, UK law, 227

financial services, 44, 111, 112
Finland, 169
food labelling, 232
France:
  consumer protection, 34
  contract, 146, 147, 152, 153
  copycat packaging, 210–11
  delictual liability, 152, 154
  distance selling, 236–8
  ill-gotten gains, 249–50
  legal model, 64, 239
  unfair competition law, 169, 182,
    198n15, 210–11
free movement principle:
  broadcasting services, 3–4
  Cassis de Dijon, 125, 126, 128, 129,
    130, 131, 132, 162
  consumer protection and, 162
  ECJ case law on commercial prac-
    tices, 108, 162–5
  ECJ view of consumers, 123–33
  exceptions, 125, 162
  rule of reason, 162
  UCPD legal basis, 119
  uneven domestic standards, 13
frustration, 155

general prohibition (Article 5):
  autonomy, 27
  average consumers *see* average con-
    sumers
  conditions, 21–2
  generally, 20, 21–8
  material distortion of behaviour,
    22–4, 155
  misleading and aggressive practices,
    28
  new regulatory technique, 103, 139
  professional diligence, 21, 22, 108,
    154
  text, 265
geographical denominations, 43
Germany:
  collectivist world-view, 177
  copycat packaging, 187, 206–8
  cross-border enforcement, 245, 247,
    248

distance selling, 236–8
  legal model for CEE countries, 64
  pharmaceutical products online, 165
  trade marks, 206
  unfair competition
    1909 UWG legacy, 176, 177, 178–
      9, 182
    and antitrust law, 174
    comparison with UK, 177–80
    concept, 33–4, 40, 198n15
    consumer protection and, 184
    legislative history, 166–8
    model, 52, 57, 62, 64, 167, 184,
      249–50
    Unfair Competition Act, 37, 46,
      52–3, 169
good faith:
  English law, 154, 155–6
  French law, 153–4
  UCPD requirement, 154–7
Goyens, Monique, 129
Greece, 167, 169
Green Book on Consumer Protection,
  245

harassment, 221–2
harmonisation of laws:
  advertising, 55, 181
  competence, 1, 92–3
  competition, 170
  consumer law, 1–3, 180
    competence, 92, 119
    general character, 94–6
    minimum harmonisation, 219
    patchwork, 94–5, 120
    scope, 117–20
  contract law, 1–3, 122, 143, 144
  full harmonisation *see* maximum
    harmonisation
  minimum harmonisation, 13–14, 219
  pre-UCPD fragmentation, 51–9
    consumer empowerment v regula-
      tion, 56–9
    piecemeal harmonisation, 54–5
    search for unifying concept, 55–6
    unfair competition to consumer
      protection, 52–4

unfair competition, 180, 181
health and safety, 16, 44, 113
Hungary:
    American technical assistance, 63
    competition law
        as consumer protection, 67
        case law, 66
        Competition Act, 77
        pre-EU accession, 62, 63
    consumer fraud, 76
    Office for Economic Competition,
        65, 77, 80
    UCPD transposition, 87
    unfair competition law, 60, 62, 64,
        169

ICPEN, 245, 253
ill-gotten gains, 235, 248–52
immovable property, 44, 113
impact assessment, 13
implementation of directives
    see also implementation of UCPD
    generally, 216–18
    indirect effect doctrine, 228
    Injunctions Directive, 240
    minimum harmonisation, 219
implementation of UCPD:
    affected legislation, 220–2
    CEE countries, 86
    challenges, 168–9, 219–20
    deadline, 5, 160
    maximum harmonisation *see* maxi-
        mum harmonisation
    post-implementation issues, 99–101,
        231–2
    transition periods, 44, 84, 113
    United Kingdom, 222–31
        average consumers, 223, 228
        DTI steps, 231–2
        individual consumer actions, 230–1
        remedies, 229–31
        strict liability, 229
        terminology, 223, 224
        Trade Descriptions Act and, 225–8
        transactional decisions, 223–4,
            228, 229
indirect effect doctrine, 228

industrial property, 162, 163
injunctions:
    collective interests, 142–3
    copycat packaging, 202
    cross-border injunctions, 19, 238–44
        OFT v Duchesne, 19, 241–4, 248–9
    Directive, 58, 236, 238–44
    mutual recognition, 58
    UCPD remedies, 235
insurance, 153–4, 155
intellectual property:
    anti-competitive function, 183
    copycat packaging and, 196, 200–3,
        205
Internal Market
    see also harmonisation of laws
    Article 4 of UCPD, 18–20, 94
        critique, 110–12
        original clause, 110
        text, 264
    deregulatory approach, 123–4
    diversity and, 118–19
    exceptions, 15, 113, 125, 131, 135,
        162
    Green Paper, 56
    mutual recognition, 18, 19, 35–6
    sales promotions, 161, 171
    Services Directive, 96–9
    UCPD objective, 13, 91
Internet:
    spam, 107, 109
    unfair practices, 15, 21
interpretation of UCPD, 99–101, 231–2
Ireland, 53, 113, 168–9, 183
Italy, 169, 182, 211, 211–13

jewellery parties, 132
judiciary, transition countries, 65
jurisdiction rules, 113

labelling, 17, 232
languages, 253
Latvia, 62, 67, 72, 76, 80, 86, 169
Letowska, E, 67
lex specialis derogat lex generalis, 17,
    44–5, 95

liberalisation of markets, 37
Lithuania, 62, 72, 74, 77, 80, 86, 87, 169
look-alikes *see* copycat packaging
Luxembourg, 12

McLoughlin, Patrick, MP, 200
Malta, 169
market liberalisation, 37
material distortion of behaviour, 22–4, 155
Max Planck Institute, 34, 35, 52, 53, 181
maximum harmonisation:
  Commission procedure, 111
  country of origin principle or, 96–7
  UCPD, 7–8, 14–15
    choice of law and, 19, 97
    v domestic prohibitions, 113
    effect on national laws, 43–5
    feasibility, 45–6
    implementation challenges, 219–20
    issues, 103
    policy debates, 108–9
    practice, 113–14
    radical departure, 140
mens rea, false statements, 227–8
mergers, 170
Micklitz Report, 176n3, 179, 180–4, 189
misrepresentation, damages, 147
modem hijacking, 21
mutual recognition principle:
  injunctions, 58
  Internal Market, 18, 19, 35–6
  standing to sue, 239–40

national treasures, 162
nationality discrimination, 27
  see also free movement principle
Netherlands, 169, 204–5, 217
new rules and techniques, 5–10

OECD, 245
OFT v Duchesne, 19, 241–4, 248–9
ombudsmen, 166, 167

package travel, 2
packaging
  see also copycat packaging
  importance, 195–6
Paris Convention, 52, 167, 169, 182
passing-off:
  copycat packaging, 42, 196–7, 202, 214
  unfair competition and, 191
  United Kingdom, 8, 187, 191
PHARE, 71, 72
pharmaceutical products, 44, 165
Poland:
  American technical assistance, 63
  competition law, 60, 62, 66
  Competition Office, 74, 80
  Consumer Protection Act, 73
  enforcement techniques, 64
  UCPD transposition, 86, 87
  unfair competition, 62, 169
Portugal, 169
precious metals, 112
predatory pricing, 171, 180
premium offers, 171
private international law, 98–9
prize competitions, 171
product liability, 2, 118
professional diligence, 21, 22, 108, 154
professional regulation, 44
proportionality, 24, 84
public health exceptions, 98, 125, 131, 162, 165
public morality exceptions, 162
public policy exceptions, 98, 125, 162
public security exceptions, 98, 125

quasi-timeshares, 14

registered designs, 201
Roman law, 152
Romania, 62, 66, 67

sales promotions:
  automatically unfair practices, 160
  definition, 171

post-UCPD national laws, 170–1
Sales Promotion Regulation, 61, 104, 171
Schulte-Nolke, Hans, 198–9n15
Schulze, Reiner, 198–9n15
scope of UCPD:
    Article 3, text, 263–4
    business-to-business
        exclusion, 33, 41–3, 111–12
        indirect protection, 176, 194
    business-to-consumers, 15, 33–5, 85, 88, 89, 160, 165–6, 175–7
    commercial practices, meaning, 35, 166, 170
    competition, 17
    competitors' interests, 41–3, 176
    confusion, 93–4
    contract law, 9, 16, 44, 113, 139–58
    copycat packaging, 17, 42, 191, 193–4, 197–200
    economic interests, 36, 84, 109, 194, 221
    effect on national provisions, 43–5
    excluded fields, 112–13, 221
    financial services, 44, 111, 112
    Framework Directive, 93, 104, 143, 219
    generally, 15–18, 33–46
    health and safety, 16, 44, 113
    immovable property, 44, 113
    implementation and, 220
    jurisdiction rules, 113
    level of protection, 37–41
    professional derogations, 44
    relations with other directives, 34–5
        sector specific directives, 8, 17, 44–5, 85, 95
        Services Directive, 96–9
    revolution, 47–8, 140
    taste and decency, 9, 15, 113, 135
    unfair competition, 17, 62–4, 170, 171–4, 176
    unfairness concept, 108
self-regulation:
    copycat packaging, 195–6, 203
    role and limitations, 28–30
    UK reliance on, 198

Services Directive, 96–9
skimming off, 235, 249–52
Slovakia, 62, 64, 74, 86
Slovenia, 62–3, 66, 86, 87, 169
Spain, 169, 208–10, 249–50
spam, 107, 109
stalking, 221–2
standing to sue, mutual recognition, 239–40
strict liability, 229
Stuyck, Jules, 136
Sweden, 12, 37, 164, 167, 169, 250
sweepstakes I, 236–8
sweepstakes II, 19, 241–4, 248–9

taste and decency, 9, 15, 87, 113, 135
telephone marketing, 107
television, 45, 55, 135
Terryn, E, 136
timeshares, 2, 14, 142–3
tobacco, advertising, 3–4, 44, 92–3, 119
trade descriptions, 195, 225–8
trade marks:
    copycat packaging and, 196, 200, 206
    Germany, 206
    UK law, 187, 195
trade names, 163
trade secrets, 180
transactional decisions:
    meaning, 146–7, 223
    UK implementation, 223–4, 228, 229
transition countries *see* CEE countries
translations, 237, 253
transposition *see* implementation of UCPD

UCPD remedies:
    adequate remedies, 191
    CEE countries, 87–8
    cross-border, 19–20, 235–6
    individual consumer actions, 235
    injunctions, 235
    interim relief, 235

national procedures, 30–1
penalties, 235–6
public and private remedies, 197–200
UK implementation, 229–31
Ulmer, Eugen, 52, 183, 189
Ulmer project, 34, 52, 57, 181, 182
unconscionability, 155
undue influence, 107
unfair commercial practices:
  benchmark, 6
  burden of proof, 40
  CEE countries
    effect of EU membership, 78–81
    pre-EU accession, 59–68
  copycat packaging *see* copycat packaging
  cross-border practices *see* cross-border consumer protection
  ECJ jurisprudence, 108, 162–5
  general prohibition, 20, 21–8, 139, 155, 265
  insurance, 153–4
  list *see* black list of unfair practices
  meaning, 21–2
  pre-UCPD fragmentation, 51–9
  proportionality, 24, 84
  self-regulation, 28–30
  UCPD standards, 40–1, 108
  uneven standards, 6, 12–13
Unfair Commercial Practices Directive (UCPD):
  2001 Green Paper, 49–50
  amendment procedure, 21
  broad approach, 5
  CEE countries and, 83–8
  challenges, 5–10
  coherence, 83–5, 88–90
  competence, 91–4
  context, 91–101, 159–61
  critique, 105–9
    missed opportunity, 103–14
    unfair competition and antitrust, 159, 161, 174
  ECJ interpretation, 99–101, 231–2
  enforcement *see* UCPD remedies
  general prohibition, 20, 21–8, 139, 155, 265

harmonisation model *see* maximum harmonisation
horizontal approach, 48
impact assessment, 13
legislative process, 4–5, 11–15, 35, 104
  travaux préparatoires, 93, 143
origins, 4–5, 11–12, 180, 181
scope *see* scope of UCPD
structure, 20–1, 104, 105, 139–40
text, 255–80
unfair competition:
  and antitrust law, 170, 171–4
    CEE countries, 62–4
  consumer protection and, 181–4, 189
  copycat packaging *see* copycat packaging
  definition, 167
  EU legislative lacuna, 159, 176
  from unfair competition to consumer protection, 52–4
  Germany *see* Germany
  harmonisation of laws, 180, 181
  Micklitz Report, 176n3, 179, 180–4, 189
  national laws, 160, 166–70
  UCPD and, 16–17, 170, 171–4, 176
unfair terms in consumer contracts:
  Directive, 2
    Dutch implementation, 217
    UK implementation, 157
  ECJ jurisprudence, 114, 231
  list of terms, 100
  regulatory mechanism, 141–2, 143
  role of consumer organisations, 141
United Kingdom:
  advertising regulation, 113
  consumer protection tradition, 183–4
  contract, 146, 147
  copycat packaging, 193, 194–7, 198–9, 200–4
  food labelling, 232
  implementation of UCPD, 222–31
  Office of Fair Trading, 198n15
  OFT v Duchesne, 19, 241–4, 248–9
  passing-off, 8, 187, 191, 196

Protection from Harassment Act 1997, 221–2
retail market, 197
self-regulation, 198
Trade Descriptions Act 1968, 195, 225–8, 227
UCPD
  English law challenges, 154–7
  filling legal lacuna, 103
  implementation, 222–31
  remedies, 149, 153, 199
unfair competition
  comparison with Germany, 177–80
  lacuna, 34, 53, 113, 168–9, 183, 191

United States:
  deceptive practices, 23
  ill-gotten gains, 249, 250
  private enforcement, 252
  technical assistance to CEE countries, 63
  unfair competition, 178

Van Dyck, T, 136
VIEW, 240, 241
vulnerable groups, 39, 116, 123, 134–7

withdrawal rights, 14

Yugoslavia, 60, 63